1 MONTH OF
FREE
READING

at
www.ForgottenBooks.com

By purchasing this book you are eligible for one month membership to ForgottenBooks.com, giving you unlimited access to our entire collection of over 1,000,000 titles via our web site and mobile apps.

To claim your free month visit: www.forgottenbooks.com/free1040868

ISBN 978-0-331-24266-9
PIBN 11040868

Histrionic Montreal

*Annals of the Montreal Stage
with Biographical and Critical
Notices of the Plays and Players of a Century.*

BY FRANKLIN GRAHAM

*"—for the which supply,
Admit me Chorus to this history."*
HENRY V. Prologue.

" Lovell, look that it be done! "
RICHARD III. Act 3., Sc. IV.

SECOND EDITION

MONTREAL :
JOHN LOVELL & SON, PUBLISHERS.
MCMII.

Origin and Progress of Dramatic Art.

❧ ❧

It does not take a great stretch of imagination to conceive the idea of the origin of the drama—a step from the drama of nature to the drama of humanity—a stride from the natural to the imitative—and so with the existence of primitive man, when first surrounded with scenes and objects, we have the origin of the drama. As the centuries continued to roll back upon the past, and as the dawn of civilization receded, man advanced. Not satisfied with merely imitating his own acts, he soon acquired the art of reproducing the acts of his fellows, and by the time we arrive to Greece and Rome we find man an intellectual being, and the drama fully developed. From this it is easily traced from the written records. From the ancient it is plain reading to the mediæval age ; from the mediæval to the Elizabethan ; and from the Elizabethan to the Victorian. Not until Cosmos decays, or when it changes its features wherein man must disappear before the formation of a new genesis, then, and then only, will the drama cease to be.

> " Thespis, inventor of the dramatic art,
> Conveyed his vagrant actors in a cart ;
> High o'er the crowd the mimic tribe appeared,
> And played and sung, with lees of wine besmeared."

Taking Herodotus as our authority, we find that the origin of the drama was during the reign of Pissistratus, and the first representation of Iampic dialogue in the sacrifice to Dionysius in the year B.C. 535. Thespis was the founder and first enactor of plays, and "Alcestus" the name of the first tragedy performed, during the festival of Bacchus.

The records of the Olympian games indicate many winners of the tragic prize, foremost of whom are Thespis, Chœrilus, B.C. 523 ; Phrynichus, B.C. 511 ; Æschylus, B.C. 499 ; Sophocles, Euripides and Aristophanes.

454948

Next in line came the Romans with Quintius Roscius and
Clodius Æsopus as the foremost representatives of comedy
and tragedy respectively.

The dramatists were Terence, Livius, Cæcilius, Andronicus
and Ennius.

" When Roscius was an actor in Rome."

THE DRAMA IN FRANCE

can be said to have virtually had its incipiency with the establishment of the Comedie Francaise.   Its origin dates back to
the reign of Henri Quatre, when some comedians came and
established themselves near the Hotel St. Paul, Paris, and
founded the Theatre du Marais.   A few years later other
comedians built a new theatre, which Corneille and Rotrou
soon rendered illustrious ; this was the Theatre of the Hotel
de Bourgogne.   Next we find the theatres of the Petit Bour-
bon and the Palais Royal, where Moliere's pieces were first
played, and Racine's maiden piece, " La Thebaide."   In 1673
Moliere died and his company divided.

In 1680 there were three theatres in Paris—the Theatre du
Marais, the Company of the Hotel de Bourgogne and that
of the Theatre Guenegaud.   The two latter were united in
August of that year, a grand performance of " Tartuffe " be-
ing given to celebrate their union.   " It is the intention of
His Majesty," says the register, " that there shall be hence-
forth no company but this, and it shall be called the Comedie
Francaise."

Performances were held at the Hotel Guenegaud, and
eighty-one new pieces were produced in the first ten years,
the authors most in fashion being La Fontaine, Dancourt and
Boursault.   Under Louis XV. the subvention granted to the
house was doub'ed, and until 1770 the theatre was permanently established in the Rue des Fosses.   During these ninety
years all that was illustrious in French literature was contributed to its glories.

It remained here until 1760, when new quarters were found
in the Palace of the Tuileries.   Twelve years were spent
there, and then a new theatre adjoining the Luxembourg was
selected.

The Comedie Francaise was still here when the Revolution
came, and in the bitter feeling of the time a feud arose between Talma and his Republican followers and the aristo-

cratic element of the company.   It was then that Talma
and his party went to the Varietes Amusants.   There they
were later joined by their former companions, and there has
been the home of the Comedie Francaise ever since.   It faces
the Place du Theatre Francais at the foot of the Avenue de
l'Opera, and at the corner of the Rue St. Honore and the Rue
de Richelieu, immediately adjacent to the Palais Royal.

In 1812 Napoleon drew up the celebrated Moscow decree
by which its organization has since been regulated.   Scribe
was first played there in 1822 ; Alexander Dumas, the elder,
in 1829 ; Victor Hugo in 1830.   Eight years later Rachel
made her debut as *Camille* in " Les Horaces."

It was a heavy financial loss at this period, and it was not
until M. Emile Perrin replaced as manager M. Edouard
Thierry in 1871 that the tide began to turn in its favor.
Since then it had more than regained its old place.   Edmond
Got, the most thoroughly humourous actor in France, had
long been its main support. ·   Coquelin, the elder, whose
brilliancy was in it, as Sarcey said, " *Un je ne sais quoi
d'cpique*," was incomparable as a comedian.   Delaunay,
aged as he was, still played the sighing lover with the fervour
of youth.   Mounet-Sully in tragedy, Shiron in comedy, Feb-
ore in domestic drama, were each unrivalled in their respec-
tive walks , while Mme. Arnould-Plessy, grandest of *Grandes
Coquettes* ; Mlle. Favart, most intense of *Fortes Premieres* ;
and Sophie Croizette, memorable in the " Sphinx " and " Le
Demi Monde," led a company of actresses whom all the other
theatres combined could not hope to rival.

The Theatre Francais was gutted by fire 8th March,
1900.   Inseparably associated with its history are the names
of Racine, Corneille, Moliere, Talma, Duchesnois, Rachel,
Bernhardt, Got, Mounet-Sully, Mars, Coquelin, and, rich with
the spoils of time, it contained a priceless treasure in its collection of sculpture, paintings and precious relics.

Of the galaxy of the Francaise's immortals, Montreal has
seen, Bernhardt, Coquelin, accompanied by his brother,
Jean,—Duquesne and Madame Barety, at the Academy of
Music in March, 1889, and again week of 14th May, 1894.
During this tour Coquelin was seen with his brother and
Jane Hading.   Jean Mounet-Sully also appeared at the Aca-
demy, supported by Mmes. Hading and Segond-Weber, week
14th May, 1894.

THE DRAMA IN ENGLAND.

The earliest authentic account we have of theatrical performances in England is in the year 1119, when the miracle play of "St. Katherine" was performed at Dunstable. It was written and produced by one Geoffrey. On the night of its production, by a strange coincidence, his house was totally destroyed by fire, and, thinking it to be a judgment from heaven, the playwright assumed the *habitum religionis*, and subsequently became the Abbott of St. Albans, dying in the year 1146.

In Fitzstephens' "Life of Thomas à Becket" mention is made of regular theatrical performances, and miracle plays continued to be performed until about the year 1400, when minstrelsy and interludes gradually increased.

Richard the Third, however, was the first king to take interest in theatricals. King Henry VIII. was also very partial to these amusements, and had plays mounted in every detail of elegance. The first tragedy was produced before Queen Elizabeth in 1561. It was written by Thomas Sackville. assisted by Thomas Norton, and was called "Ferrex and Porrex," but perhaps better known as "Gorboduc." To Nicholas Udal, however, belongs the distinction of having written the first English comedy, and although "Gorboduc" was produced a year before "Roister Doister," the latter had been written first. Shakespeare had not then completed his second year, and it is an interesting fact that the birth of the drama in England and the dramatist who gave it everlasting life should be exactly contemporaneous. Immediately afterwards came the plays of Lyly, Marlowe, Heywood, Middleton, Rowley, Marston, Chapman, Dekker, Webster, Beaumont, Ford, Fletcher, Massinger—and the giant that towers over them all, the pride of England and the greatest of the human race—Shakespeare.

Richard Burbage was the first great actor England had. He was a contemporary of Shakespeare, and the original conceptions and traditions of these two masters were in turn handed down from actor to actor.

Those most prominent to survive Burbage were Joseph Taylor and John Lowin. In the year 1647, when fanaticism ruled the laws of England, the theatre was for the first and only time abolished by Parliament. The players were driven into the country, but after twelve years of civil strife Charles

II. landed in England and the surviving players wept for joy. Many of these had taken arms against the Roundheads, notably Michael Mohun, Charles Hart and Nicholas Burt. Two theatres were established under the direction of Sir William Davenant and Thomas Killigrew. The foremost actor of this period was Thomas Betterton, surrounded by such a coterie as Sandford, Smith, Harris, Underhill, Doggett, Mrs. Bracegirdle, Mrs. Barry and Nell Gwynne. It was during this epoch that women were substituted for the boys who had heretofore played the female roles. This innovation, at a time when the morals of the Court were on a level with the pavement, defiled the otherwise literary period of Dryden, Wycherley, Vanbrugh, Farquhar and Congreve, also rendering immortal the memory of that delightful old gossip, Samuel Pepys. Only Thomas Betterton and his wife, by the purity of their lives, not less than the greatness of their careers, stand forth as shining lights in that age of profligacy. On an income of $800 a year Betterton accumulated a modest fortune. He died in 1710, aged 75.

The production of Addison's " Cato," three years later, introduces the succeeding group of actors, Barton Booth being the most distinguished player of the reign of Queen Anne. Political influences between Whigs and Tories were such as to render the production of the tragedy memorable. The cast comprised the representative actors and actresses of the day : Barton Booth, Colley Cibber, Robert Wilks, George Powell, John Mills, Lacy Ryan, Bowman, Kean, Mrs. Barry, Mrs. Oldfield and Mrs. Porter. Booth retired in his forty-sixth year on account of declining health, and died in 1733.

The first and second Georges, with strong preferences for bear-baiting and tight-rope dancing entertainments, did nothing to foster the favorable conditions of the drama achieved during the days of Anne. The most conspicuous figures of the theatre were Charles Macklin, famed for his performances of *Shylock* and *Sir Archy*, as well as for having had the distinction of playing *Macbeth* after he had attained his one-hundredth birthday ; James Quin, Mrs. Elizabeth Barry, Lavinia Fenton, Mrs. Pritchard and Kitty Clive, until the advent of the great reformer, David Garrick, who, at a single bound, outdistanced Quin, the established tragedian of the day. He had been famous for his *Falstaff*, *Cato* and *Coriolanus*, but, realizing his defeat, gracefully retired. Macklin, who died in 1797, aged 107, had been something of a re-

former, he being the first actor to rescue the character of
Shylock from the list of comic parts to play it seriously.   In
1744 he produced " Othello," after announcing that the chief
character would be " dressed after the custom of his country," for up to that time, and for a long time afterwards,
Othello wore an English officer's uniform.

David Garrick, a little wine merchant, within a week after
his first London appearance (1741) was known to all England, and for a period of thirty-five years was the idol of the
stage.   His school was the closest yet to nature, and his
many needed reforms led the way to the since elevated condition of the stage.   Actors were not permitted to address
the audience across the footlights with insolent familiarity;
nor would he allow certain spectators to commingle with the
performers on the stage ; and he it was who first introduced
footlights by the use of candles.   Strange, however, that he
should not have given closer attention to the details of costume, choosing to play all his characters in the Court dress
of the period.   His closest rival was Spranger Barry, the
silver-toned, who stood foremost in the bright galaxy of the
period, including Mrs. Woffington, Mrs. Abington, Mrs. T.
Cibber, Mrs. Bellamy, Anne Barry, Mrs. Yates, Samuel
Foote, Edward Shutter, John Moody, Thomas Weston, Wm.
Smith, Henry Mossop, Thomas King, Thomas Sheridan,
Charles Bannister and West Digges.

In 1779 Garrick was laid in Westminster Abbey, to sleep
with kings and heroes, and for a short time John Henderson
drew public attention by the excellence of his *Hamlet* and
Falstaff.   About his generation were clustered Wm. Lewis,
Henry Johnston, John Palmer, Mrs. Hartley, Mrs. Inchbald,
Miss Linley and Miss Pope.

Probably the most interesting group of *stars* in the an-
nals of the British stage came in immediate succession, headed
by Mrs. Siddons and her brother, John Philip Kemble, their
most illustrious contemporaries being Geo. F. Cooke, Joseph
G. Holman, R. W. Elliston, John Fawcett, Wm. Farren,
Mrs. Jordan, Miss Eliza O'Neill, Wm. Dowton, Munden and
Charles Mayne Young, Kemble's most distinguished disciple.
Closely following are included Charles Kemble and Edmund
Kean.   With Mrs. Siddons and John P. Kemble many reforms in costuming were brought about, and in his management of Drury Lane, Kemble otherwise contributed materi-
ally to the advancement of the drama.   Cooke was his most

formidable rival. Byron said that of actors Cooke was the most natural, Kemble the most supernatural, Kean the medium between the two, but Mrs. Siddons was worth them all put together. She died in 1831, having survived her brother eight years. Kemble retired from the mimic scene in 1817, when many worthy representatives were meeting with more or less success, among whom were : Junius Brutus Booth, John Vandenhoff, Alex. Rae, J. W. Wallack, sen., and W. A. Conway. The mantle of Kemble, however, was reserved for W. C. Macready, whose efforts in the line of theatrical administration culminated in the achievement of a glorious career to the time of his retirement in 1851. His revivals were the most artistically complete seen until those of Irving.

A close second to Macready was Samuel Phelps, during eighteen years of management of Sadler's Wells Theatre from 1844, wherein he produced thirty-one of the Shakespearean series, besides many of the old and modern classical plays. In 1878 the theatre was pulled down. The same week Phelps died, aged 72.

Then came the laudable efforts of Charles Kean, at the Princess Theatre in 1850, whose marvels of scenic splendor were unfortunately marred by over-elaborate trappings ; and lastly the Lyceum productions of Sir Henry Irving, who has eclipsed them all in point of artistic perfection and effect.

THE DRAMA IN AMERICA.

As early as 1538 dramatic performances in the new world were given at Tlascala, Mexico, under the direction of Fray Toribio de Benevente, as recently recorded by John Malone. The French in Louisiana also presented plays long before the establishment of the English drama in America.

David Garrick was in the zenith of his fame in England when William Hallam, as manager of Goodman's Fields Theatre, became bankrupt in 1750. His creditors, holding him in high esteem, left him in possession of his theatrical wardrobe and sufficient capital to start anew in life. He was one of four brothers, the others being Admiral Hallam, Lewis, who subsequently accompanied him to America, and the fourth, also an actor, was accidentally killed by the tragedian, Charles Macklin. William and Lewis Hallam picked out a company of twelve adult performers, and in May, 1752, the troupe of adventurers embarked on the "Charming Sally," Capt. Lee, and after a voyage of six weeks, landed at York-town, Va. The company included William, Lewis, Mrs., Miss and Master Hallam, Miss Palmer, Messrs. Rigby, Clarkson, Singleton, Herbert, Winnel and Malone. During the voyage they had passed over many tedious hours in re-hearsing on deck some twenty plays, so that by the time they reached the Western country they were pretty well organized. Their first performance was given 5th September, 1752, the play being "The Merchant of Venice." This was the first company of any note in this country, but the credit of the original English performance in America is due to another English company just twenty years before, when perform-ances were given three times a week in a large room in the upper part of a building occupied by the Hon. Rip Van Dam in New York. They played during the month of September, 1732, closed in October, resumed in January, 1733, and dis-banded a month later. The Hallams, however, may be pro-perly styled the promoters of the American stage.

In 1756 Lewis Hallam, sen., the manager, died, and shortly afterward his widow married David Douglass, who there-upon assumed the management of the company. After a long circuit throughout the West Indies and the Southern States, Douglass decided to bring his company North again, and in 1758 they arrived in New York. Such, however, was the discouraging reception there that after an indifferently successful season they determined to try their fortunes once more in the Quaker City, despite the strong opposition they were assured of meeting.

Accordingly, Douglass obtained permission from Governor Denny to erect a theatre in Southwark, and on 25th June, 1759, the "new theatre on Society Hill" was opened under as favorable auspices as could be expected with the tragedy of "Tamerlane," followed by the farce, "The Virgin Un-masked, or an Old Man Taught Wisdom," with singing by Mrs. Love, a talented member of the company, in the inter-mission.

April 24. 1767, is marked as the notable day upon which was produced the first American play acted in America, the "Prince of Parthia," by Thomas Godfrey, jun., the son of the inventor of the quadrant.

During the winter cf 1769-1770 the company passed a com-paratively uneventful and successful season at the "South-wark," but did not appear again till October, 1772, when they found the city stirred by dark omens of the coming con-flict. The great event of this season was the presentation on February 17 of the second original American drama ever performed on an American stage, "The Conquest of Canada, or the Siege of Quebec," the exact authorship of which is, however, unknown.

Officers of the British army and navy took part in the play, having with them artillery, boats and other suitable paraphernalia. The doors were opened at 4, and the play be-gan at 6. Whether or not the play was a signal success has not been recorded. The last season in Philadelphia before the Revolution was for two weeks only, in November, 1773, notable for two facts—the little interest shown in the stage and the sad death of Mrs. Douglass.

An attempt was made by the company to give perform-ances in 1774, but owing to the resolutions of the Continental Congress, then sitting, discouraging every species cf extra-vagance, the only entertainment was a semi-dramatic *melange* including "The Lecture on Heads," and a recitation, "Bucks Have at Ye All."

The next time the curtain rose to a play in the Southwark Theatre it was before a foreign audience of red-coats, and it was to be many long years before the members of the Ameri-can company were again to speak from the old familiar boards.

There being no inducements to visit Canada owing to the likelihood of trouble there, the company embarked for the West Indies, the more loyal colonies of George, where the climate, however, cut the thread of life of nearly two-thirds of this original company.

Lewis Hallam, jun., destined to reorganize theatricals after peace had been declared, went to England.

Let us then bid adieu to these faithful colonial actors, for when we meet them again they will be owing allegiance to another master. They did their part nobly, suffered patient-ly, labored unceasingly, and were throughout courteous, re-fined and courageous.

MONTREAL IN 1786.

" The memorials and things of fame,
That do renown this city."

Twelfth Night, Act 3, Sc. 3,

The Canadian metropolis, with its wall built by King Louis
of France sixty-two years before, enclosing a population of
some five thousand inhabitants, scarcely promised its noble
aspect of a century later, with its beautiful storied scenes and
picturesque panorama so closely dotted with the steeples of
magnificent temples, homes and warehouses so far as eye can
reach, from the easy slopes of the mighty St. Lawrence to
the abrupt ridge of Mount Royal, and ever and anon rich in
bits of garden ground, in season so gorgeous with the lilac,
geranium and rose tree, shaded by rows of the tremulous
leaved maple. If the quaint old town is not so fair to look
upon in 1786, much different is the pageant from right and
left beyond its contracted area of one hundred acres. Here
and there small cottages and tree-bowered roads are alternated by richly laden corn fields and the yellow sheaves of
barley (the first crop in the new France), while upon the nearest slopes directly across the broad blue line of the St. Lawrence, between ridges of wooded hills, small white cottages
nestle on lawns of emerald velvet in close proximity to the
superbly rising parish chapel, its spire gleaming as of burn-
ished silver in the benediction of the golden sun. Close by,
and in the shadow of the chancel, lies the garden of hallowed
rest. Beyond, vast ranges of wooded acclivity are discerned,
on the line of horizon, the grisly mountains of the Adiron-
dacks, faintly enwreathed in silver mist, while south-west a
flood of crystal light reveals the Lake of St. Louis ; also the
stream of the Ottawa glistening and gliding through wood
and dale to its tributary confluence.

" —— like to the Pontic sea,
Whose icy current and compulsive course
Ne'er feels retiring ebb, but keeps due on
To the Propontic and Hellespont."

Then the golden light fades into that passing star-lit
shadow so distinctive of a Canadian summer gloaming. En-

suing years have beautified the City, but this pageant is little altered, blending so softly between past and present.

From the altitude of Mount Royal, seven hundred feet, as one looks towards the town, is heard the distant rumble of traffic over stone-paved and narrow streets, *"the spirit-stirring drum"* rattling the old iron shutters, *"the ear-piercing fife"* and *"the swollen bagpipe, singing i' the nose,"* for Montreal is a military town, and on the Champ de Mars parades are in daily routine. The glittering appearance of a thousand tin-covered roofs, rendered dazzling by a burst of sunshine through clouds of silver and bronze, has not changed materially to this day. From the base of the mountain in a direct line to the creek (Craig St.) are to be seen fields under cultivation ; gardens, groves of the poplar, pine and maple ; the lingering ploughman and the sleek cattle. As we arrive at the St. Anne suburbs, a Sulpician father is seen to raise his hands and bless a group of frolicsome children as the *Angelus* is sounded by *le gros bourdon.*

Within the precincts of the City proper, six months later, much excitement is rampant at intelligence received and duly published in Montreal's only newspaper, "The Gazette," that the wall, being obsolete and an eye-sore, is threatened to destruction, and that the harbor, so dangerous and difficult of access, is to be improved. It is also rumoured that a fellowship of players is on its way to the town, and that carpenters are fitting up and enlarging the quarters in use by the amateur dramatic corps of the militia, under direction of the colonel, who has long been expecting the arrival of the troupe.

> " ⸻ *it so fell out that certain players*
> *We o'er-raught on the way; of these we told him;*
> *And there did seem in him a kind of joy*
> *To hear of it."*

The regiment located in Montreal in 1786 was the 44th Foot, now the First Battalion, Essex Regiment, and its two senior officers were Colonel Henry Hope and Major Bryan Blundell.

Over such a scene the British flag had been waving twenty-three years, and that relict of French defence, the wall, had but fifteen more years of exhibition. A decade had passed since Washington in his protest against the misgovernment of King George, finding himself in desperate straits for munitions of war, commissioned the spirited Brigadier Arnold to

capture Quebec.   The intrepid Arnold climbed the heights of
Abraham, as Wolfe had done ; but got no further.   In the
meantime Montreal had fallen before Montgomery, who then
joined Arnold and reversed his experience by falling before
Quebec.   We are familiar with the facts of the retirement of
the American forces ; how the scourge of small-pox decima-
ted their ranks, and, receding step by step, abandoned Canada
by the end of the year—brave victims of merciless circumstances in heroic realities of loyal love.

THE DRAMA IN MONTREAL.

" The actors are come hither, my lord."—Hamlet, Act 2, Sc. 2.

During the last days of February, 1786, a company of
comedians arrived in Montreal from Albany, where they had
been located since the early part of December, 1785. The war
of the Revolution was not at that time so far forgotten that
there still existed a bitter feeling against the mother country,
and the fact that these players were English, and on their way
to Canada to meet better friends, was sure to arouse public
feeling against them.   They had much difficulty in being permitted to perform at Albany, but they finally succeeded and
gave their first performance 9th December, 1785.   They produced several pieces, " until the season for passing the ice "
arrived, when they departed for Montreal, where they performed in the quarters used for such purposes by the regi-
mental amateurs.

The members of the company were Messrs. Moore, Bentley,
Worsdale, Duncan, Bellair, Pinkstan, Allen, Mrs. Moore,
Bentley, Allen and Pinkstan.

The first performance given was on Monday, 27th Febru-
ary, the play being Oliver Goldsmith's "She Stoops to Con-
quer," written in 1773.   The cast was as follows: *Young Mar-
low*, Mr. Moore; *Hardcastle*, Mr. Bentley; *Hastings*, Mr. Wors-
dale ; *Tony Lumpkin*, Mr. Allen ; *Servants*, Messrs. Bellair and
Duncan ; *Mrs. Hardcastle*, Mrs. Bentley ; *Miss Neville*, Mrs.
Pinkstan ; *Maria*, Mrs. Moore ; *Miss Hardcastle*, Mrs. Allen.
This to conclude with Mr. Colman's droll comedy, "The
Deuce is in Him."   *Dramatis personae : Colonel Tamper*, Mr.
Allen ; *Doctor Prattle*, Mr. Moore ; *Major Bedford*, Mr. Bent-
ley ; *Servant*, Mr. Bellair ; *Mlle. Florival*, Mrs. Pinkstan ;
Emily, Mrs. Bentley ; *Belle*, Mrs. Allen.

"The performance at six o'clock precisely. Tickets to be had at the inn ; no money to be taken at the entrance. Admission to first places, eight shillings ; second, four shillings; rear, two shillings. The room will be comfortably warmed."

The company's repertoire consisted of O'Brien's farce, " Cross Purposes," " Taming of the Shrew," " George Barnwell," the merits of which the manager set forth at length in its salutary influence in warning young men of the dangers that beset the path of him who follows after the strange woman,—" The Countess of Salisbury," a tragedy by Hall Hartson ; Colman's farce, " The Deuce is in Him" ; William Lyons' " The Wrangling Lovers "; Mrs. Centlivre's " Busy Body "; Otway's " Venice Preserved "; " She Stoops to Conquer"; Macklin's "Love à la Mode"; John O'Keefe's "The Fair American," " The Citizen," " Lethe," and " The West Indian." It will be noted that, weak as the company appeared, they did not allow the legitimate to stagger them.

Of the *personnel* of the company little is known, except that it is supposed that Mr. and Mrs. Allen were the parents of the eccentric Andrew Jackson Allen, afterwards dresser to Edwin Forrest.

Bentley was a member of the orchestral corps at Philadelphia.

No records exist to show how long they remained ; but presumably for a short season, as Montreal's English population was very low, in the units of thousands, and possessed no theatre, besides which the Revolution's wave of adversity must have been still keenly felt.

After a short sojourn at Quebec they re-appeared in Montreal *en route* to New York, where they disbanded.

Several of this company's members had been associated with Lewis Hallam, jun., at the first feeble attempts at histrionism made in New York after the Revolution. Coming back from the West Indies, the players had spent a few unprofitable months in Philadelphia, and then a feeble detachment came on to New York with Hallam and opened the John Street Theatre, 24th August, 1785. So pronounced was the opposition to plays at that time, that the entertainments were advertised as a series of lectures to begin with a prologue and end with a pantomime, the music selected and composed by Mr. Bentley. On 20th September they came out boldly with a play and produced " The Citizen," the first drama

played in New York after the Revolution. The season closed
1st November, and Hallam, being encouraged to bring on his
main body of artists, did so, and opened with them 21st November, whereupon his advance guard, slightly recruited, went
up the river to Albany and Montreal.

Such is the story of the first regular company that came
to Montreal.

> " To thine and Albany's issue
> Be this perpetual."

It will be interesting to note that theatricals and the first
Presbyterian organization in Montreal were precisely contemporaneous, the first denominational service originating 12th
March, 1786, just a couple of weeks following the first dramatic representation here.

Another coincidence between church and stage was the
baptism, 6th June, 1779, of WM. B. WOOD, the first native-
born Montrealer to achieve pronounced success in American
theatricals. This actor records that the ceremony was performed by Rev. D. C. Delisle, the first Protestant minister resident in Montreal. Mr. Wood's parents had come to Montreal prior to the breaking out of the Revolution, returning
to the United States just in time to see the embarkation of the
last of the English troops on the cessation of hostilities. The
actor has left a record of the Philadelphia stage, but has unfortunately made no other reference to the city of his birth.
After the departure of the original troupe there was a long
dearth in matters theatrical, excepting the amusement of amateurs, principally military, nor do we know of any plays being regularly presented until we come to

THE FALL OF 1798,

when Rickett's Equestrian and Comedy Company of Philadelphia arrived, and gave both equestrian and dramatic performances in this city. Their season was spread through the
winter months, and it having been such a long period since
the citizens had been visited by an attraction of this kind,
they gave the performances their very best patronage, and
the management made money, for Ricketts returned to Philadelphia with his troupe thoroughly satisfied in having ventured a journey then considered to be most extraordinary.

The spot chosen was the south western corner of St. Paul and Bonsecours streets.

The members of the troupe were : *Equestrians,* Mr. Ricketts, F. B. Ricketts, Master Hutchins, Signor Spinacuta and Mr. Franklin. *Histrions* and *Pantomimists,* Thompson, Chambers, Matthew Sully (died 1812), John Durang, Jones, Tompkins, Coffie, Miss Robinson, Mrs. Chambers, Mrs. Durang and Mrs. Tompkins.

JOHN DURANG was the father of Charles Durang, the historian of the Philadelphia stage. He was born in Lancaster, Pa., 6th January, 1768, and died 28th March, 1822.

FIRST THEATRE 1804-5.

Ricketts' Circus revisited Montreal on several occasions, and there is no doubt that the officers of the various military corps stationed at Montreal organized clubs for the purpose of giving amateur theatrical performances long before Mr. Ormsby arrived here from New York and Albany, and, with the assistance of local sympathizers, undertook the construction of stage appurtenances in the upper part of a large and long stone warehouse standing next door to the Post Office, then situated on St. Sulpice Street, near St. Paul Street, and somewhat isolated. This was Montreal's

FIRST THEATRE (1804),
St. Sulpice street, near St. Paul.

Mrs. Centlivre's " Busy Body " (based on Dryden's " Sir Martin Marall," 1667), first produced in 1708, and Bickerstaff's " Sultan," first produced in 1775, were the two pieces presented on the opening night, 19th November, 1804. The following advertisement appeared in the issue of the *Gazette* on the morning of the performance :

THEATRE.

BY PERMISSION

"Mr. Ormsby, from the Theatre Royal, Edinburgh, respectfully informs the ladies and gentlemen of Montreal that he intends (with their approbation) establishing a company of comedians in Canada to perform in Montreal and Quebec alternately. The theatre in this city is fitted up in that large and commodious house, next door to the Post Office, where will be presented this evening (19th November, 1804) a comedy in five acts called ' The Busy Body,' to which will be added the much-admired farce called ' The Sultan.' N.B.— Particulars in advertisements for the evening. Boxes, 5s. Gallery, 2s 6d. Tickets to be had at Mr. Hamilton's Tavern, Montreal Hotel and at the theatre, where places for the boxes may be taken."

A number of old comedies were produced during a short and unprofitable season. Mr. Ormsby returned to New York.

MR. ORMSBY had been in America a few years when he appeared in Montreal. He had been for a long time connected with the Edinburgh stage, and after coming to America was, in 1800, the manager of the Albany Theatre. We again find him there in 1808. There is no existing record to show that he ever returned to Montreal. He never rose to any prominence in America, and soon returned to his native country.

Lambert, in his book of travels, is the historian for the two following years, and in writing of

CANADIAN THEATRICALS OF 1805

says : " An attempt was made to introduce a company from Boston in conjunction with the Canadian performers. I went one hot summer evening to see them perform in ' Katherine and Petruchio,' but the abilities of the Bostonians were nearly eclipsed by the vulgarity and mistakes of the drunken *Katherine*, who walked the stage with devious steps and convulsed the audience with laughter, which was all the entertainment we experienced in witnessing the mangled drama of our immortal bard."

The Bostonians did well in Canada during that season, their clothing and " sleek " appearence being noted by Lambert.

In the absence of clearly authentic records disclosing the *personnel* of this *corps dramatique* from Boston, it may not be misleading to choose certain names from the following list, which comprised that portion of the roster attached that year to the Boston house as being the most likely to have undertaken so arduous a venture as to come to Montreal. The managers of the Boston company were Charles S. Pownell and Mr. Dickson. The others were Mrs. Jones, Mrs. Harper, Mrs. Pownell, Mrs. Dickson, Miss Bates and Mrs. Young; Messrs. Harper, Usher, Taylor, Barrett, Bignall, Kenny, Wilmot. S. Pownell, Wilson, Chalmers, Fox and Sauberes.

Several subsequently became familiar figures on the Montreal boards.

Mr. and Mrs. C. S. Pownell were also for many years connected with Halifax theatricals. He died there in 1810.

LAMBERT SAYS OF 1806 :

"There is a theatre in Montreal, but the performers are as bad as the worst of our strolling actors ; yet they have the conscience to charge the same price, nearly, as the London theatres. Sometimes the officers of the Army lend their assistance to the company, but I have seen none except Col. Pye and Capt. Clark, of the 49th, who did not murder the best scenes of our dead poets. It may be seen how despicably low the Canadian theatricals must be when boys are obliged to perform the female characters ; the only actress being an old superannuated demi-rep, whose drunken *Belvideras, Desdemonas* and *Isabellas* have often enraptured a Canadian audience."

MONTREAL IN 1806.

"Will you walk with me about the town ?
Peruse the traders, gaze upon the buildings ?

Comedy of Errors, Act 1, Sc. 2.

Our clean-shaven friend with his silk hat and garment of
formal contemporaneous cut, after arriving from the United
States by stage, would notice in his walks about the town
that the city in 1806 possessed a Presbyterian church and an
unfinished Episcopalian church, two Catholic chapels, three
nunneries, Hamilton's city hotel and a primitive theatre.
If he took time to count the number of houses in the city he
would have found 1,578, and if his theatre had been large
enough to accommodate every resident, its walls would have
contained 5,014 females and 4,554 males, or a total of 9,568.
The only mode of conveyance he had between Montreal and
Quebec was by means of stages and batteaux, until 3rd November, 1809, when John Molson, of Montreal, sent the first
steamboat, "The Accommodation," to Quebec with ten pas-
sengers.

Several members of the 1806 company undertook performances during 1807, but met with little or no success, and it
was not until the following year that our playgoer became
more fortunate in the class of attractions presented.

Seth Prigmore was the next manager. He arrived late in
the Fall of 1807, and at once began the reconstruction of the
existing theatre, which he re-opened as

THE MONTREAL THEATRE

on 7th January, 1808.

In reference to the Prigmore   season the *Gazette* of 4th
January, 1808, says: "Mr. Prigmore presents his respectful
compliments to the ladies and gentlemen of this city and its
vicinity, and begs leave to inform them that on account of the
holydays he has been able to keep his carpenters to that
work, as was his first calculation; in consequence of this and
other unavoidable circumstances, he is obliged to postpone
the opening of the new theatre until Thursday next, the 7th.
He therefore humbly hopes this will meet the approbation of
his patrons and the public in general, conscious he has and
evermore will exert the utmost of his abilities to merit their

patronage and support." A packed house greeted the company in Colman's "Heir-at-Law" on the opening night. The
interior had undergone considerable repairs and embellish-
ments; stoves had been placed in different parts of the house,
the gallery frequenters were kept in strictest subjection, and
no intoxicants sold. On 18th February "The Tempest" was
produced, the principals in the cast being : *Prospero*, Mr.
Prigmore, and *Miranda*, "by a young lady of the city, being
her first appearance on any stage. Between the play and the
entertainment, a favorite song, to which will be added the
musical entertainment called 'The Purse, or the Benevolent
Tar,' Mr. Prigmore as *Will Steady*. Doors to be opened at
5 o'clock and performance to begin at 6. Boxes, $1; pit, 50c;
gallery, 25c." This performance was repeated by request.
The young lady referred to is believed to have been the
daughter of Hamilton, the inn-keeper.

Several other plays were produced under the Prigmore
management, and on 28th May the following announcement
appeared in the *Gazette:* [6]

"THEATRE.—The public are respectfully informed that the
theatre will be opened for a few nights longer. On Friday
evening, 27th May, will be presented a celebrated tragedy written by W. Shakespeare, called :

" OTHELLO."

MOOR OF VENICE.

Characters : *Othello*, Luke Usher ; *Iago*, Seth Prigmore ;
Cassio, Mr. Taylor ; *Roderigo*, Mr. Kennedy ; *Montano*, Hop-
kins Robertson ; *Gratiano*, Benjamin Carr ; *Desdemona*, Mrs.
Robinson ; *Emelia*, Miss Hamilton.

To which will be added the favorite farce called the

" REGISTRY OFFICE."

Characters : *Gulwell*, Mr. Taylor ; *Donald McIntosh*, Mr.
Robertson ; *Pat O'Carroll*, Mr. Prigmore ; *Frenchman*, Mr.
Carr.

"Doors open at 6.30 and performance at precisely 7.30.
Tickets to be had from Mr. Brown's book store until four,
afterwards at the theatre. Places for the boxes may be taken
as usual : Boxes, 5s. ; pit, 2s. 6d. ; gallery, 1s. 3d. No liquor

to be sold in the theatre." This was the first professional performance of " Othello " in Montreal, and marked the first appearance here of Usher and Robertson.

The following editorial also appeared : " We understand
that on Friday evening next will be presented Shakespeare's
celebrated tragedy of " Othello." The principal character
will be played by Mr. Usher, from the Boston Theatre, who,
for a long time in that company, has played the principal
characters with distinguished success. We doubt not, now
we find order and regularity observed in the theatre, that success will attend it ; and from the attractions both of pieces
and performers we do not hesitate to say there will be a
numerous audience."

In reference to a benefit performance to Mr. Usher, the
following personal appeared in the *Gazette* of 23rd June, 1808:
" Mr. Usher respectfully informs the public, that understand-
ing a large party of ladies and gentlemen will be assembled
on St. Helen's Island on Thursday afternoon, by a special invitation he has been induced by the request of a few friends
to postpone the entertainments advertised for Thursday until
Friday evening, 24th June, when will be presented a celebrated play in five acts (translated from the German of Schiller)
called 'Abaellino, the Great Bandit.' This play is universally allowed to be the *chef d'oeuvre* of Frederick Schiller,
whose fame as a dramatic writer has so resounded through
the continent of Europe that he was particularly called 'the
Shakespeare of Germany.' It has been performed in London
and in the different theatres of the United States with distinguished approbation. *Abaellino,* Mr. Usher ; *Rosamunda,*
Miss Hamilton, to which will be added the favorite farce of
'Raising the Wind': *Diddler,* Mr. Prigmore; *Sam,* Mr. Usher, in which he will introduce the song of the 'Farm Yard.'
The windows of the theatre will be kept open, and every attention paid to keep the place cool and comfortable."

Prigmore found after one year's management that his
efforts were not sufficiently profitable to warrant his continuance of the management. When he came here he had already advanced in years, and as an artist had lost considerable
of his old-time brilliancy.

SETH PRIGMORE was an Englishman who came to America
in the Fall of 1792. His first appearance on the stage in this country
was at Philadelphia, where he remained four months, after which he

went to New York, opening at the John St. Theatre, 28th January, 1793, as *Lord Scratch* in the comedy of "The Dramatist." He subsequently appeared in all the leading cities of the East, chiefly in the lighter comedy roles, but never succeeded in establishing himself in the front rank of his profession.

Mr. Prigmore played generally the comic old man; but his grimaces and low buffoonery made him far from acceptable to the judicious. Yet he was a favorite with the gods of Olympus. He was ever annoying in private life and offensive to the well-bred actor and gentleman. In a tour in Lower Canada in 1809, Durang says: "We met Mr. P. in a huge sleigh near Trois-Rivieres· He was wrapped up in a buffalo robe, a *bonnet rouge* was on his head, such as the Canadian peasantry wear ; a wampun belt was buckled around his waist, and Indian moccasins were on his feet. With his red face and burly form, he appeared like one of the ancient French landed proprietors, or like one of the half-breeded chiefs. He had some three or four persons with him, whom he called his company, and was then *en route* to play at Quebec."

Bernard thus describes Prigmore: A man of some vanity and little merit, whose opinion of himself was in inverse proportion to that of the public." One of the peculiarities of this person was to suppose (though he was neither handsome or insinuating) that every woman whom he saw, through a mysterious fatality, fell in love with him. There was a very benevolent widow in respectable circumstances, who frequently went to the theatre and was kind enough to enquire into the pecuniary condition of the players. Among others she asked about Prigmore and was told that he had a very small salary and made a very poor appearance. Hearing of this she remembered that she had a pair of her late husband's indispensables, which she resolved to offer him· A servant was dispatched to the object of her charity, who met one of the actors and partly disclosed his business. The latter went in search of Prigmore and exclaimed, " Prigmore, my dear boy, here's your fortune made at last, a rich widow has fallen in love with you and wants to see you." Prigmore was led to the servant in a state of bewildered rapture, and was told to call on the lady. His friend circulated the joke in the green room, and several waited on Prigmore to extend congratulations. Prigmore, as may be supposed, passed a sleepless night and spent an extra hour at his *toilette* next morning. He was ushered into the widow's parlor and began to felicitate himself at the aspect of his future home. The lady at length appeared· She was upon the verge of forty, a very fashionable age at that time, which, resting upon the shoulders of a very comely looking woman, seemed to be in character with her dwelling. She acquainted him that she had heard his situation was not as agreeable as he could wish, and that she was desirous of doing him all the service that lay in her power. Prigmore, considering this as an express declaration of her affections, was about to throw himself

at her feet, when she suddenly summoned her servant and said,
" Rachel, bring the breeches !" They were brought before the as-
tounded Prigmore, and as the lady folded them she remarked that they
were as good as new and begged his acceptance of them.

" And was it for this you sent for me, madam ?"

" Yes, sir."

He put on his hat and walked to the door.

" Won't you take the breeches, sir ?"

"Wear them yourself !"

The reader must pardon this little digression·

" **NOBLE** " **LUKE USHER** had a most retentive memory, being
able to memorize from twelve to fourteen lengths (42 lines to a
length) in a day and repeat the words ,verbatim from the text. He
first appeared on the American stage at Washington, D.C., in 1800,
and during the same year married Miss Snowden, *nee* L'Estrange,
in Philadelphia, where he played a short engagement. The couple
then went to Boston, becoming members of the company there, subsequently coming to Montreal· After closing his Montreal engagement, he went to Kentucky, where at Lexington, in the month of October, 1808, he opened the first theatre in the "Western country,"the
opening piece being "The Sailor's Daughter," and the characters performed by the Thespian Society. Returning to Montreal in 1809-10,
he became associated with Mills in the management of the theatre. In
1812 he opened the first theatre in Frankfort, Ky. In 1814 he made
his New York appearance for the first time at the Anthony Street
Theatre as *Gloster* in Richard III.

Usher organized a company to play in Kentucky and died on his
way thither the same year. He was buried at Lexington.

MRS. LUKE USHER, *nee* Harriet L'Estrange, was the daughter
of the actress, Mrs. L'Estrange, who died at Annapolis, 26th August,
1799. Mr. L'Estrange died at Baltimore in 1804. Miss L'Estrange
was on the stage in Philadelphia in 1796. She was of a tall figure, lady-
like in appearance and manners. Her complexion was dark and her
face handsome. She was thin in person and seemed physically delicate. Mr. Snowden, a young Philadelphian, fell in love with her in
her early life as an actress, and they were married. After his death
she married Usher in 1800. She held a lease of the Quebec theatre
for a time (1809-1810), playing occasionally with the officers. One of
these, Durang says, a Lieut· Wood, was a capital performer, and a
good scenic artist. Mrs· Usher died 28th April, 1814, at Louisville,Ky.

HOPKINS ROBERTSON was greatly liked for the excellence
of his work in serious roles and for his delineation of Scottish characters. He had been for several years at the Park Theatre, where he
had been greatly esteemed· By his presence of mind, at the burning
of the Richmond Theatre in 1811, he succeeded in saving many lives.
He died in his forty-eighth year in New York, 10th Nov., 1819.

MR. TAYLOR was an Englishman who gained many laurels in America for the excellence of his acting in the leading roles. He attained some notoriety on the occasion of his first appearance in Boston in 1794 as *Octavian* in " The Mountaineers," by wearing a natural beard grown for the occasion.

BENJAMIN CARR came from England to reside in Philadelphia, where he first engaged as a music dealer and publisher. Being a thorough musician and having a pleasing voice, he went on the stage, first in New York in 1794, in " Love in a Village." After several years he returned to teaching music in Philadelphia, where he died 24th May, 1836.

MR. ALLPORT, IN 1809,

was Prigmore's successor as manager of the theatre. He was a scene painter and a good oil portrait artist, but a very poor actor. He engaged Mr. Mills in June to play leads. The others in the company were Charles Durang, John Johnson, Horton, John D. Turnbull, Anderson (an Englishman who acted as prompter), Mrs. Mills, Mrs. Allport, who afterwards became Mrs. Horton, and Mr. and Mrs. Young. Mrs. Young subsequently became the great Mrs. Hughes.

The theatre during the season was only opened as occasion served. During the month of July, John Bernard, a well-known English comedian, visited Montreal, and describes the situation of its theatricals.

" I found a company playing at Montreal as deficient in talent as in numbers. Johnson, their acting manager, whom I had myself brought on the stage and laid under some obligations; Mills and Usher, the only actors of merit, were both from my own company and had left Boston, the former a month and the latter a year previous, and with the same object, that of anticipating me in securing the Canadian circuit, they having learned from my own lips that I intended to apply for it on the expiration of the lease of the Boston Theatre. Usher had so far succeeded as to obtain the Quebec house in the name of his wife for five years, but Mills had done nothing here, as the public were crying out for a new theatre and he had neither the money to erect one or friends to do so for him. Having many letters to the first families in the town, I at once delivered them, and, returning home highly gratified with the reception I had met with, I addressed a note to the theatre, expressing my wish to perform for a few nights, but received no answer. In consequence of this neglect, at which, however, I was not surprised after the attempt that had been made to forestall me, I gave out my bills for an evening's entertainment, and the news of my arrival soon spreading, was waited on a few hours

later by several gentlemen of the town to know why I did not perform. I referred them to the management, to whom therefore a note
was immediately forwarded, acquainting them that there would be no
attendance at the theatre unless I was engaged. A low fellow (Allport),
a scene painter, was accordingly sent to me to treat for terms, who actually offered me the whole concern for $300; but, not inclined to talk
of this, I told him I would engage with them on my usual terms, viz.:
to perform six nights for a clear benefit, which was agreed to. As
from their slight pretensions to support, the company had hitherto
met with but little success, they resolved to take benefits during my
six nights as their only remaining chance of indemnification. The
houses proved all good and my own an overflow, an assurance to me
what Montreal could do for a manager when any proper inducement
was offered to it. Mr. Mills had declined my services on the night
of his benefit, but being much in debt, had not found its profits to relieve him, and therefore made interest with some friends in the town
to get a second. They told him it would be of little use unless I stayed
to play for him, which was not more a compliment to my talents than
a proof of the wretched condition of the company. Much against his
inclinations, therefore, he was obliged to come to me with a stooping
neck to ask the favor. Though I felt that I might have justly retal-
iated, I chose rather to appeal to the man's better feelings, so agreed
to play for him, with the result that he cleared more money than had
been in the house altogether on the previous evening."

John Bernard terminated his Montreal engagement 20th
July, and on his way to Quebec stopped off at Three Rivers,
where he was the guest of General Sheaf, who, with his wife,
are mentioned by the comedian as clever amateur musicians.
At Quebec he was under the patronage of Col. Pye, who was
then at the head of the Amateur Association in the Rock
City. Judge Sewell also manifested interest in Mr. Bernard,
whom he had known some twenty-eight years previously at
Bristol. Six performances were given at Quebec, his characters being *Vapid, Gregory, Gubbins, Sir Robert Bramble, Allapod* and *Dashwood*, with *Lord Ogleby* and "The Liar" for his
benefit, which netted £95, not including ten guineas which
Governor Craig sent him for his ticket.

JOHN BERNARD was the first actor of prominence to visit
Montreal. He was gifted with superior talent both as an actor and as
an author. He was born in Portsmouth, England, in 1756. His father
was a naval officer, and a relative of Sir Francis Bernard, a British
governor of Massachusetts, who was so unpopular in that colony
that, when he was recalled in 1769, Boston celebrated his departure
by salvos of artillery and general demonstrations of public joy.

In 1774 John Bernard began a professional career destined to
last with honor, if not with profit, for half a century.

JOHN BERNARD.

He was a member of a strolling troupe for a short time, but soon gained admittance into the regular company which served the Norwich circuit. Here he met Mrs. Cooper, an actress of great versatility, whom he married in 1774. In the winter of 1777-78 Mr. and Mrs. Bernard joined the company at the Bath Theatre, then the most important in England outside of the metropolis. There they made their first appearance as *Gratiano* and *Portia* to the *Shylock* of Henderson. There they played *Sir Benjamin Backbite* and *Mrs. Candor*, in the first performance of "The School for Scandal," out of London. From 1780 until 1784 Bernard acted in Ireland, where he was associated with such stage giants as Miss O'Neill and John Kemble. On the 19th of September, 1784, Bernard made his first appearance in London and at the Covent Garden Theatre, playing *Archer* in the "Beau's Stratagem," Mrs. Bernard taking the part of *Mrs. Sullen*. In London Bernard made many friends ; his associates were Sheridan, Selwyn, Fox and the leading wits and men about town; and in 1789 he was elected secretary of the famous Beefsteak Club, an honor of which he was always very proud.

His first wife having died, he married again, in 1795, a Miss Fisher, who had a short and unimportant career on the stage, dying ten years later in America, to which country he carried her in the summer of 1797. His engagement was with Wignall, the Philadelphia manager, at a salary of £1,000 a twelve-month, at that time an unusually large amount; and he made his first American appearance on August 25, 1797, at the Greenwich Street Theatre, New York, as *Goldfinch* in "The Road to Ruin." During the six years Bernard spent in Philadelphia he played, besides the comedy parts for which he was engaged, *Shylock, Falconbridge, Hotspur* and others in the absence of a leading tragedian in the company. He went to Boston in 1803, where, in 1806, he became joint manager with Powers, of the Federal Street Theatre, and sailed for England in search of new attractions for his company. With a third wife, a Miss Wright, he returned to Boston the same year, and remained there at the head of affairs in the Federal street house until 1810. After professional tours in Canada, he acted in the Thespian Hall at Albany, N.Y., and opened January 18, 1813, the first regular theatre—that on Greene street—which Albany possessed. In 1816 he went upon a tour through the United States, being one of the earliest moving "stars" in the American theatrical firmament. In the autumn of 1817 he returned to the stock company of the theatre in Boston, and took his farewell of the American stage in the "Soldier's Daughter," April 19, 1819, delivering a farewell address, and going home to England as heartily liked and as sincerely regretted as his colonial relative of half a century before was hooted and despised. He died in London, November 29, 1828, in very poor circumstances.

MR. and MRS. WM. S. TURNER were born in England, and came to America as the early pioneers of the drama. In 1815 he opened the first theatre in Cincinnati. He was originally a printer.

but his individual merit was said to be in cooking canvas-back ducks. He returned to printing in 1830, in partnership with his son Frederick, in Philadelphia, where he died.

Sophia Turner was ladylike in her deportment on the stage, and showed great professional culture. She died in 1853.

JOHN MILLS, IN 1810,

managed the affairs of the theatre, being at the head of a small company which also included Messrs. Douglass, Johnson, Bernard, Harper, Kennedy, and Mrs. Mills, Turner, Harper and Cipriani. On 9th April a benefit was tendered Mrs. Harper, when the comedy of "Ways and Means" was produced together with the melodrama of "Tekell, or the Siege of Mongatz," written by Theodore E. Hook. On Shakespeare's birthday, 23rd April, Kennedy took a benefit in Schiller's "Robbers" and "The Indian Princess." This was followed by another benefit performance on the 30th for Joseph Harper in "Clemence and Waldemar" and "Tekell."

On 16th July Kennedy took his benefit, Mrs. Inchbald's "Lovers' Vows" being the bill, with the following cast : *Baron Wildenheim*, David Douglass; *Count Cassel*, John Mills; *Fred Friburg*, Mr. Kennedy; *Anhalt*, John Johnson; *Verdun*, John Bernard ; *Agatha Friburg*, Mrs. Eliza Mills; *Amelia Wildenheim*, Mrs. Sophia Turner; *Cottager's Wife*, Mrs. Cipriani.

Concluding with a farce called "The Jew and Doctor."

On 19th Mrs. Turner's benefit was in "Laugh When You Can," with the farce, "The Spoiled Child."

It is most interesting to note the appearance of David Douglass during this season, he having been the successor of Lewis Hallam, the organizer of America's earlier theatricals.

DAVID DOUGLASS, born in London in 1730, first appeared prominently in theatricals in Philadelphia about 1756. He married the widow of Lewis Hallam in 1758, and was for many years an active manager in Philadelphia and New York. He is believed to have taken the first regular company to Albany in 1769, but I have not been able to find any record of his having come to Canada prior to 1810. Mrs. Douglass died in 1773. She was one of the first actresses who crossed the Atlantic, and was possessed of great dramatic talent. A monument should have long since been erected to her memory by her profession. Douglass died in Jamaica shortly after his retirement from the stage in 1812.

JOSEPH HARPER appeared in New York with his first wife as members of the first company that acted after the Revolution, 25th November, 1785. He enjoyed the distinction of being the original *Falstaff* in America (John Street Theatre, 5th Oct., 1788), in which part he was favorably compared to John Henderson and James Quin. His labors were devoted entirely to the Eastern theatres, and at various times he managed the affairs of the Boston and Rhode Island houses. He was undoubtedly a talented actor, playing in a wide range of parts, and was highly esteemed as not more indefatigable in the discharge of the duties of his profession than meritorious in performing the obligations of social and domestic life. He was born in Jamaica, W.I. His first wife (Miss Smith) came from England. She was an admirable actress, performing the routine of old ladies very acceptably. She died in New York, 3rd October, 1791.

Joseph Harper ended his long career in New York in 1835.

John Mills and a party of actors from Montreal took

THE THEATRE OF QUEBEC

from Mr. Usher in the Fall of 1810, and did well with it. Durang, who was a member of the company, records that on the opening night Mills acted scenes from "Macbeth," although the company did not possess means beyond the compass of a farce. In the dagger scene he used two white-handled dinner knives borrowed from Mrs. Armstrong, a good-natured, little, fat lady who kept the tavern under the theatre. The kilt was borrowed from an officer and fellow-lodger. Taken as a whole, the play, as presented on this occasion, was a direful affair. It had not the redeeming merit of being ludicrous or funny, unless the amusement was furnished by a very tall Scotchman with a huge aquiline nose and a bald head, the very personification of a bald eagle topping a human skeleton. He was six feet four inches high, and delivered the words of the " gracious Duncan " in a vile Scotch jargon. This *autre* representative of majesty was a professional by courtesy, and named Sobey. He was a man of extensive information. In the farce that was played on the same evening, Mills acted *Dr. Lenitive*. The Governor-General and his pretty young wife were there. All the married officers and their wives were present, besides the fashion of Quebec. A collection of refinement that had been used to the most superb theatres of Europe were thus assembled in a large upper storey of a building which was in a state of dilapidaton. It was fixed up with tiers of boxes, but the auditors could shake hands across the area. The ladies in their brilliants and beauty, and the splendid scarlet uniforms of the officers, with silver and gold trimmings, made an array of magnificence not often witnessed in larger and more pretentious modern theatres. This brilliant audience, although they seemed to enjoy the performance with becoming grace and good humour, gradually withdrew after a Highland fling had been danced, and missed a treat by not waiting. Several not accompanied by ladies remained to enjoy the laugh. In the course of the farce there is a duet between *Dr. Lenitive* and *Label*, wherein runs between the lines little symphonies to be executed by the orchestra. There was no music there, but Mills resolved to sing the duet, although *Label* as pertinaciously refused, but was obliged to yield. During the verses Mills and his companion *fal la lud* the orchestra part, which was too much for one of the officers, who rose in his box and said, " Come, that's too ridiculous. We stood your *Macbeth*—a wench as *Lady Macbeth*, and the rest ; but I'll be damned if we stand your singing the symphonies of your songs." Mills, who was witty himself, and often the cause of wit in others, replied to the officer and audience in a very good-humored manner, having the tact to do this very cleverly. He worked upon their risibles, and concluded by saying to the officer, " No doubt you have acted yourself in your time for your amusement, sir, and have been put to your shifts." This set all in a roar of laughter, for this officer, it seems, had been a principal actor in their amateur club, and had perpetrated the very same expedients that he now stopped Mills for. The performance, however, ended merrily, and the band of the 8th Regiment played " Rule Britannia."

JOHN MILLS (by Charles Durang). He was one of my old friends and was a brother to Mrs. Woodham, whom he strongly resembled. Both were handsome and talented. Mrs. Cunnningham, of the Philadelphia Theatre, was his mother. The family had been brought out from England by the elder Warren. Mills was early at the Chestnut Street Theatre, Philadelphia, and afterwards doing leading business at Boston, possessing great versatility of talent, and if not great, was at least respectable in all. His disposition, however, was too convivial, although his liveliness and spirit of anecdote gave him an *entree* everywhere. In 1809 he went to Canada, where we met him in a theatrical corps at Montreal, under the management of Mr. Allport. During the severity of the winter the theatre was closed, and

Mills, with his family, moved into the theatre, making the green room his parlor and the adjacent dressing-rooms his chambers. Early in 1809 (Mr. Durang means 1811) he was taken seriously ill with the yellow jaundice. and, growing worse, died. On the night after he died a severe snowstorm came on, and such was the extent of the storm that on the following morning we could not open the door of the theatre, and it was noon before we were relieved by the snow clearers. We had nothing to eat or drink all this time. The death of poor Mills under these appalling circumstances was a melancholy reflection. But few friends any of us had. Montreal was not large then. Stone houses, tin roofs, iron doors and window shutters gave it the appearance of huge prisons, and the narrow streets, blocked with snow, were dreary avenues leading to the doors of the various cells. A few Canadian *habitants* roving through the streets with their grey *capots*, legings and *tuques*, were all the persons you would meet with, excepting an occasional group of soldiers and a guard. However, when it was known that poor Mills was no more by the English merchants and officers of the army, we were cheered by the general sympathies which were elicited on the occasion. A Boston merchant, Mr. Holmes, who had a branch at Montreal, came forward in the most handsome manner and offered his services and purse and wrote a beautiful obituary eulogy on Mills. On the day of the funeral Col. Proctor, commander of the 41st, signified his intention of attending. The body was placed in a mahogany coffin, and deposited on sleigh runners, drawn by one horse, followed by some half dozen actors and a dozen gentlemen of the city to the place of burial in the Quebec suburbs. As we passed the Champ de Mars, Col. Proctor and his officers joined the *cortege* on foot. As we left the old French fortified walls, then in a state of dilapidation, the cathedral of Notre Dame, with its snow-covered towers in the distance, the tops of the houses just seen above the walls. Montreal looked a town buried in the snow by some tremendous avalanche. The distant bugle and drum which were heard at the barracks, with the military array following the hearse, added to the impressiveness of the occasion. An Episcopal minister (Dr. Mountain) performed the ceremonies at the grave. Poor Jack, once the pride of the stage, the delight of the ladies and the admiration of men, now lies without one mark to point to his last resting place. Thou wert

> " A safe companion and an easy friend,
> Unblamed through life, lamented in thy end."

Mills was related to Mrs. Ternan, who subsequently appeared here, but by marriage only, Mrs. Mills being her aunt. He published some poetry in which he lauded the precocious talent of Fanny Jarman, later Ternan.

Mr. Durang has given us a very interesting reminiscence, and has left little for me to add. Mills came to America in 1806, making his first appearance in Baltimore as *Bob Tyke*,

4th October of that year. He first appeared in Philadelphia 3rd December in the same part. He was a good comedian, and well known in Boston, Philadelphia and New York. Mrs. Eliza Mills was a fair walking lady who possessed an excellent voice.

JOHN JOHNSON, a man of most exemplary character, and an actor of long provincial experience in England, where he was born in 1759, made his American appearance in Boston in 1795. His wife, who came with him, first appeared that year in Baltimore. Johnson visited England in 1798 (returning four years later), and again in 1806. He was a favorite *Sir Peter Teazle*, and Mrs. Johnson equally admired in the *vis-a-vis* role. Johnson died in New York, 25th Oct., 1819. Mrs. Johnson, who was many years his junior, is regarded to have been a very tall, beautiful and graceful actress. She died at Whitestone, L.I., 16th June, 1830.

JOHN JOHNSON, IN 1811,

succeeded the late Mr. Mills as lessee of the theatre. He was given a benefit, 6th May, and the programme indicates the members of the season's company. The performance was Morton's comedy, "A Cure for Heartache," just written, and this was its original production in Montreal.

Cast : *Old Rapid*, Mr. Robertson ; *Young Rapid*, Mr. Johnson ; *Vortex*, Mr. Young ; *Sir Herbert Stanley*, Mr. Coles ; *Charles Stanley*, Mr. Horton ; *Bronze*, Mr. C. Durang ; *Heartly*, Mr. Anderson ; *Farmer Oatland*, Mr. Allport ; *Waiter*, Mr. Harley ; *Frank Oatland*, Mr. Thompson ; *Miss Vortex*, Mrs. Young ; *Ellen Vortex*, Mrs. Allport ; *Jessie Oatland*, Mrs. Mills.

Mr. Young was given a benefit May 13th.

The threatening aspect of the reations between England and the United States at this time caused an extreme commercial depression, which greatly affected the profits of the theatre.

MR. ANDERSON, who had appeared here as early as 1809, and as late as 1818, died in Albany, 30th April, 1823.

THE WAR OF 1812

seems to have interfered with Montreal's regular theatricals, representations being very few and scarcely noteworthy. But Ceyatano's Circus did good business during the early winter months, closing at the end of April. On 10th February a benefit performance was given for the poor of Montreal, the total receipts being £93, less £14 expenses, leaving £79 8s 9d. Of this two-thirds was given to the Roman Catholic priest, one-sixth to Rev. Dr. Mountain (Episcopal), and one-sixth to Rev. Dr. Somerville (Presbyterian, St. Gabriel church).

This incident is worthy of special note, inasmuch as it records so early in the history of the city the mark of good-fellowship which should more closely exist between church and player, bound by the ties of *humanity*, which is greater than all the creeds, greater than all the books. The admirable spirit shown by the poor circus performers, all of whom lost their lives within a few months, invites for repetition the incident of the courtesy of the Recollet Fathers, as recorded by Rev. Dr. Campbell, when, in 1791, they placed their chapel at the disposal of the Presbyterian congregation, refusing any remuneration, although finally induced to accept a present of two hogsheads of Spanish wine and a box of candles as a slight acknowledgment of their courtesy.

CEYATANO & CO. were Spanish managers who arrived in this country in 1810, and exhibited extensively in specially erected board pavilions. In 1812 the entire outfit, including the company, was lost at sea, on their passage from New Orleans to Havana. This was probably the first regular touring circus in America.

CHARLES DURANG was a clever writer, as well as actor, and has left a valuable record of the Philadelphia stage. He not only appeared in Montreal, but his father, John, was also seen here in 1798. Charles was born in Philadelphia in 1795, and first appeared on the stage 1803. He married an actress named Mary White. He died in 1870.

THE YEAR 1813

was devoid of theatrical interest, the only entertainment of importance having been given by amateurs, 25th March. It consisted of Cumberland's comedy, " The Natural Son," with the farce of "The Review." The proceeds were for the benefit of the "widows and orphans of our fellow subjects who fell in the late battle in Upper Canada."

The few players who chanced to come to Montreal during the next five years found it almost impossible to attract the citizens, owing to the wretched condition of the play-house, which had not been originally erected for theatrical purposes, and, as there was little disposition manifested to improve this condition of affairs, Montreal was for five years practically without a theatre. A few itinerant players of little prominence gave occasional representations.

In time, however, the public began to cry out for a new temple of Thespis. Accordingly, in 1817, the erection of a new play-house was begun. It was situated at 2 College street, in a block of stone buildings bounded by St. Henry street and Longueuil lane. It was known as the Mansion House block, and built by William Johnson Holt. The central portion was called the Mansion House. The theatre, which was itself a wooden structure, extended back of the main building about sixty feet, and, small as it was, was amply roomy in those days for the English population of 8,000, having a seating capacity of 700 or 800. The entrance to the Mansion House and theatre was through a large arched doorway. This play-house was formally opened as

THE SECOND MONTREAL THEATRE

on 16th February, 1818, under the management of John D. Turnbull. The season was a memorable one, introducing to Montreal the tragedian, Frederick Brown, destined to become a favorite actor-manager here. The company was a strong one, including Messrs. Baker, H. A. Williams, Kennedy, Doige, Turnbull, Anderson, Huntley, McCleary, Thornton, Richards, Wells and Mesdames Williams, Kennedy, Shottwell, Dorion and Misses Denny and Grant. Admittance to the boxes was five shillings, and pit two and six. The doors opened at six and the curtain rose at seven. The opening bill was Lillos' "George Barnwell." It was on this occasion that Mrs. Dorion first appeared here in the role of Maria. A series of standard plays was produced, the second being "Venice Preserved," in which Mr. Baker was a debutant. This tragedy was cast as follows : Jaffier, Mr. Baker ; Pierre, Mr. Richards ; Belvidera, Mrs. H. A. Williams ; Duke of Venice, John D. Turnbull; Priuli, Mr. Kennedy; Renault, Mr. Doige; Spinosa, Mr. Anderson.

Mrs. Williams, who was as good in tragedy as in comedy, subsequently played *Mrs. Haller* in Kotzebue's " Stranger " to the *vis-a-vis* role assumed by Baker.

On Easter Monday, 28th March, Coleman's " Mountaineers," with two after-pieces, was presented. Mrs. Williams took a benefit on the 30th, in Dimond's " The Foundling of the Forest,' and farce, "The Budget of Blunders." Farquhar's " Beaux's Stratagem " was given for a benefit to Doige, 13th April. It was on this occasion that Fred Brown made his *debut* in Montreal in the following cast : *Aimwell,* Frederick Brown ; *Archer,* Mr. Baker ; *Sullen,* Mr. Thornton; *Sir Charles,* Mr. Richards ; *Fogard,* Mr. Anderson ; *Gibbett,* Mr. Huntley ; *Hornblow,* Mr. Doige ; *Bagshot,* Mr. Wells ; *Boniface,* Mr. McCleary ; *Scrub,* Mr. H. A. Williams ; *Lady Bountiful,* Mrs. Thornton; *Dorinda,* Mrs. Baker; *Mrs. Sullen,* Mrs. Williams ; *Ginsey,* Miss Grant ; *Cherry,* Miss Denny ; with the after-piece of "The Blind Boy." Among other productions was " Romeo and Juliet," 11th May, with Baker as *Romeo*; McCleary played *Mercutio* ; Thornton the *Apothecary*; Miss Denny, *Juliet,* and Mrs. Williams the *nurse,* in a benefit performance to Mr. and Mrs. Thornton. " The Man of Fortitude" was the after-piece.

The old favorite, John Bernard, appeared for three nights, opening 25th May, as *Allapod* in "The Poor Gentleman," and as *Michael* in the after-piece, "The Adopted Child." Another comedy, " The King's Birthday," was produced 4th June.

Several members of the old company left about this time, but were replaced by Messrs. Sierson, Morrison, Mrs. McDonald and Mrs. Green. Bernard took a benefit 9th June in "A School of Reform," and again 30th in "The Clandestine Marriage." Mrs. Green had a benefit 7th July, in "A Cure for Heartache." Mr. Green made his first appearance at this performance, singing " Robin Adair," and John Bernard was the *Oatland*. "Bluebeard" was produced 15th July for Mrs. Bernard's benefit, and on the 30th John Bernard recited at a benefit concert to Prof. Smith. The theatre was then closed until 21st October. It had been repainted, etc., and presented a neat appearance. The opening bill was Tobin's " Honeymoon." Lewis' tragedy of " Adelgitha " was given 16th November with the following people in the cast : Messrs. Carpenter, McCleary, Morrison, Richards, Brown, Sinclair and McMillen, Misses Denny and Moore,

Mrs. Cunningham and Dellawater. Baker made his reappearance 30th November in "Hamlet" and 7th December in " Pizarro." Most of the members of the company then dispersed, their places being filled for the remaining few productions of the season by " gentlemen amateurs." " Lovers' Vows " was given 14th December in aid of the Female Benevolent Society, and a benefit to Carpenter, the acting manager, in Sheridan's "School for Scandal," and "The Falls of Clyde," on 21st December, brought a rather successful season to a close.

JOHN D. TURNBULL was born in England, and made his American debut at Boston in 1799. He was first seen in Montreal under the Allport management as early as 1809, and just nine years later assumed the lesseeship of the new Montreal theatre. He was the author of "The Wood Demon." His daughter, Julia A., and a son were also histrionical. The former died in New York, 11th Sept., 1887.

FRANCES ANNE DENNY-DRAKE was born at Schenectady, N.Y., 6th November, 1797. Her parents moved to Albany when she was quite young. Ludlow is my authority in stating that her first appearance on the stage was at Cherry Valley as *Julia* in " The Midnight Hour," in the Spring of 1815. In 1818-19 we find her in Montreal as noted, and in 1820 she appeared at the Park Theatre, New York. She married Alexander Drake, a son of the old Southern manager, in 1823. During the season of 1829 she was playing in opposition to Fanny Kemble at New Orleans. After the death of her husband, in 1830, she became Mrs. G. W. Cutter, but they soon separated and she continued to act as Mrs. Drake. She died on her son's farm near Louisville, Ky., 1st Sept., 1875. Her career was a successful one artistically, she being considered one of the best actresses in the legitimate walks.

MR. and MRS. H. A. WILLIAMS were the parents of " *la petite* Augusta." After Mr. Williams' death Mrs. Williams, in 1828, became the wife of R. C. Maywood.

W. H. DYKES, IN 1819,

leased the theatre, and opened 14th January with "Othello," Frederick Brown playing the title role. He was accompanied by his wife, also an actress of merit. He played a round of characters, *Othello* thrice, *Hamlet, Shylock, Macbeth, Sir Giles Overreach, Octavius, Mortimer, Rolla, Glenroy, Coriolanus* and *Richard III.* A benefit was tendered Mrs. Brown, 8th February, in " The Suspicious Husband," and on 15th Manager Dykes took a benefit in " Jane Shore." Baker,

who had been ill for some time, recovered in time to take a
benefit, 17th, when he played *Iago* to Brown's *Othello*. Brown
reappeared on Easter Monday, 29th March, lending his services for the benefit of the company in Holcroft's " Road to
Ruin." Some little difficulty arose in connection with this
performance, owing to Miss Denny refusing to appear. She
was the favorite actress, and had asked for a benefit, but the
company would not agree to it, and her absence displeased
the public. Miss Denny gave a concert in the parlors of the
Mansion House, 5th April. Frederick Brown closed his season with " The Gamester," 9th April. The audience was
very enthusiastic and the house crowded. Brown recited
" Alexander's Feast," and made a speech. Mr. and Mrs.
Dykes took a benefit, 4th May, in " Speed the Plough," and
a similar testimonial was accorded Baker, 7th May. Miss
Denny, who had become reconciled to the company, took a
benefit, 11th May, in " The Honeymoon." Anderson benefited 14th May, and the season closed with a benefit to Richards and Sinclair in "The Broken Sword." There is also
a record of Mrs. French having given a concert in the Assembly Rooms of the Mansion House, 22nd July. After concluding his Montreal engagement, Brown appeared in Boston, where he had made a very favorable impression in 1816.
Being called upon to play in support of Cooper and Wallack,
he went through his parts with such indifference that he was
rebuked by press and public. The former accused Brown of
using expressions disrespectful to a Boston audience, and,
early in December, the managers, fearing a riot, allowed
Brown to depart for Montreal, where he inaugurated a short
winter season, 20th December, during which were produced
Rev. Maturin's " Bertram," " Brutus," " George Barnwell,"
"Othello," "Manuel," etc.; but the illness of the *star* brought
the season to a speedy close. Mr. and Mrs. George Bartley,
English actors, gave an entertainment at the Mansion House,
15th November, 1819. They had been in America one year,
and had come to Montreal in the company of Mr. Brown,
from Boston, where their abilities had not been fully recognized by the miscellaneous audience.

MR. and MRS. BARTLEY enjoyed high esteem in England. He
had played *Richard, Shylock* and other leading roles in tragedy and
comedy. He married Miss Smith in 1814. Her talents were equal
to his, and their public readings were much appreciated, Mr. Bart-

ley retired from the stage as late as 1853. He had several times given
readings before Queen Victoria. Mrs. Bartley died 14th Jan., 1850,
aged 64. George Bartley followed 22nd July, 1858, in his seventy-
fourth year.

W. H. DYKES, an eccentric actor-manager, was too much of a
rolling-stone to trace. He was here, there and everywhere, and had
been of the Boston company prior to his advent in Montreal. While
there he married Miss Brailsford.

THE SEASON OF 1820

was a short and unimportant one, opening 24th January with
"The Honeymoon," under the patronage of Lieut.-Col. Burer,
of the 37th Regiment. Miss Denny, assisted by officers of
the regiment, took part, with the permission of the theatre's
manager, Mr. Turnbull. Brown reappeared, 7th February,
in "King Lear," and after giving three performances, the
season practically closed. During the year some amateur
performances were given, and some magicians and musicians
gave entertainments at the Mansion House assembly rooms.
From this time the annuals of this theatre practically ceased.

In 1831 we find the Congregationalists using the hall as a
place of worship. The main building became known as the
Eagle Hotel, kept by Francis Duclos. The hotel gradually
sank into a low lodging-house, known as "Noah's Ark," and
during the smallpox epidemic of 1885 it was found to be a
veritable pest-hole, with its one hundred and ten human in-
mates. The place was cleared out by the police, and has
since been used for manufacturing purposes. All that remains of the old theatre is the arched front entrance on
College street (now part of St. Paul street).

THE THIRD MONTREAL THEATRE

stood on Notre Dame street, opposite the Recollet Barracks.
It was opened 21st January, 1821, with Kenny's farce,
"Raising the Wind." C. W. Blanchard, of circus fame, was the
manager. The following was the cast: *Plainway*, Mr. C. W.
Blanchard ; *Diddler*, Mr. Hiven ; *Fainwould*, Mr. Greene ;
Sam, Mr. Woodruff ; *Richard*, Mr. G. Blanchard ; *Peggy*,
Mrs. Greene ; *Miss Durable*, Mrs. Thornton. Two after-

pieces, "Day After the Wedding" and "The Village Lawyer," were also in the evening's bill.

This company met with very fair business during the season, owing to extensive repairs going on at the Mansion House and Theatre. This new house had a career of three seasons.

THE NEW MARKET THEATRE,

or Roy's assembly rooms, stood on Jacques Cartier square, and was used for theatrical purposes as early as 1822.

Late in the summer a small company attempted to support the young "American Roscius," George Frederick Smith, a youthful prodigy eleven years of age. He was seen as *Norval, Octavian, Richard* and *Romeo*, when he departed for Albany.

GEORGE FREDERICK SMITH had been well drilled in his characterizations, and elicited a fair amount of praise. He was born in Cork, Ireland, 29th Dec., 1811. He appeared in New York in 1821. After a short career on the stage he settled in New Orleans as a dentist.

This theatre was the scene of little interest, until late in the spring of 1824. Most of the members of the company had already been seen here. The feature of the season was the production of Kenny's comedy, "Ellen Rosenberg," for the benefit of Mr. Wilkins, 20th May. The cast shows the *personnel* of the troupe : *Rosenberg*, Mr. Emanuel Judah ; *Col. Mountfort*, Mr. Charles Webb ; *Elector*, Mr. Modely ; *Flutterman*, Mr. Wilkins ; *Storm*, Mr. J. D. Turnbull ; *Stephen*, Mr. J. Turnbull ; *Ellen Rosenberg*, Miss Smith ; *Christine*, Mrs. Dorion ; *Mrs. Flutterman*, Miss Johnson. "The Review" was the after-piece. A ventriloquist, Taylor, also performed. The performance began at 7.30. "Ellen Rosenberg" became a favorite piece in Montreal, and was subsequently produced at the Royal Circus. This place of amusement was short-lived.

On 17th January, 1823, tenders were asked for masonic and carpentering work for the proposed new theatre on St. Paul street, by order of the committee and George Auldjo.

THE ROYAL CIRCUS.

On 24th March, 1824, West and Blanchard opened their circus on Craig Street, in rear of the present site of the St. Lawrence Hall. The principals of the troupe consisted of Messrs McDonald, Turner, Miss Elizabeth Blanchard, Mrs. Blanchard, as well as West and Blanchard. Meeting with good patronage, they erected a stage in the spring, and began giving dramatic performances as well, producing "Timour, the Tartar," "Inkle and Yarico," "The Forty Thieves," " Maid of Magpie," "Lodiska," together with other equestrian dramas.

The season closed 8th October with a benefit to Mr. Blanchard.

EMANUEL JUDAH was born in New York and was connected with the Southern theatres during the early part of his career. He first appeared in New York as *Bulchasin Muley* in "The Mountaineers." at the Pavilion Theatre, 18th August, 1823. In 1824 and 1825 he played in Montreal. He was well known at the minor theatres of New York. In 1829 he was at Albany under Vernon's management. His last metropolitan engagement was at the Franklin Theatre in 1837. Two years later he was drowned in the Gulf of Mexico. His wife, Sophia, a well-known actress, died in New York in 1865. She was the grandmother of the famous Worrell sisters.

CHARLES WEBB, a native of Philadelphia, never attained to prominence. After a career of many vicissitudes he jumped from a bridge in Wheeling, Va., in March, 1851.

The year 1825 saw the opening of Montreal's sixth theatre, the first

THEATRE ROYAL,

which was built on the site now forming the western end of Bonsecours market on St. Paul street. It cost $30,000, the amount being partly raised by subscription, and the Hon. John Molson was the principal shareholder. Mr. Forbes was the architect. The building was a commodious one for the period, and presented an attractive interior as well as exterior. It was two stories high, with a Doric portico. Inside it had two tiers of boxes, the pit and a gallery. It was

FREDERICK BROWN.

opened under the management of the old favorite, Frederick
Brown, the tragedian, and T. S. Brown (no relation) in his
" Memoirs " chronicles the fact that the company, which
numbered seventy-one people, broke down at the end of the
season from its own weight. It is more reasonable, however,
to consider this figure somewhat fabulous. The opening of
the theatre was on Monday, 21st November, with Reynolds'
comedy, " The Dramatist." The principal actors during the
season were Mr. and Mrs. F. Brown, Watkinson, Laws, Lear,
Morton, Brewster, Judah, Horton, Essender, Herbert, Clark,
Heyl, Talbot, Master Talbot, Harris, Logan, Mr. and Mrs.
Forbes, Mrs. Meline, Miss Eliza Riddle, Mrs. Brazier, Mrs.
Talbot, Mrs. Wm. Riddle, Mrs. Brundage and Miss Turner.

Following the opening piece were produced successively the
following throughout the balance of the season : " Speed the
Plough," "The Wonder, or a Woman Keeps a Secret," "Town
and Country," " Richard III.," " The Stranger," " Douglas,"
with Miss Riddle as *Young Norval* ; "Hamlet," "The Way to
Get Married," for Miss Riddle's benefit and farewell appearance, 7th December, concluding with "The Pages; or "Frederick the Great," " Merchant of Venice," "Adelgitha." Miss
Riddle was re-engaged 14th December, appearing as *Virginia* to Brown's *Virginius*, this being the original representation of Knowles' sublime tragedy in Montreal. On 19th
was produced "Coriolanus," followed by Tobin's "Honeymoon," "The Wandering Boys," "Heir-at-law," "King Lear,"
28th; and on 30th, for Miss Riddle's benefit and last appearance, " The Road to Ruin," closing the season.

FREDERICK and SOPHIA BROWN. Mr. Brown was born in
England, and was there rocked and nurtured in the cradle of Thespis.
His father was D. L. Brown. At a very early age he was known as
the Liverpool Roscius, and gave remarkably precocious signs of extraordinary excellence. The prophesies then made were never fully
realized; yet he obtained a most respectable rank in all the walks to
which he aspired, and it was only his own weakness that caused his
vaulting ambition to " o'erleap itself," and left him as the waif of the
common. He stood well in England, and married Sophia DeCamp,
a sister to Vincent, and to Mrs. Charles Kemble. Mrs. Brown was a
fine actress and an accomplished woman, but, to use a common word,
a homely one. At first glance one would conceive her to be very ugly;
yet so fascinating was her brilliant conversation that a few minutes in
her presence would transform her face into one of great beauty of
expression, reflecting pleasing intelligence. Frederick Brown was

equally imbued with all these faculties, and in person (although small in stature) was affable and gentlemanly. They were engaged in England by Mr. Dickson, the Boston manager, for the Federal Street Theatre, and made their appearance there about 1816. After establishing the Theatre Royal, at Montreal, the house for a time paid, but eventually the manager fell into bankruptcy. He conducted things royally, in accordance with the supremacy of the name of his house, but he was extravagantly inclined and neglected the balance sheet of his accounts. He played tragedy or comedy as required. His *Don Felix* in " The Wonder " was excellent, and in parts of that nature he was neatness and elegance combined. He had much chaste vivacity and clear judgment, never "o'erstepping the modesty of nature." His tragedy performances may be estimated by the same rule. They were chaste and discriminating to a fault. Although of slight physical powers, he was not without force and tragic expression of intensity, possessing a face of no marked constructiveness, but rather common in form; yet it was not without its passionate or various reflection of inward feeling, though genius was not present—that powerful lever of the great in art. Brown was conventional in all he did; thoroughly bred in the Kemble school, he never transcended its doctrines. But though his colouring was of the drawing-room tint, he would not use the dagger with the complacency of Joseph Surface when handing a chair to Lady Teazle: the emotional would harmonize with the action of the terrible. Without annoying rant, his forte, like a soft impressive picture, lay in the *chiaro oscuro*. In May, 1821, Kean was engaged to act at the Boston Theatre. On one occasion, when billed for Richard, the great actor would not go on, the house being too slim, he said. Brown was sent for and gave great satisfaction. He was stage manager for Gilbert at Charleston, S.C., 1824, and went South again in 1830, accompanied by James E. Murdoch, who must have gained good instruction from the English actor. Brown was an excellent reader, and combined with large literary acquirements, the government of a refined, cultivated mind.

In the summer of 1834. Brown was associated at Wilmington. Del., with a corps of comedians somewhat genial in mind. Charles Durang, among others. Many pleasant walks were taken around the romantic environs of that beautiful place. Brown would often stroll into the old graveyard of the Swedes' Church, which stood on an elevated slope on the right bank of the picturesque winding Christiana creek. The church was then in a deplorable condition of dilapidation, less from age than from want of care. The cemetery was overrun with weeds and grass. Here and there an old, rude-cut headstone would peep over the weeds, inscribed with the name of some one who had died during the reign of Charles, William, Mary or Anne, etc. Poor Brown became impressed with the scene, as the buried dead at his feet reminded him of his country's history. He believed the fane worthy of some preservation, and in his contempla_ tions penned a few affecting poetical lines descriptive of its hallowed ground and history, now being destroyed through neglect. The editor of the Wilmington paper published the verses, which had the effect of causing the construction of an enclosure around the burying ground. Subsequently the ancient church was repaired. so that service was again heard within its once deserted walls. Thus a poor performer and his muse did some good to religion, in restoring a deserted sacred edifice, wherein the country's earliest forefathers had worshipped, to prayer and religious history.

Frederick Brown, from necessity, became a wanderer in the world, ending his life of sorrow in an obscure town in North Carolina in the year 1838.

Mrs. Brown, during her later years, had a pupil by the name of Miss Meadows, whom she schooled in a series of characters. With this girl, who had merit, Mrs. Brown travelled through the South and West, realizing a little money by the effort. Mrs. Brown afterwards took an engagement to play the old dames of comedy, and died at Mobile, Alabama, in 1841.

The foregoing sketch of Brown was written by Charles Durang, who, having been personally acquainted with the tragedian, is the best authority I have been able to find. On 9th March, 1819, he appeared as *Hamlet* at New York. In 1826 he supported Edmund Kean during the latter's engagement in Montreal, and was still lessee of the Theatre Royal, which he opened a year previously.

MISS ELIZA L. RIDDLE was the daughter of the comedians, Mr. and Mrs. Wm. Riddle, and was born in 1809. Her first appearance was not a distinct success, but she made rapid headway, and became a leading lady of acknowledged ability. During the season 1831-32, she appeared in the original representation of Knowles' "Hunchback" in this country, assuming the role of *Julia* at the Arch Street Theatre, Philadelphia. In 1836 she married Joseph M. Field.

LEWIS HEYL possessed a sweet voice, and as a singer gained considerable popularity. He was a native of Philadelphia, where the final call was made in 1839.

During the year

THE ROYAL CIRCUS

did a fair business under the management of George Blanchard. On 13th October "The Romp" was produced, and on the following night a benefit was given to Mr. Roper in "The Forty Thieves." The company at that time included Messrs. Roper, Schinotti, Gale, Simmonds, Martin, Johnson, C. Blanchard, G. Blanchard, Lawson and Brazier, Mrss. Talbot, Carnes, Brundage, Honey, Parker and Brazier. "The Cobbler's Daughter" and "Sylvester Daggerwood" were presented 17th October. On this occasion Mr. Simmonds played *Daggerwood,* and introduced imitations of the popular actors of the day. On the following evening Mrs. Carnes benefited in "No Song, No Supper." Cast : *Robin,* Mr. Roper; *Crop,* Mr. Schinotti ; *Endless,* Mr. Simmonds ; *Frederick,* Mr. Martin ; *William,* Mr. Johnson ; *Thomas,* Mr. C. Blanchard ; *Dorothy,* Mrs. Talbot ; *Margaretta,* Mrs. Carnes ; *Nelly,* Mrs. Brundage ; *Louisa,* Mrs. Honey. This closed the season.

MR. and MRS. JAMES ROPER. Mr. Roper was early in the equestrian business. His dramatic efforts were mostly important as prompter. Mrs. Roper (maiden name Cooke) was genteel and lady-like, but of no great pretensions to talent. She died of consumption at Philadelphia in 1835.

MRS. TALBOT came to America with her first husband in 1820, but separated from him and married Chas. Page. She died in Philadelphia in 1838.

MARY ANNE BRUNDAGE first appeared in New York in 1815. She married McDonald Clarke, from whom she eventually separated.

THE SEASON OF 1826

was one of the most memorable in Montreal's theatrical annals, and opened early in the year with F. Brown again at the head of affairs. Robert Campbell Maywood appeared in February in a round of legitimate characters, and became quite popular here. His engagement closed 20th February, when he took a benefit.

Maywood's engagement in Montreal was followed by that of Thomas S. Hamblin, then in his twenty-sixth year. He made his first appearance here in the character of *Hamlet,* 22nd February, and played a return engagement, 28th March, in "William Tell."

THOMAS S. HAMBLIN (*as Coriolanus*).

THOS. SOWERBEY HAMBLIN was born near London, 14th May, 1800, and first appeared on the stage as *Truman* in "George Barnwell," at Drury Lane Theatre in 1819. The illness of Alexander Rae brought Hamblin out in *Hamlet* two or three seasons later at the same theatre with considerable success for so young an actor. He married Elizabeth Blanchard in 1825, and in the early fall of that year came to America under the auspices of Price and Simpson, making his first appearance in his favorite character of *Hamlet* at the Park Theatre. After remaining in New York about a year, he and his wife began starring. He revisited England, and in 1830 leased the Bowery Theatre, New York, which he managed with but few intermissions until his death, 8th January, 1853. He died in New York and is buried in Greenwood Cemetery. During his managerial career, he gave the total nightly receipts of his theatre over 160 times for the benefit of charities. As an actor he had forgotten more than most actors knew and still remembered enough to teach the best of them. To see him dressed for *Brutus, Coriolanus* or *Virginius* was a study for a painter. A singular fatality seemed to pursue him through life, that was, the loss of his theatres by fire no fewer than four times, and by a strange coincidence there were four Mrs. Hamblins in his history. At his death he left eight heirs, each of whom received $10,000. A daughter, Constance Hamblin, has been frequently seen here in support of legitimate stars.

R. C. MAYWOOD was born in Scotland in 1786. He first appeared on the American stage in 1819 at the Park Theatre, New York, as *Richard III.*, and at Philadelphia, 6th Nov., 1828, at the Arch Street Theatre, as *King Lear*. In April, 1832, he became manager of the Walnut Street Theatre, Philadelphia, in conjunction with Pratt and Rowbotham. He subsequently managed the Chestnut Street Theatre. In 1840 he relinquished the management and took his farewell benefit. He died 1st Dec., 1856, at Troy, N.Y.

Probably the greatest actor who ever visited Montreal appeared during the midsummer season. I refer to Edmund Kean.

The following letter appeared in the *Gazette* of 21st January, 1826 :

To Edmund Kean, Esq:

SIR,—It is not without considerable interest that your fellow subjects in this province have heard of your arrival in America. Whatever may be the motives that induced you to make so long a voyage, they hoped that the ocean would have buried all references to them forever, and that your reception on the American Atlantic shores would have been such as your professional talents ought always to command and secure. If your fellow subjects in Canada have been partially disappointed, they rejoice that such disappointment is counterbalanced by the exercise in two great and enlightened cities of

those feelings of humanity which are due to the stranger in every
country, and of those honors which genius will ever command among
every polite and civilized people. The purport of this is to invite you
on your powerful character to Canada. I can assure you that this
invitation does not proceed from a solitary individual. It is the voice
of both provinces, which, if obeyed, would hail you with a welcome
that would resound from Niagara to Montmorency. In the city an
elegant and convenient theatre has lately been built. The present
manager, Mr. F. Brown, is a gentleman of professional and private respectability, and I venture to assure you that your appearance on our
boards would be at once gratifying to your feelings as a man and to
your expectations as an actor, In proof of this I could present you
with long extracts from all the newspapers published in this country,
every one of which has borne out ample testimony to proper sentiments of joy at your success and regret at your disappointment in the
United States. I, in common with many other persons of respectability, who have witnessed the homage paid to your great talents by the
sages, the philosophers and the poets of your mother country, at least
hope that as soon as convenient you will enable a loyal and hospitable
people, proud of their country, to do justice to those sentiments which
they entertain regarding you. Should your eye chance to meet this
letter, some notice would greatly oblige many thousands besides, sir,

Your obedient servant,

PHILO EURIPIDES.

It is too late in the century to learn whether is was the
composition of the letter or the anticipation of a good business that finally induced the great actor to visit Montreal,
which he accordingly did, making his *debut* 31st July, in his
great character of *Gloster* in " Richard III." On 2nd August
he played the role that first made him famous—*Shylock* ; and
on the following night he electrified our grandfathers in
Othello. On that occasion the following was the distribution
of characters: *Othello*, Mr. Edmund Kean; *Iago*, Mr. Frederick
Brown ; *Cassio*, Mr. Wm. Lee ; *Rodrigo*, Mr. Thos. Placide ;
Desdemona, Miss Riddle ; *Emelia*, Mrs. F. Brown. His farewell appearance and benefit was in "King Lear," 9th August.

A public dinner was tendered the distinguished artist,
who was otherwise lionized and feted during his stay.

One, T. S. Brown, in his memoirs, recites an incident of
Kean's visit, for the truth of which I do not vouch, as he errs
greatly in his data, etc., but here it is for what it is worth :

"When Edmund Kean came to this city in 1827, the theatre was
closed, but the citizens were so anxious to see him, that a company
was formed with Mrs. Barnes(Carnes), and some circus preformers,
who happened to be in the city at the time, and he gave four performances. In the last one he was extremely drunk. He was playing the
part of 'Daggerforth' (Daggerwood) in a comedy, and during the
performance had to stand on his head on a chair. The gallery liked
this, and shouted 'Another tumble, Mr. Kean !' Kean thought they

said 'Another tumbler, Mr. Kean !' and he got furious and rushed off the stage and out of the theatre. The gallery in its turn got angry, and started to smash things generally. Kean was hastily sent for, and was found in bed at the Masonic Hall (Hotel). He was dressed and brought back to the theatre where he made a graceful apology to the audience, winding it up, however, by saying : 'As for the man who told me to take another tumbler I despise him !' This was given in his deepest and most tragic tones, and fairly brought down the house."

Edmund Kean had been in America since the previous November, making his appearance at the Park Theatre, New York, as *Gloster*, 14th November, 1825, but owing to an indiscretion on his part in a reference to America and its people, while on his first visit in 1820, he was confronted by a turbulent audience, which would not hear the apology the actor wished to make. This rioting also continued at Boston. but he was rather more favorably received at Philadelphia in January, 1826, after having again appeared in New York a few days previously to a more satisfactory welcome.

Before departing for Quebec, Kean was entertained at a public dinner at the Masonic Hall Hotel, and in the course of a speech, made in reply to the drinking of his health, spoke of his departure from England in a manner that serves to throw fresh light upon his many-sided character.

"I was scarcely from the land," he said, "when reason told me I had lost a portion of my respectability as a man, and my chief resources depended on my exertions as an actor. I assumed, therefore, a callous indifference, played for a time the character of misanthrope, knit my brows, and pretended contempt for the world, but it was merely acting. Deeply I felt the loss of that society I had for years associated with, and every little act of kindness penetrated the brazen armor I had borrowed for the occasion. The searching eye could even discern smiles without mirth, and pastime without pleasure."

At Quebec his advent excited unusual interest. He had been announced to perform on Monday, 8th September, and expected to arrive on the previous Thursday. Not having appeared by Sunday, the disappointment of Quebecers greatly increased the sensation. On Monday, however, news was brought that he was positively on the tug-boat *Hercules*, which was towing a vessel into the harbour, when a number of citizens went down to meet and give him a hearty welcome ; and the manager, learning that he was able and willing to play that night, sent the public bellman about town to announce the fact. The theatre was crowded ; the Governor, Lady Dalhousie and suite occupied boxes, and Kean was enthusiastically applauded.

During his engagement at Quebec an incident occurred which greatly delighted him.   Becoming aware of the excitement his performances were creating, a number of Indians attended the theatre, when Kean, gratified by their visit, and pleased by their picturesque appearance, desired to become better acquainted with them.   Introductions, therefore, followed.   He was no less an object of wonder and admiration to them than they to him.

He entertained them hospitably, recited, sang and played to them ; rode with and tumbled for them, and finally expressed his desire to become one of their tribe, and leave the ways of the white man forever.   The Indians made him a chief, and with much ceremony invested him with a costume such as they wore (something more than a pair of overalls and a blanket) and gave him the name of *Alanienouidet*.   He then disappeared with them.   Subsequently speaking of this period to his friend Grattan, he declared he had gone mad for several days, and having joined the Indians in their camp, he was pursued by some friends, who carried him back. and for a time treated as a lunatic before he was allowed to leave for New York.   He always declared that he valued the honor the Hurons had conferred on him above the highest triumphs he had achieved at Drury Lane.

He reappeared in New York, 18th November, 1826, playing *Richard*, but in a few days the severe mental and physical strain he had endured culminated in a serious illness.   His great powers had declined, and his friends believed that he had not long to live. He made his last appearance in America, 5th December, 1826, in New York, in the part of *Richard*, reappearing in London as *Shylock*, 8th January, 1827.

It was painfully evident he was a physical wreck; that the spirit which had kindled his audiences to fervor was often absent, while traces of suffering were but too visible.   To commemorate his return to Dublin, the management of the theatre commissioned an artist named Meyer to paint a full length portrait of Kean, representing him, at his own request, as an Indian chief; and when he took his benefit, 2nd April, it was announced he would not only play *King Lear*, but deliver a farewell address in the character and costume of *Alanienouidet*, chief of the Huron Indians, which name and title were conferred upon him by the Hurons at Quebec on 7th October, 1826.

EDMUND KEEN.
From the Gebbie collection.

EDMUND KEAN was one of the greatest actors the world has produced. Byron compared his acting to reading Shakespeare by flashes of lightning, and Mrs. Garrick recognized in him a worthy successor to her David, and the only one fit to wear his sword. Castle street, Leicester square, was the scene of the actor's birth, 4th Nov., 1787. His reputed father was Aaron Kean, a stage carpenter, and his mother a strolling actress named Nancy Carey, grand-daughter of that Henry Carey, the dramatist, who wrote the charming lyric, " Sally in Our Alley." It was a tidy actress, named Miss Tidswell, who seems to have picked young Kean from the gutter to make him the consummate flower of the British stage; she too was credited with being his mother, but it seems she was able to prove an alibi. She gave the poor little waif some schooling, and what was more to his profit, an introduction to the stage.

He appeared very early as a representative of cupids, monkeys and devils, and on one occasion when an unfortunate step caused the downfall of sundry fellow-devils he wittily excused himself to the angry manager by stating that he had never appeared in *tragedy* before.

Then his mother, discovering that he had a gift, made use of it. She spirited the child away to attract crowds, while she sold her pack or told fortunes. The boy carried the tramp's pack, and at farm-houses and among the gentry recited the lines Miss Tidswell had taught him. He thus happened to appear before an eminent physician, Dr. Young, father of the afterwards celebrated actor, Charles Young. The doctor introduced the lad to a lady who was passionately enamored of the stage—a Mrs. Clarke. This lady, having a grand company, invited the boy to entertain her guests. When the little ragged boy appeared in the grand dining-room the lady asked: "Are you the boy who recites so well?" The child bowed with great dignity. "What can you recite?" " Richard the III.;" "Speed the Plough;" " Hamlet;" " Harlequin," answered the unabashed youngster. The lady took him to her dressing-room and made a composite costume for the little actor; presently he did, sure enough, declaim all the parts he had named. The guests rewarded his efforts by a shower of silver pieces, which the boy proudly declined to pick up. Mrs. Clarke was so struck by this trait that she at once set about educating the little genius. He was placed at school, and instructed in all the elementary studies of the day. This lasted two years, when one day, having visitors, Mrs. Clarke invited them to the theatre and the boy as well. "What !" cried the snob of the party; "does he sit in the box with you ?" Kean's face flushed crimson; he quit the table, and that night disappeared from his benefactor's home.

Then he resumed the tramp life with Nancy Carey, alternating with sojourns under the wing of Miss Tidswell. On one occasion his acting in a country show at Windsor so impressed the King that he sent for the little man and made him a present of two guineas. Next the longing for the sea seized him, and he succeeded in shipping as cabin boy for a voyage to Madeira. But the life of the ship was not what he had imagined, so he returned to tramping as soon as the voyage brought him back. Then followed vicissitudes such as a realist in romance would hardly venture to devise for a social outcast. He found himself afterwards in Belfast, Ireland, cast with the great Mrs. Siddons, who condescended to speak with tolerance of his acting, little suspecting that the poor wretch who was playing secondary parts was in a short time to seize the tragic sceptre from the hands of the great Kemble in his own theatre.

Mrs. Siddons said that he played well, but that there was too little of him to make a great actor. He was, in person, five feet four inches in height. In 1808 he married Miss Mary Chambers, the leading lady of Beverley's company, of which he was also a member. She was nine years his senior.

Sometimes the record is too harrowing to retrace, the man of genius and the wretched wife trapsing over the country roads, living on charity or nothing at all.

It was when fortune was at its lowest, when in utter destitution, the wretched couple had begged a theatre at Exeter, and when the curtain rang up there was but a sprinkling of people in the seats, that fortune was beaming with its broadest smiles. In spite of the depressing house, Kean gave loose to his genius, and played with divine fire, After the play, Kean, in his dressing room, heard some one inquiring about him, and then, after some explanatory phrases, heard the startling words; "I am the manager of Drury Lane." The manager of Drury Lane had discovered the divine gift in the overworked, unappreciated actor, and that was the beginning of the greatest tragic career in the annals of the British stage.

The fateful opening was set down for the 26th January, 1813, while the British were still inebriated over the miraculous conquest of Napoleon by the allies after the campaign in Germany. Everything seemed to be done to make the fateful appearance a failure; the poor man could get but one rehearsal, and then his fellow-actors sneered at his slender figure and his extraordinary innovations in the traditions of the part. For the first time in six months Kean had meat for his meal that day, and as he was quitting his wife he exclaimed: "My God, if I succeed I shall go mad !"

He carried his entire costuming outfit in a small bundle in his hands and excited the derision of his fellow-actors by his miserable figure. The manager was desperate, for the theatre had been steadily losing money for months. and Kean was a last desperate resort. When he emerged from his dressing room in a black wig, instead of the traditional red wig, the actors broke into a guffaw of derision. The night was hideously depressing, snow covered the ground and the house was very meagrely filled, until late in the evening, when the overflow from Covent Garden served to patch up the gaping emptiness. The "first night" audience took its time in judging the debutant; but his voice

E. KEAN (*as Alan*).

In the dress presented to him on the occasion of his being chosen
a chief of the Huron tribe of Indians, by the name of Alanienouidet,
at Quebec, 7th October, 1826.

Painted by Meyer, and engraved by Storm. Reproduced from an
original proof in the possession of Franklin Graham.

won the approval of some of the old heads. He made *Shylock* more human and artistic than his predecessors, and by the third act Kean was a dazzling success. In the scene where he learns of *Jessica's* escape, the staid audience rose from their places and acclaimed an amazing outburst of passion, such as had never been witnessed on the stage before. The trial scene was the most astonishing evidence of the power of one human being over many ever recorded in the annals of acting; even the actors flocked to the palpitating, fainting man and strove to make up for their past gibes.

He fled like a madman through the slushy streets to his wife, who was faint with expectation and terror, and shouted : " Mary, the pit rose at me; I've won; you shall ride in your carriage." In a thousand contemporary memoirs you shall find the comments of all sorts and conditions of men over the wizardry of this extraordinary actor, who, springing from no one knew where, had in one night eclipsed the fame of the greatest who had ever illustrated Shakespeare.

For eighteen years his income was over £10,000 yearly, but he died in debt.

At Drury Lane, 24th Jan., 1825, his reception was most boisterous. It was some weeks before peace was restored. His first American tour was opened at the Chatham Theatre, New York, 29th Nov., 1820, re-opening at Drury Lane, 23rd July, 1821.

Unfortunately, as is the usual case with genius, Kean became so dependent on the use of stimulants that the gradual deterioration of his great gifts was inevitable. Still, even in their decay, his powers triumphed during the moments of his inspiration over the absolute wreck of his physical faculties, and compelled admiration when his gait had degenerated into a weak hobble—when the lightning brilliancy of his eyes had become dull and bloodshot, and the tones of his matchless voice were marred by rough and grating hoarseness.

He made his last appearance at Covent Garden, 25th March, 1833, playing *Othello* to the *Iago* of his son Charles. The senior became greatly affected after the speech in the third act :

Farewell the tranquil mind ! farewell content !

After a protracted pause at its termination, instead of the articulate vehemency usual with the words, Kean muttered indistinctly:

" *Villain — be sure — you — prove* "

then he groaned, and whispered, "Oh, God ! I am dying ! Speak to them, Charles." His son caught him in his arms, and he was borne from the scene. Edmund Kean's career was cancelled 15th May, 1833, in his forty-sixth year ending his strange eventful history, so replete with heart-breaking vicissitudes.

" *After life's fitful fever he sleeps well.*"

During the same season the Montreal company included Thomas Placide, who subsequently became a famous comedian and manager on the United States side.

THOMAS PLACIDE was a boisterous performer who never rose to much distinction. He greatly resembled his brother Henry, but his work did not begin to compare with the latter's. Thomas was born at Charleston, S.C., in 1808. His stage career began early, and his regular *debut* was at the Chatham Street Theatre, New York, in 1828. He was manager of the Park Theatre for several seasons, and in 1853 became a member of Wallack's company, retiring a few seasons later, and dying 20th July, 1877. He was the first man to wear paper collars in Montreal, not being in good credit standing with his laundry, and set a fashion followed out some years later.

The next season was without importance in a theatrical sense, the circus and amateur performances being much in vogue.

The chief dramatic recreation of the year appears to have been catered by the amateurs of the 71st Regiment, the famous Highland Light Infantry, under patronage of Colonel Jones.

THE YEAR 1828

was marked by the appearance of Mr. and Mrs. Edward Knight, of Drury Lane Theatre. Mrs. Knight had recently changed her name from Miss Povey, and was a great favorite on the other side. They gave a concert at the theatre, 7th July, and subsequently organised other entertainments. Several other English comedians also appeared during a very short season, including Miss George, of the Haymarket Theatre, an interesting ballad singer, who later became Mrs. Oldmixon ; Mrs. Gill, of the Theatre Royal, Bath ; Mrs. Austin, of Drury Lane Theatre ; and Mr. Horn. They gave entertainments 26th July and 5th August.

MRS. EDWARD KNIGHT was born Mary Ann Povey, in England, 1804. Though not beautiful, she was a " plump and pleasing little person, light in complexion, round face and expressive blue eyes, with a rich and powerful voice." She was good in comic opera, and later in life assumed a wider range of characters, when she became attached to the Park Theatre. In 1845 she lost her only child, a beautiful girl of seventeen, and in May, 1849, returned to England, having become partially blind, induced by excessive weeping. She died in 1861. Mr. Knight was a musician, and died young.

THE SEASON OF 1829

was more successful, and was opened early in the year by the "English," "Gentlemen Canadian" and "Garrison Amateurs."

The fact of three amateur clubs existing shows that considerable interest was beginning to be given to the drama.

The regular season of 1829 was opened up 3rd June, under the management of

. VINCENT DE CAMP.

In his management of the theatre during the 1829 season, Mr. De Camp was surrounded by Mr. and Mrs. Armand Vestris, Mr. and Mrs. Knight, Mr. and Mrs. Achille, Clara Fisher, Mrs. Fred. Brown and Messrs. Fisher and George Holland. Mr. and Mrs. Vestris opened their engagement, which extended from 3rd to 10th June, in "A Hundred Pound Note," and during the performance the Achilles appeared in their celebrated "shawl dance," the whole concluding with the farce of " Mons. Tonson." Mr. George Holland subsequently made his appearance in " The Lottery Ticket."

The most important debut of the season was that of Clara Fisher, 20th July, in " The Belle's Stratagem," Miss Fisher as *Letitia Hardy*, and Mr. De Camp as *Doricourt*.

Following Miss Fisher's first appearance came the comedies, " She Would and She Would Not," " The Wonder," "The Invincibles," and "A Bold Stroke for a Husband." The remainder of the season passed without interest.

Mrs. Knight began an engagement of four nights, 7th September, in " Guy Mannering," " Fontainebleau " and " Le Mariage de Figaro." De Camp's first season closed 26th, with a complimentary benefit to his sister-in-law, Mrs. F. Brown, when " The Rivals " was staged. On this occasion the garrison amateurs lent their assistance.

VINCENT DE CAMP, of the Theatre Royal, Drury Lane, and Haymarket Theatre, London, was a brother-in-law to the great Chas. Kemble and to Frederick Brown, and was known as a veteran of the London stage, but in America he failed to make the impression he had anticipated. He was born in Vienna, Austria, in 1777, and went to England in early life with his father, who was a musician. He first appeared on the boards of Drury Lane Theatre in children parts, but when he reached manhood made his regular debut as *Vapour* in the farce of " My Grandmother." He was for some time subsequently considered a useful performer of *fops*, *coxcombs* and *gay footmen*. His American *debut* was at the Park Theatre, New York, 24th November, 1823, as *Gossamer* in " Laugh when You Can " and " The Three Singles." He had only recently given up the management of the Bowery Theatre, New York, when he came to Montreal to assume the management of the Theatre Royal. He last appeared in Montreal in 1834. His last appearance in New York, as an actor, was in 1828. During 1837-38, he played at Mobile, Ala., under the management of Ludlow and Smith, and died in Texas, 27th July, 1839. During one part of his life he had been a great London favorite, lived in handsome style, kept his carriage, moved in good society and lived in every way like a gentleman. He played the violin, and sang and danced well. As he advanced in years, however, he displayed amusing peculiarities, one of which was to deal in milk. At Mobile he was known to rise early, deliver his milk in time to attend rehearsals, and after the performance hurry away to do his milking for the next day's delivery. At the time of his death he was prospecting in Texas with an idea of coming across an ideal El Dorado.

CLARA FISHER MAEDER was called the female Charles Mathews of her day. She was born in England, 14th July, 1811, and made her first appearance when at the age of eight, in a burlesque of "Richard III," at the Drury Lane Theatre, at once springing into fame.

She came to America in 1827, first appearing at the Park Theatre in New York, and after appearing at Boston and Philadelphia, came to Montreal. The theatre-goer of the present day would find it difficult to realize the extraordinary interest which Clara Fisher created in the cities of the United States and Canada, and for a period of six or eight years afterward she was the favorite star of every city she visited. Her "Hurrah for the Bonnets of Blue," "The Dashing White Sergeant," "Buy a Broom," etc., became universally popular; her name became a household word, children were named after her, and young ladies affected her lisp and manner.

She not only performed leading parts with Cooper, Vandenhoff, Forrest, Hamblin and Charles Kean, but also appeared prominently in opera with the Woods, Mrs. Knight, Horn, Braham, Sinclair, Pearman, Miss George, and all the famous vocalists of her time. On the Park stage she was the original representative of nearly fifty parts.

In December, 1834, she married James Gaspard Maeder, an Irish musician, and at his instigation she ventured to appear in opera, but with only qualified success. Mr. Maeder died 28th May, 1876. She was seen in Montreal during several seasons, and latterly as a member of the first Buckland *regime* stock company at the Theatre Royal, in 1852 and 1854. Her sister, Ida (Mrs. Geo. Vernon), also a well-known actress, was seen in the 1853 company here. Mrs. Maeder last appeared on the stage in 1889, when she accepted an engagement with Richard Mansfield's company for ten months, but which only lasted about ten days. Mrs. Maeder states that she could not get along with Mr. Mansfield or he with her, somehow. She then became a member of that part of Daly's company then travelling under the management of Arthur Rehan. It was with this organization that she made her last appearance, presenting *Mrs. Jeremiah Joblots*, in "The Lottery of Love," at Baltimore, in 1899."

She died at New Brunswick, N.J., 12th Nov., 1898.

CLARA FISHER.

THE ACHILLES came to New York in 1828. They were very fine dancers, the Madam being by some thought fully equal to Hutin. She was as graceful, but not as dexterous and daring. For many years she kept a dancing school in New York, after having been deserted by her husband, who became the part proprietor of a café in Marseilles.

GEORGE HOLLAND was distinctly an actor of the old school, invariably introducing even into modern characters its traditions and conventionlities; his effects were broadly given, and his personality was essentially comical.

He was born in London in 1791, adopting the stage as a profession in 1817. Ten years later he appeared at the Bowery Theatre, and for many years afterwards was recognized as a welcome *star* comedian. He died 20th December, 1870. The Church of the Transfiguration (Rev. Dr. Houghton) came into theatrical prominence by this event. Joseph Jefferson, tells the story as follows :

"Upon the announcement of the death of George Holland, I called at the house of his family, who desired the funeral to take place from the church.

"I at once started in quest of the minister, taking one of the sons of Mr. Holland with me. On arriving at the house, I explained to the Rev. Mr. Sabine the nature of my visit, and the arrangements were made for the time and place at which the funeral was to be held· After some hesitation he said that he would be compelled, if Mr. Holland had been an actor, to decline holding the service at the church·

"I rose to leave the room with a mortification that I cannot remember to have felt before or since· I paused at the door and said :

" 'Well, sir, in this dilemma is there no other church to which you can direct me, from which my friend can be buried."

"He replied that there was a little church around the corner where I might get it done; to which I answered:

" 'Then, if this be so, God bless the little church around the corner ;' and so I left the house.

"The minister had unwittingly performed an important christening, and his baptismal name of ' 'The Little Church Around the Corner " clings to it to this day."

So warm was the feeling on the subject of the dead comedian's treatment that the theatrical community organized special benefit performances, by which $15.352.73 was raised and devoted to the support of the actor's widow and children·

MADAME VESTRIS, *nee* Lucy Eliza Bartolozzi, born in 1797, married Armand Vestris in 1813, and C. J. Mathews in 1838, when she came to America and appeared at the Park Theatre. She last appeared on the stage in 1854 in London, and died in 1856. She was a fine musical comedienne.

The same company with few exceptions

APPEARED IN 1830.

Miss Emery being a new acquisition. During the season
Clara Fisher again appeared as *Letitia Hardy* in "The
Belle's Stratagem," *Lady Teazle* in the "School for Scandal,"
and other old English comedies. Among other pieces were
produced "Actress of All Work," "The Four Mowbrays,"
"Man and Wife," "The Spoiled Child," "The Wonder,"
"The Invincibles," "The Young Widow," "The Rivals,'
"Le Mariage de Figaro" and "Fontainebleau," in which
Mrs. Knight achieved considerable success. She made three
appearances from 11th September. On 14th September Mr.
De Camp announced in the columns of the press his intention
of opening the theatre for a limited winter season of ten weeks
by subscription, giving two performances weekly. Gentle-
men, 20 nights, boxes, $14 ; ladies, $12 ; pit, $7 and $6. The
venture was not successful, however, and Mr. De Camp closed
his season with a benefit to F. Brown, 17th September. The
Garrison Amateurs also tendered a benefit to Mr. and Mrs.
Brown, 24th, with "The Rivals" as the bill. In November
Miss Emery, supported mostly by members of the circus company, gave "Isabella" and "The Mountaineers." In the
support appeared Messrs. Thos. Grierson, Schinotti and Mrs.
Kent. On 11th November, Mr. Wells appeared in " Timour-
lane, the Tartar," in which production the horses belonging
to the circus were introduced. This incident was much criti-
cised by the press, who, "aware of the present low state in
dramatic taste in Montreal, should not profane boards con-
secrated to sock and buskin by equestrian performances."
Wells also appeared in "Cerenza." This profanation of the
Temple of Thespis, however, resulted in profitable business
being done for a season of two weeks. The theatre was then
turned over to the Garrison Amateurs, who, on 29th November, produced Morton's "Speed the Plough." The following
night Colman's " Heir-at-Law " was presented for the benefit of the General Hospital. During the month of August,
Mrs. Feron gave several concerts at the theatre.

MISS EMERY (Mrs. Burroughs), born in London, Eng., first
appeared on the stage at the Surrey Theatre in 1827. She promised
to be a great artist, playing tragic roles with grand effect. She was
a remarkably large and beautiful woman, but her life's story was one

of the saddest known in the annals of theatrical biography. Her first appearance in America was at the Chestnut Street Theatre, Philadelphia. 31st October, 1827, as *Belvidera*. On 17th March, 1828, she made her New York *debut* at the Chatham Theatre. Her remarkable talents were not appreciated in America, probably owing to the condition of a rather over-crowded stage as much as to becoming enslaved by alcohol. Step by step she declined; her magnificent wardrobe was sold, and in time her lodgings were in a miserable garret. This once brilliant and magnificent woman was latterly a well-known street figure, begging stray quarters from former associates in the profession. Her death, in 1832, occurred under pitiful circumstances, resulting from a quarrel with a couple of drunken creatures. She managed to drag herself to a market-house, and laid down and died.

MRS. FERON was the most celebrated European vocalist who had up to this time visited America. She was a brilliant singer of the most florid Italian school. She has been engaged at the San Carlos Theatre at Naples at a salary of $5,000, but in this country did not create a great sensation, being neither young nor beautiful, the lack of which attributes was just as unfortunate for the singer seventy years ago as it is to-day.

MR. SCHINOTTI used to glide through an Indian war dance with native character well marked. He was also a clever pantomimist. His wife died in 1829, in her twenty-second year.

WILLIAM G. WELLS, born in London, came to America in 1827. He was a clever dancer and ballet master, dancing in connection with his sister, who was a pretty little creature. She subsequently married and, returning to England in 1846, soon after died. Wells retired from the mimic scene early and taught dancing in Pittsburg. He died in Mexico in 1841.

THOS. GRIERSON came to this country on the "Britannia," having as *compagnons de voyage* Mrs. John Drew, then Louisa Lane, aged seven, her mother and Master and Miss Wells, dancers. Mrs. Drew records that they enjoyed an exceptionally fine voyage of four weeks, landing in New York, 7th June, 1827.

Grierson was a tall and rather ungainly young actor at this time, with ambitious aspirations for tragic walks, although unassuming in his general demeanor. He was a native of Liverpool, and like all English actors, was accurate and diligent in his methods. He did not remain long in this country, returning to England, where he inherited property from his mother, which made him comfortable for the few years he lived.

THE SEASON OF 1831

was notable for the appearance here of Mr. and Mrs. Wm. R. Blake, Mrs. Charles Bernard, Jas. H. Hackett, Mr. and Mrs. Fred. Brown, V. De Camp, R. C. Maywood, E. Forrest, W.

Duffy and Clara Fisher.   The Garrison Amateurs and the Scotch Amateurs also gave representations, the former producing " A Roland for an Oliver " and " The Miller and His Men," 12th January, for the benefit of the General Hospital, and "The Honeymoon," 12th February.   The Scotch Amateurs presented Allan Ramsay's "The Gentle Shepherd" and " Village Lawyer " on the 18th of March, the proceeds also going to the General Hospital.

The City Amateurs produced " Barbarossa " on the 14th April, for the benefit of the Orphan Asylum.   Mr. and Mrs. Knight were given a benefit on the 23rd June, in " Luke the Laborer" and Pocock's "Zembuca," taking another benefit on the 25th in " Spectre Bridegroom."

Vincent De Camp was again at the head of affairs when the season opened on the 4th of July.   The opening bill was "Virginius," with Frederick Brown in the title role.   He appeared, 7th, in " Damon and Pythias."   " The Dramatist " was presented on the 9th, together with " The Lottery Ticket," De Camp assuming the role of *Wormwood*.   The feature of the season was the initial bow in Montreal of Mr. and Mrs. Wm. Rufus Blake on the 11th July, in Tobin's " Honeymoon." They subsequently appeared in "Paul Pry," "Katherine and Petruchio," "The Road to Ruin," "The Stranger," "The Gambler's Fate," and " The Spoiled Child," in which Mrs. Charles Bernard appeared.   Another important event occurred when James H. Hackett made his debut here, on the 22nd of July, as *Solomon Swap* in " Jonathan in England."

Hackett appeared 28th, at a benefit performance to the Blakes in "Speed the Plough," and, 29th, in "Rip Van Winkle " and " Down East."

"Pizarro " was staged 30th, with the following cast, made especially interesting in including the name of Edwin Forrest, destined to become America's greatest representative of rugged tragedy : *Pizarro*, Edwin Forrest ; *Rolla*, Fred Brown ; *Alonzo*, Wm. Duffy ; *Elvira*, Mrs. F. Brown ; *Cora*, Mrs. C. Bernard.   The Blakes made their farewell appearance, 1st August, in "Wives As They Were."

" Othello," with Forrest as the *Moor*, Brown as *Iago*, Duffy as *Cassio*, Mrs. Brown as *Desdemona*, and Mrs. Bernard as *Emelia*, was produced 2nd August.   Mrs. Bernard took a benefit 3rd August in " Ambroise Gwinnett."   *Ambroise Gwinnett*, Mr. Wm. Duffy ; *Ned Gayling*, Mr. Edwin Forrest ; *Lucy Fondlove*, Mrs. Charles Bernard.   Forrest and Duffy were seen, 4th, as *Damon* and *Pythias* respectively.

EDWIN FORREST.

Mr. and Mrs. Hackett closed 6th August, in "The Comedy of Errors." Cast: *Antipholus of Syracuse*, Mr. Preston; *Antipholus of Ephesus*, Mr. Hardy; *Dromio of Syracuse*, Mr. De Camp; *Dromio of Ephesus*, Mr. Hackett; *Adriana*, Mrs. Hackett; with "Giovanni in London" as the after-piece, Hackett in the title role. Mrs. Brown had a benefit, 15th, in "The Honeymoon" and "Family Jars," assisted by the members of the "Buskin Club." Whatever induced Forrest to visit Montreal, unless to accompany his friend Duffy on a summer tour, we are not likely to ever know. He was then in his twenty-fifth year, and had already made his mark in the United States, having been a star since 1825. During the October following his incursion to Montreal, Forrest first produced "The Gladiator" in Philadelphia. Clara Fisher and F. Brown were seen in "The Wonder," 16th, as *Violante* and *Don Felix;* "Therese," 18th; "The Miller's Maid," 22nd; "The Idiot Witness," 24th.

Charles Kean, son of Edmund Kean, made his first appearance in Montreal, 25th August, as *Sir Giles Overreach* in Massinger's "A New Way to Pay Old Debts," and farce, "Lovers' Quarrels." He was seen as *Shylock*, 26th. De Camp had a benefit, 27th, in M. G. Lewis' play, "Castle Spectre," on which occasion Mrs. Hughes (late Mrs. Young) made her first appearance as Mrs. Hughes in the character of *Angela*. This closed the season, but Charles Kean was re-engaged from 3rd to 20th October, appearing in *Richard;* *Othello*, 4th; *Hamlet*, 7th; *Sir Giles*, 8th; *Mortimer*, 12th; *The Stranger*, 14th; *Othello*, 15th; and, by command of His Excellency, Lord Aylmer, "Richard III.," 18th, with a prelude, "Pay Me for My Eye"; and, again by command, *Hamlet*, 20th. This was his last appearance. A benefit to Essender and Hardy, under the patronage of Col. Macintosh, was tendered, 22nd, in "Paul Pry" and "The Irish Tutor."

Late in the season the celebrated Lydia Kelly had large audiences for a short season, after a very successful American sojourn. From Quebec she returned to England.

EDWIN FORREST was, by Lawrence Barrett, conceded to be greatest in such Shakespearean characters as *Lear, Othello* and *Coriolanus*. He was greater, however, in such roles as *Virginius, Spartacus, William Tell* and *Metamora*. Poor Forrest never felt a happy moment after his wife's base ingratitude had rent his great soul, and as he grew older, other kings had arisen on the stage, to whom his old subjects showed a reverence once all his own; the mockery of his diadem only remained. Sitting after a performance of "King Lear" one night, a friend complimented him on his playing of the role. Whereupon the veteran, feeble in health, almost indignantly replied, rising slowly, and even laboriously from his chair, to his full height: "*Play Lear !* I *play Hamlet, Shylock,* if you please ; but, by God, I *am Lear !*" Nor was this wholly imaginative. Had his suit succeeded when he tried to secure the hand of Jane Placide, very different would have been his lot. Edwin Forrest was the first American actor of greatness to appear on the English stage, on 17th October, 1836. Then he was praised and welcomed by Macready, but when the latter visited America seven years later for the second time, and found himself compared unfavorably with the robust Forrest, envy entered his heart. In 1845 it found its vent, or at least Forrest thought it did, in influencing the English writers against the American actor during the latter's second visit. No one persisted in unjust persecution of the visitor more than Macready's particular friend, Forster, the critic of the London *Examiner*. He went so far as to review Forrest's work as follows: "An old friend, Mr. Forrest, afforded great amusement to the public by his performance of 'Macbeth' on Friday evening, at the Princess Theatre. Indeed, our best comic actors do not often excite so great a quantity of mirth. The change from an inaudible murmur to a thunder of sound was enormous, but the grand feature was the combat, in which he stood scraping his word against that of *Macduff*. We were at a loss to know what this gesture meant, till an enlightened critic in the gallery shouted out, ' That's right, sharpen it !' "

Forrest called on Macready no more, and, unfortunately for both, during a performance of "Hamlet" by the Englishman at Edinburgh, Forrest injudiciously hissed some of the business in the play scene. Then the storm burst. England and America tossed the question of courtesy back and forth, and international feelings ran high. The climax was reached during Macready's last visit to America, when occurred the disgraceful riots at Astor Place Opera House, New York, 10th May, 1849. Macready was presenting "Macbeth" on this occasion. The rioters broke all the windows and doors of the theatre.

The militia was called out to quell the disturbance, and, after the Riot Act had been read twenty times, command was given to fire a volley. Twenty-one people were killed, thirty-three wounded and sixty-three were placed under arrest.

Forrest's last public appearance was in Boston as a reader of "Othello." While the audience was dispersing, the doorkeeper said: " I hope we shall have you with us long, Mr. Forrest." "Oh, yes, he replied, "all week." "I didn't mean, here in Boston, but in the world." " Ah, as to that," rejoined the old tragedian, "how uncertainn and vague it all is !" The next week he was dead. He died of apo_ plexy on the 12th of December, 1872. Mr. Forrest accumulated a vast fortune and established the institution for aged actors, called " The Forrest Home."

May the remembrance of his follies not check a tear that should flow to his memory, for who is faultless ?"

WILLIAM DUFFY and Mr. Forrest were great friends. He played secondary parts to Forrest before entering into a managerial career, and it is said that, had he chosen to star instead, he would have been a great actor. He was born in Albany in 1803. His parents came from Londonderry, Ireland. He first joined Caldwell's company in the South, but his regular *debut* was made in Albany, 19th July, 1827, as *Bertram*. He afterwards managed theatres at Albany and Philadelphia. He was murdered in 1835, by an actor named Hamilton, who was afterwards acquitted.

JAMES HENRY HACKETT was essentially a comedian, although he attained some distinction as a tragedian. His principal comedy characters were *Justice Woodcock, Sylvester Daggerwood, Mons. Morbleau, Dromio, Rip Van Winkle, Nimrod, Wildfire, McSycophant*, and, far beyond all others, *Falstaff*.

He played *Lear* and *Hamlet* in 1840 for the first time, and very seldom thereafter, for he made no impression in tragic parts· This comedian was born in New York, 15th March, 1800. At the age of nineteen he married the actress, Catherine Lee Sugg, who died in 1840. In 1866 Mr. Hackett contracted a second marriage, and died in 1871, survived by his widow and son, James K. Hackett, now a prominent *star*.

MR. and MRS. BLAKE.—William Rufus Blake was born in 1805 at Halifax, N.S., where he was educated, and made his first essay as an actor as the *Prince of Wales* in " Richard III." He made his New York *debut* as *Frederick* in "The Poor Gentleman·" in 1824. A year later he married Mrs. Waring· He starred not only in America, but also in England. While playing *Sir Peter Teazle* at Boston, 21st April, 1863, he was taken suddenly ill and died the next day· He was of fine appearance when young, but after reaching forty, he became corpulent, which obliged him to change the roles of sighing lovers to those of old men, in which he was excellent. Mrs. Blake, *nee* Caroline Placide, sister to Henry and Thos. Placide, was born (1798), at Charleston, S. C. In 1812 she married Leigh Waring, an English light comedian, who died five years later. She was an excellent *Lady Teazle*, which she played to her husband's *Sir Peter*.

MRS. CHARLES BERNARD married a circus clown, named Walter Williams, who was commanding a large salary, but she soon wearied of him and was divorced. Her maiden name was Tilden, and she came of a well-connected Baltimore family, but the death of her father led to her mother adopting the stage, and Miss Tilden in time followed· In 1824 we find her playing at Charleston, S.C., and in

1828 was married to Charles Bernard, a descendant of John Bernard. He, however, soon died of consumption. and Mrs. Bernard tried a third husband in the person of Dr. Tucker, of Philadelphia. She was a fine looking and dashing actress of general comedy parts.

LYDIA KELLY, one of the greatest melo-dramatic actresses of her day, was the daughter of Captain Kelly, known as "facetious Joe." Meeting with great success in London, she came to America, where, at the Park Theatre, New York, she proved to be a strong card, from 17th Sept., 1824, until 26th July, 1831. Upon returning to England, she married a French baron.

CHARLES JOHN KEAN was the second but only surviving son of that great genius, Edmund Kean, and was born at Waterford, Ireland, 18th January, 1811. The fortunes of his father at this time were at their lowest ebb, but the tide changed, when, in his third year, his father came home, flushed with his triumph at Drury Lane, and exclaimed: " Charley, my boy, you shall go to Eton." It was not until 1824 that he was entered at Eton.
. His father's reverses obliged him to discontinue his studies three years later, and in order to provide for his mother he embraced the stage as a profession, making his first appearance at Drury Lane, 1st October. 1827. in the character of *Norval*. in "Douglass." The press gave him no encouragement, but he persisted and won some applause in the provinces. He came to America in 1830, appearing as *Richard*, in the fall, at the Park Theatre. He was in his twenty-first year when he visited Montreal. On his return to England in January, 1833, he fulfilled several short engagements, and on 25th March was the *Iago* to his father's *Othello*, at Covent Garden, when the sire collapsed. Charles Kean soon became a provincial favorite, and by 1838 was recognized in the metropolis as well. He again visited America in 1839, and married Ellen Tree in 1842.

In 1846 they ventured on a production in America of "King John" and "Richard III," on a scale of splendor never before witnessed in this country, and conceived the idea of giving those spectacular presentments, chiefly Shakespearean, that suit all the world, to the Princess Theatre, in 1850. and which continued for a period of nine years. In 1849 Kean lost the mother he loved so much. Mrs. Kean thought her Charles the greatest actor that ever lived, not excepting his father. This opinion the dear old lady sought to impress on all visitors and friends. Kean once gave a dinner party to some distinguished persons, and begged his mother to abstain from her usual enconiums at table. This she promised, but her son, to make sure, arranged that if she forgot he would touch his shirt collar as a warning.

At dinner a noble lord was seated next to Mrs. Kean. They discussed various topics of the day, politics, etc. His lordship spoke in praise of Macready's *Richelieu*. This fired Mrs. Kean.

CHARLES JOHN KEAN.
(Gloster.)
From a painting by Reid, in the possession of John Tullis & Co.

" My Charles is—"
(Shirt collar touched—pause.)
" Yes?" exclaimed the lord.
" Is the best—" continued Mrs. Kean·
(Collar raised again—another pause)
"Beg pardon," said the lord.
"Well, then, my Charles is the best actor that ever trod. There !
It is out. Charles, and it's no use to pull your collar up to your eyes."
In 1863 Mr. and Mrs. Kean set out on a tour around the world,
taking in America on their return *route* in 1865, Kean paying a visit
to Montreal after an absence of 32 years. Their farewell appearance
was in May, 1867, at Liverpool. Kean died 22nd Jan., 1868, his wife
surviving him twelve years.

Chas. Kean had by nature every bad quality an actor could possess
—a bad figure and voice and an impediment in his speech. But he had
fine taste and an iron will: tireless industry, and, if he had no genius,
he had splendid talents with ambition as high as Hope's great throb-
bing star above the darkness of the night.

MRS. HUGHES was born near Albany in 1792, of humble parentage, and in her early life her father moved to Montreal. She was noticed by John Bernard during a visit here, and four years later became
his leading lady, when he opened up the Albany Theatre, 18th January, 1813. Her first husband died in Albany, and she afterwards
married Mr. Hughes. Her career was a long and successful one, and
she became an actress of the first rank. As she advanced in years
she played "old women" at Burton's, for many years, and on 14th
June, 1852, was given a benefit there, being announced as the oldest
native actress on the stage. She retired in 1860 to her farm, near
Sandy Hill, N.Y., where she died 15th April, 1867, from the effects of
an accident.

MR. HUGHES possessed classical features, and a noble figure,
standing six feet high. He had an excellent education and a mind
well stored with extensive reading, the intellectual evidence of which
was made manifest in his conversation. He was well known on the
Boston and Philadelphia stage. His *Pizarro* was excellent, as was
also his *Henry IV.* He died in the South, his wife surviving him.
Hon. Charles Hughes, State Senator of New York, is their son.

The frightful epidemic of

CHOLERA IN 1832

which killed several hundreds of Montreal's citizens practically suppressed theatricals that year. On 9th April a concert
was given by Mr. and Mrs. Anderson, of Drury Lane Theatre
and the Italian Opera House, London, in the parlors of the
British American Hotel. A few amateur performances were
also given.

THE SEASON OF 1833

was an especially notable one, introducing to Montreal the
great Charles Kemble and his daughter, Fanny Kemble. The
Browns and R. C. Maywood finished a short season in July,
being followed, 24th, by the Kembles. Their brother-in-law,
De Camp, was the manager during the season. In the support were Messrs. Barton, C. K. Mason, Knight, and C. Mestayer; Misses Clara Fisher, Meadows (pupil of Mrs. Brown),
Mestayer and Smith and Mrs. Sefton. The opening performance was in "Venice Preserved" : *Jaffier*, Mr. Kemble ;
Pierre, Mr. Barton ; *Belvidera*, Fanny Kemble. On the 25th
the bill was "Fazio," in which Mr. Kemble did not appear,
he deeming the title role insufficiently prominent. It was assumed by Mr. Barton ; *Bianca*, Fanny Kemble ; *Abdobella*,
Miss Smith ; *Clara*, Mrs. Sefton. "The Wonder," 26th ;
"The Gamester," 29th ; "The Stranger," 30th ; "Much Ado
About Nothing," August 1, with Kemble as *Benedict*, Fanny
Kemble as *Beatrice*, and De Camp as *Claudio*. "The School
for Scandal" followed, 2nd, and the engagement closed, 3rd,
with Scott's "The Lady of the Lake." It is recorded that the
houses were so crowded that people sat on the stage.

The Kembles visited Quebec after terminating their Montreal engagement, and played there for two weeks, but re-
appeared during August in a couple of performances.

John Sinclair, of the Theatre Royal, Drury Lane, gave a
concert, 16th August, assisted by Messrs. Madotti, Signor
Cioffi, Kyle, Herwig and Greenwood. It was repeated 19th.

The theatrical season re-opened after the company's return
from Quebec, 22nd August, with "The Maid of Milan" and
"Katherine and Petruchio," with Mrs. Brown and Mr. Barton in the title roles of the after-piece. "Guy Mannering"
and "The Day After the Wedding" were also produced.

Fanny Kemble was the means of preventing the elder
Charles Mathews from visiting Montreal in 1834-5. In reply
to his inquiry as to conditions theatrically in Canada, she
wrote the following letter to him, under date of 21st December, 1834 :

"We went to Canada, I believe, upon the same terms as everywhere
else—a division of profits. Vincent de Camp had the theatres there,
and of all the horrible strolling concerns I could ever imagine, his
company and scenery and getting-ups were the worst. He has not
got those theatres now, I believe, but they are generally open only for
a short time, and by persons as little capable of bringing forward de-

CHARLES KEMBLE.

cent dramatic representations as he, poor fellow, was. You are, however, so much less dependent upon others than we were for success. Heaven knows the company would have been blackguardly representatives of the gentry in "Tom and Jerry;" you can fancy that they were in heroicals. Our houses were good; so, I think, yours would be; but though I am sure you would not have to complain of want of hospitality, either in Montreal or Quebec, the unspeakable dirt and discomfort of the inns, the scarcity of eatables and the abundance of eaters (fleas, bugs, etc.), together with the wicked (limb) dislocating road from St. Johns to Laprairie would make up a sum of suffering, for which it would be difficult to find adequate compensation. In the summer, the beauty of the scenery going *down* (?) the St. Lawrence to Montreal, and of the whole country around Quebec, might, in some measure, counterbalance these evils. But unless Mrs. Mathews' and your own health were tolerably good at the time, the hourly inconveniences you would have to endure would render an expedition to the Canadas anything but desirable. The heat while we were in Montreal was intolerable—the filth intolerable—the bugs intolerable—the people intolerable—the jargon they speak intolerable. I lifted my hands in thankfulness when I again set foot in these United States. The only inn existing at Montreal was burned down three years ago, and everything you ask for was burnt down in it."

Whew ! What a roasting ! Mr. Mathews, whose health was in a precarious condition, preferred not to undertake so arduous a journey.. He died 28th June, 1835, shortly after his return to England.

MR. BARTON, the tragedian, came to America in 1830. He was an Englishman, and met with some success in this country. He was a gentleman in every sense of the word, and a sensible and classical artist. He was very particular as to stage business, and was enthusiastically fond of his profession. He acted as stage manager for James H. Caldwell at New Orleans. His last appearance in this country was at New York in 1839, after which he returned to England. He was unfortunate in suffering from intense nervousness, as well as asthmatic troubles, which eventually caused his death, in 1848. It was at his suggestion that the great Charlotte Cushman first undertook the study of serious roles.

CHARLES KEMBLE, one of the most notable actors who ever came to Montreal, was born 25th Nov., 1775, and received his education at Douai. His first regular stage appearance was as *Orlando*, at Sheffield. In 1806 he married Maria Theresa, a sister of Vincent De Camp. As an actor, he became excellent in a line of characters which he made his own in such roles as *Archer, Doricourt, Charles Surface* and *Ranger*. His *Laertes* and *Falconbridge* were equal to the *Hamlet* and *Coriolanus* of his brother, John P. Kemble, and his *Cassio* as fine as the *Othello* of Kean or the *Iago* of Cooke. His imposing person, classical countenance and tuneful voice enabled him to be also highly successful in the lighter tragic roles. Attempts at management of Covent Garden Theatre resulted in severe loss, but he was saved from ruin by the talents of his daughter, Fanny, who enabled him to pay off debts of $60,000. She accompanied him to America in Sept., 1832, to reap a golden harvest. Returning to England in 1835 he engaged chiefly in giving readings from Shakespeare, frequently by royal command, but increasing deafness compelled his retirement. Mrs. Kemble died in 1838, and in 1841 a loss of $20,000, which he had invested in the United States Bank added to his misfortunes. He was appointed examiner of plays by the Lord Chamberlain, and held this office up to the time of his death, 12th Nov., 1854.

FRANCES ANNE KEMBLE, beautiful and gifted, was the daughter of Charles Kemble, the grand-daughter of Roger, and niece to John Phillip, George Stephen Kemble, and their sister, the great Mrs. Sarah Siddons. Fanny, as she was called, was born in London, 27th Nov., 1809. The fortunes of her father being at a low ebb she went on the stage, making her *debut* as *Juliet* to the *Romeo* of Wm. Abbott, at Covent Garden, 5th Oct., 1829. For nearly three years she attracted large audiences which replenished her father's exhausted treasury, by her splendid talents, which were equally appreciated on an American tour in 1832-33. In the full tide of triumphant success she left the stage in 1834, to make an unhappy alliance with Pierce Butler, of Philadelphia, who took her—an ardent abolitionist—to his Georgian plantation. In 1845 she became divorced from Mr. Butler, and in the company of her sister, Adelaide Kemble Sartoris (died 1879), undertook continental travel until 1847, when she commenced her famous readings, with unvarying success both in America and in England. The last of these was given in Steinway Hall, New York, in Oct., 1868. Mrs. Kemble-Butler died at her daughter's residence in London, 15th January, 1893.

CHARLES KEMBLE MASON, nephew of Charles Kemble, was born in England in 1805, and became a well-known Covent Garden Theatre favorite. His first New York appearance was as *Beverley*, at the Park Theatre, 4th Dec., 1839. His last regular engagement was in support of Mrs. Scott Siddons, in 1869.

JOHN SINCLAIR was the father of Catherine Sinclair, who married Edwin Forrest in 1837. He was born at Edinburgh in 1790, and died in 1857.

THEATRICALS IN 1834

were at a low ebb, and the professional season short and unprofitable. The military amateurs presented several of the old favorite pieces, but a second outbreak of the cholera rendered further theatrical representations impracticable.

THE SEASON OF 1835

was marked by the appearance of a number of people new to the city, the principal being Tyrone Power, the famous Irish

FANNY KEMBLE.

songster and comedian. The use of the theatre was tendered gratuitously by the Hon. John Molson, 9th April, to the amateurs of the 24th Regiment, when "The Miller and His Men" and "The Irishman in London" were produced for the benefit of the theatrical fund. The principals were Sergt. Malin, Corp. Greer, Nickinson and Fields. Greer spoke a prologue of some forty lines.

The regular season was opened under Mr. Logan's management, 5th June, when Tyrone Power made his first appearance here in the character of *Murtoch Delancy*, in which he introduced the song, "The Boys of Kilkenny." He also appeared as *Terry O'Rourke alias Dr. O'Toole*, and sang "The Groves of Blarney." "The Irish Tutor" was also given. Mrs. Rogers was the chief support, and the amateurs assisted. On 11th June Power made his second and last appearance as *Sir Patrick O'Plenipo* in "The Irish Ambassador" and farce of "The Review." On this occasion Mrs. Spiller, being indisposed, a gentleman amateur was called to assume her role, but Power protested, and Mrs. Spiller finally consented to appear, ill as she was. Power's action highly incensed the amateurs, but everything was finally amicably arranged.

At the close of Power's season, Manager Logan left for the United States to ascertain the cause of the delay of the new company's arrival, with the result that he entered into arrangements with the principal performers of the Chestnut Street Theatre Company, Philadelphia. In addition to the members of the stock company, he announced the engagement of Madame Celeste, the famous *danseuse* and pantomimist. The regular company included Mr. and Mrs. Rowbotham, Mr. and Mrs. Rogers, E. Hamilton, Thorne, Pickering and Logan. On 11th July "The Honeymoon," and farce "Turn Him Out," were played to poor business. Subsequent performances were in " Charles II.," " The Hunchback," " School for Scandal," " The French Spy," and on 21st July Madame Celeste made her Montreal *debut* in " The Wizard Skiff," and on 24th " The Wept of the Wishton Wish." This piece closed the season 31st July. Logan and the company then left for Quebec. On their return a benefit was tendered Mrs. Rogers in " The Heir-at-Law," 25th August. The season had not been remunerative to Logan. Mr. and Mrs. Rogers had come here directly from Ireland, where

they both enjoyed a large share of public favor, and had been
noticed most prominently in the Irish press. This was the
first instance of an actress of Mrs. Rogers' pretensions having chosen the British province for her debut. A performance of " The Heir-at-Law " was given with the assistance of
the Garrison Amateurs, and on September 1st a benefit was
again given to the Rogers, shared by E. Hamilton, of the
Philadelphia theatre. " Black Eyed Susan " and " Love in
Humble Life " were the bills.

During the month of July, J. W. S. Hows gave a reading
from Shakespeare at Rascoe's Hotel, where also appeared the
Siamese Twins.

About this time began to flourish

THE MILITARY THEATRE,

situated in a secluded spot in the Artillery Barrack Yard. It
was of modest dimensions, yet very well equipped with the
requisite appurtenances; the officers, commissioned and non-
commissioned taking part. On 15th September, 1835, "The
Maid of Genoa " was produced at this playhouse by the amateurs of the 32nd Regiment, and on the 13th November they
again appeared in " The Innkeeper of Abbeville," repeated
16th.

THE SIAMESE TWINS, Chang and Eng, were born at Banga-
sean, Siam, 15th April, 1811, and died near Mount Airy, N.C., 17th
January, 1874. Their father was Chinese, and their mother Chino-
Siamese. They came to America in 1825, and were exhibited here
and in England twenty-five years. After accumulating $80,000, they
settled as farmers in North Carolina. In 1866 they married two sisters, by whom they had eleven children, Chang six, and Eng five.
Two of these were deaf and dumb, but the others had no malforma-
tions or infirmities. After the war they again resorted to public exhi-
bitions, but were not very successful. Their lives were embittered by
their own quarrels and the bickering of their wives. They returned
home with their tempers much soured and their spirits greatly de-
pressed after a declaration by the most skilful and eminent European
physicians that the severing of the band (which they desired) would
prove fatal. Notwithstanding this, they always maintained a high
character for integrity and fair dealings, and were esteemed by their
neighbors. In 1870 Chang had a paralytic stroke and was weak and
ill, while Eng's health was much improved. Chang died first, probably
of a cerebral clot, during the night, and when Eng awoke and found
his brother dead, his fright, together with the nervous shock acting

on an enfeebled heart, caused a syncope, which resulted fatally two and a half hours later. The twins differed considerably in size and strength, as well as disposition, Chang being considerably the larger and stronger, but also the more irritable and intemperate. Their bodies were taken to Philadelphia, where a careful examination showed that a division of the band would have been fatal to both.

JOHN W. S. HOWS first appeared on the stage in New York, in 1835, as *Shylock,* but retired, and for many years taught elocution.

MARIE CELESTE, born in Paris, 16th August, 1814, made her first appearance on any stage at the Bowery Theatre, New York, in 1827, as a dancer. A year later she married Henry Elliott, the son of a wealthy farmer, who soon spent all his money and separated from his wife. She returned to England and made a high reputation as an actress in melodrama. She revisited America in 1851, and again in 1865; retired from the stage in 1866, but appeared again in London in 1874. She died in Paris, 12th Feb., 1882.

H. H. ROWBOTHAM was born in Bath, England. He was a good actor in a wide range of parts. His first American appearance was in Philadelphia, 13th May, 1828, in "Jane Shore." His *Rob Roy* was a very good performance, and although his tragic powers were not of the first rank, yet he often soared above mediocrity· He died in Philadelphia, where he had been connected with the management of the Chestnut Street Theatre, 14th February, 1837. He was very concientious and honest in his dealings.

MRS. ROWBOTHAM was originally a dancer at the Italian Opera House, London· She was a handsome woman, and was always received by the public with delight· Her maiden name was Johannot, and she was born in London. In Philadelphia she was a great favorite. In 1838 she married Robert Hamilton, and died a year later.

TYRONE POWER was born at Kilmacthomas, Ireland, in 1797, and made his professional *debut* at Newport as *Alonzo* in "Pizarro" in 1815.

He married two years later, and becoming possessed of his wife's fortune, left the stage in 1818. Unfortunate speculations forced him to return to the stage, when he made his first appearance at London, in 1822. in "Man and Wife." He first appeared on the American stage, 28th August, 1833, at the Park Theatre. New York, as *Sir Patrick O'Plenipo* and *Teddy the Tiler.* His last appearance on any stage was 9th March, 1841, at the same theatre as *Gerald Pepper* and *Morgan Rattler.* T. N. Talfourd epitomized the comedian's methods in the following expression : " This actor, if not the richest, is to my taste the most agreeable of stage Irishmen. He buzzes about the verge of vulgarity and skims the surface of impudence with a light wing and a decent consideration for fastidious nerves."

Tyrone Power was in Petersburg, Va., in 1841, and was observed one morning roaming about the old Blandford church grounds· A few days after his departure the following lines were found, and are still preserved on a wooden tablet. As no one ever claimed their authorship they are generally attributed to him:

" Thou art crumbling to the dust, old pile,
Thou art hastening to thy fall,
And round thee in thy loneliness
Clings the ivy to thy wall.
The worshippers are scattered now
Who knelt before the shrine,
And silence reigns, where anthems rose
In days of ' Auld Lang Syne.'

" How doth ambition's hope take wing ?
Where oft in years gone by
Prayers rose from many hearts to Him,
The Highest of the High,
The tread of many a noiseless foot
That sought the aisles is o'er,
And many a weary heart around
Is still forevermore.

" How doth ambition's hope take wing ?
How droops the spirit now ?
We hear the distant city's din,
The dead are mute below ;
The sun that shone upon their paths
Now gilds their lonely graves,
The zephyrs, which once fanned their brows,
The grass above them waves.

" Oh, could we call the many back
Who've gathered here in vain,
Who've careless roved where we do now,
Who'll never meet again.
How would our very hearts be stirred
To meet the earnest gaze.
Of the lovely and the beautiful,—
The light of other days."

He was lost on the steamship "President," which sailed from New York, 21st March, 1841. No monument rears its chaste marble to inscribe thereon his name and fate, that future generations may know that such a man had lived, and as he lived so he perished in a " sea of troubles." No requiem to sing his soul to rest but the eternal moaning of the mighty ocean.

CORNELIUS A. LOGAN, author and comedian, was born at Baltimore, and was first a printer, then studied theology, but finally went on the stage making his *debut* as *Bertram,* in 1825, in Philadelphia. He first appeared at New York. at Burton's Theatre, in 1849, in his own farce of " Chloroform." He also wrote " Yankee Land." He was the father of Olive, Celia and Eliza Logan. He died of apoplexy on board a steamer on the Mississippi, 23rd February, 1853. He is buried in Spring Grove, Cincinnati· On the headstone is engraved his name, also the solitary line :

"*Our father who art in Heaven.*"

IN THE SPRING OF 1836

the Theatre Royal underwent considerable repairs, some needed improvements being also added. Preparatory to the regular opening of the season a number of amateur performances were given in the Military Theatre, where Mrs. Spiller was given a benefit 3rd March.

The house was leased by Manager Thomas Ward, of the Washington Theatre. The company included Mr. and Mrs. Thomas L. Ternan, William Abbott, John Nickinson, John Reeve, J. S. Balls, C. Eberle, Lewellyn, Mr. and Mrs. H. Knight, Mrs. Hughes, Madame Celeste, Herr Cline and Garner. Mr. Dinsmore, of the Chestnut Street Theatre, Philadelphia, was to have been associated with Mr. Ward, but could not get away from home affairs.

Thomas L. Ternan, styled the "celebrated tragedian," opened the season 27th June in "Fazio," he in the title role and his wife as *Bianca*. They also appeared in the after-piece, entitled "Personation," in which Mrs. Ternan sang "Come Love to Me," accompanying herself on the lute with very pretty effect. They subsequently appeared in "The Wonder" and "La Somnambula."

William Abbott, the English tragedian, made his Montreal debut 5th July as *Hamlet*. He appeared as *Daran* in "The Exile," 7th, and as *Macbeth*, 8th, Mr. Rogers being the *Macduff*, Mr. Ward *Banquo*, and Mrs. Hughes *Lady Macbeth*. His last appearance for the season was on the 9th, when he played *Charles Surface* to the *Joseph Surface* of Mr. Ternan and *Lady Teazle* of Mrs. Ternan in "The School for Scandal." He became a favorite here, although he experienced poor business during his visit.

Herr John Cline performed on the elastic cord during week of 11th July.

On 20th July, John Sefton made his initial bow here in his original character, *Jemmy Twitcher*, in the "Golden Farmer," a favorite piece at the time, written by Benjamin Webster. The performance concluded with the farce of "John Jones."

It was about this time that Mrs. Watts, the first wife of John Sefton, made her first appearance here on any stage.

On the 23rd was produced " Therese, or the Orphan of Geneva," together with "Catching an Heiress." Sefton was seen as *Lavigne* and *Tom Twigg* in these pieces, being his last appearance for the season.

Mr. and Mrs. Rogers produced " Charles XII. of Sweden," 4th August, assisted by amateurs.

John Greene, the Irish character comedian, came to Montreal after having played an engagement at Quebec, making his first appearance 15th August in Buckstone's " Married Life," and as *Murtoch Delaney* in "The Irishman in London." On the 16th he was seen as *Pryce Kinchella* in "Presumptive Evidence," with the farce, "Lady and the Devil."

Herr Cline performed on the wire at each performance.

Mr. Ward was given a benefit in " Married Life," 19th, and on the following night another benefit was given, Mr. and Mrs. Knight being the recipients, with " The Lady of the Lake " as the attraction.

The special event of the season was the appearance of England's great comedian, William Dowton, on the 2nd, 3rd and 6th of September. The opening bill was "The Rivals," cast as follows : *Sir Anthony Absolute*, Mr. William Dowton ; *Bob Acres*, Mr. John Reeve ; *Faulkland*, Mr. Thomas L. Ternan ; *Captain Absolute*, Mr. Ward ; *Sir Lucius O'Trigger*, Mr. Rogers ; *Lydia Languish*, Mrs. Ternan ; *Mrs. Malaprop*, Mrs. Rogers.

Mr. Dowton's second appearance was as *Falstaff* in "Henry the Fourth," on which occasion Ternan was the *Hotspur*. The comedian's last appearance was as *Sir Peter Teazle*, in " The School for Scandal," Mr. Ward benefiting, 6th September.

Under the patronage of Major Wingfield and officers of the 32nd Regiment, "The Recruiting Officer" and "Black-Eyed Susan " were presented at a benefit performance to John Nickinson, 7th September, on which occasion Mr. Ward read a farewell address written by Mr. Weston. John Greene also appeared in his character of *Looney McTwolter*, and Mr. Nickinson as *Caleb Quotem* in " The Review."

The following day saw the departure of the company for Washington for the opening of the season there. John Nickinson also left to fulfil an engagement at the Bowery Theatre, New York. The season had not resulted in financial gratification to the management, nor had the patronage of the l public been at all flattering to the talents of the artists who had appeared.

The Amateurs gave two more performances that year in the Military Theatre.

THOMAS WARD, born in Liverpool, 16th May, 1799, first appear-ed on the stage in 1816. In America he was known as an active man-ager.

JOHN REEVE was a well-known player and a favorite *Bob Acres*. His American *debut* was at the Park Theatre, New York, 30th Nov-ember, 1835. He was chubby, large and fat, and very laughable as "'Cupid." He also gave capital imitations of *stars*, and could turn a *pirouette*, large as he was. He was born in London in 1799. His American tour was not pofitable and he soon returned to England, where he died 24th January, 1838.

WILLIAM ABBOT was born at Chelsea in 1789, and made his first appearance on the stage at Bath, in his seventeenth year, as *Alonzo* in " Pizarro," He was then engaged by Mr. Diamond for three or four seasons, finally making his London *debut* at the Hay-market' Theatre, in the summer of 1810, as *Frederick* in "Lovers Vows." He was the *Romeo* at Covent Garden, on the occasion of Fanny Kemble's *debut* as *Juliet* in 1829. He made his first New York appearance at the Park as *Beverley* in "The Gamester," 28th Sept., 1835, and re-appeared there as *Hamlet* 9th April, 1836. He was the author of "The Youthful Days of Frederick the Great" and "Swed-ish Patriotism." He made several visits to Montreal, and his last appearance on the stage was at the Park Theatre, 29th May, 1843, when he played *Hemeya* to the elder Booth's *Pescara*, when he was seized with an apoplectic fit and died 7th June, at Baltimore. He married an American actress, Miss Buloid; she died 15th December, 1858.

HERR JOHN CLINE presented an address and gentlemanly gracefulness on the rope that was new here, and his work was the general theme of eulogy. He was highly polished in style and atti-tude, copying classical statues of ancient masters. He subsequently appeared at Guilbault's Gardens, situated on St. Lawrence street, above Sherbrooke street, for a short time. His brother, Andre, was the Louis Cyr of that period. Herr Cline was born in London, Eng., and made his American *debut* at the Bowery Theatre in 1828. He retired in 1862, but, having lost his savings, was compelled to return to rope dancing at an age when most others are satisfied to be able to walk at all.

FRANCES ELEANOR TERNAN, *nee* Fanny Jarman, was born at Hull, England, in 1802, and was already a great stage favorite at Bath before she reached her fifteenth year. After playing through the provinces she appeared for the first time at London, at Drury Lane, Feb. 7, 1827, as *Juliet*. She came to America with her husband in 1845, making her *debut* at the Chestnut Street Theatre, Philadelphia, 18th November, 1834, as *Juliet*. Her last appearance on any stage was at the Lyceum Theatre, London, in 1865, as *Alice* in "The Master of Ravenswood," She died in London, 30th October, 1873.

THOMAS LUKE TERNAN was born in Dublin in 1799, and made an early appearance on the stage. He was well received in the English provinces as a *star*. His first American bow was at the Chestnut Street Theatre, Philadelphia, in Nov., 1834, in the character of *Richard III.*, and in New York the following month as *Romeo* to his wife's *Juliet*. They went South in 1835, and came to Canada in 1836. They subsequently starred all through the principal eastern cities! Their last appearance in America was at the Walnut Street Theatre, Philadelphia, 11th December, 1836, in Talfourd's " Ion," Mrs. Ternan as *Evadne*. They returned to England, becoming favorites at Drury Lane Theatre. He died in London, 17th October, 1846.

JOHN SEFTON was a celebrated comedian of the second rank, born in Liverpool 15th Jan., 1805. He first appeared in America, in Philadelphia, in June, 1827, and remained a prominent stage figure until his death, 19th Sept., 1868.

He first married Mrs. Watts, and afterwards Miss Wells, the mother of his daughter, Angela, born 1840.

WILLIAM DOWTON was an artist of the natural school. His passionate *old men* were pronounced faultless, nothing being more true to nature, for it was the comedian's nature, he having been known to snatch off his wig in an outburst of temper and fling it into the fire. He died in 1851, aged 87.

J. S. BALLS was a dashing young English comedian, born in 1799. His first London appearance was in 1829, and at the Park, New York, 15th October, 1835. His *Vapid* in " The Dramatist" was very good. His last appearance in New York was in 1840. He died in Dublin in 1844.

CHARLES EBERLE was a low comedian who lost his life on a steamer on his way to Boston in 1840. His first appearance on the stage was at Frankfort, Ky., in 1822.

MR. and MRS. HENRY KNIGHT were well-known and esteemed players here. He was a brother to Edward Knight, already noted, and the son of Edward ("little") Knight, a popular London actor, who died in 1826. Harry was accidentally killed in 1839. Mrs. Knight then married George Mossop, but was divorced, and married a non-professional named De Costa, and, retiring, lived in Philadelphia. She was formerly Miss Eliza Kent, and was an excellent actress in all the walks of comedy, possessing a fine figure and good in-telligence. She was first seen on the stage under Hamblin's manage-ment at the Broadway.

Harry Knight used to sing "The Poachers," and was very fond of the song· It is said that he used to enter the boxes, unobserved, and cry out "Knight !" "Knight !" in order to be called on to sing, imme-diately dodging behind the scenes to answer his own call.

JOHN GREENE rose to positive excellence as an exponent of Irish character. He was born in Philadelphia, and brought up to be a printer, but it was the old story; he became " infirm of purpose" and went on the stage. He was an early companion of Forrest, and made his first stage appearance in 1818; died 28th May, 1860. His wife was also an actress· Her maiden name was Annie Muskay, and she was born in Boston, 23rd March, 1800; died 19th January, 1862. She had a commanding figure and pretty features, but became quite deaf in later years.

"OLD" POWELL, a well-known English actor, is recorded to have died here 13th May, 1836, aged eighty-two.

THE CIVIL STRIFE OF 1837,

together with the memory of the previous year's unsatisfac-tory business, did not encourage the return of a professional company that year for anything like an extended season. There is, however, a record of the first appearance here of Joseph Proctor, then a rising young actor, in a round of legiti-mate roles, apart from whom a few amateur performances were noted; in fact, it was not until 1840 that anything like keen interest in Montreal's theatricals was once more revived.

JOSEPH PROCTOR was born in Marlboro, Mass., May 7, 1816, and made his *debut* on the stage November 29, 1833, in the Warren Theatre, Boston, acting *Damon* in "Damon and Pythias," E. S. Con-ner playing *Pythias*. He went to Albany and opened in the Pearl Street Theatre, under the management of Wm. Duffy, October 16, 1834, as *Damon*, and subsequently joined the stock company. Later he played through the West and in Canada until 1837, when he en-gaged at the Walnut Street Theatre· E. S. Conner was also in the company, and between them great rivalry sprang up. After their joint performance in " Thalba," the patrons of the theatre became divided, and were known as the Proctor and Conner factions.

At the Bowery Theatre, in 1839, Mr. Proctor made his first appear-ance in New York, acting *Nathan Slaughter* in "Nick of the Woods," or the "Jibbenainosay." Mr. Proctor played in it upwards of two thousand times.

In 1851 he went to California, and after starring in the principal towns, embarked in management in the American Theatre, San Francisco. Subsequently he built the Sacramento Theatre, which in 1876 became a Chinese Theatre. Mr. Proctor frequently played *Othello* to the *Iago* of the elder Booth, and *Iago* with Edwin Forrest as the *Moor*. His repertory also included *Virginius, Macbeth, King Lear, Richelieu, Jack Cade* and other legitimate roles. After playing a farewell star engagement in 1859, at New York, he sailed for England. He made his *debut* in London, at the Standard Theatre, where he played one hundred nights in a round of Shakespearean characters, "Nick of the Woods" and other dramas. He then made a tour through Ireland and Scotland. In the company of the Theatre Royal, Glasgow, he met Henry Irving, who played *Macduff, De Mauprat, Cassio* and *Roland Forrester* ("Nick of the Woods") with him. Returning to London, he fulfilled engagements in the Surrey and Marylebone Theatres. He came back in the fall of 1861, making his re-appearance in the Howard Athenaeum, Boston, and then made a starring tour of the country. From the Spring of 1873 until the Fall of 1875 he was off the stage, devoting his attention to a patent he had purchased of the inventor. He was said to have lost $70,000 in that venture. He again re-appeared before the public with a company on the combination plan and retired from the stage some years before his death, which occurred in Boston, 2nd October, 1897.

THE FEATURE OF 1838

was the occasion of the first appearance in Montreal of Ellen Tree, afterwards the wife of Charles Kean. Miss Tree made her *debut* here on Wednesday, 22nd August, in the character of *Julia* in "The Hunchback," and after a short season proceeded to Quebec.

Between 1836 and 1839 Miss Tree visited every large town in America, realizing the sum, large for that time, of £12,000. Her next visit to Montreal was after an absence of twenty-six years.

ELLEN TREE (Mrs. Charles Kean) was one of four sisters, the eldest of whom, Maria, was a vocalist of considerable ability, and it was at her benefit that Ellen Tree, when seventeen years of age (1822), made her first appearance, in the character of *Olivia*. Her talents had won for her an independence within twenty years, when she married Charles Kean. Thereafter she stood at her husband's side, his best adviser and his strongest support. It is not necessary to recall all the triumphs which were obtained. Mr. Kean acted for the last time in May, 1867, after which they both retired from the stage, he dying during the following January; she, in 1880. It seemed hard that after laboring so long and so strenuously they should not have been longer spared to each other in their well-earned retirement. There have been few actresses, who, like Mrs. Kean, could undertake the whole range of character and excel in so many. There is a wide distance between *Ion* and *Violante*, between *Rosalind* and *Portia ;* but few had seen either more delightfully portrayed than by her. Poetry and pathos, gaiety and force alike never demanded in vain, a dramatic tact which mounted to genius, and a mastery of blank verse, which few actresses have attained, were but parts of her gifts. Her domestic character was as admirable as her public career.

DURING 1839

we find the Amateurs as the leading feature, the Garrison Amateurs presenting " X. Y. Z."; or, " Old Sandgliter's Coffee House," on 11th January for the benefit of the widows and orphans of the volunteers killed at Odelltown. "Othello According to Act of Parliament," was the after-piece. On 22nd January they produced " My Husband's Ghost," " The Unfinished Gentleman " and " Frank Fox Phipps."

The most notable *star* engagement was that of Miss Jean Margaret Davenport, then in her twelfth year. On 5th August she appeared as *Richard III.,* supported by her father and mother ; *Shylock,* 7th ; *Norval,* 9th ; *Sir Peter Teazle,* 12th; *Norval* and *Paul Pry in Petticoats,* 14th; "The Dumb Boy," 19th; *Shylock,* 20th; " The Child of Nature," 26th; and a repetition of " The Dumb Boy," 27th.

While in London Miss Davenport had been presented with Kean's hat after her performance of *Richard,* and in New York she was given a gold watch and chain.

MRS. LANDER (*nee* Jean Margaret Davenport) was born in England, 3rd May, 1829, and made her *debut* in her eighth year at New York as *Little Pickle* in " The Spoiled Child." She was successful and her parents put her through a course of studies in a well-selected repertoire. From being a youthful prodigy she subsequently made a distinct hit as an actress of intense roles. In 1860 she married Col. Fred. W. Lander, who was killed in battle two years later. Mrs. Lander then returned to the stage, after ministering for many months to the sick and dying soldiers. She was the original *Camille* in this country. Her last appearance was in Albany, under Mr. Albaugh's management, when a version of Hawthorne's " Scarlet Letter " was produced.

AMATEUR PERFORMANCES IN 1840

began early in the year. The Raines Family, Tyrolese Minstrels, gave a concert in Roscoe's Hotel, 20th June, and remained until 13th July.

THE COMPANY OF 1840

was managed by Fuller and Weston, and included W. C. Drummond, Latham, Tuthill, Clifford, Mr. and Mrs. Harry Hunt, Mrs. Hughes and Miss Shaw. Mrs. Creswick, wife of Wm. Creswick, the tragedian, made her first appearance here on the opening night of the regular season, 11th July, when "The Barrack Room" was performed. On 14th July Harry Hunt and Mrs. Hughes made their bows here in "Charles II." Then followed productions of "The Maid of Croissey," "Paul Pry," "Love in the East," etc. The subsequent appearance of the operatic artists, Mr. and Mrs. Edward Seguin and Mr. Horncastle in "The Barber of Seville," "Fra Diavolo," "Cinderella," was a treat to lovers of music.

Mrs. Creswick, who had come here direct from Mad. Vestris' Theatre, New York, some weeks previously, was joined by her husband, he making his first appearance here on 8th August in "The Iron Chest." Cast : *Sir Edw. Mortimer,* Wm. Creswick; *Adam Winterten,* Thos. Fuller; *Orson,* H. Tuthill; *Lady Helen,* Mrs. Louisa Hunt; *Blanche,* Mrs. Elizabeth Creswick; *Barbara,* Miss Shaw. "Simpson & Co." was the after-piece.

Montreal was favored with the appearance of another good actor during the short period of the Creswick engagement, in C. K. Mason of the Covent Garden Theatre, who made his *debut* here as a *star,* 11th August, in *Othello,* with Creswick as *Iago.* "The Stranger," "Rob Roy" and "William Tell" followed on 12th, 15th and 18th August. Mason had been here in 1833. Mr. and Mrs. Creswick took a benefit on 24th August in Bulwer's "The Birthright." On 25th August the Seguins produced "Cinderella," and on 26th August Knowles' "Love" was presented with "La Somnambula." "Douglas" was produced on 1st September and on 3rd September. The Seguins closed the season with "La Gazza Ladra," but re-appeared at an amateur performance of "Der Freischutz" on 8th September, this being their last appearance for the season.

Rockwell's Amphitheatre Co. opened a circus season on 21st September.

A cursory glance at the foregoing cast of "The Iron Chest" may not elicit much interest until its importance is realized when we consider that it records the appearance of the late Mrs. John Drew, who was first married to Harry B. Hunt in 1838.

HARRY B. HUNT, a young Irish comedian, possessed a fine voice, and was in demand as the singing hero in the melodramas and light operas of the time. He had been a member of the fast set which had surrounded George the Fourth before his ascent to the throne, and was a gentleman of dashing manners and great animal spirits. He died in New York 11th Feb., 1854.

MRS. JOHN DREW, *nee* Louisa Lane, was the daughter of Mr. and Mrs. Thomas F. Lane, English players, and was born in London, 10th January, 1820. Her mother brought her to America in 1827, when she was known as a child prodigy.

In 1848, after securing a divorce from Harry Hunt, the popular actress married George Mossop, a fairly good actor of Irish birth, who was chiefly remarkable because he could not speak without stuttering badly off the stage, although before the footlights his language was as smooth and flowing as that of an orator. He died a year afterward, and in 1850 Mrs. Mossop met and married John Drew, the best comedian in America in Irish parts, and those requiring elegance and dash and broad humor. Like Hunt and Mossop, he was a native of Dublin, and was twenty-three years old at the time of his marriage.

In 1853 was born the present John Drew, and on 21st May, 1862, the senior Drew died. Mrs. Drew's mother, who had been married to Mr. Kinloch, died in 1887, aged 91. The Arch Street Theatre, Philadelphia, was opened for the first time under Mrs. Drew's direction, August 31, 1861, with "The School for Scandal" and "Aunt Charlotte's Maid," which plays were presented by one of the best stock companies ever organized.

A history of the house during Mrs. Drew's management would be almost an epitome of the activity of the American stage during this period. Few, indeed, were the representative American plays and players that were not seen at the Arch Street Theatre while Mrs. Drew was manager.

Old favorites made last appearances there, and young actors and actresses—fledglings who were destined to soar high—made their *debuts* upon that stage.

When Mrs. Drew relinquished the management in 1892, after thirty-one years of service, she had not made a fortune, but she had given her theatre and herself a glorious record of artistic achievement.

Mrs. Drew played the part of *Mrs. Malaprop* in "The Rivals," for the first time on February 22, 1879, when Joseph Jefferson revived the old comedy at the Arch Street Theatre. This is, perhaps, the character with which she is most closely identified in the minds of the present generation of theatre-goers, and upon that first night the artistic delicacy and quaint humor of Mrs. Drew's portrayal brought her a share of the honors equal to that of Mr. Jefferson as *Bob Acres*.

Mrs. Drew appeared at the Academy of Music, Montreal, week 22nd May, 1893, in "The Rivals." The following was the cast:

Mrs. Malaprop, Mrs. John Drew; *Sir Anthony*, McKee Rankin; *Lydia Languish*, Mrs. Sidney Drew; *Capt. Absolute*, Maurice Barrymore; *Bob Acres*, Sidney Drew; *St. Lucius*, Edmund Lyons.

Mrs. Drew re-appeared here in June 1894. She died 31st August, 1897, and is buried in Glenwood, Philadelphia, within easy view of my window, as I draw this record to a close. A ray of starlight is streaming on that beautiful hillside, gleaming on a tomb whereon is inscribed the memory of a brilliant actress, a most excellent woman and a devoted mother—the tribute of a loving son.

THOMAS FULLER was born at Dracut, Mass., and made his *debut* in March, 1838, at the Tremont Street Theatre, Boston. He was the manager and lessee, in Montreal, during 1838-9-40-41, coming from Albany, whence he escaped, being cudgelled by an actor named Eaton. Fuller, to avoid him, hid in a garret until evening, when he slipped into a carriage, was driven down to the river and taken on board the night boat in a skiff, and so left Eaton dissatisfied and Albany without a manager. While in Albany Fuller had been outwitted by a printer, who was his heaviest creditor. He printed tickets for the last performance, sold them himself and kept the money. Those were hard days for our theatrical friends.

MR. and MRS. EDWARD SEGUIN.—Mr. Seguin was superior to any previous basso in America. He was born in London in 1809, and, after appearing in minor engagements, made his regular London *debut* in 1831, and in America at the Broadway Theatre, 13th October, 1838. Died of consumption 13th December, 1852.

Mrs. Seguin, *nce* Annie Childe, was also born in London, appearing on the stage at a very early age. Her first appearance in New York was at the Park in 1841, and last appeared in 1882. She died 24th August, 1888.

WILLIAM CRESWICK, although not one of the giants of art, was certainly the very first of the second rank. Born 27th December, 1813, in the immediate neighborhood of Covent Garden, he frequently saw the most eminent players of the time, and although intended for a mercantile career, he soon evinced a decided predilection for the stage. In 1831 he accepted an engagement at a small theatre on the Commercial Road, London, and soon afterwards joined a small company at Suffolk. In 1834 he was playing leading business in the York circuit, where he met Miss Elizabeth Paget, of the Olympic Theatre, whom he subsequently married, and who died 16th February, 1876, aged 67. Returning to London, he made his first prominent appearance 16th February, 1835, as *Meredith* in Jerrold's "Schoolfellows," at the Old Queen's Theatre. He visited America in 1840, and remained three years, playing heavy tragedy. He was subsequently associated with Phelps, Macready and Helen Faucit, and a trip to Australia added greatly to his fame. He revisited America in 1871 with Jams Bennett and Walter Montgomery for his associa-ates. Creswick took his farewell to the stage 29th October, 1885, when a complimentary benefit was given the esteemed actor at Drury Lane Theatre, when he appeared in a scene from " King Lear." He died 17th June, 1888, his remains being laid close to those of his friend Macready, in the old catacombs of Kensal Green Cemetery?

W. C. DRUMMOND, born in London, made his first American appearance on the stage in Baltimore in 1810. This was in the ballet of "Cinderella," he having originally been a dancer. He was the first husband of the beautiful Anne Henry.

It is said that his wardrobe was unequalled during his palmy days. To him all passions came as easily—to weep, to laugh, to sigh or to rage. He died in New York 21st February, 1871.

The year 1841 brought Mons. Alexandre, on 23rd January, in four representations in French and English of "The Devil on Two Sticks," and during the spring the Garrison Amateurs gave a few representations.

THE SEASON OF 1841

was regularly opened in July under the management of Fuller & Weston. We find in the company Mrs. Hughes, Miss Mc-Bride, Mrs. Hautonville, Mrs. J. A. Smith, Messrs. J. A. Smith, Nickinson, Stafford, Merryfield, Weston and Fuller. The first night of the season was on 9th July, when "Laugh When You Can" and "The Lottery Ticket" were presented. Wm. Abbott began a four nights' engagement 10th July in "The Lady of Lyons," "Romeo and Juliet," "The Stranger," and terminated on 13th July with a repetition of the opening night's bill. Mrs. Hautonville made her first appearance on 12th July as *Juliet* to Abbott's *Romeo*. The old operatic favorites, the Seguins, returned this season, appearing on 15th July in "La Somnambula." Abbott played a return engagement in "The Sea Captain" and "Richelieu" on 27th and 28th July, which was extended into August. "Catching an Heiress" and "The Old English Gentleman" were staged, and on 16th August "Nicholas Nickleby" was produced with Abbott in the title role. "The School for Scandal" was followed by "Hamlet," 19th; and "Mazeppa" was also presented. The famous singing comedian, Braham, had appeared at a concert in Rascoe's Hotel, 11th August, and was engaged to appear at the theatre 2nd September for two nights in "Love in a Village." Abbott, assisted by the amateurs, presented "Charles XII. of Sweden" for a benefit on 7th September.

Fanny Fitzwilliam, a celebrated comic actress of London, appeared on the following evening in "The Irish Widow," and was followed by the first appearance in Montreal of the celebrated comedian and sketch writer, J. B. Buckstone, 9th September, as *Selim Pettibon* in his own piece, "A Kiss in the Dark." Abbott made his last appearance for the season as *Frank Heartall* in "The Scottish Widow." Buckstone, supported by Fanny Fitzwilliam, appeared in several of the comedian's sketches. "The Irish Widow" was repeated 16th September for a benefit to the managers. The season closed on 17th September with "The Banished Star," when the company left for Quebec.

JOSEPH ALFRED SMITH was born in Philadelphia in 1813, and, when a young man, was a favorite member of the first stock companies in that city, in Boston and in New York. During his long career he played in support of nearly every noted artist of the time. By every player with whom he was associated he was beloved, and his kindly manners earned for him, in the old days, the title of "Gentleman Joe."

He retired from the stage in 1884, after playing during the latter years of his career in travelling companies. From that time up to the period of his passing away, 1st August, 1899, he had been a guest at the Forrest Home, where, with the friends of his youth about him, he passed the happiest period of his life. To the aged players there his death was a severe blow indeed.

JOHN BRAHAM, born in 1774, was the son of a Portugese Hebrew. His first appearance in America was at the Park Theatre, New York, 21st December, 1840. He died in 1856.

MRS. HAUTONVILLE (Mrs. Bradshaw), known as the beautiful Miss Cross, of the Chestnut Street Theatre, Philadelphia. first appeared there in 1831 as a member of the ballet, and later became a good actress.

J. M. WESTON, who had been joint lessee with Fuller during 1840-41, played small parts. He was born in Boston in 1817, and first came out as *Richard* under Pelby's management in New York. "Dr." Weston was a useful actor, with good judgment; but his *forte* was as a stage director. We find him managing the magician Macallister from 1852 to 1856, when, after the latter's death, Weston married the widow. He was for a time acting as agent for A. J. Neaffie, the tragedian. His wife died in South America in 1859, aged 27. Weston certainly was a bird of passage.

JOHN BALDWIN BUCKSTONE may be said to have played almost all the principal low comedy parts of the English drama. His name is inseparably associated with some of the most amusing char_ acters in the higher range of old English comedy, for example: *Grumio, Speed, Touchstone, Sir Andrew, Aguecheek, Zekiel, Homespun, Scrub, Tony Lumkin* and *Bob Acres.* It may be added that the varied attributes of those characters have invariably received at his hand the happiest illustration. Mr. Buckstone was born at Hoxton, near London, in September, 1802, and died 31st October, 1879. ˋ

JOHN NICKINSON, who first appeared here during the season of 1836, and who was manager and lessee in 1843, was a great favorite in Canada. He was born in London in 1808, and at the age of fifteen enlisted in the British Army as a drummer boy. His regiment subsequently came to Quebec, where he took part in amateur performances, having a strong bent in that direction· His *corps* was afterwards stationed in Montreal, where he made a number of professional friends, bought his discharge and entered on a theatrical career· In 1852 we find him at the head of a company touring Canada, and among its members were W. J. Florence, C. M. Walcot, jun., and Charles Peters. They appeared in Quebec, Montreal and Toronto. In Toronto Nickinson was induced to take a lease of the theatre, which he relinquished in 1858. He was subsequently manager of the Utica Museum and the Albany Museum, and was also well known in New York city. He died in a drug store in Cincinnati, 8th February, 1864. He left a widow and five children : Charlotte, Eliza (who married Charles Peters), Virginia (who married Owen Marlowe in 1857 and died in New York city, 7th March, 1899), Isabel (who married C. M. Walcot, jun.), and John.

Mr. Tuthill was lessee of

THE THEATRE DURING THE YEAR 1842.

Several new faces were seen, Mr. and Mrs. John Sloman making their *debut*, 26th May, in Knowles' "Hunchback," Mr. Walter Leman being the *Master Walter*; William Wheatley as *Sir Thomas Clifford*; Mrs. Sloman as *Julia*; and Mrs. A. W. Penson as *Helen.* Other members of the company were Mr. Byrne, Mrs. Brown, Mrs. Henry and Mr. W. C. Drummond·

Mr. Drummond appeared as *Jaffier*, Mr. Wheatley as *Pierre* and Mrs. Sloman as *Belvidera* in "Venice Preserved," 27th May.

The event of the season was the appearance of the people's novelist,

CHARLES DICKENS.

I reproduce in full a copy of the bill announcing the event,

and programme, the only known original being in the possession of Henry Hogan :

THEATRE ROYAL.

For this night only.

The manager has the honor to announce a performance in
which Charles Dickens, Esq., together with the distinguished
Garrison Amateurs (whose successful performance on Wednesday last created such unbounded admiration), will appear
this evening, Saturday, May 28, 1842.   The performance
will commence with "A Roland for an Oliver."   *Sir Mark
Chase*, Hon. P. Methaen; *Alfred Highflyer*, Mr. Chas. Dickens; *Wm. Selbourne*, Earl of Mulgrave; *Fixture*, Capt. Willoughby ; *Gamekeepers, etc.* ; *Maria Darlington*, Mrs. A. W.
Penson ; *Mrs. Selbourne*, Mrs. Brown ; *Mrs. Fixture*, Mrs.
Henry.   After which "Two O'Clock in the Morning."   *Snobbington*, Mr. Chas. Dickens; *The Stranger*, Capt. Granville,
23rd Regiment.   To conclude with "High Life Below Stairs."
My Lord Duke, Dr. Griffin, 85th Regiment; *Sir Harry*, Capt.
Willoughby, 23rd Regiment ; *Lovell*, Capt. Torrens, 23rd
Regiment; *Coachman*, Capt. Granville, 23rd Regiment; *Free-
man*, Earl of Mulgrave; *Shilep*, Mr. Chas. Dickens; *Kingston*,
Mr. Thomas; *Tom*, Mr. Hughes; *Mrs. Kitty*, Mrs. A. W. Pen-
son ; *Lady Bob*, Mrs. Henry ; *Lady Charlotte*, Mrs. Brown ;
Chloe, Miss Heath.   The performance to commence at half-
past seven.

On Monday evening Mr. and Mrs. Sloman's third appearance."   Montreal, May 28th, 1842.—*Gazette Office*.

The performance had been preceded by a strictly amateur
and select production a few nights before, which Dickens
fully described to his friend, Forster, as follows:

"The play came off last night; the audience, between five and six
hundred strong, were invited as to a party, a regular table with re-
freshments being spread in the lobby and saloon. We had the band
of the 23rd (one of the finest in the service) in the orchestra, the theatre was lighted with gas, the scenery was excellent, and the properties were all brought from private houses. Sir Charles Bagot, Sir
Richard Jackson and their staffs were present, and as the military
portion of the audience were in full uniform, it was really a splendid
scene. We 'went' also splendidly through with nothing very remarkable in the acting way. We had for *Sir Mark Chase* a genuine
odd fish, with plenty of humor, but our *Tristam Sappy* was not up to
the marvellous reputation he has somehow or other acquired here. I
am not, however, let me tell you, placarded as manager for nothing.
Everybody was told they would have to submit to the most iron des-

potism; and didn't I come Macready over them ? The pains I have taken with them and the perspiration I have expended during the last ten days exceed in amount anything you can imagine. I had regular plots of the scenery made out, and list of the properties wanted, and had them nailed up by the prompter's chair. Every letter that was to be delivered was written; every piece of money that had to be given, provided; and not a single thing lost sight of. I prompted myself when I was not in; when I was I made the regular prompter of the theatre my deputy; and I never saw anything so perfectly in touch and go as the first two pieces. The bedroom scene in the interlude was as well furnished as Vestris had it: with a 'practicable' fireplace blazing away like mad, and everything in a concatenation accordingly. I really do believe that I was really very funny; at least I know that I laughed heartily myself, and made the part a character such as you and I know very well—a mixture of F. Harley, Yates, Keeley and *Jerry Sneak*. It went with a vim all through; and, as I am closing this, they have told me I was so well made up that Sir Charles Bagot, who sat in the stage box, had no idea who played *Mr. Snobbington* until the piece was over. But only think of Kate playing ! and playing devilish well, I assure you ! All the ladies were capital, and we had no wait or hitch for an instant. You may suppose this, when I tell you that we began at eight and had the curtain down at eleven. It is their custom here to prevent heartburnings in a very heartburning town, whenever they have played in private, to repeat the performance in public. So, on Saturday (substituting real actresses for the ladies), we are to repeat the two first pieces to a paying audience, for the manager's benefit. I have not told you half enough. Wasn't it worthy of *Crummels* that when Lord Mulgrave and I went out to the door to receive the Governor-General, the regular prompter followed us in agony with four tall candlesticks with wax candles in them, and besought us with a bleeding heart to carry two apiece, in accordance with all the precedents."

With all due respect to the memory of Mr. Dickens, his account would lead us to believe that he had been the "whole show"; in fact, the *dickens* and all, and the others nonentities.

Milman's "Fazio" followed 30th; "Lady of Lyons," 31st: "The Honeymoon," 1st June; "Victorine," for Sloman's benefit, 2nd June; "Therese," 3rd; "Victorine," 4th; and benefit to Mrs. Sloman, 6th, in "Isabella." "The Heir-at-Law" was produced 7th, and on 9th, by command of His Excellency the Governor-General, "The Poor Gentleman" was presented. J. H. Hackett began a short engagement on 10th in "Henry IV.," followed by "Rip Van Winkle," "Yankee in England," and closed 14th June. On 15th was noted the first appearance of Mrs. Seymour in the character of *Mrs. Haller* in "The Stranger," with Wheatley in the title role. "The Lady of Lyons," "A Child of Nature," "Mabel's Curse" and Bulwer's "Money' followed. Mrs. Sloman closed with "Romeo and Juliet," 20th, playing *Juliet* to Wheatley's *Romeo*. Miss Melton was a *debutante*, 21st, as *Letitia Hardy*, followed by productions of "The Englishman in India," "Paul Pry," and Mrs.

Seymour reappeared, 24th, in "The Captive Maniac." Miss Melton was seen, 25th, in "The Wonder" and "Charles XII.," and closed with a benefit, 27th, with "Faint Heart Never Won Fair Lady." An interesting feature of the season was the appearance of T. D. Rice, 28th June, in "Deaf and Dumb," "After the Sarcophagus" and "Jumbo Junior," introducing the famous song "Jim Crow." He took a benefit, 4th July, in "Bone Squash Diavolo." Miss Melton, who had returned from Quebec, was seen in "The Englishman from India," 5th July. Rice re-appeared for Latham's benefit, 6th, taking part in the after-piece, "The Virginia Mummy," to Boucicault's "London Assurance," which was repeated several nights. "Douglas" and "Money" were again staged, and on 13th Wheatley was tendered a benefit.

On 18th July, under military patronage, was performed "Henri Quatre" and "Ambroise Gwinette." A benefit to the "needy of the steamboat disaster" took place the following evening in "Charles XII. of Sweden." A revival of "George Barnwell," 22nd, was followed 23rd by a benefit to Manager Tuthill in "The Rivals," Miss Melton as *Lydia Languish* and Latham as *Bob Acres*. This performance closed the season. The Steyermark Family of musicians opened 8th of August.

ANNE J. HENRY-DRUMMOND-BARRETT was born in Philadelphia in 1801· At the age of sixteen she married W. C. Drummond, from whom she was subsequently divorced, leaving him with two daughters. In 1825 her extraordinary charms of mind captivated George H. Barrett, to whom she was wedded, but the brilliant union was in time disturbed; this fascinating beauty, whom Fanny Kemble described as "a faultless piece of mortality in outward loveliness," had acquired an insane craving for stimulants that it at times placed her in such positions as would even question her honor. In 1840 Mr. Barrett secured his divorce. In 1842 we find her in Montreal as Mrs. Henry, and, as fate would have it, in the same company as Mr. Drummond· Through proper influence the poor woman mended her ways and was restored to society. She renewed the triumphs of her former years, and commanded the admiration of all by her marvellously preserved beauty, which even at the age of fifty seemed as fresh and as charming as in her girlhood. She died 22nd December, 1853, and lies buried at Mount Auburn, under a monument bearing the lines :

> "With fairest flowers
> We'll sweeten thy sad grave. Thou shalt not lack
> The flower that's like thy face, pale Primrose. nor
> The Azured Harebell, like thy veins, nor leaf
> Of Eglantine, not sweeter than thy breath."

MISS MELTON, a clever Englishwoman, made her first American appearance on the stage at Burton's Theatre, Philadelphia, in 1840. She married and retired from the stage.

MR. and MRS. JOHN SLOMAN.—Mr. Sloman was an apostate London Jew, and became an English buffo. "We do not know what 'buffo' means," said the critic of the Albany *Advertiser,* but he is an English "buffo." After playing for many years in England and America, he finally established his residence at Charleston, S.C., where he died in January, 1858. His forte was farce comedy. A daughter, Jane, also possessed dramatic ability.

Mrs. Sloman, daughter of Wm. Dowton, was a tragic actress, correct and lady-like, but too coldly classical to suit the multitude. She died 8th February, 1858, aged 59.

WALTER M. LEMAN had high aspirations towards the tragic walks. He was born in Boston, where he began as a call boy in 1828, and made his first regular *debut* in Montreal as *Master Walter* in "The Hunchback," 26th May, 1842, to the *Julia* of Mrs. Sloman. Returning to Boston, he became manager of the National Theatre, and afterwards drifted to California, where in San Francisco, on 16th December, 1878, a benefit was tendered him to commemorate the fiftieth anniversary of his professional career. He died in that city 31st December, 1890.

THOMAS D. RICE was born in New York in 1808, and made an early appearance on the boards. He met with great success in England in 1836. He never forfeited the respect of the public or the goodwill of his fellowmen. He died in 1860.

WILLIAM WHEATLEY was an accomplished actor, and, although he was capable of playing the entire range of legitimate roles, was most excellent in such impersonations as *Captain Absolute, Charles Surface, Doricourt* and *Young Mirable.* He made his first stage appearance as *Albert* to the *William Tell* of Macready, at the Park Theatre, New York, in 1826. He so pleased the great tragedian that he was taken on tour. He subsequently fulfilled a number of successful engagements, and after closing his Montreal season he became manager of the Walnut Street Theatre, Philadelphia, shortly afterwards retiring from the stage to go into finance on Wall Street. He soon returned to his first love, however, and was afterwards mostly engaged in managerial ventures, retiring altogether in 1870. He died 3rd November, 1876, aged 59.

HENRY TUTHILL was a gentlemanly, high-souled fellow, and a native of Dublin, where his father had been a wealthy hotelkeeper, who established Harry in the silk business in 1823, but he became bankrupt in 1830, and afterwards went on the stage, a vocation he had always liked. He came to America in 1832. In 1852 he was in California. He died in Dublin, 14th April, 1863.

THE YEAR 1843

brought to Montreal Mr. and Mrs. Chas. J. Hill, both of whom became great favorites. They were the parents of Barton and Rosalie Hill, the latter appearing with her parents during the season. Mr. and Mrs. Nickinson also appeared, together with Miss Mary Rock, Miss Bailey, J. W. Wallack, jun., Geo. Graham, Baker and Geo. H. Andrews. Nickinson was the manager, and the season opened 5th June with "John of Paris" and "The Four Sisters." The Boucherville fire sufferers had a benefit, 24th, in "Beauty and the Beast." Then followed productions of "The Rivals," "Black-Eyed Susan," "Jack Sheppard," "Robert Macaire," "The Honeymoon." J. W. Wallack, jun., made his first appearance here 8th August as *Melnotte* to the *Pauline* of Mary Rock in "The Lady of Lyons"; Mrs. Sutherland was the *Widow*, and Mrs. C. Hill *Mad. Lachapelle*. The French Opera Co., from New Orleans, opened a season 11th August, closing 21st for the season. Rockwell and Stone's circus did a good business during the season.

GEORGE GRAHAM, an excellent low comedian, born in Manchester, England, made his first American appearance on the stage at Mitchell's Olympic Theatre, New York, in 1840. He died in Boston in 1847.

JAMES W. WALLACK, jun., was a handsome, popular and talented actor. He was the son of Henry Wallack, brother to Fanny, and cousin to Lester Wallack. He came to America in 1819 with his father, being then a year old, and first appeared on the stage at three as *Cora's* child in "Pizarro," in Philadelphia. In 1838 he was the leading actor in his uncle's (J. W. Wallack, sen.), theatre in New York. In 1842 he married Mrs. W. Sefton, formerly Miss Waring. He visited London in 1851, playing there and also in Paris. From that time up to his death, which occurred 23rd May, 1873, he starred with Mrs. Wallack in the legitimate drama. In referring to him, Jefferson says: "Young, vigorous and handsome, he was the most romantic looking actor I ever saw; there was a dash and spirit in his carriage, too, that was charming. I say he was at his best in those days, because in after years the acting of Macready, whom as an artist he idolized, had an unfortunate influence upon him, as he ultimately became imbued with the mannerisms of the English tragedian, which were so marked that they marred the natural grace of the imitator."

MRS. WALLACK, the daughter of Leigh Waring and Caroline Placide, afterwards Mrs. W. R. Blake, was born in 1815. Her first appearance on the boards was at the Chatham Theatre, 27th September, 1828. In 1837 she married W. Sefton, who died two years later, and after remaining a widow three years, was married to J. W. Wallack, jun , with whom her subsequent stage career was associated. She was a powerful and intelligent actress. Joseph Jefferson says of her : "All who remember Mrs. J. W. Wallack, jun., will attest the force of her tragic acting. In the quality of queenly diginity I think she even surpassed Charlotte Cushman, though she lacked perhaps the spirit and fire of the latter."

MARY ROCK was another Clara Fisher, to whom she proved a powerful rival. After the death of her parents in London, when she was very young, she was adopted by a wealthy aunt in Dublin. As she verged into girlhood, she met the best society under her aunt's roof, such as Tom Moore, O'Connell, Shiel and others. Reverses, however, sent her to Edinburgh, where she taught music, and at the age of twelve she was brought out on the stage as *Tom Thumb*, and soon known thorugh the provinces as "The Little Fairy." Sir Walter Scott was an early friend, as was also Charles Mayne Young, the English tragedian, who encouraged her to play heroic roles. Always *petite*, she shrank from assuming that pretentious line, but Young said, " My wife was no larger than you, but when she played *Lady Macbeth* —and he accompanied his words with such pantomimic power that the picture could be seen—she was a giantess !" Miss Rock first appeared in America at Boston's Federal Street Theatre, under the management of tragedian William Pelby, in 1827. Her last appearance at New York was in support of Forrest, at the Bowery Theatre, 2nd October, 1840, as *Julie* to his *Cardinal*. During her Montreal engagement in 1843 she met Capt. Murray, of the English Army. He was Sir John Murray, Baronet, and a man of wide and varied acquirements, had travelled much, but did not possess the qualifications of a good husband. A physician found that it was necessary for the captain to cross the water for the benefit of his health some time after his marriage with Miss Rock, and the faithful wife scraped together her hard-earned means, entrusted the whole to the captain, together with her jewels, etc. He set out for England, "but never came back." She then for several years taught music in New York and Albany, fighting the battle of life nobly, but now, in her old age and poverty, is almost forgotten, and yet this remarkable woman had such universal versatility as permitted her the entire range of farce, comedy, tragedy and opera. Truly the avenues of life are often darkened by overwhelming tribulation, yet often in some manner inexplicably surmounted by indomitable grit.

GEORGE H. ANDREWS, born in London, 1798, made his American stage *debut* as *Bob Acres* in Boston, 1827. He died in New York, 7th April, 1865.

THE FIRST ROYAL'S DOWNFALL.

We have now arrived to the last season of the old Theatre Royal, its downfall having been in consideration for some time in order to erect the present Bonsecours Market. Early in the month of May, 1844, the material was sold by auction to Mr. Footner, architect, for $150.   It was not demolished until after the regular season, however, which was the most notable since the appearance of Edmund Kean, eighteen years previously, in presenting to Montrealers the great William Charles Macready.   The opening was in June, when Mrs. George Jones and Mr. Rodney appeared in a repertoire of standard pieces, the most interesting production being "Pizarro," with Mrs. Jones as *Belvidera* and Mr. Rodney as *Rolla*.   Leander Rodney was lessee and manager, and the company included Mrs. William Isherwood, Mrs. Robinson, Messrs. J. S. Silsbee, Jas. N. Robinson, Samuel Johnston, Chas. A. King, J. B. Vanstavoren, Thos. A'Becket, J. B. Phillips and T. F. Lennox.   Mrs. Gibbs, a good singer and *comedienne*, also appeared.   On 8th July Mrs. Jones presented her first appeal to the Montreal public, under the patronage of His Excellency Sir C. Metcalfe, in Knowles' "The Wife" and "Love's Sacrifice."   Macready's engagement was announced by Mr. Robinson, acting manager of the Theatre Royal, to commence 15th July in *Hamlet*, but owing to the illness of the distinguished visitor he could only open 17th.   He was supported chiefly by Mrs. Jones, Mr. Ryder and Mr. Rodney. He was seen as *Richelieu*, 19th; *Werner*, 22nd, when His Excellency the Governor-General was present ; and *Macbeth*, 24th, for Macready's benefit, he playing the title role to Mrs. Jones' *Lady Macbeth*, Ryder's *Macduff* and Rodney's *Banquo*. First and second boxes, 5s. ; pit, 3s. 9d. ; gallery, 1s. 10½d. Doors open at 7; performance at 8.

Mr. Macready had been in the city from 6th July, and it was during his Montreal engagement that he made the following well-known entry in his diary : July 17th.—*Acted Hamlet; lay on my sofa at the hotel ruminating upon the play of Hamlet; upon the divine spirit which God lent to that man Shakespeare to create such intellectual realities, full of beauty and of power.   It seems to me as if only now, at fifty-one years of age, I thoroughly see and appreciate the artistic power of Shakespeare in this great human phenomenon; nor do any of the critics, Goethe, Schlegel, or Coleridge, present to me in their elaborate remarks the exquisite, artistical effects which I see in this work, as long meditation, like long straining after light, gives the minutest portion of its excellence to my view.*

"The Falls of Clyde" was given, 31st, at a benefit to Mr. Lennox, and Mrs. Jones received a similar testimonial, 6th August, in "Fazio," previous to her departure for Europe. On this occasion the lady was the recipient of an address. The last performance given at the old Theatre Royal was on 8th August, when Shakespeare's "Comedy of Errors" was presented at a complimentary benefit to the manager, Mr. Rodney.

R. C. Maywood, under vice-regal patronage, gave an entertainment at Roscoe's Hotel, 18th June, 1845, entitled "Lights and Shadows." This was his first appearance here in several years.

JOSEPH B. VANSTAVOREN, a native of Philadelphia, began his theatrical career there at the Walnut as a call boy in 1838. He became a useful actor of limited range, and died in 1852 in New York.

MRS. WM. ISHERWOOD (daughter of John Clark) first appeared on the stage in New York as *Pirt* in "London Assurance," and died there 29th June, 1850.

Her husband, in partnership with McKenzie, opened the first theatre in Chicago in 1837. He died in 1841.

THOMAS A'BECKET had the distinction of making his first stage appearance on board an English frigate at Valparaiso, S.A., and in the U.S. in 1836 in New York. He was born in Rochester, England.

JOHN B. PHILLIPS was an admirable prompter, and a genuine comic genius.

Off the stage his wit at times was hardly unworthy a Hood or a Jerrold.

It is told that Forrest, the tragedian, coming among the list of "stars," Phillips was assigned the part of *Horatio* in "Hamlet." At rehearsal during the first act a difficulty arose from Phillips being unable to give the emphasis Forrest wished conveyed to *Horatio's* line, "I warrant it will." The progress of the rehearsal was interrupted, and many times the following dialogue repeated, without producing the desired effect :—

> *Hamlet.*—"I will watch to-night,
> Perchance 'twill walk again."
> *Horatio.*—"I warrant it will."

"No, no, no," roared Forrest; "deliver it in this way, Mr., Mr., Mr.—Phillips."

Then giving the line with the required force and expression, he paused and glared at Phillips, who was coolly and deliberately answered, "No, sir; if I could deliver it in *that* way my salary would be five hundred dollars per night." The humor of the remark was too much for Forrest's gravity even; with a characteristic grunt (such as only Forrest could utter), the tragedian walked to the "prompt table," and with a smile said to the manager, "let Mr. Phillip's salary be doubled at my expense during my engagement." Night came, and poor Phillips, elated with good fortune, and over-anxious to please Forrest, ruined everything.

"I will watch to-night,"

said *Hamlet.*

"Perchance 'twill walk again,"

quickly replied *Horatio,* taking the sentence out of *Hamlet's* mouth. Forrest with difficulty restrained his passion, and when he came off the stage, fuming with rage, roared, "I will give one hundred dollars per week for life to any one who will kill Mr. Phillips."

He was a brother to H. B. Phillips, so well known for several seasons as acting manager here for Mr. Buckland. J. B. Phillips married Annie Myers, and died in Baltimore (the scene of the occurrence of the foregoing anecdote), 12th July, 1862.

MRS. GEORGE JONES became prominent in subsequent Montreal theatricals. She was the wife of the very erratic Jones, better known to professionals of the present day as Count Johannes. Mrs. Jones was a favorite and capable actress, and was the recipient of a flattering compliment from the great Macready, whom she supported here during the 1844 season. She last appeared in 1870 in Niblo's stock company. Mrs. Jones died in Boston, 12th December, 1875. Her maiden name was Melinda Topping.

JOSHUA S. SILSBEE was a clever impersonator of "Yankee" character. He was born in Steuben county, N.Y., 1st December, 1813, and first appeared on the stage in his 25th year. His New York *debut* was made in 1843. He starred for several seasons, and in 1850 went to England, remaining abroad three years. He died in California 22nd December, 1855.

THOS. F. LENNOX was a character actor of Scottish peculiarities, and well known on both sides of the line. He was born in Scotland and made his American *debut* at the Chatham Theatre in 1829 as *Rob Roy.* He died in October, 1849, at Memphis, Tenn.

THOS. RYDER, Macready's leading man, and an actor of considerably note, died 31st December, 1872, aged 61.

WILLIAM CHARLES MACREADY was born in London 3rd March, 1793. His father was a theatrical manager, and in his seventeenth year William managed a company of players at Newcastle, Wm. A. Conway being the star. Macready was educated for the church, but it was owing to Mrs. Siddon's suggestion that the pulpit lost a gifted speaker. The senior was shocked at the idea. "Well, then, your son will live and die a curate on £50 or £70 a year," said the greatest of actresses, "but, if successful, the stage will bring a thousand a year." The wily manager took the hint, and in 1811 his son made a successful *debut* as *Romeo*. After being advanced on a tour through the provinces, he made his initial London bow as *Oreste*, 16th September, 1816,

Richardson, an old showman, was always very proud of having numbered Edmund Kean among his company. When Macready's name had become well known, Richardson was asked if he had ever seen him. "No, mister," he answered, "I knows nothing about him; in fact, he's some wagabone as nobody knows—one of them chaps as ain't had any eddication for the thing. He never was with me, as Edmund Kean and them riglars was." Macready made rapid strides, and the great popularity of Knowles' "Virginius," which he was the first to bring out, added immensely to his own. In 1824 he married Miss Atkins. His first visit to America was in 1826; his second in 1844, and his third and last in 1849, when occurred the fatal Astor Place riots, which resulted in the death of 22 persons. The trouble arose over the jealousy of Edwin Forrest, and broke out during a representation of "Macbeth," by Macready, 10th May. Macready made a public statement, pledging his sacred word of honor that he had never shown any hostility to "an American actor." This called forth a public letter from Forrest, in which he confessed and gloried in having hissed the English actor, but denied having assisted in any systematic organization against him, adding, with an insolence entirely unworthy of Edwin Forrest, that his advice had been to let "the superannuated driveller alone." In the sketch of Edwin Forrest the tragic results were narrated. Macready was glad to escape to Boston in a covered carriage, and returned to England. His farewell to the stage took place 26th February, 1851, when he played *Macbeth*. A public dinner was given him under the management of Charles Dickens and presidency of Lord Lytton. The remaining twenty-two years of his life were engaged in superintending the education of his children and schemes for the welfare of the poor.

Chivalrously he hearkened to the call sounded by the mystic trumpeter from death's pale realm, and, surrounded by those nearest and dearest to him, between smiles and tears, he reached his journey's end.

> "*Farewell, Macready ; moral, grave, sublime ;*
> *Our Shakespeare's bland and universal eye*
> *Dwells pleased through thrice a hundred years on thee.*"

Montreal's seventh play-house was called

THE ROYAL OLYMPIC THEATRE.

It stood on the present site of the Riendeau Hotel, on the west side of Jacques Cartier square, near Notre Dame street, on property belonging to Mr. Roy, and was built by subscription. George Skerrett was lessee and manager. The opening was on the 23rd of June, 1845, when Goldsmith's "She

Stoops to Conquer " was presented. Then followed " The Ladies' Club," "Married Life," "Minister of Finance," "The House Dog," "His Last Legs," "A Match in the Dark," "The Heir-at-Law," etc. On 21st July R. C. Maywood began an engagement in Macklin's "A Man of the World," in which he appeared in his great role of *Sir Archy MacSycophant.* He next appeared in "John Bull," ' The Hunchback," "The Merchant of Venice," and "Time Works Wonders." Miss Clarendon appeared for the first time 19th August in "The Lady of Lyons," "The Honeymoon," 20th, and "The Stranger," 21st. Mr. and Mrs. Charles Hill took a benefit 22nd in "The Dream at Sea"; George Skerrett, the manager, followed with a benefit in "Speed the Plough" to a full house. Skerrett delivered a poetic address as a farewell, and the first regular season of the new theatre was brought to a close. The house was re-opened 8th September with Signor Mazzochi as manager and Van Praag as stage manager. Julia Vincent and Mrs. C. Howard were featured in several spectacular performances, and a number of light comedies were also staged. They closed 27th with a benefit to Signor de Begnis. George Skerrett was again at the head of the 1846 company and lessee of the Royal Olympic Theatre. With a few exceptions his associates were the same as in the previous season, and the attractions of the year would not suggest noteworthy comment.

GEORGE and EMMA SKERRETT were clever players and great favorites here, as well as at Albany, where they were also managers. George Skerrett was born in Liverpool, 21st May, 1810. He married Emma Palmer, who was born in Glasgow in 1817. They came from England in 1844, making their initial bows at the Park Theatre, New York, Mrs. Skerrett's *debut* being 3rd September, as *Gertrude* in "The Loan of a Lover," and Mr. Skerrett's on 14th September. He died at Albany, 17th May, 1855, of consumption. Mrs. Skerrett afterwards married Harry L. Bascombe, from whom she separated in 1857. She died in Philadelphia, 27th September, 1887. Their daughter, Rose, born 1838, married L. R. Shewell in 1860, and a son, George, died in New York city lately.

THE NEW THEATRE ROYAL,

or Hay's Theatre, was the eighth in the city's annals, and was situated at the rear of the building known as the "Hay's Block," at the corner of Notre Dame street and Dalhousie square, and extending back into Champ de Mars street. The location of the building was at that time in the most fashionable quarter of the city. Several companies of artillery and infantry were then located at Montreal, their barracks being on ground now covered by the Canadian Pacific Railway Depot. The officers of the militia were the *lions* of society, and St. Denis street was then to Montreal what Sherbrooke street is now.

The Hays' Block was built in 1846-7 by Moses Hays, of the firm Hays & Hawiks, hatters anl furriers. It was a block of four and a half stories, stone front. The front portion of the building was tenanted by the Free Masons. John Wells was the architect. George Skerrett was the manager and R. J. Jones assistant manager. The opening was on 10th July, 1847, with Shakespeare's "Much Ado About Nothing." On this occasion James W. Wallack, jun., appeared at the head of the company. The cast was as follows : *Benedict*, Mr. Wallack; *Claudio*, John Dyott; *Don Pedro*, Mr. Palmer; *Don John*, Mr. Ward; *Dogberry*, Mr. Skerrett; *Leonate*, Mr. Pardey; *Boraccio*, T. B. DeWalden; *Friar*, Mr. MacDonald; *Beatrice*, Mrs. Skerrett ; *Hero*, Miss Maywood ; *Ursula*, Mrs. Flynn ; *Margaret*, Miss Frazey. The performance was preceded by the National Anthem and an address by Mr. Skerrett. Miss St. Clair introduced dances, and "Tom Noddy's Secret" concluded the whole. Wallack appeared as *Shylock*, 12th; "The Wife," 13th; "The Wonder," 14th; "Much Ado," 17th; and again in a benefit performance to himself in "Hamlet," with "Katherine and Petruchio" as an after-piece. He was then re-engaged, and appeared in "The Brigand," "The Rent Day," "Don Cæsar de Bazan" and "The Hunchback."

Wallack's engagement was followed by another equally notable, in that of James R. Anderson on 2nd August in "Othello." Mrs. Bland, late Harriet Faucit, had been specially engaged to support him. On 3rd was produced "The Lady of Lyons"; "Macbeth," 4th; "Lady of Lyons," 5th; "Macbeth," 6th; and Anderson's benefit 7th in "The Elder Brother." He opened his second week in Schiller's "Robbers." 9th; "Othello," 10th; "Hamlet," 11th; "The Robbers," 12th; "Macbeth," 13th; and closed 14th with "The King of the Commons."

JAMES ROBERTSON ANDERSON was born in Glasgow 8th May, 1811, and died 3rd March, 1895. He first appeared in strolling companies and became manager of the Leicester, Gloster and Cheltenham circuit during 1834-5 and '36. He first appeared under Mac-

ready at Covent Garden as *Florizel* in " The Winter's Tale," 30th September, 1837. He made rapid progress, and at the same theatre 23rd
May, 1842, he first appeared in a star part, *Othello*. He came to America in 1846-7, part of 1848, and again in 1853. In 1867 he made an
Eastern tour. He last appeared before the American public early in
1860, when he concluded a tour that had continued since 20th October,
1858. Writing in the Newcastle *Chronicle* a history of his early engagements, Mr. Anderson thus described his impressions: Monday,
26th, found me *en route* for Montreal. I slept at Niagara Falls, and on
Tuesday took the steamer on Lake Ontario, touching at Kingston, a
melancholy looking place, and bearing away for the River St. Lawrence. Wednesday, got out of my berth at 4 o'clock in the morning
to witness the steamboat run down the famous and dangerous rapids.
It was a grand sight to see her descending at such fearful speed, with
six Indian pilots at the wheel to keep her steady in her course. The
slightest deviation in steering the boat would have driven us against
the huge perpendicular rocks that lined both sides of the river, and
dashed us to pieces without a chance of life. Our pilots, however,
brought us safely through those frightful dangers, and landed us in
Montreal at 9 o'clock on Thursday evening. I found good quarters
at Daly's hotel.

They had a fine large theatre in Montreal, of which Mr. George
Skerrett was manager. I opened in "Othello;" the play was very
fairly acted, the house well filled, the audience judicious and liberal in
their approval. I was called for, and received with much applause. I
was pleased with my reception. I ran through the first six nights,
acting the old plays to very good business—so good that the manager
induced me to renew the engagement for six nights more, which turn
ed out equally well; and on settling day he handed me in gold and
notes $1.250. Not bad for the month of August, with the ther-
mometer at 90 degrees in the shade. The exchange in money between
Canada and the United States was heavy at this time, but it was better
to do it in Montreal than in New York. I bought a bill for $1,000,
and sent it to my friend, W. P. Chapman, to be placed to my credit
in "The Union."

Montreal was a handsome, lively, bustling city, and being somewhat
Frenchified, reminded one of New Orleans. It is beautifully situated
on the noble river St. Lawrence, and the surrounding country is picturesque and lovely. At the back of the town " the ride round the
mountain is perfectly unique."

The forty-eight Viennoise children opened a short season
16th August, closing 25th. The troupe was under the direction of Josephine Weiss, from the Imperial Theatre, Vienna.
Nothing prettier than the dancing of these children had been
seen here. Their grace, precision and artlessness left an impression which remained for a long time on the minds of
those who saw them.

Mrs. Seguin, after an absence of three years, appeared, 26th, in opera, supported by a small musical company. During the season Miss St. Clair, a clever dancer, entertained between intermissions, and on the last night, 29th Septemebr, took a benefit in Boucicault's "London Assurance," she dancing her usual *pas seul*. The seasons 1848, and 1849 passed without noteworthy incident, excepting that De Walden, the stage manager, retired in 1848, and that the Government Legislature met at the theatre for a short time after the destruction of the Houses of Parliament by the mob in 1849.

T. B. DE WALDEN was born in London in 1811 and first went on the boards as a professional early in 1844. His American *debut* was in December of that year. He retired from the stage about 1857.

JOHN DYOTT, equally capable in tragedy as in comedy, was a native of Dublin, where he was born in 1812. In 1837 he married Miss Watson, and seven years later made his initial appearance in America as *Iago* to the *Othello* of J. R. Anderson in New York. He retired twenty-five years later to his farm at New Rochelle.

H. O. PARDEY, an Englishman, born 16th September, 1806, retired from the stage in 1855 to write plays, some of which were successful. He was found dead in a street in Philadelphia, 3rd March, 1865.

It was in the winter of 1849 that

THE GARRICK CLUB

came into existence and gave a series of performances at the Theatre Royal, the first, "Rob Roy," being for the benefit of Jos. Smith Lee, who had been dismissed from a lucrative Government position through having incurred the wrath of the existing powers. Mr. Lee was a Shakespearean scholar, and a favorite generally. This was the year of the riots in Montreal, which resulted in the mobbing of Lord Elgin by the Tory side, party feeling running very high. Encouraged by their success, the members of the Garrick Club rented a brick building on St. Jean Baptiste street, now occupied as a warehouse by the firm, Evans Sons & Co., and opened it as the Miniature Theatre, also known as the Garrick Theatre, and lastly as Skerrett's Bandbox. On the opening night, 12th October, 1850, "The Tower of Nesle," with the comedy of "State Secrets," were presented. The President, J. H. Isaacson, read an address in rhyme. Mr. Isaacson claimed its draft. Inasmuch as it marks an historic event in Montreal's theatrical annals, I herewith reproduce it, although it is not my intention to note at length performances by amateurs.

Ladies and gentlemen, I wish to say
Just a few words to you before the play;
In fact, the truth with candor to confess,
I'm going to speak the " Opening Address."
It's mentioned in the bills, and so—and so—
Of course, I must deliver it, you know,
The Club decided that it should be done;
The Secretary said he'd be the one
To write it. That decided, came the question
who would speak it. I offered the suggestion
That Mr. Baxter was extremely fit
And proper for the office—" De'il a bit !"
But all cried out (I told them they would rue it)
"Oh, you're the President, and you must do it."
Now Presidents have generally a supply
Of talk quite inexhaustible, but I
Of public speaking am extremely shy.
Indeed, at first, I felt inclined to vow
I wouldn't do it ; yet here I am. So now,
'Sith I am entered in this cause so far,' I pray,
Lend an attentive ear to what I have to say.
'Twill not be very long; the words are few ;
We merely wish to give a general view,
To tell you what we are and what we mean to do.
First, of our little play do not suppose
That with presuming vanity we chose
That honored name of Garrick—our intent
Was merely to express the—what we meant
Was—just—I really do. I must confess,
Forget what he intended to express.
But never mind; we'll let that matter go :
What I desire is that you all should know
That we are modest, feel our own demerits,
And do not think we're Garricks. Keans or Skerretts,
But some who hear me now are thinking, p'rhaps :
"Oh, yes ; you're quite a modest set of chaps ;
Extremely modest ; Shakespeare, nothing less,
Will suit your taste. We rather guess·
You'll make of that a pretty decent mess."
Stay. gentle friends : allow me to remark,
You're, metaphorically. in the dark.
We are not actors, and we therefore may
Not fully act the business of the play.
The frantic rushes and the sudden pauses
We have not practised much ; they're of the causes,
You will admit, of unreserved applauses,
But, though not actors, we can tell a tale
Of gentle Shakespeare's and, I think, not fail
To interest our hearers·
Enough, no doubt, of my discourse you've heard,
And yet I've spoken scarce a single word
Of what I meant to say—which seems absurd.

But, you know, I told you I was never
At speech-making particularly clever.
Pardon my faults, kind friends, and I will try
To speak a little better by-and-by.
We'll meet again in Venice ; pray you there
Give me and all who speak a hearing fair.

Among the members of the Club were J. H. Isaacson, F.
T. Judah, George Smith, brother of the designer of St. Andrew's Church; Henry Stearnes, brother of Hon. Henry
Stearnes ; Captain Lovelace, afterwards Colonel Lovelace ;
Matthew Baxter, F. J. Locke, John Sharpe, B. Christopherson, R. Thomas, J. S. Lee, J. Driscoll and a man named Paris.
Messrs. Christopherson and Sharpe generally assumed female
roles, having stage names of Miss Kitson and Miss Dudley
respectively.   During the few years of the Club's existence
were produced, "The Heir-at-Law," "The Canadian Settler,"
"The Tower of Nesle," "Merchant of Venice," "Lady of
Lyons," "The Honeymoon," "Othello," "Douglas," and a
comedy by Jerrold called "The Bride of Ludgate," exclusive of a large number of farces which were performed as
after-pieces.   Performances were given twice each week during the winter season, the Club's efforts receiving great encouragement from the citizens.

Mr. Matthew Baxter is the only surviving member.

The opening of the regular season of 1850 at the Hays'
Theatre occurred late, but several transient troupes had appeared previously.   Sand's American minstrels appeared 4th
and 5th February.   The Ravels began a two weeks' engagement 15th July.   Mons. Adrian, the magician, was seen 14th
August, and, as already noted, the Garrick Club appeared
12th October.   The regular season was begun 30th October.
The manager was Henry W. Preston, already well known in
Montreal, having at one time been a member of De Camp's
company, and afterwards for a short time his successor in the
management of the old Theatre Royal, on St. Paul street.
Preston had for associates in his new venture, Messrs. Lyne,
Barton, Marshall, Cushman, Brookton, Newton, Hastings,
Taylor, and Masters Hastings and Taylor ; Mrs. Isabella
Preston, Marshall, Hastings, Melville, and Fanny Mow-
bray, a famous *danseuse*.   "The Stranger" was the open-
ing bill 30th October, Miss Mowbray introducing dances.
The band of the 20th Regiment was also in attendance.
A series of standard plays was subsequently staged, "The

Maid of Croisy," " The Honeymoon," " Bertram," and, on 6th November, Lyne appeared as *William Tell* at his own beneht. On 11th November Mrs. Preston had a benefit in " Lady of Lyons," when she assumed the role of *Claude Melnotte* to the *Pauline* of Miss Mowbray. Lyne was seen as *Shylock*, 30th, and the company was further enforced at this time by the addition of Messrs. H. F. Read, John Nickinson, H. W. Smith, A. Muire, Mortimer, Charles D. Pitt, Misses Anna Howland, Fanny Wallack and Charlotte Nickinson. Several of the old company left. "The Soldier's Daughter" was among the first pieces to be presented, and Lyne played *Richard* III., December 6. Anna Howland's first appearance was in "The Lady of Lyons," 11th December. On 30th December we find Lyne playing *Shylock* for the Garrick Club. He appeared on several occasions during the following month. By a strange co-incidence, the Hays' Theatre was destroyed by fire very shortly after the erection of its successor, the present Theatre Royal, seemingly not willing to outlive its usefulness. on 9th July the building was set on fire. The supposition at the time was that the incendiary was a soldier, who wished to vent his spite on Mr. Hays for some imagined wrong. This unfortunate act resulted in the destruction of 1,100 houses, rendering 8,000 persons homeless, and causing damage to the extent of over a million of dollars. A small quantity of scenery was saved, including the familiar Windsor Castle scene drop-curtain, all of which was purchased by Mr. Joseph, and used at the new theatre; in fact, the curtain did duty until some years ago, when it was replaced by the presetn design. The Hermann Concert Company were giving a performance at the time of the fire, and some of its members were injured in making their escape.

HENRY W. PRESTON was born in Ireland and was originally a hatter by trade. His real name was Patrick Hoy. He was divorced under his original name from his wife, Mrs. Nichols. He was a fair actor, but frequently did some strange things on the stage when un_der the influence of liquor. Once while playing *Polonious,* the boys in the gallery became noisy, whereupon the Danish prime minister made a stirring appeal to " the dacency of those devils beyant." His end was tragic. He was seen on the night of 3rd April, 1859, stand_ing by the river at Albany, and on being asked why he did not go home, he replied : " I have no hcme; the worms have holes to crawl into, but poor men are without shelter." A few minutes later a splash told the last of Preston. During his career he had managed several theatres.

FANNY WALLACK was a daughter of Henry Wallack, and like all his family, picturesque in attitude and action. Her American *debut* was at the Chatham Theatre, New York, 23rd December, 1839. She died in Edinburgh, 12th October, 1856, not long after she became Mrs. Moorhouse.

CHARLES DIBDIN PITT, an English tragedian of considerable prominence, came to this country in 1847, remaining for four years. Returning to England, he became lessee of the Sheffield Theatre, until 1866, when he died, 21st February, aged 47.

THOMAS A. LYNE was born in Philadelphia, 1st August, 1816, and made his first regular stage appearance at the Walnut Street Theatre there, in March, 1829, as *William Tell*. In 1835 he appeared in New York.

Lyne made a nice little sum out of Mormon patronage, and by methodical investment managed to keep himself in comfortable circumstances the rest of his days. Lyne was a very good actor of what has been denominated the " Forrest school." He passed away in 1890.

The most interesting feature of 1851 was the opening of the Garrick Theatre in July by George Skerrett as

SKERRETT'S BANDBOX,

with a very small company to be in keeping with a very small theatre. The orchestra comprised three pieces.

Here, on 7th July, was begun a short season of comedy in which Mrs. Skerrett had opportunity of displaying her *soubrette* talents.

On 1st July the Heron Family appeared at St. Lawrence Hall for two weeks, the ball-room being converted into a temporary theatre. Skerrett not finding that his "bandbox" afforded sufficient accommodation, leased the hall of the St. Lawrence Hall, and on 28th July presented to Montrealers the peculiar and eccentric comedian, Sir William Don, in "Used Up" and "The Rough Diamond." He re-appeared 29th in "Pillicuddy." It was at this time that Barton Hill and his wife, Olivia Crook, made their first stage appearance in Montreal. On 4th August Mrs. Barton Hill made her first appearance in "The Serious Family." This company. also included Mrs. Charles Hill. Several entertainments were given at the Odd Fellows' Hall during the year.

SIR WILLIAM DON was a Scotchman, who stood six feet four inches in height. He first appeared in America at the Broadway Theatre in November, 1850. In 1857 he married Emily Sanders. Don was a whole-souled but erratic genius, yet withal a very entertaining comedian, and had played in all the theatres of America. He died at Hobart Town, Tasmania, 19th March, 1862, aged 36. Lady Don died 20th September, 1875.

SALLE BONSECOURS

was in popular utilization at this epoch for concert purposes, and is specially referred to in these annals for having first introduced to Montreal the future great Patti, then in her ninth year. She was announced as "The Musical Prodigy, ADELINE PATTI," appearing in two concerts 3rd and 5th May, 1852, given by Emma G. Bostwick, Signors R. Pico, Vietti, Mr. Ebben, flutist, and Herr Mueller, pianist.

THE ST. JEAN BAPTISTE THEATRE

(Garrick) was used by the Canadian Amateurs throughout the same season.

On 30th July John Wells, the architect, asked for tenders for the building of the new Theatre Royal on Cote street. The Hays' Theatre had become altogether unfit for the proper setting and production of plays, and it had become necessary that a better condition of accommodation should exist. The present

THEATRE ROYAL

on the eastern side of Cote street, above Craig street, was completed early in 1852, and has always been the property of Mr. Jesse Joseph. It was built entirely of brick, had two galleries, and a seating capacity of about 1,500. A small quantity of scenery, including the old familiar drop-curtain representing Windsor Castle, was saved from the Hays' Theatre fire, and purchased by Mr. Joseph, the curtain doing duty until some ten years ago, when it was replaced by another design.

John Wellington Buckland was the first lessee and manager. The Theatre was opened 31st May, 1852, by the celebrated *prima donna*, Catherine Hayes, at the head of a concert company.

Mr. Buckland managed the affairs of the house until 1869 (at times represented by Ben De Bar), when John W. Albaugh took the lease for one year, being succeeded in 1870 by Buckland during the early part of the season, and by James

A. Herne during the latter part. Ben De Bar, represented by J. W. Albaugh, held the lease in the early part of 1871, and Kate Ranoe during the latter part. Mr. Buckland resumed 1st January, 1872, for a short season. He died 20th November of that year. In those days the pit (where the orchestra chairs now are) was the cheapest part of the house. It extended clear from the stage to the back of the house, and the admission was two York shillings, or twenty-five cents. In June, Ben De Bar leased the house until the end of the year, when George Holman took up its management, 1st January, 1873, closing in March. When Ben De Bar came on from New Orleans, he brought with him a number of new ideas, and proceeded to re-model the theatre. He abolished the twenty-five cent pit, and replaced it with orchestra chairs, and turned the family circle into the gallery; then the noisy "pit-tites" became the "gods." Mrs. Buckland was the next lessee, under the management of Ben De Bar, for the remainder of the year, resuming in 1874 with Harry Lindley as the manager. The same arrangement existed during 1875, and with the close of the season also closed Mrs. Buckland's long connection with the old house. She retired to private life. It was during the management of Harry Lindley that the "Montreal Dramatic Club" was organized, and gave occasional performances at the Royal. The officers of the Club were: J. B. Burland, director; Chas. Wand, business manager; Geo. Grant, treasurer; Geo. Franklin, stage manager; and Carl Thorbahn, band leader. Other members of the Club were: H. P. Gradbury, Harry Earle, Frank Williams, T. Brock, C. E. A. Patterson, David Battersby, W. Hamilton, P. Jones, W. Wilson, J. Jackson, Alf. Isaacson, Charles Chester, Miss Kate Browning, Miss Laura Villiers and Miss Williamson. The prices of admission to the performances given by the Dramatic Club were: Boxes, $3; dress circle, 50 cents; family circle. 37½ cents; and pit, 25 cents.

We find George Holman lessee and manager during the 1876 season, he continuing until the summer of 1878, when the management passed into the hands of O'Brien and West. J. B. Sparrow's name became first prominent as lessee and manager of this house, 8th Sept., 1879. He continued to be sole manager until the middle of January, 1884, when he became associated with H. R. Jacobs. Their subsequent success in catering to the public at such popular prices of 10, 20,

30 and 40 cents is well known, and has proved profitable in every respect to this day. Early in 1898 Mr. Sparrow again became sole lessee.

With the season of 1900-01, the old Theatre Royal has been turned into a pretty playhouse. Beyond the fact that the walls and galleries are the same, the place is entirely new from top to bottom, and Mr. Sparrow commenced the 1900-01 season under auspicies that promised the most successful season he had ever known.

There have been very few contemporary actors and actresses of note who have not strutted and fretted their brief hours on this stage.

With this preliminary, we shall now pass on to the detailed annals of this eventful house.

Following the opening, 31st May, 1852, by Catherine Hayes, a French Vaudeville Company appeared 1st June. Ole Bull, accompanied by Alfred Jaell, assisted by the German Musical Society, gave concerts 14th, 16th and 19th. A benefit performance in aid of the fire sufferers of a week before was given 14th July, the piece being "The Serious Family." Kate Horn (Mrs. Buckland) appeared as *Widow Delmain*, and Wm. P. Davidge as *Amidal Sleek*. The regular opening, however, was on 15th July, with Sheridan's comedy, "The Rivals." As the curtain rose on the first act, it revealed Mrs. Buckland in the character of *Lydia Languish*. Cast of characters: *Mrs. Malaprop*, Mrs. Clara Fisher Maeder; *Sir Anthony Absolute*, Mr. Wm. P. Davidge; *Lydia Languish*, Mrs J. W. Buckland; *Capt. Absolute*, Mr. George Jordan; *Bob Acres*, Mr. Andrews ; *Sir Lucius*, Mr. Bland ; *Faulkland*, Mr. Trevor ; *David*, Mr. Thompson; *Fag*, Mr. Connor; *Lucy*, Miss Western

In the season's company were also included: Mrs. Ponisi, Mrs. H. Bland, Miss Emily Lewis, Charlotte Nickinson, Annie Walters, Julia Gould and Geo. W. Lewis, stage manager. Mr. Hilliard, a relative of Fanny Kemble, was the first scenic artist. During the performance, Julia Gould sang "Kate Kearney," and Annie Walters danced "El Zapatedo."

Prices of admission were, dress circle, 75c; family circle, 50c; parquet, 25c; and private boxes. $5. The box office was at Herbert's piano store on Notre Dame street.

Following the opening performance of "The Rivals," as already noted, was produced in the following order: "All that Glitters is not Gold," "The Heir-at-Law," "Married Life,'

"London Assurance," "The Rivals," "School for Scandal," "Lady of Lyons," "The Ladies' Battle," "Country Squire," "She Stoops to Conquer," benefits were tendered Mrs. Buckland, 7th August, in "The Ladies' Battle"; Mr. Davidge, 14th, in "Paul Pry"; Mr. Jordan, 19th, in "The Rent Day," and "Robert Macaire"; Mr. G. W. Lewis, 21st, in "Rob Roy." This performance is memorable for the fact that it first introduced to Montrealers Wm. J. Florence, Charles Peters and C. M. Walcot. "Delicate Ground," "Captain of the Watch," were subsequently staged. On 27th August Miss Nickinson had a benefit, and the season closed 28th with a benefit to Mrs. Buckland in "Mons. Jacques" and "Follies of a Night," together with the travesty of "Antony and Cleopatra."

JOHN WELLINGTON BUCKLAND died in this city 20th November, 1872, aged 57. He was born in London and was one of a family of twelve sons and six daughters. He was a graduate of Heidleberg, and spoke French and German with the same facility as he did English. His father held an important position in the financial house of Rothschild, and he himself began his business career under the auspices of that firm. He was shortly afterwards transferred to Quebec with one of the partners, and was before long in the employ of Pembleton Bros., of that city. After remaining with that firm several years he went to Buffalo and first embarked on an independent career in association with one Brown, under style of Brown, Buckland & Co. He was then married to Miss Kate M. Horn, who was ever to him the true and faithful partner, not only of his gains, but also of his labours. He went to New York where he became a member of the banking firm, Buckland, Brown, Truscott, Greene & Co. Here he met Mr. Corbin, who had intended to be the lessee and manager of the Theatre Royal, and negotiated a loan to the latter, but Corbin was unable to finance the matter any further, and in order to save himself Mr. Buckland assumed the lesseeship of the theatre as noted. His wife, Kate M. Horn, was a charming actress, and had then been a member of Wallack's Stock Company for some years. It was in that way that a number of that company were induced to come to Montreal during the summer season, and, the first venture proving profitable, the company repeated its visits during several following seasons. When the Bucklands came to the city, Montreal was a garrison town, and among the officers was a Major Lye, who was a cousin to Mr. Buckland. The major, therefore, introduced Mrs. Buckland to his brother officers as his "American cousin," and it is said that this was how the play of that name, in which Sothern made the great hit in the character of *Lord Dundreary*, got its name.

He was a man of retiring habit and exceedingly grave demeanor, while Mrs. Buckland was of a sprightly disposition and a great talker. When she would say to him, "John, why don't you talk more?" he would answer. "Why, Kate, you talk enough for both of us."

MRS. BUCKLAND (Kate Horn), first apeared on any stage as Miss Neville in the " School for Scandal " when she was under sixteen years. She had been left an orphan at this early age, and had gone on a visit to Charleston, N.C., with a Mrs. Tim, a soubrette, whose husband was a musical conductor, where she appeared as stated. Her first regular engagement was with the Park Theatre, New York, where she was the companion and friend of Mrs. John Drew.

On January 20, 1842, she appeared at Mitchell's Olympic, as *Sophia* in "The Rendez-vous." Her first appearance at the old Park Theatre was March 24, 1845, as *Seraphina*, in " Fashion." She first acted in Philadelphia, August 26, 1850, at the Walnut Street Theatre, as *Helen* in " The Hunchback." Clara Fisher Maeder, Mrs. Buckland, George and Annie Jordan and William Davidge were in the stock company that first acted at Brougham's Lyceum, December 23, 1850. Geo. C. Jordan, Charlotte Cushman. Emma Skerrett, Clara Fisher Maeder, Mary Taylor and others, were in the company. On April 25, 1852, she acted *Helen* in " The Hunchback," at Barnum's Museum, for the benefit of H. F. Daly. As *Helena* in " A Midsummer Night's Dream." on February 3, 1854, she appeared at Burton's Chambers Street Theatre. She commenced at the old Broadway Theatre, New York, September 17. 1855. as *Lady Anne* to E. L. Davenport's *Richard*, and on February 18, 1856, she played *Geraldine* in " Herne, the Hunter," at the same theatre. She was considered one of the most beautiful women on the stage, and in company with Charlotte Cushman scored many brilliant triumphs. She was the only member of her family who adopted the stage.

After the death of her husband, Mrs. Buckland lived a retired, quiet, but happy and contented life. She loved to talk over the scenes and trials of her active life on the stage, and it was one of the greatest of pleasures to hear her recite the scene from " London Assurance," where *Lady Gay Spanker* describes how the race was won. The vim and spirit she would put into it, even in comparatively recent years, would carry the memories of her old admirers back to the fifties when she was in her prime. A story is told of Mrs. Buckland's great spirits when a young woman. While in a furniture store on Broadway, Miss Horn very much admired a large easy chair, which a gentleman friend offered to purchase for her if she would carry it down Broadway to her home. Miss Horn accepted the offer, and won the chair, after exciting the curiosity of hundreds of pedestrians. Mrs. Buckland died 10th September, 1896, at Strong's Hospital. She left $14,000 to various Montreal charities.

JULIA GOULD, who sang " Kate Kearney " on the opening night of the Theatre Royal here, was born in London, 1827, and was first seen in opera in 1840. After coming to America she was seen in all

KATE HORN (MRS. J. B. BUCKLAND),

as *Lydia Languish.*

From a daguerreotype in the Wallack collection.

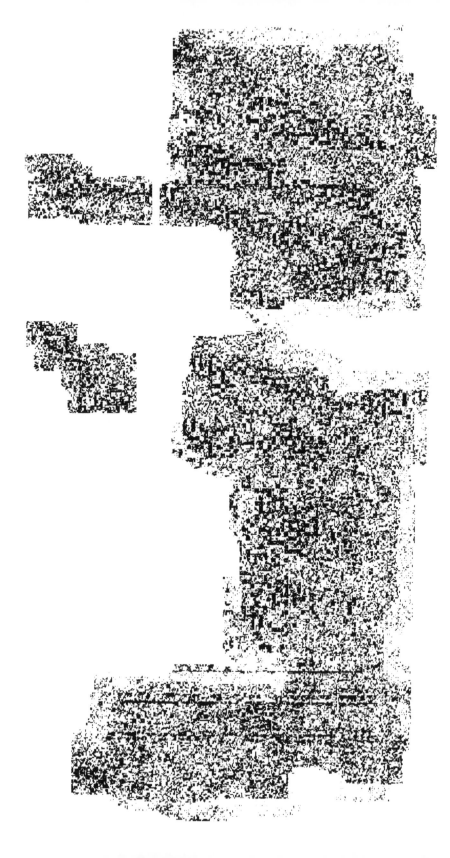

parts of the country, and in 1860 joined Buckley's Minstrels. She went to California in 1864.

ANNIE WALTERS, who danced " El Zapetedo," on the opening night of the Theatre Royal, married Geo. C. Jordan in 1858, and was very soon afterwards divorced.

CATHERINE HAYES was born in Limerick, Ireland, in 1820, and was called "the Irish Swan." She showed marvellous talent and power of song as a child, and was given a good early training. Her *debut* in opera was at Marseilles in 1845, when she sang in "Les Huguenots." In 1846 she was heard at Vienna, and in 1849 she made her first appearance at Covent Garden, coming to America in 1851 at the head of a concert company. While here she was engaged by P. T. Barnum to give sixty concerts during an Australian tour for a consideration of $50,000. She died in 1861.

OLE BORNEMANN BULL, one of the earliest attractions at the Theatre Royal, was born at Bergen, Norway, 5th February, 1810. His career as a great violonist began in his twentieth year, and his 1853. His tours were very profitable, and he made a great deal of 1853. His tours were very profitable, and he made a great deal of money, all of which he lost in an attempt to found a Scandinavian colony in Pennyvania. He was considered half genius, half charlatan. He died 17th August, 1880.

WILLIAM PLEATOR DAVIDGE was one of America's representative comedians. He was born in London, 17th April, 1814. His *debut* was at Nottingham in 1836. In 1842 he married Elizabeth Clarke, an actress. His first appearance in America was at the Broadway Theatre, 19th April, 1850, as *Sir Peter Teazle.* He remained there five years and then in various stock companies. From Wallack's he joined Daly's in 1869, remaining eight years. He was the original *Dick Deadeye* in the first New York production of " Pinafore." His last engagement was with the Madison Square Theatre Company. His book, " Footlight Flashes," is well known. Mr. Davidge died 6th August, 1888, in a passenger car while *en route* to California to fulfil an engagement.

GEORGE JORDAN was a capable and pleasing actor, and when he first appeared here was the very pink of an Adonis, enchanting the hearts of the ladies. He was born in Baltimore in 1830, and began life as a printer, subsequently making his first appearance at the Museum under the management of John E. Owens. He made a very favorable impression in 1852, when he came to Montreal. Mr. Jordan afterwards met with success in England. He died 14th Nov., 1873.

HUMPHREY BLAND, an English actor, born in 1812, came to this side in 1844, making his *debut* at the Park Theatre, New York. His appearance in Philadelphia was in 1850, where, at the Arch Street Theatre, he played *Joseph Surface*. He was thrice married. Harriet Faucit, his second wife, died in 1852, and in August, 1853, he was married to Emily Lewis. Mr. Bland died 17th January, 1869.

GEORGE W. LEWIS died at sea in January, 1853, aged twenty-six.

MADAME PONISI (Mrs. Elizabeth Wallis), an estimable lady and talented actress, was born at Huddersfield, England, 15th December, 1818, and at an early age made her *debut* on the stage at Barnard Castle, as *Amy* in " Father and Son." She acted several years in the English provinces before reaching London.

Madame Ponisi arrived in this country September 22nd, 1850, and faced the American audience for the first time, October 7, 1850, at the Walnut, as *Marianne* in " The Wife." After playing a week in Philadelphia she went to New York, and at the Broadway Theatre, November 11, 1850, made her metropolitan *debut*, playing *Lady Teazle* to the *Charles Surface* of Sir William Don, who had then but recently made his American *debut*. Mme. Ponisi was successful at the Broadway in such a measure that she was at once given leading business, and that position she held almost continuously until the old house was torn down in 1859. She joined Wallack's Theatre, making her first appearance as a member of the stock company at that house, November 13, 1871, as *Tabitha Stork* in "Rosedale." From that time the history of Mme. Ponisi's career was wholly identified with that of the Wallack Stock Company.

From time to time she appeared at other houses, notably at Booth's Theatre, April 2, 1877, supporting John McCullough. Madame Ponisi was married in England prior to 1848 to James Ponisi. She was divorced from him towards the close of 1858 (he died some years ago), and in Feb., 1859, she married Samuel Wallis, the property man, with whom she lived happily until his death, November, 29, 1884.

She retired from the stage in 1892, and died in Washington, 21st February, 1899.

H. B. PHILLIPS died September 26, 1896, in Brooklyn, N.Y. He was born May 19, 1819, at Charleston, S.C. In 1828 his parents moved to New York.

In 1837 Phillips was treasurer for C. R. Thorne, sen., at the old Franklin Theatre, Chatham Square, N.Y. He made his first appearance on the stage for Mr. Thorne's benefit, as *Alonzo*, in " Pizarro." He was at the Astor Place Opera House when the Macready riot occurred. When Brougham's Lyceum opened he went there, where he remained for ten years. During the summer months of that period he managed the Theatre Royal, Montreal, for J. W. Buckland. At the time of President Lincoln's assassination he was acting manager of Ford's Theatre. He then took to playing old men roles, in which line he continued for many years. In 1853, he married Mary Taylor. He was the father-in-law of Kate Castleton.

THEATRE ROYAL FAVOURITES FORTY YEARS AGO.
GEO. VANDENHOFF.   AGNES ROBERTSON.   MRS. CONWAY.
CHAS. FISHER.   MARY GANNON.
ELLEN TREE KEAN.   J. W. WALLACK, JR.
IDA VERNON.   GEO. JORDAN.
C. W. COULDOCK.   F. B. CONWAY.
JOHN DYOTT.   W. R. BLAKE.   CHAS. PETERS.

THE SEASON OF 1853

was preceded, week 20th June, by Italian Opera. Mr. Buckland was manager and lessee, and Charles Walcot, stage manager. The company was again a powerful one, comprising Messrs. Davidge, Chas. Fisher, F. Chippendale, F. A. Vincent, jun., F. B. Conway, Crocker, Reynolds, Culbert, H. B. Philips, Tyle, F. Lyster, Jackson, Bernard, Denman, Thompson, Chas. Reed, machinist, Mr. and Mrs. Chas. Walcot, Mrs. Conover, Mrs. George Vernon, Mrs. Howard, Mrs. F. B. Conway, Mrs. Buckland and Annie Walters. The opening was 7th July, when Fred. B. Conway was first seen in Montreal, in the character of *Alfred Evelyn* in Lytton's "Money," with Davidge as *Stout* ; Mrs. Conway as *Clara Douglass*; and Mrs. Vernon as *Lady Franklin.* The following pieces were successively presented: "The Hunchback," "The Stranger," in which Mr. Crocker was seen as *Count Winterson*; " London Assurance," " Naval Engagements," " Black-Eyed Susan," " Othello," " The Rivals," " Merchant of Venice," "School for Scandal," "Rob Roy," "Paul Pry." On 11th August, Conway had a benefit in "Macbeth," on which occasion Charles Wheatleigh made his first bow to Montreal. Mr. and Mrs. Conway closed 13th, when Mrs. Conway had a benefit in "Hamlet." Mr. Hale made his first appearance in this production. Subsequent productions followed of " Don Caesar de Bazan," "Katherine and Petruchio," "The Golden Farmer," and "Hamlet," 25th, for a benefit to Mr. Wheatleigh. The season closed 27th August, but re-opened for a short time in September, in order to present Agnes Robertson and her husband, Dion Boucicault. Their first appearance in Montreal was the event of the season, anl also marked the first appearance of Miss Robertson in America.

AGNES ROBERTSON commenced her theatrical career in her thirteenth year at Hull. She was born at Edinburgh on Christmas day, 1833, and, before she was eleven years of age, gave public concerts. She eventually became a *protege* of Mr. and Mrs. Chas. Kean, first appearing at the Princess Theatre in January, 1851, as *Nerissa* In January, 1853, she married the celebrated dramatist, and in the spring crossed over to America, opening in Montreal. Her success became phenomenal, tickets being sold as high as five and six dollars, and such was the enthusiasm she created among the ladies of Boston that her promenades through the streets were beset with crowds following her, while the corridors of her hotel were blocked with fair admirers. She appeared chiefly in roles cut out especially for her by her husband. The talented couple subsequently separated as man and wife. Miss Robertson was a graceful and intelligent actress of natural and sympathetic power, with an abundant fund of delicate humor and touching pathos.

The name of

DIONYSIUS LARDNER BOUCICAULT is a strong one in the list of the present century's dramatists. He was born in Dublin, 26th December, 1822, educated at University College, London, and became world famed in his nineteenth year as the author of "London Assurance." He also obtained some distinction as an actor. In 1860 he produced the "Colleen Bawn," which was the first of several popular Irish dramas. He wrote more than 140 original pieces and adaptations. He last appeared at the Academy of Music, Montreal, week of 20th December, 1886, in his own play of "The Jilt," supported by his second wife, Louise Thorndyke, whom he married in Australia 9th September, 1885, having deserted Agnes Robertson about 1879. He died in New York, 18th September, 1890.

FREDERICK CHIPPENDALE, son and grandson of famous actors, is the grandfather of those clever artists, Affie, May and Leonore Warner, daughters of Mr. and Mrs. Neil Warner. A family of actors and actresses for four generations!

The direct subject of this sketch informs me that he was born in 1820 at Ayr, Scotland. His father, William H. Chippendale, who died 5th January, 1888, at the ripe age of 87, had the distinction of having played the role of the old courtier, *Polonius*, to the *Hamlet* of Edmund Kean, John P. Kemble, Chas. M. Young, Henry Johnston, Macready, John Vandenhoff, Chas. Kean, Barry Sullivan, Forrest, Edwin Booth, Wm. Creswick and Henry Irving. He was the son of a capable and well-known actor, and was himself an artist of rare ability and intelligence. His wife, Mary J. Snowdon, began her professional career in 1855. Frederick Chippendale was always regarded as a most finished and reliable actor, his special forte having been in the "old men" of the knickerbocker order. During a long career in this country he supported all the leading celebrities of his day. His daughter, Belle Chippendale, married Neil Warner in 1874. Mr. Chippendale retired from active service a few years ago, owing to his having become quite deaf. The veteran is in otherwise perfect health, and is a merry member of that happy and select community at the Forrest Home, Holmesburg, Pa.

DENMAN THOMPSON was not the celebrated actor he is to-day when he was first seen on the Montreal stage; neither has he visited the city for many years, for reasons best known to himself. His real name is Henry D. Thompson. He was born at Beechwood, Erie County, Pennsylvania, 15th October, 1833, his parents being farmers.

DION BOUCICAULT.

In 1850 he went to Boston to find employment. and there joined Troyon's circus as property boy. In the course of the season he rode in the opening pageant and developed ability as an acrobat. During the winter of 1850 he made his first stage appearance as a super-numerary at the Howard Athanaeum, Boston. For a while he worked in his uncle's dry goods store at Lowell, Mass. In 1852 he appeared as the *Oarsman* in " The French Spy," at the Lowell Museum, and after that acted for a season at Worcester, Mass. Then he became an itinerant player, belonging at different times to wandering companies. In 1856 he was a member of the Royal Lyceum Theatre at Toronto, Canada. In 1862 he went to England, hoping to secure a chance to play *Salem Scudder* in " The Octoroon." Failing to obtain the engagement, he returned to Toronto, and acted there till 1868, when he again appeared with travelling companies· It was while confined to his bed in Pittsburg with an attack of rheumatism that he conceived the idea of playing a Yankee character. The result was his appearance at Harry Martin's Varieties in Pittsburg, in February, 1875, in a twenty-five minutes' sketch called " Joshua Whitcomb." The title of the sketch is a combination of the Christian names of Mr. Thompson's great uncle, Josh, and of General Whitcomb, a well-known character at Swansea. After " Joshua Whitcomb " had run its successful career from Maine to California, a new version of the play was written and called " The Old Homestead," which attained equal success, and ran for a number of seasons. The play has been several times produced here. headed by Archie Boyd.

CHARLES PETERS was born in Birmingham, England, 15th April, 1825, and came to America in the fall of 1849. His first engagement was at Niblo's in 1850. He moved about for some time, and in 1852 we find him touring Canada under the management of his father-in-law, John Nickinson. having as companions his brother-in-law (Chas. Melton Walcot, jun.,) and W. J. Florence. In 1858 he was the original *Binney* in "Our American Cousin," just played in Laura Keene's Theatre at New York, 18th October of that year, running until the 19th of March, 1859. On the 4th of October, 1864, Mr. Peters was accidently run over by a Third avenue car at New York, receiving serious injuries, but recovered, and realized some $4,000 from a benefit performance tendered him by professional friends. He died on the 2nd of November, 1870. leaving a widow. who is still on the stage, as well as a daughter, Maud, and son, Frank. By this marriage with Eliza Nickinson he became brother-in-law to Owen Marlowe and C. M. Walcot, jun. Charles Peters was a cousin to Mr. John Peters, the genial cashier of Messrs. R. G. Dun & Co., Montreal.

FELIX A. VINCENT was born in London in 1831: came to Boston. Mass., in 1849, and was known as a good stock actor.

FREDERICK BARTLETT CONWAY was what is called a good "all-round" actor. His *Evelyn* in "Money" was one of his best impersonations and he was considered the best *John Mildmay*, in "Still Waters Run Deep," on the American stage. He also gave an excellent characterization of *Armand* in "Camille." He was born in London, 1819, made his *debut* at Birmingham in 1839, and, after achieving a respectable success in England, came to New York in 1850, when he opened as *Charles Surface.* In 1852 he married Sarah Crocker, and together they starred throughout the States until 1860, when they visited England, and were well received. They returned in 1863, and a year later Conway became lessee of the Park Theatre, Brooklyn, which he successfully managed until the time of his death. He died 7th Sept., 1874, at his summer residence, Manchester, Mass.

MRS. F. B. CONWAY, *nee* Sarah Crocker, was a sister of Mrs. D. P. Bowers. Her first appearance in New York was at the National Theatre. Col. Brown says she was one of the best actresses of her time, being gifted with an intellect of strong analytic power, sufficient to fit out half a dozen leading ladies. She died at Brooklyn, 25th April, 1875.

Lester Wallack tells a good story of Conway, who was once approached in a very familiar manner by Goffee, an "acrobatic monkey," whom he had known in former years. "Suppose we 'ave a benefit together," said Goffee: "you do a Roman part and I'll do my scene as the hape between the hacts, and we'll draw lots of money." Conway, who always stood upon his dignity, lost all patience, and retorted : " Sir, I have endured the ups and downs of life in my time, and have met with various indignities. I can stand a great deal, but *Cato* and a ring-tailed monkey—never."

CHARLES FISHER was born in London, 1816, and after a good apprenticeship on the English stage, came to America in 1844, where he was welcomed at Burton's Theatre. He took high rank from the first. In 1858 he visited London, playing a brief engagement there and in Dublin. On his return he joined Wallack's company, remaining twenty years, when he became a member of Daly's company, with which organization he was associated until his retirement from the stage, a short time prior to his death, which occurred 11th June, 1890. He will be remembered as a genial and courtly gentleman, of whose character nothing could be said save in praise, and in whose personality the predominant features were sweetness and gentleness.

MR. and MRS. WALCOT.—Mr. Walcot is sixty-three years old and a native of Boston. His father was an actor before him, and the son began as an amateur when he was seventeen and a student at St. John's College, Fordham. He went on the professional stage as soon as he graduated, and has played so many different parts that he has never tried to set down the sum of them. While at Laura Keene's Theatre in New York, forty years ago, he was married to Isabella Nickinson, daughter of the comedian, John Nickinson. She was only sixteen at the time, having been on the stage six months.

During their long career the Walcots have taken part in some memorable performances. In 1846 they played *Cassius* and *Calphurnia* respectively, in the New York production of "Julius Caesar," containing in the casts the three Booths—Edwin, Junius Brutus and John Wilkes. Soon afterwards they were *Horatio* and *Ophelia* in Edwin Booth's record-breaking hundred nights run of "Hamlet" at the Winter Garden. Mrs. Walcot was the *Lydia Languish* the first time Mrs. John Drew would consent to play *Mrs. Malaprop* in "The Rivals."

The Walcots are sterling artists, both. There is a rugged strength in their method of acting that makes the most trifling part convincing.

IDA FISHER VERNON was an actress deserving of more than passing attention. She was born at Brighton, England, in 1796. Her maiden name was Jane Merchant Fisher, she being a sister to Clara Fisher, who made her first Montreal appearance in its early stage history. Mrs. Vernon came to America in 1827, making her *debut* at the old Bowery Theatre, New York, 11th Sept., as *Cicely Homespun* in the "Heir at Law." She married George Vernon 6th October, and subsequently becoming a member of the Wallack Co., remaining until 5th April, 1869, when she appeared for the last time in the mimic scene as *Mrs. Sutcliffe* in "School." She was a lady of extraordinary intellectual endowments, of the purest morality and refinement. She died in New York, 4th June, 1869.

CHARLES WHEATLEIGH was not a great actor, but was artistic in his methods and capable. He died in New York, Feb. 14, 1895. Mr. Wheatleigh was born in London, and from his earliest recollections had a tendency toward the stage. His *debut* took place in Brighton, where he was favorably received as *Romeo*. His first London appearance was in September, 1848, at the Marylebone Theatre, as *Captain Cleveland* in "Is She a Woman?" The following year he came to this country, and was for a long period identified with the management of the Lairds. His first appearance in New York was on August 31, 1852, at Niblo's as *Doricourt* in "The Belle's Stratagem." Several years afterwards Mr. Wheatleigh joined Mr. Daly's company.

The principals of

THE 1854 COMPANY

were Messrs. Fisher, Cunningham, Stoddart, Jordan, Hale, Stewart, J. Moore, Miss Mary Gannon, Mrs. Maeder, Mrs. Stewart, Mrs. Hale, Miss Walters, Mrs. Lebrun and Mrs. Buckland. Mr. Moore was stage manager, and, as heretofore, Mr. Buckland lessee and manager. The regular season opened 31st May with Kotzebue's "Stranger," Jordan in the titular role and Mrs. Buckland in the *vis-a-vis* character, *Mrs. Haller.* The following plays were staged during the season :

"Loan of a Lover," "The Lawyers," "The Poor Gentleman,"
"Lady of Lyons," "The Honeymoon," "Black-Eyed Susan,"
"Merchant of Venice," "State Secrets," "The Gamester,"
"Rent Day," "Richard III," "Sir Cupid," "Othello," with
Fisher as the *Moor* and Jordan as *Iago*; "London Assurance,"
"Wild Oats," "Love Chase," "Rob Roy," "School for Scan-
dal," "Hamlet," with Jordan as the *Dane*; "The Hunchback,"
"Macbeth," "Sweethearts and Wives," "Paul Pry," "The
Iron Chest," "Corsican Brothers " (its first production here);
"The Rivals," "Money," 26th July, for Jordan's benefit ;
"Love's Sacrifice," "Mary, Queen of Scots," 29th, and "Asmodeus," 30th, for Fisher's benefit, closed the season. Several
transient companies subsequently appeared, but were of little
importance. On 20th September Frank S. Chanfrau made
his first Montreal appearance in "Toddles " and "The Stage-
struck Darkey." Mrs. Buckland and Mlle. Albertine also
appeared.

FRANCIS S. CHANFRAU was born in New York, 1824. He
made his first hit as *Jerry Clip* in " The Widow's Victims," and followed this with " Mose, the Fireman," but his most permanent success
was as *Kit* in " The Arkansas Traveller." In 1858 he married Henrietta Baker, one of the most refined and intelligent actresses on the
stage. He died 2nd October, 1884.

CHARLES B. HALE, a useful and reliable stock actor, was born
in England 23rd June, 1819, and first appeared on the stage at Here-
ford, as *Thessalus* in " Alexander the Great." His metropolitan *debut*
was in 1849, and his first American appearance was in 1852, at the
Broadway Theatre, New York, as *Sam Warren* in " The Poor Relation." He died 29th January, 1893. His wife, Charlotte France, died
6th December, 1865.

MARY GANNON was born 28th October, 1829, and went on the
stage in her third year. In her tenth year she appeared in a company
of children in " Gulliver in Lilliput." She rose in the profession step
by step until she became the *comedienne* of Wallack's company. Her
last appearance on the stage was 27th January, 1868, when she had
great difficulty in performing her part, and on 22nd February following she died.

JAMES HENRY STODDART is the second son of an equally
famous actor of the same name. Born at Barnsley, Yorkshire, 13th
October, 1827, he received strict schooling in the Scotch fashion. His
theatrical career began at the Theatre Royal, Glasgow, under the tutel-
age of his father. At eighteen he left that city and became a stroller
until 1853, when he came to America. He joined Wallack's company

first, and then various other stock organizations. He was a character actor in every sense of the word, and a roll-call of his impersonations alone would fill a column. Mr. Stoddart married the lady favorably known as Miss Canover. In Sept., 1901, Mr. Stoddart began a prosperous tour in Rev. Dr. Watson's "The Bonnie Brier Bush." In his long career he has given no better picture that that of the hard, religious, upright old Scotchman, strong in his faith, and then broken in his sorrow. It is an interpetation artistic in every way, perfectly consistent, and signally successful.

Those who figured during

THE 1855 SEASON

were W. R. Blake, Wm. P. Davidge, F. S. Chanfrau, Chas. Peters, Jas. Bennett, John T. Sloan, Harry Hall, Mr. and Mrs. John Wood, Mr. and Mrs. F. B. Conway, John Brougham, Morris Barnett, C. Fisher, Mary Agnes, Miss Albertine, Miss Reignolds, Mrs. Hale and Mrs. Buckland. The regular opening was the 4th June, with a production of the comedy, "Legerdemain," introducing Harry Hall, an English actor, and Mrs. Buckland. W. R. Blake opened a short season, 18th, in "School for Scandal," "The Rivals," "Heir-at-Law," and Davidge opened for six nights, 9th July, in a round of comedies. Mr. and Mrs. F. B. Conway were seen, 16th, in "Macbeth," followed by "Hamlet," "Othello," "Ingomar," "Willow Copse." The event of the season was the first appearance of the English tragedian, James Bennett, who opened 13th August as *Shylock*; *Sir Giles Overreach*, 14th; "Damon and Pythias," 15th; "Richard III.," 16th; "Hamlet," 17th; and "Pizarro," 18th. Mr. and Mrs. John Wood appeared 20th. The season closed 8th September, when was produced "A Model of a Wife." MacAllister, the magician, appeared shortly after for a few nights.

Kate Reignolds, in her recollections, has been pleased to refer to Montreal in an interesting and favorable manner :—

"Canada was always a delightful place to visit. My first trip thither was under the care of Mrs. Buckland, to play in Montreal. My last, a happy halcyon month in fascinating Quebec, hospitably entertained by Consul Howells and his pleasant family. The French element makes a delightful, sympathetic and discriminating audience, but the English military, when they were garrisoned in Canada, were the most valuable patrons of the theatre. The officers in Montreal had private theatricals all the winter, under Mr. Buckland's management, which naturally placed them on the most friendly terms with him, so that in his summer season they strolled into his box, or office, and had *entree* behind the scenes. At one time, when I was in Montreal, both the famous Guards regiments had their quarters at St. Lawrence Hall, and half the mess were men of title. A benefit night under "patronage" was a pretty sight; red coats in the pit, officers in the boxes; English women looking as only English women do in full dress, and the band of the regiment massed in the orchestra."

MR and MRS. JOHN WOOD.—He was an Englishman, and first appeared on the stage in boyhood. He married in early life, and he and his wife played their first important engagement at Manchester. His *Touchstone* and her *Audrey* were well liked. Their American *debut* was 11th Sept., 1854. at Boston, he as *Bob Acres*. They visited California in 1859, and afterwards separated as man and wife. He died in Vancouver, 28th May, 1863.

Mrs. Wood (*nee* Vining), after accompanying her husband to California in 1859, became the manageress of the American Theatre in San Francisco, and in 1860 also that of the Olympic Theatre, New York.

In 1859-60 she was associated with Mr. Jefferson at the Winter Garden, when that house was under the management of Boucicault and Stuart. Here it was that Jefferson first played *Caleb Plummer* to the *Tilly Slowboy* of Mrs. Wood in Boucicault's version of "The Cricket on the Hearth." Six years later she returned to London, but again visited America in 1871-2, and afterwards managed the St. James Theatre, London.

MACALLISTER, the magician, first visited New York from Havana in 1849, and was subsequently seen all over the United States and Canada. He died, 1st Sept., 1856. at Keokuk, Iowa. His young widow then married J. M. Weston, and died in 1859.

KATE REIGNOLDS was born in England in 1832. Her grandfather was a staff officer of Wellington at Waterloo, where he lost his life. She was first regularly introduced to the stage by Forrest as *Virginia* in New York. Her first husband, Henry Farren, died in 1857. In 1860 she married Erving Winslow, of Boston, and has since lived in retirement. She still resides (1900) in Boston.

M'LLE. ALBERTINE, a prime favorite for many years as a clever dancer, in time became forgotten. She lived for some years in destitute circumstances in New York, unable to follow her vocation owing to total blindness. She died 6th Oct., 1889. at New Bedford, Mass. Her first public appearance was made in Philadelphia, 15th March, 1850, at the Arch Street Theatre.

JOHN BROUGHAM was born in Ireland. 1810, and first appeared before the public in 1830. Keese in his life of Burton, says: " He possessed exuberant vitality, keen sympathy and appreciation, rare personal magnetism, and you have before you glorious John. whose hearty voice it was always a pleasure to hear. His *Sir Lucius O'Trigger* was famous. He died in New York, 7th June, 1880.

JOHN THOMAS KENT SLOAN, born in England, 4th March, 1813; died in Liverpool 20th May, 1861. First appeared on the stage in 1832, and ten years later made his London *debut* at Drury Lane. He came to America in 1849.

JAMES BENNETT was not a distinct success in this country. Col. Brown describes him as being below the medium height and in general appearance reminding one of Fechter. He had the ungainly stage walk of Sullivan and Irving, as well as a painful rolling of his eyes. On his second visit to America in 1871, he was specially engaged to play *Richard III.* in a grand spectacular production at Niblo's 10th April, but was a lamentable *fiasco*, although supported by a very powerful company. After the first week, Neil Warner played *Richard*, which enjoyed a run of three weeks.

At the outset of Barry Sullivan's career, he and Bennett were once brought into close rivalry under one management, to the eventual defeat of Sullivan. Many years later, during a London engagement Sullivan met with an accident, and an understudy assumed his role of *Gloster*. He was a wan, grizzled and wistful looking man. No one appeared to know him. Approaching a group of old friends in a restaurant after the performance, he surprised them by asking if they did not remember—James Bennett. "Ah, well," he muttered bitterly, "no one knows Bennett now !" In 1888 Sullivan was striken with paralysis. About the same time Bennett became totally blind. Happily he quickly passed from pain to peace.

Mr. Buckland opened

THE 1856 VENTURE

in the middle of May. He had been very unfortunate in his management of the Howard Atheneum, Boston, and the Montreal season, which closed in August, was even more unprofitable. The company from Quebec under the management of Henry Farren was seen in Montreal during the season. It included: F. Lyster, *basso*; Francis Trevor, *tenor*; and Rosalie Durand, *prima donna*, in operatic efforts; and there also appeared, Messrs. Donaldson, H. C. Ryner, Henry C. Jordan, Mrs. Jordan and Fanny Morant.

An autumn season was inaugurated by Mr. Buckland, when Celia and Olive Logan appeared with much success which was repeated in Quebec, compensating the manager somewhat for the losses he had sustained earlier in the season.

MORRIS BARNETT died in Montreal, 18th March, 1856, aged 56.

The following season also passed without much interest being taken by the public in theatricals, and the management was not encouraged to provide sufficiently strong *star* attractions to draw our ever over-exacting public.

IN 1857

Mr. Belton was acting manager. The most important appearances, during a short season, were those of Kate Reignolds, and James Bennett, the English tragedian. The latter appeared in a round of Shakespearean characters, beginning 10th August. Mr Belton also undertook the management of the Quebec Theatre, which had a short and unprofitable season.

Kate Reignolds records that she had a narrow escape from death after terminating her Montreal engagement in 1857. Fearing that she had taken a wrong train, she, in a moment of excitement, jumped off, and, upon being picked up, was found to be badly bruised.

F. E. BELTON was an Englishman of considerable managerial experience. He was the brother-in-law of Richard Graham, the tragedian. After a short sojourn in the United States, where he was for a time identified with the Boston theatre, he returned to England, and became manager of the Exeter theatre.

THE YEAR OF 1858

was most notable, bringing Charles Mathews before a Montreal audience for the first time, in "Cool as a Cucumber," "A Game of Speculation," and "Trying it On." This was 1st June, on the night of the regular opening for the season. H. B. Phillips was the stage manager. The famous comedian closed 26th, in "Madeline."

Mr. and Mrs. Sloan appeared in "Jessie Brown," 9th June, and, on 14th, Miss Angela Sefton made her first appearance in "The Dumb Boy of Manchester." Her father, John Sefton, appeared with her. The favorite, Jane Coombs, made her first bow here, 1st July, in "The Lady of Lyons." "The Sea of Ice" was staged 7th.

Mrs. Buckland made her second appearance this season, 8th, as *Calanthe*, in "Damon and Pythias," supported by Messrs. Elmore, Phillips, Loveday, Stoddart, Selwyn, Barrett, C. Hale, Josephine Manners and Mrs. Sylvester. Charles W. Couldock first appeared here 12th July as *Luke Fielding*, in "The Willow Copse." He played a round of legitimate characters, and closed 17th in "Othello." On 22nd was staged "The Courier of Lyons."

CHARLES JAMES MATHEWS.

Mr. and Mrs. D. W. Waller began, 26th July, in "Lady of Lyons," following in "Hamlet," "Macbeth," and "Patrician's Daughter," closing a successful week, 31st, with " Castle Aldabrand."

Beginning 2nd August, came E. Blanchard's Canine Paradox; and on 16th Sallie St. Clair appeared in "The French Spy."

George Vandenhoff was heard in Shakespearean readings at the Mechanics' Hall, 9th and 11th June.

The visit of Henri Vieuxtemps, the celebrated violinist, marked an important musical event, 7th July.

CHARLES JAMES MATHEWS played in most of the countries of the world, and was the author and adapter of forty-three plays, and the creator of 161 parts. He was the only son of the celebrated comedian after whom he was named. He made his *debut* in 1835, and married Madame Vestris in 1838, when he came to America. He was the original *Dazzle* and his wife the original *Grace Harkaway,* in "London Assurance." Madame Vestris died in 1856, and a year later Mathews re-visited America, where he married Lizzie Weston Davenport the day after she was divorced from her husband, A.H. Davenport. For this the comedian was publicly horsewhipped by Davenport in New York. Mathews died 24th June, 1878, aged 75. Mrs. Mathews (*nee* Jackson) had married Davenport in 1854. She died at Brighton, England, 3rd January, 1899.

JOHN H. SELWYN (Josephs) was a native of England, where he was born in 1836. He first appeared on the American boards in Boston, 1854, and three years later married Miss J. Hayes. He afterwards managed Selwyn's Theatre in Boston.

JOSEPH LOUIS BARRETT, a brother of Lawrence Barrett, was born 14th July, 1831. He first married Emily Viola Crocker, niece of Mrs. D. P. Bowers and Mrs. F. B. Conway.

Mr. and Mrs. Barrett were seen in the Montreal Stock Company during several seasons. She died 21st Oct., 1869. For some years prior to his death, Mr. Barrett had been a member of Ada Gray's company.

CHARLES WALTER COULDOCK frequently appeared here, and had been seen in all his great roles. He was born in London, England, 26th April, 1815, and came to America in 1849 in Charlotte Cushman's company, making his *debut,* 8th October, the *Stranger* to Miss Cushman's *Mrs. Haller.*

After a brief tour as leading support to Miss Cushman, he settled down in Philadelphia, at the Walnut Street Theatre, for four seasons as leading man. While there Mme. Celeste played a *star* engagement (1852), and during the time did "The Willow Copse," a new drama

brought to this country by her. So well pleased was she with **Mr.**
Couldock's performance of *Luke Fielding* that she presented him with
a copy of it, with the right to produce it. For four seasons he travelled as a *star* with this play.

For about twenty years, from 1859, he was one of our best *stars*.
When the Madison Square Theatre was dedicated, February 4, 1880,
Mr. Couldock played *Dunstan Kirke* in " Hazel Kirke." He had created the character when the play was first produced under the title
of "An Iron Will," at Low's Opera House, Providence, R.I., October
27, 1879. He continued to act it at the Madison Square Theatre until
the play was withdrawn, May 31, 1881, after its hour hundred and
eighty-sixth consecutive representation.

Mr. Couldock's *Iago* and *Hamlet* were his best performances thirty
years ago. His greatest fame, however, was achieved in the role of
Louis XI. Later on he adhered to a new line of dramatic work,
known as the domestic drama.

His last appearance in Montreal as a *star* was week 7th January,
1889, in "Hazel Kirke," at the Theatre Royal. He re-appeared at
the Academy of Music in support of Wilton Lackaye in " Dr. Bel-
graf," in the spring of 1897.

For many months he sat in the deepening twilight, waiting for the
dawning of the grander day, while in his still vigorous brain were
clustered the hallowed memories of many years. He died in New
York, 27th November, 1898.

GEORGE VANDENHOFF was a son of John Vandenhoff, and
was born in Liverpool in 1816. He was educated for the bar, and finally admitted, but much against his father's wishes he decided to go on
the stage, making his *debut* at Covent Garden Theatre, 14th October,
1839. His *debut* at the Park Theatre, New York, was 21st September,
1842, as *Hamlet.* In January, 1853, he returned to England on account
of ill-health, returning in August, 1855, three days after which he married Miss Makeah, a lady who had appeared at the Winter Garden
Theatre. She died 20th April, 1885. In November, 1858, Mr. Vandenhoff was again admitted to the bar· He possessed a commanding
figure and an open and manly countenance, a voice of strong and
pleasing quality and he walked the stage with grace and dignity. As
a reader he was very fine, and appeared in Montreal on several occasions at the Mechanics' Hall· He died at Bennington, 10th August,
1884.

MARCUS ELMORE, an English actor, was doing the leading
business during the season, appearing in "Othello," "William Tell,"
"Pizarro," "The Stranger" and other standard productions. Mr.
Elmore was an actor of strong legitimate methods. He came to this
country from the St. James Theatre, London, and made his American
debut 2nd June, 1856, at the Broadway Theatre as *Huon* in "Love."
He returned to England, where he died some years ago. His wife,
Mary Hannah Elmore, died 25th January, 1899.

. **DANIEL WILMARTH (WALLER)**, the son of a New York merchant, made his stage *debut* in his seventeenth year in Philadelphia as *Hamlet*. Meeting with some success, he went to England, where in 1849 he married, and in 1851 returned to America. In 1853 Mr. and Mrs. Waller made a tour of Australia. He died 20th Jan., 1882.

EMMA WALLER, born in England in 1829, first studied in France and Italy for the operatic stage, but abandoned this course, and in 1848 appeared on the dramatic stage.

Her first appearance in London was made at Drury Lane in 1856, as *Pauline*, in " The Lady of Lyons." Prior to that time she had acted in provincial theatres, and there is a record of her appearance at Melbourne, in 1855, with G. V. Brooke, in " Macbeth." On October 19, 1857, she appeared in Philadelphia, playing *Ophelia*, and on April 5, 1858, she made her advent on the New York stage, acting with her husband at the old Broadway Theatre, as *Marina*, in " The Duchess of Malfi "—a version of that dark and terrible play having been made for her especial use by her friend, Richard Hengist Horne, the noble old poet of "Orion." After that time, during several seasons, she made starring tours of the country, and she was everywhere received with favor.

Wm. Winter says that in her day she was a tragic actress of the first rank , and worthy to be named with Mrs. Duff, Charlotte Cushman. Charlotte Crampton, Mrs. Warner and others of that exalted lineage. the queens of the tragic stage.

Mrs. Waller's great performances were those of *Lady Macbeth, Meg Merrilles* and the *Duchess of Malfi*, but she also played male characters, and her clever impersonations of *Hamlet* and *Iago* were admired. She was a woman of stately presence and of a most expressive countenance; she possessed dark, piercing eyes. a pallid complexion and a voice of unusual depth and compass; her temperament was in the highest degree emotional; and, whether in repose or in movement, her demeanor was impressively indicative of a self-centred mind. deep feeling perfectly controlled and great physical power. In the character of *Meg Merrilles* she was perfection. She died in New York, 28th February, 1899.

JANE COOMBS was a pupil of Clara Fisher-Maeder, and made her New York *debut* 27th Oct., 1855. In 1862 she appeared at the Haymarket Theatre. London: she married F. A. Brown in 1864. and lived in retirement for a time, but is again touring. Harry Lacy tells rather a good one on himself and Jane Coombs. " I'll never forget one performance in John Elseler's Theatre in Pittsburg. The play was "Romeo and Juliet." To give effect to a few of the strong scenes. I wanted a little slow music. I said to the German leader: 'Now when *Romeo* and *Juliet* walk to the altar to be blessed by *Friar Laurence*, play something slow and tender." When the time came the Teuton took the cue all right, and began: "*Birdie, I am tired now, so put me in my little bed.*" It was a most ridiculous sittuation, and Miss Coombs turned and gave him a look that almost withered him."

THE SEASON OF 1859

was notable in bringing the famous Irish tragedian, Barry Sullivan, to Montreal. J. W. Buckland was lessee and manager; H. B. Phillips, stage manager ; T. B. MacDonough, prompter ; Hawthorne, scenic artist; and Geo. Wilson, machinist. Miss Jean M. Davenport (Mrs. Lander) opened a six nights',*starring* engagement, 13th June, in "Charlotte Corday," following in "Adrienne Lecouvreur," etc. "The Jealous Wife " and Sandford's Ethiopian Troupe subsequently held the boards. Barry Sullivan began a two weeks' engagement from 27th June, opening in "Richelieu." The *personnel* of the season's stock company will be seen by the following support to Mr. Sullivan in the " Richelieu " cast: *Cardinal Richelieu*, Barry Sullivan; *De Mauprat*, Harry Copland; *Baradas*, Charles Fisher; *Gaston*, T. B. MacDonough; *Louis XIII.*, Geo. Lingard; *De Beringhen*, Harry Thompson; *Friar Joseph*, H. B. Phillips ; *Francois*, J. L. Barrett ; *Hugnet*, W. J. LeMoyne ; *Governor*, T. Owens ; *First Secretary*, Mr. Lee ; *Second Secretary*, Mr. Wallack; *Gaoler*, Mr. Lawson ; *Julie de Mortemar*, Alice Gray; *Marian de Lorme*, Mrs. Sylvester. During the engagement Mr. Sullivan appeared in the following successively: " Macbeth," " Richard III.," " Money," " The Lady of Lyons," " King Lear," " Don Caesar de Bazan," "Hamlet" and "The Merchant of Venice." Mr. Sullivan's engagement was by no means a financial success here. C. Hale, J. H. Jack, Miss A. France, Miss Pritchard, Miss R. France and Mrs. Eckhardt were also members of the stock company.

Mr. Sullivan's extensive repertoire seems to have been a heavy strain on the supporting company, and the tragedian was greatly provoked at being forced to act as prompter as well as *star*. Mr. George Horne, of this City, records that in one of his death scenes the actor was so discomfited by his support forgetting the lines of the text that, springing to his feet, he roared, "Am I to prompt you when I am *dying?*" He then rushed off the stage, and it was several moments before he could be induced to return and finish *dying*.

William E. Burton was another bright *star* to appear, opening 1st August in "An Englishman in France," "Pillicoddy" and other light comedies. His engagement closed 12th August, and he shortly afterwards retired from the mimic scene.

Susan Denin and Kate Denin Ryan, supported by the comedian, S. E. Ryan, began a limited engagement 15th July in repertoire. This noteworthy engagement was followed by another not less so: Helen and Lucilla Western (the *"Star Sisters"*) began a week's engagement on the 1st of August, in "Flowers of the Forest." The cast was as follows: *Starlight Bess,* Lucille Western; *Cynthia,* Helen Western; *The Wolf,* Charles Fisher ; *Cheap John,* C. Hale ; *Kinchen,* H. Thompson; *Hugh Lairock,* H. B. Phillips; *Alfred,* J. L. Barrett; *Lemuel,* Alice Gray. Lucille had a benefit, 4th, under the patronage of Sir Francis Williams, K.C.B., commander of the British forces in North America. "Flowers of the Forest" was last played at Montreal week 10th January, 1887, by Lindley's Company, at the Lyceum Theatre, under the title of "Ishmael." Sallie St. Clair opened the 5th of September for one week, assuming five different characters in her production of "The Female Brigand." The stock company then appeared in "As You Like It," and on 10th October the Cooper Operatic Troupe began an engagement for one week in a series of standard grand operas. The principals were Brookhouse Bowler, Aynsley Cook and Mr. Rudolphsen.

ALICE GRAY, who was seen as leading lady in Montreal in 1859-'62-'63, was born in Boston in 1833. Her real name was Dehan. Her *debut* was made in Buffalo in 1855. and possessing considerable talent as well as personal charms she soon rose to leading roles. subsequently becoming a member of Daly's company. Miss Gray married Wm. L. Lawson at Haverhill, Mass., on 29th March, 1887.

WILLIAM J. LE MOYNE has now become one of America's representative stock actors. He was born in Boston about 1831, and first appeared on the stage at Portland. Me., in 1852. He was in the civil war. During the past two decades Mr. Le Moyne has been associated with New York stock and travelling companies. He married Sara Cowell, who has been a *stellar* card for two seasons in "The Greatest Thing in the World."

THE DENIN SISTERS.—Kate Denin was born in Philadelphia in 1837, and soon developed histrionic tendencies. She married C. K. Fox, and the next day left for the west, leaving Fox behind. She afterwards married Sam Ryan, and in 1857 went to Australia. On her return she starred in all the cities of importance in the United States and Canada.

Kate Denin is a member of Charles Frohman's forces. She is recalled in Boston as a member of the Museum Company in the sixties,
She eloped from that theatre with Mrs. Vincent's young husband,
handsome John Wilson, who was afterwards Kate Denin's third husband.

Susan Denin, who was two years younger, is said to have been
the more talented. Her London *debut* was made 20th of March, 1869.
She became Mrs. Theodore Morris, and died 4th December, 1875.

SALLIE ST. CLAIR was born in England in 1831 and was brought
to America in her infancy. She was first seen on the stage as an infant and giving a speaking part for the first time at Philadelphia in
1846. In 1860 she married Chas. M. Barras, and died 9 h April, 1867.

THE WESTERN SISTERS were born in New Orleans, Lucille
in 1843 and Helen in 1844. The latter died in 1868 when the best days
of Lucille may be said to have begun. Their father, a tobacco merchant, died in 1859 and Mrs. Western married W.B. English. a theatrical manager, who in time brought his step-daughters before the
public, they being known as the " Star Sisters " Lucille. in after
years, became celebrated in "East Lynne" a part which she at first
refused to even rehearse, but which eventually brought her over a
quarter of a million dollars all of which was frittered away by
others. Her life was one of incessant toil without fruition. Had her
great powers been properly directed, much different would have been
her record. She became the wife of James H. Meade, and died in
Philadelphia, 11th January, 1877, while playing a *star* engagement.

Helen who first married a Baltimore lawer'was married to James
A. Herne, in August, 1865, in Montreal. She died in her 24th year,
in 1868. Jane English, their mother, died in the Forrest Home, 31st
October, 1898.

JAMES H. MEADE. The passing away of this well-known character, May. 10, 1898, in New York city, brought to mind many episodes
in a most remarkable career. Lucille Western, the famous actress,
made her Montreal *debut* August 1. 1859. She was then sixteen years
of age. The following year she met and married "Jim" Meade, her
senior by thirteen years. Although little more than a child. the actress gave promise of genius, which afterwards made her acting in
" East Lynne " a feature of the American stage, which will long remain a memory. Meade managed his wife's dramatic tours and performed his duties ably.

They lived together for a number of years, leading a somewhat
checkered existence, and then in that easy way which stage folks have
they mutually agreed to disagree, and separated. Before the pre-ar-
ranged divorce was secured. Lucille Western died, a victim to a passion which dominated over her genius.

At the time that Lucille Western was first creating a furore in the
Quaker City, one of its most beautiful young girls was Susannah P.

McComb, a daughter of Samuel McComb, a well-known bookbinder. She was considered one of the prettiest girls in a city famous for the beauty of its women. Miss McComb in time met Willam D. Edson. The young man possessed rare business qualities and made quite a large fortune in the boot and shoe business. But with rapidly acquired riches came taste foreign to one who had been brought up in the quiet atmosphere and the staid ways of a Quaker household. Flying steeds frequently give wings also to the money of their owners. Even Edson's wealth could not stand the strain of his extravagances, and one day the firm of which he was the head failed ignominiously. In fact, there were circumstances connected with it which caused him to travel to Canada. Before or about this time Edson met Susannah McComb. He had been married and had two sons living, but succeeded in procuring a divorce from his wife. He took the beautiful Susannah to his bosom, and some time afterwards in Montreal they were married. Eight months after, Edson sent his second wife back to Philadelphia, promising to join her there. Having thus disposed of his second wife, he sent for the first partner of his woes and afterwards lived with her. In 1872 Susannah McComb ceased to be Mrs. Edson. The ground upon which the legal separation was procured was that of desertion, and one of the witnesses who gave testimony before the examiner appointed by the Court was Jas. H. Meade, who even at that time was conscious of the charms of the beautiful plaintiff. Eighteen years afterward, when he, although in the full vigor of life, was well advanced in the sixties, and Susannah McComb, still a beautiful woman—they were made man and wife. She now survives him, and one who saw her in Philadelphia recently, said : "Although a becoming gray tinges her hair, her beauty is still absolutely dazzling." James Meade had been identified with numerous theatrical ventures. He was a man of such rugged constitution, although small and spare of frame, and carried his years so lightly, that his death came as a surprise to those who never thought of him in connection with the dread destroyer.

WM. EVANS BURTON.—This comedian was born in London in 1802, and was educated for the church, receiving a classical education. At the age of eighteen he took charge of his father's printing office· At twenty-three he became an amateur actor, his *forte* being tragedy. Before this, in 1823, he had married, and in 1825 his father died· He carried on the printing business until 1830, when he went on the stage, soon afterwards coming to America, and in 1834 was seen as *Dr. Allopod* at the Arch Street Theatre, Philadelphia. He became a great comedian, appearing in a number of Dickens' characters. He possessed wonderful facial power (not even surpassed by Charles Mathews), a strong physique, and great elecutionary powers. In 1856 he married his second wife, Mrs. Hilson, and in 1859 retired from the stage, dying 10th February, 1860. During his stage career he had been for some years in the managerial line, one of these efforts being the management of Burton's Theatre, New York.

JOHN HENRY JACK is a well-known stage figure and one of the best *Falstaffs* of to-day. He was born in Philadelphia 1st Feb., 1836, and has played in almost all the large cities of the United States and Canada. In 1879 he made a tour of the world, making his re-appearance in America at the Park Theatre, Philadelphia, 13th Aug., 1880. His most recent work has been in the support of Mrs. Fiske and Joseph Jefferson.

EUPHEMIA (EFFIE) GERMON was always a great favorite here, although not appearing in anything but *soubrette* roles as a rule. She was born 13th June, 1845, at Augusta, Ga., and made her professional *debut* in 1857. While here she kept the "Johnnies" busy. Many old theatre-goers will remember her song, "The Captain with the whiskers took a sly glance at me." Miss Germon was four times married, first to a brother of Patti, then to Burk, to Albert Roberts, and, finally, to Fiske.

THOMAS BARRY SULLIVAN was not noted for personal beauty, for volume of voice, or variety of tone in speech, yet he filled heroic roles with dignity and force. His features were deeply furrowed by small-pox and also gave evidence of his having received a pistol shot, which accident occurred on the stage. Firm set jaws, teeth of remarkable whiteness, dark hair, huge bushy black eyebrows and fine piercing eyes of Irish blue completes his portrait.

He was given to exaggeration in action at times, and to straining for originality in his readings. His *Hamlet* declared that he knew a *hawk from a hjrne* (*hjrcn*), adding pettishly to express his dislike for the courtiers, "*Pshaw!*" He played *Hamlet* 3,500 times.

Sullivan was born in Dublin in 1824, and died in London, 3rd May, 1891. His *debut* was at Cork in 1840, and after acting through the provinces made his London appearance 7th February, 1852. He came to America in 1858, making his first appearance at the Broadway Theatre, New York, 22nd Nov., as *Hamlet*. He fulfilled *star* engagements in all the principal cities of the United States and Canada in a round of characters, including *Claude Melnotte, Macbeth, Hamlet, Shylock, Lear, Richelieu* and *Richard III.*, returning to England in the summer of 1860. He shortly afterwards visited Australia and again came to America in 1875. His finest impersonations were *Falconbridge* in "King John," *Macbeth* and *Richard III.*, these performances being full of originality.

His last appearance on the stage was at the Royal Alexandria Theatre, Liverpool, 4th June, 1887, as *Richard III.*

It was at Shewsbury, during the last act of *Richard*, on one occasion, just after he had repeated the line :

"*My kingdom for a horse!*"

that someone in the top gallery asked him if an ass would do as well Barry was angry, but quickly replied. "Yes, just come around to the stage door."

While playing *Hamlet* in Philadelphia, Sullivan, on one occasion, had among his audience Edwin Forrest, who showed to every one around him how much he despised the innovations of the Irish actor. Espe_cially was this pronounced when the actor spoke the words, "*I know a hawk f.om a h.ron—psh.w!*' Sullivan might well resent the insult; and as he subsequently took the courtiers aside he pointed his finger straight at Forrest in the box, and in the words of the text, exclaimed with emphasis, "*Do you see that great baby yonder? He is not yet out of his swaddling clouts.*"

The audience cheered and hissed, admired the quick wit, but resent_ed the attack. Forrest should have remembered the terrible sequel of his having previously hissed Macready. He certainly felt Sullivan's rebuke very keenly.

Although of abstemious habits, Barry Sullivan was striken without warning and suffered greatly for nearly three years before his great soul took its eternal flight. He rests among poets, patriots and states_men in Glasnevin cemetery, Dublin, where a statue of the actor as *Hamlet* marks the spot.

His tomb is built where the sunbeams rest
When they promise a glorious morrow;
And they'll shine on his grave like a smile from the west,
O'er his own loved Island of Sorrow"

THE SEASON OF 1860

was opened by the French Company in repertoire during April, and was regularly inaugurated 28th May, when Agnes Robertson, who had first appeared here seven years before, was seen in "Andy Blake" and "The Young Actress." The *personnel* of the stock company appears in the cast of "Andy Blake": *Andy Blake*, Agnes Robertson; *General Daly*, Charles Fisher; *Ignatius Mulrooney*, C. Hale; *Dick Daly*, J. L. Barrett; *William*, Mr. Harrison ; *Mrs. Blake*, Mrs. Sylvester ; *Mary* (first appearance), Mary Miller; *Lady Mountjoy*, Mrs. C. Hale. Agnes Robertson produced several other comedies during her engagement. The other members of the season's stock company not appearing in the foregoing cast were: Fred G. Maeder, George Lingard, George Becks, White, Howell, H. B. Phillips, T. B. MacDonough, Ernestine Hendrake, Henry Wright and Viola Crocker.

Mr. and Mrs. F. B. Conway made their first appearance in three years in "Macbeth," 11th June. On 21st "Romeo and Juliet" was produced, with Mrs. Conway as *Romeo*, Viola Crocker as *Juliet*, Mr. Conway as *Mercutio*, Charles Fisher as *Friar Laurence*, C. Hale as *Peter*, H. Wright as *Tybalt* and J. L. Barrett as *Benvolio*.

The next important production was "Our American Cousin," first seen in Montreal on Friday, 29th June, with the following cast : *Asa Trenchard,* C. Hale ; *Lieut. Vernon,* F. G. Maeder; *Capt. de Boots,* Mr. Lee; *Abel Murcotte,* C. Fisher; *Buddicombe,* Mr. Harrison ; *Lord Dundreary,* J. L. Barrett ; *Sir Edward Trenchard,* H. Wright; *Coyle,* George Lingard; *Binney,*T. B. MacDonough; *John Whicken,* Mr. White; *Florence Trenchard,* Mrs. F. B. Conway; *Mrs. Mountchessington,* Mrs. Sylvester; *Augusta,* Miss E. Hendrake; *Mary Meredith,* Mary Miller; *Georgiana,* Miss Viola Crocker. This play was first produced at Laura Keene's Theatre, New York, 18th October, 1858, running until 19th March, 1859. It was frequently seen here, Barton Hill becoming a very capable delineator of the character of *Dundreary,* which role made E. A. Sothern famous in the original productions.

Marcus Elmore re-appeared after two year's absence, and did leading business until the close of the season, being seen in "Othello," 4th July, following in standard legitimate dramas. The Italian Opera Co. was heard 16th July for a short season, and the French Company, from New Orleans, began a six nights' engagement 6th August. Other English productions followed, "London Assurance" being presented 17th for C. Hale's benefit. Marcus Elmore was also tendered a benefit in "Green Hills of the Far West," with Acts 2 and 3 of "Rob Roy"; and on 3rd September the season closed with a benefit to Mr. and Mrs. Buckland in "Follies of a Night," "Green Bushes" and "The Merry Wives of Montreal."

John C. Heenan, the pugilist, appeared 8th November, assisted by Aaron Jones, of London; Ned Price, of Boston; and Monsieur Gregoire, the then "strongest man in the world."

FRED G. MEADER was a son of the great Clara Fisher-Meader. and was born 11th Sept., 1840. It was in Montreal that he first essayed dramatic authorship. presenting Dickens' "Great Expectations" in dramatized form. Mr. Maeder wrote more plays than any other American dramatist. He was joint author with McKee Rankin of "The Canuck;" and this was one of his last productions, he dying 8th April, 1891.

Adelina Patti made her first appearance in Montreal during September of this year, on the occasion of the grand reception and ball in honor of the Prince of Wales, now King Edward VII. The diva was accompanied by Carl Formes, Amelia Strackosch, Amoch, Barili, Susini and Signor Brignoli, appearing in a building specially constructed on St. Catherine street west known as the Crystal Palace. She was then in her twentieth year. Her first appearance in Montreal was in 1852 in the Salle Bonsecours.

ADELINA MARIA CLORINDA PATTI was born in Madrid, Spain, 19th Feb., 1843. While she was an infant her parents came to America, where she early exhibited very remarkable musical talent. At the age of sixteen she appeared in opera, in New York, with great success. Two years later she appeared at the Royal Italian Opera House, London, and was once acknowledged to be one of the greatest dramatic vocalist that ever appeared, which reputation she has since maintained.

She met her husband, the Marquis de Caux, in 1867, during a soiree at her own house. He followed the prima donna all over Europe. The marriage was opposed by Salvator Patti and de Caux's mother, but on July 29, 1868, the ceremony was performed at Clapham.

It was at Homburg that Patti met Nicolini. The tenor, with his wife and five children, dwelt close by Mme. Patti, and the prima donna evinced a strong dislike for him. Nicolini and de Caux became warm friends, but the prima donna's dislike for Nicolini seemed to increase. It is not told how or when her feelings changed, but the climax was reached when one of Nicolini's letters fell into de Caux's hands. He sued for divorce, and she took the same step against her husband. Mme. Patti then transferred her allegiance to the tenor. In 1886, some years afterwards, they were married. Since then Mme. Patti has been for the greater part of the time in retirement at her castle of Craig y nos, in Wales. Signor Nicolini died at Cannes on January 19, 1898. His real name was Ernest Nicholas.

Adelina Patti was married at Brecon, Wales, to Baron Cederstroom, 1899.

Baron Olaf Rudolf Cederstrom is a young Swedish nobleman of good family but small fortune. He was 29 years old and an athlete, and Patti is said to have fallen in love with him when seeing him perform on the bars at his gymnasium in London.

Patti has made six triumphal tours in America, her last ending in March, 1894.

THOMAS B. MACDONOUGH, a capable actor and manager, was born at Philadelphia on the 8th of December, 1835. His introduction to the stage as a professional actor was at Norristown, Pa., in 1854. During the war he served for the Southern cause. He first appeared in New York in 1863.

Mr. MacDonough died 3rd February, 1899, in Philadelphia.

THE SEASON OF 1861

introduced that very pleasing English tragedian, Charles Dillon. Woods' Minstrels came 14th January. From 16th April to 25th Buckland was associated with E. Bertrand, and during that time appeared a French company, including Paul Labas and Mlle. Sen as principals. A troupe of Spanish dancers held the boards during the latter part of May, closing 1st June. On 3rd and 4th June the Strakosch Grand Opera Company appeared, including Carlotta Patti, sister to Adelina, and Sig. Brignoli, Sig. Barili and Amelia Strakosch. The regular season opened 11th July with J. W. Buckland as manager. The opening bill was "Everybody's Friend" and "Jenny Lind." Charles Fisher made his first appearance this season, 12th, in "She Stoops to Conquer." Charles Dillon appeared 13th in his great role of *Belphegor* in "The Mountebank," and the after-piece, "The Artful Dodger." This was Mr. Dillon's first appearance here. On 15th he was seen in "Virginius," "Belphegor," 16th; "Othello," 17th; "Damon and Pythias," 18th; "Brutus," and "Corsican Brothers," 20th; "Hamlet," 22nd; "Three Musketeers," 23rd; "Money," 24th and 25th; "Merchant of Venice," and "Katherine and Petruchio," for the closing of his engagement, 26th.

"Mazeppa" and "Dick Turpin" followed, and from 8th August to 24th the Nelson Sisters appeared in a repertory of standard plays. Laura Honey appeared 26th in Boucicault's "Colleen Bawn," and on 2nd September Eliza Webb in "All that Glitters is not Gold," and "Lalla Rookh."

Charles Dillon re-appeared, 4th September, as *Sir Giles Overreach*; "Richelieu," 5th; "The Gamester," 6th; "Macbeth," 7th; "King Lear," 9th; and "Richard III.," 12th. The supporting stock company during the season was cast as follows in "King Lear": *King Lear*, Charles Dillon; *Edgar*, S. C. Dubois; *Edmund*, Mr. Van Deren; *Duke of Kent*, H. B. Phillips; *Duke of Gloster*, C. Merton; *Oswald*, E. Lamb; *Fool*, Effie Germon; *Duke of Albany*, F. G. Maeder; *Duke of Burgundy*, Mr. Carland; *King of France*, W. Pope; *Duke of Cornwall*, Mr. Lee; *Rhys*, E. B. Holmes; *First Knight*, Mr. Ward; *Cordelia*, Eliza Webb; *Regan*, Mrs. Van Deren; *Goneril*, Mrs. Wilkins. Mrs. Buckland was the *Portia* in the production of "The Merchant of Venice," a character which she played admirably. During the performance, Mr. Dillon found it necessary to appeal to the respectability of the uniforms of a few

officers occupying a box, who repeatedly interrupted the per_
formance. The latter for a moment seemed likely to pro_
voke the quarrel further, but the angry "pit" took sides with
the tragedian, and the performance went on without further
trouble. Marie Henderson and her sisters, Carrie and Sara
Nelson, were seen in a repertory for a week from 16th, fol_
lowed by Laura Honey, 23rd. Miss Honey appeared 26th
with W. P. Davidge in "Married Life." "The Lancers" and
"The Jewess" followed. Mr. Fauvel had a benefit November.
The Nelson Sisters re-appeared in December, the principal
production being "The Honeymoon." On 27th the Quebec
Garrison Amateurs presented "Charles XII., King of
Sweden."

During the season

NORDHEIMER'S HALL AND MECHANICS' INSTITUTE HALL

were leased to small companies, Sam Cowell's (died 11th
March, 1864, aged 43) Vaudeville Company appearing at the
former 8th, 9th and 10th July, and the Holman Opera Com_
pany at the latter 12th August, this being the first record of
their appearance in Montreal. Christy's Minstrels also ap_
peared at Mechanics' Hall, October 28 and 29.

CHARLES DILLON was one of the most intense actors of this
century. Harry Lindley says that in *Belphegor* he brought tears as
the deserted husband; his grief and momentary bewilderment at the
loss of his wife, to the full agony of its realization, was not only ren_
dered with force but also with most subtle and delicate touches. As
he made his exit from his abandoned room, with sunken frame, feeble_
ness of limb, and the semblance of mute despair upon his face, yet di_
vested of extravagance, he showed the finest traits of tragic intensity
He was not so happy in the great creations of Shakespeare, although
his *Hamlet* had novel innovations which pleased the public. In char_
acters calling for manly pathos he never had a superior. The abler
critics said he "lacked in intellectual gifts." Dillon was born at Diss,
England, in 1819. Prior to his London *debut*, he had made quite a
reputation in the large provincial cities. He first appeared in London,
at Sadlers Wells' Theatre as *Belphegor*, in 1856, when he scored a very
flattering success. He visited America in 1861 and became a favor_
ite. From thence he went to Australia in 1862, returning by way of
America in 1865, when his wife died. He returned to England in 1866.
In 1873 he made a success as *Jean Valjean* in Hugo's "Les Misérables."
He dropped dead in England 24th June, 1881. It was at Hawick
that the summons came. On the opening night he played "Othello,"

and although there was a wretched house, amounting to barely a few pounds, it was remarked that he acted with all the old grace and fervor. After the play, when he had finished dressing, he came out and sat upon the stage, waiting for the manager to bring him the miserable pittance which constituted his share of the receipts. The primitive orchestra consisted of a piano, on which *entr'actes* were played behind the scenes by a member of the company. Evidently the chief was in a despondent mood, for he remained silent and saturnine. Noting this, one of the young fellows of the troupe sat down to the piano and began to play some lively airs. When he had finished, Dillon muttered; "You have a light heart—a light heart, sir; how I envy you." With that he sighed and turned away. Could he have had a presentiment that the end was so near? Next morning he went down to the theatre to enquire if there were any letters. He was now elate and confident. Although the house had been so bad on the previous night, the impression created upon the audience was so favorable that a capital week's business was anticipated. After his usual custom, he took the company to an adjacent tavern and stood drinks of humble malt all around, told them some piquant story of America and Australia ; then they sallied forth to explore the town. As they reached the middle of High street, laughing and talking, he paused suddenly, put his hand to his head, as he was wont to do in *Beverley*, and exclaimed : *"God ! can this be death ?"* As the words left his lips he fell dead without a groan. His muscles had been so strained to harmonious motion that habit had become second nature, and one who stood beside him in that supreme moment assured me that in the very *rigor montis* he instinctively fell in an attitude of classic grace, even as *Cæsar* might have fallen beneath the steel of *Brutus*, and the others at the base of *Pompeii's* statue. It was best that the end came as it did, for the aspirations which had been more than fulfilled in the summer of his existence died out in its dreary autumn, and the future was a hopeless blank. His list of characters was extensive, but his great roles were *Hamlet, King Lear, Othello, Richelieu, Macbeth* and *Belphegor*.

LAURA HONEY, an English actress, first appeared on this side in Boston, 3rd September, 1858, at the Howard Athenaneum, in the "Child of the Regiment."

THE NELSON SISTERS, Carrie, Marie and Sarah, were the daughters of an English composer. They visited Australia, thence to California and to New Orleans. They appeared in New York in 1860 in musical burlesque, and returned to England in 1861.

SAMUEL CONIER DU BOIS died in Philadelphia, 17th January, 1898, aged 64. He was a call-boy in the Walnut in the early fifties, subsequently managed a theatre in Pittsburgh, returned to the Walnut as an actor, and retired from the stage in 1870, about which time the general abandonment of the stock company system had began. He had played frequently with Edwin Forrest during his Walnut days ; so, when he determined to return to the stage, he possessed an equipment for the classics that made him a valuable man in support of Mc-Cullough, Warde, Collier and Edwin Booth. He never gained particular fame as a player; but he never quite lost his love for the theatre, and was indefatigable for years in the devising and superintendence of festivals and celebrations that called into requisition his taste and talent. One of his notable achievements was the management of a festival, some years ago, in Cincinnati, in which Booth, Barrett, Murdoch, Mary Anderson, Clara Morris and Fanny Davenport participated. He was active in the arrangement of much of the pageantry of historical significance that marked the opening of the World's Fair.

E. B. HOLMES, after the close of his Montreal engagement, met Lizzie Macgregor in the West Indies, and they were married. She appeared with him here the following season. He was born in New York 2nd June, 1840.

THE SEASON OF 1862

again found the Bucklands at the head of affairs, with Alfred Nelson as acting manager. The names of the members of the company will appear further on in the cast of "Nick of the Woods." Knowles' play of "The Hunchback" was the opening bill, 9th June, followed by "The Wonder," "Married Life," "A Kiss in the Dark," "As You Like It " and "Our American Cousin." "Nick of the Woods" was produced 21st June. Cast: *The Jibbenainosay, Bloody Nathan, Nick of the Woods, Avenger, Reginald Ashburn*, Barton Hill; *Ralph Stackpole*, Vining Bowers ; *Richard Braxley*, Mr. Mardyn ; *Col. Bruce*, E. B. Holmes ; *Big Tom*, W. Pope ; *Abel Doe*, Mr. Ward; *Roland*, C. Merton; *Wenonga*, A. Nelson; *Piankashaw*, H. Chitty; *Little Tom*, Mr. De Vere; *Tellie Doe*, Alice Gray; *Edith Forrester*, Marian Watts ; *Mrs. Bince*, Mrs. C. Hill ; *Phoebe Bruce*, Effie Germon : *Nelly Bruce*, Lizzie Macgregor. Julia Bennett-Barrow, the celebrated actress, opened, 23rd June, in " As You Like It." *Rosalind*, Mrs. Barrow ; *Jacques*, Barton Hill ; *Touchstone*, Vining Bowers. Mrs. Bennett-Barrow was seen in an extensive repertoire during her engagement. Following came productions of " The Jealous Wife," " The Love Chase," "Angel of Midnight," "Family Jars," "Colleen Bawn," "Dundreary Abroad," etc. Ada Laurent, a dancer, was seen during the month of June. The celebrated pianist, Gottschalk, appeared at the head of a concert company 4th and

5th July. Kate Reignolds opened 7th July for a short season, being seen in "Cricket on the Hearth," "Asmodeus," "Peg Woffington," "The Marble Heart," and "Romeo and Juliet," 8th July, Miss Reignolds being the *Romeo* to Alice Gray's *Juliet*. A French company came week of 11th, and did good business. J. H. Hackett came 21st July, opening in "Henry IV.," Macklin's "Man of the World," 22nd; "Merry Wives of Windsor," 23rd; "Henry IV.," 24th; three small farces, 25th; and a repetition of the "Merry Wives," 26th. Edward L. Davenport, the admirable tragedian, made his *debut* at Montreal 28th July in "Hamlet," with the following cast: *Hamlet*, E. L. Davenport; *Claudius*, T. E. Mills; *Polonius*, E. B. Holmes; *Laertes*, Barton Hill; *Horatio*, C. Merton; *Rosencranz*, Mr. Pope; *Guildenstern*, Mr. Chitty; *Osric*, Effie Germon; *Bernardo*, L. Monroe; *Marcellus*, R. F. Smith; *Francisco*, Mr. Mitchell; *Ghost*, Charles Fisher; *First Actor*, A. Nelson ; *Second Actor*, G. Jones ; *First Grave-digger*, Vining Bowers; *Second Grave-digger*, C. Hill; *Priest*, Mr. Amherst; *Gertrude*, Alice Gray; *Ophelia*, Marian Watts; *Player Queen*, Miss Macgregor. "Damon and Pythias" was produced 29th; "Othello," 30th; "Richard III.," 31st; "Merchant of Venice" and "Black-Eyed Susan," 1st August. Mrs. Buckland was the *Portia* to Mr. Davenport's *Shylock*. J. H. Allen was the next *star* to appear, having been specially engaged during the first part of September for a production of Edmund Falconer's picturesque Irish drama, "The Peep o' Day Boys." That production, it will be remembered, was made by Laura Keene, and was one of the most successful works accomplished under that lady's management. Cast: *The MacCarthy, The Captain of the "Peep o' Day"* (dual roles), J. H. Allen; *Squire Doherty*, Chas. Fisher; *Darby Kelly*, R. Cook; *Aleck Purcell*, George Becks; *Howard*, S. C. Dubois; *Terence McGowan*, C. Merton; *The Babby*, A. Nelson; *Capt. McNeary*, E. B. Holmes; *Thady Doyle*, W. Pope; *Dennis*, H. Chitty; *Percy McDade*, Coburn; *Larry Riordan*, Moore; *Johnny Gaul*, Peters; *Phadrid*, Hughes; *Mickey*, Davidson; *Sergeant*, Jones; *Nelly Brady*, Alice Gray; *Mary Kelly*, Effie Germon; *Helen McNeary*, Fanny France; *Patsy Moore*, Miss Macgregor; *Widow Milloy*, Mrs. C. Hill; *Molly Flaherty*, Laura Le Brun.

A CURIOUS INCIDENT.

The history of a theatre so closely bound up with the fortunes, likes and dislikes of the city as the Royal is, there are many interesting incidents to be recorded, and a chat with Mr. Chris. Acheson, the veteran doorkeeper, who has been in the employ of the Royal for forty-one years, gives one some idea of the many-sided career the people's theatre has gone through.   In old days Montreal's audiences were not so quiet and respectable as they are now; the police were not so much in evidence, and mobs did pretty much what they deemed good in their own eyes.   More especially were they touchy on religious matters, as Charles Fisher, who played the part of *Squire Doherty* in the "Peep o' Day," found out to his cost.   It appears that the gallery objected to his raising his hands and blessing the crowd in the "Fair" scene. Fisher persisted in doing it, and immediately it rained apples, turnips and eggs from all parts of the gallery, while a crowd of fully five hundred toughs gathered on Craig street to attack him as he came from the theatre.   It was only through the presence of mind of Chris. Acheson, who smuggled him into a private house, and then succeeded in getting him to his hotel by a roundabout way, that he escaped serious injury. The scene then had to be cut out, as even forty policemen were not able to maintain order.

J. H. Allen was seen as *Ingomar* to the *Parthenia* of Alice Gray, 19th September.   George Pauncefort, a very capable actor from New York, Boston and Philadelphia, made his first appearance 22nd Sept. in "A Romance of a Poor Young Man," and had an extended engagement.   About this time the name of Charles Peters also figured in the bills.   The Webb Sisters (Emma and Ada) were also seen in a series of dramas and comedies, closing 22nd November in a triple bill. C. Hill was tendered a benefit 2nd August, and shortly afterwards left for a trip to England.

ADA LAURENT made her first American appearance in Montreal in 1862, coming from England, where she was born of French parents. She was educated in a convent in Paris, but eventually took a fancy for the stage, making her initial bow at the Lyceum, London, in 1860, as *Columbine*. Her first New York appearance was in March, 1868, as a *danseuse*.

GEORGE PAUNCEFORT came from England, and made his American *debut* at the Boston Theatre as *Captain Absolute*, 11th September, 1854. He opened the Worcester, Mass., Theatre in March, 1859, as Pauncefort's Athenaeum. He married Georgiana Edward, and has a son, George, who is on the stage.

George Pauncefort, the original *Armand Duval* in this country, he originating the part simultaneously with the *Camille* of Matilda Heron. He was a happy blending of the old and new schools, a capital instructor and stage director.

In light comedy roles of the *Charles Coldstream* and *John Mildmay* type he was superb. In melodramas like "The Duke's Motto," "The Iron Mask," etc., he was very effective, and in *Hamlet* and *Macbeth* he was acceptable.

JULIA BENNETT BARROW was the actress whom Edwin Forrest esteemed as the best *Desdemona* of the stage, and who increased the *furore* over *Hiawatha* by her recitation of the poem as she stood in the picturesque costume of an Indian squaw behind the footlights, while Longfellow himself applauded her beauty and her melodious voice. With graceful figure and expressive voice, this highly-cultivated daughter of a well-to-do English actor had advanced so far in music as to be urged towards the operatic stage, but in 1841, while in her teens, she made her *debut* as an actress, and the success which met her efforts determined her course. In her twenty-first year (1845) she married Jacob Barrow, but her subsequent retirement from the stage was broken two years later by unfortunate circumstances. She returned to the theatre, and came to America to gain extended triumphs, making her *debut* at the Broadway Theatre, 24th Feb., 1851. Efforts in the managerial line proved disastrous, and gradually Mr. and Mrs. Barrow faded from the scene. They returned to England, where the exquisite and beautiful Mrs. Barrow lingered for some years a paralyzed invalid.

EDWARD LOOMIS DAVENPORT, a scholarly and most finished actor, was by many conceded to be the ideal *Hamlet*, while other critics thought him greater in *Sir Giles, Bill Sykes, Brutus,* and *William* in "Black-Eyed Susan." In all he was equalled by few, and in several excelled by none. Born in Boston, 1816, he was in the early forties a favorite actor at the Bowery Theatre, New York, as well as in Boston. Anna Cora Mowatt engaged him to support her on an English tour, which opened in Manchester on December 7, 1847. Mr. Davenport fairly shared the honors of the tour with Mrs. Mowatt, and when she returned to America he decided that it would be advantageous to himself to remain behind. In 1849 he was married to Fanny Vining (Mrs. Charles Gill), an English actress, who had played with him. Fanny Davenport, it is said, was his step-daughter.

In England he played leading and alternate business with Macready, also appearing with him on the occasion of Macready's farewell performances at the Haymarket Theatre in 1851. Returning to America in 1854, he toured through the United States and Canada, appearing in Shakespearean roles, also in several characters drawn from the muse of Dickens. Unfortunate managerial efforts dimmed the lustre of his reputation and ended in failure. He died at Canton, Pa., 1st September, 1877. Mrs. Davenport died 20th July, 1891. Two sons, as well as Fanny and Blanche, have also been on the stage.

BARTON HILL.

BARTON HILL is of Greek stature, classic in relation to this native stage, artist now as always and with reminiscences so rich that, like the favorite line in "Love's Labor Lost," *"aged ears play truant at his tales and young hearings are ravished by his sweet and vol. uble discourse."*

Like the makers of the finer watches in Geneva, where only the third generation are entrusted with tempering the main spring and setting the balance wheel, he was master of stage craft by heredity. His father was Charles Hill, actor, of Drury Lane; his grandfather, John Hill, and his name Barton flowed from a racial line whose presence is marked on the oldest play bills extant, including that of Joseph Addison's "Cato" in 1690. It so fell out that Barton Hill took a high place in his profession, and as stage manager and director of plays has long been recognized by his fellows as being far beyond the mummer degree.

Charles John Barton Hill was born in Dover, England. It was in Montreal that Mr. Hill passed the first three years of his American sojourn. His father and mother, Mr. and Mrs. Charles Hill, and sister, Rosalie, went to Montreal directly after arriving in America from England, in 1843, leaving Barton behind to complete his education in Belgium. They became members of the company playing at the old Theatre Royal on St. Paul street, which included, among others, that season, J. W. Wallack, jun., Mary Rock and George Graham, under the management of John Nickinson.

Mr. and Mrs. Hill decided to become citizens of Montreal, Mrs. Hill opening up a dancing school in a house built after her plans on the east side of St. Jean Baptiste street, next door to Robinson's livery stables. The school was the fashionable resort of the time, and thither congregated the juvenile *elite* of the city.

In 1846 Charles Hill went back to England, and on his return brought with him his son, Barton, who records that his first position as money earner was as a compositor in "The Herald" office, under Mr. Penny. He was then in his sixteenth year, and shortly afterwards joined the Sock and Buskin Club of amateurs, where his abilities as an actor soon became recognized.

The following year, after the breaking out of the epidemic of ship fever, Barton Hill forsook his printer's stick to accept the hazardous post of hospital registrar for the attractive salary of $2.50 per day. His duties compelled him to come in contact with all the patients admitted to the hospital (railway freight sheds at Point St. Charles), and it must still be a matter of much conjecture to him how he managed to escape contagion. He was one of four of a staff of fifty who did not fall victims to the scourge. The haste of the younger members of the medical staff to enjoy themselves before their convalescence was assured proved fatal to several. Young Hill was one of the very few privileged juniors to be allowed to mess with the staff of doctors, among whom are recalled : Drs. Campbell, Francis, Hall, Liddle, McCullough and Lindsay.

This experience lasted from the month of June to the following spring. Mr. Hill had in the meantime resolved to study medicine. He was accordingly entered at McGill, and Dr. Crawford, taking a fancy to the young man, became his preceptor. During this period Mr. Hill records that the first successful operation under ether was performed, he assisting Dr. Crawford in an amputation. Drs. Wright and Angus McDonald were his *confreres*. A change of political influence, however, deprived Barton Hill of his hospital position, and not wishing to be dependent on any of his friends, he decided to abandon his intention of becoming a physician.

In the summer of 1848, the Hill family, consisting of Mr. and Mrs. Charles Hill, Rosalie, Barton and Robert, began a tour of the principal towns, giving parlor entertainments, etc., but the venture was not financially successful, and after disbanding, Barton drifted to Toronto, where he returned to the font and stick at the magnificent remuneration of $2.50 per week. This occupation, however, not fulfilling the realization of his ambitions, he determined upon becoming an actor for keeps, and was fortunate enough to find an engagement in the Pittsburg stock company, where he made his *debut* November 10, 1849.

In the following year, 1851, Mr. Hill made his metropolitan *debut* at the Broadway Theatre. He was married to Olivia Crook the same year, and also made his first appearance as a professional actor in Montreal the same summer, appearing under George Skerrett's management in the old Garrick Theatre, on St. Jean Baptiste street, known that season as Skerrett's Bandbox. Mrs. Barton Hill accompanied him and was billed as "Miss Olivia."

In the company was Sir William Don, a generous but eccentric actor who stood six feet four inches. The company subsequently adjourned to the reception-room of the St. Lawrence Hall after finding that the capacity of the Bandbox was not sufficient to accommodate the public.

His first starring engagement in Montreal began in June, 1862. He had made quite a hit as Dundreary in "Our American Cousin," and it was decided to put it on the boards during this engagement. There was some difficulty to find an actor in the company able to play Asa Trenchard. Mr. Hill suggested to Manager Buckland that he telegraph Vining Bowers, whom he knew to be at liberty. It was in that way that the comedian first came to Montreal.

From 1862 to 1872 Barton Hill was an annual *star* at the Theatre Royal, missing but the season of 1870. which year be passed in London, Eng., to fulfil an engagement at the St. James Theatre in the character of Young Marlowe, making his *debut* 16th Oct., 1869.

It was the summer of 1864 that John McCullough first appeared in Montreal as leading man. Barton Hill, however, does not appear to have met him during this engagement, for he tells me that they first met in 1865.

"My first impression of John McCullough," says Mr. Hill, "was a most favorable one, and never changed during the period of the several years we were associated together here and there, but chiefly in our management of the California Theatre. I had just arrived in Montreal, and upon calling at the theatre saw that a rehearsal was on. McCullough was pointed out to me, and I at once felt drawn towards him. During the rehearsal I was chagrined to hear one of the actors using rather abusive and unbecoming language in the presence of the ladies of the company. A repetition of this I saw very soon angered the good-natured John, who finally dragged the ungentlemanly fellow to one side and threatened to inflict corporal punishment if he did not at once desist. The threat, of course, had its desired effect After the rehearsal I was introduced to Mr. McCullough for the first time. During Frank Drew's engagement, John and I went up to Ottawa, where we played "Othello." It was his desire to have a shy at *Iago*, and it was probably there that he first played that role. The theatre in Ottawa was then controlled by the Townsends. We repeated the performance in Montreal August 8. My engagement with Mr. Buckland was to have terminated on the eve of Charles Kean's opening, 14th August, but at his request I was invited to remain over a week longer to participate in Mr. Kean's revivals. "I shall always remember the season of 1866. It was early in June when I set out from Cleveland *en route* to fulfil my annual engagement in Montreal. Arriving at Ogdensburg, I was told that, owing to the Fenian scare, our boat would not be permitted to cross to Prescott. I had received a letter from Mr. Buckland imploring me not to disappoint him. So much in earnest was he that he guaranteed me $150 for the week. Naturally, I was in despair, but finally contrived to be rowed across the river with my trunks. At Prescott I was surrounded by soldiers, who insisted upon examining my entire effects. The day was excessively hot, and there on the wharf, unsheltered from the sun, I was compelled to stand by and see my trunks rummaged through. The sword I used as *Elliot Grey* in "Rosedale" was confiscated. (Mr. Hill was the original *Elliot Grey* in Philadelphia.) Through the intercession of some friends, I subsequently recovered the sword. I also managed to arrive in Montreal in time to keep my engagement. Such was the public excitement, however, that my share of the week's business actually stood at $33. Mr. Buckland wished to stand by his contract, and proferred me the full amount of his guarantee, but I declined to take advantage of his generosity, feeling that, after all, I had earned just what came to me under the circumstances. Mr. Buckland then made arrangements for a return engagement after I had played in Ottawa. The tide had changed on my return, for we had excellent business, my share amounting to $150 for the first week in an engagement that lasted to September 20th.

"In 1865 I became a member of Kilwinning Masonic Lodge in Montreal."

Barton Hill married Marian Watts, daughter of Mrs. John Sefton, in 1861. They have four children, of whom three are daughters.

It was in 1862, the year that Mr. Hill played his first starring engagement in Montreal, that he received an offer from Mrs. Garretson of the Walnut Street Theatre, Philadelphia, to take the place of Edwin Adams, that baritoned-voiced young melancholy, who left the fragrance of a beautiful memory to be refreshed until this day by the tears of those who love him still. Mr. Hill was promised all the features and honors accorded to Mr. Adams, but there was a slight difference in the salary. He answered by telegraph : "I appreciate the honors, but expect the same salary. This was granted him. He opened as *Armand Duval* to the *Camille* of Charlotte Thompson, and you who have kept the history as well as the sentiment of the play in regard know that Dumas fils had not long been author of that matinee tear shower. With one exception, Mr. Hill was the first of an apostolic succession of unfilial *Duvals* catching at in sorrow and disappointment the fragrance that no comedian has to offer. In the same year Mr. Hill went over to the Arch Street Theatre as leading man for Mrs. Drew. He remained there with few intervals for ten years, and by his high intelligence and clear and firm conception of the parts he played he secured a hold upon the affections of that city surpassed in the case of no artist, Mrs. John Drew herself alone excepted. He played a wide range of parts, but it was not only in the public estimation that he secured a high place.

Barton Hill was a member of Edwin Booth's great company during the Winter Garden Theatre season. The theatre burned down on the morning of March 23, 1867. Edwin Forrest, who had been looking for an actor to replace John McCullough in playing parts second to his own, made Mr. Hill an offer, which was accepted, and in the support of the gigantic tragedian, he met with unqualified success.

John McCullough, acting on this recognition, called him to California to manage his theatre there, and during that robust actor's successful career Mr. Hill cared for his local interests and was his partner in that splendid property so long as McCullough retained its control.

Thus It was that the acquaintance and friendship first formed in Montreal continued steadfast and unbroken to the end—twenty years.

Barton Hill's brother, Robert H. Hill, mentioned in the first part of this article, is auditor of the Lake Shore and M.S. Railway Co., a position he has held since 1858. Rosalie Hill married MacDonald Bridges, and their daughter is Mrs. Alexander Murray. Mr. Hill's home is at Paradise Valley, Munroe County, Pa.

During the past two seasons Mr. Hill has been in the company of Nance O'Neil in Australia.

His father, Charles Hill, died 23rd Sept., 1874.

INTERIOR OF THEATRE ROYAL,
1825.

F. Brown and Miss Riddle in the original performance here of "Virginius."

VINING BOWERS will be remembered as a very clever and pleasing comedian. He was for a few years closely associated with the Montreal stage, and a great favorite with theatre-goers here.

Mr. Bower's was born in Philadelphia, Pa., April 23, 1835. He began his theatrical career at the Chestnut Street Theatre, that city, in 1849, as call boy and to play small roles. Ten years later he· went to New York, where he had obtained an engagement as second low comedian at Barnum's Museum. His next engagement was at Albany. He afterwards was engaged for principal low comedy roles at Washington, Philadelphia, Cleveland, Wheeling, New Orleans and other cities. He died in New York, August·18, 1878.

Very few changes took place in the ranks of the support during

THE 1863 SEASON,

which was opened regularly 12th July. The principals to appear were Barton Hill, Alice Gray, Kate Denin, Emily Thorne and W. J. Scanlan among others. The feature of the season was the appearance of Emily Thorne in "Aurora Floyd." Other pieces produced were "Ingomar," "Our American Cousin," a play which gave Mr. Hill much scope in the character of *Dundreary*; "The Octoroon," "The Duke's Motto," "Macbeth," "The Marble Heart," "The Wife," "East Lynne," "Lady Audley's Secret," and "The Loan of a Lover."

EMILY THORNE belonged to that talented family which included C. R. Thorne, jun. A score of years has passed since Emily Thorne's brilliant performance of *Aurora Floyd* was famous in the land. To-day she lives in quiet retirement, a handsome white-haired lady of independant means, quite philosophic of the theatre with its fitful triumphs. Her first appearance on the stage was under her father's management in her eleventh year, about 1856. George C. Jordan was her first husband. After his death she married J. C. Chamberlin in 1884.

WILLIAM J. SCANLAN, at the age of thirteen, was known as "The Temperance Boy Songster," and travelled through the country on that mission. This Irish comedian and vocalist was born at Springfield, Mass., in 1836. He at one time *starred* jointly with Tim Cronin, the Irish comedian, subsequently with Minnie Palmer for two years, and in the fall of 1881 he made his first appearance as a *star*, and for the first time sang in public his famous "Peek-a-Boo." Mr. Scanlan was forced to retire from the stage from the effects of paresis, and died 18th Feb., 1898.

Small troupes appeared in 1864, the Ravels and John Denier holding the boards at the Mechanics' Hall 11th January, for one week, and Wood's Minstrels at Nordheimer's Hall, for the season commencing 4th January.

The Theatre Royal opened, 2nd June, 1864, with a French repertoire company from Niblo's Theatre, New York, for two weeks.

The regular opening night for

THE SEASON OF 1864

was 30th June. Vining Bowers acted as stage manager, and the stock company boasted of having for its leading man, the popular John E. McCullough. The opening bill was "On Delicate Ground" and "The Serious Family." John McCullough made his first bow to Montreal play-goers 1st July, having come from Niblo's Theatre, New York. His *debut* here was in "The Stranger," he in the title role and Mrs. Buckland as *Mrs. Haller*. He was afterwards seen in "The Iron Chest" and "Robert Macaire," "Lady of Lyons," "East Lynne," "Colleen Bawn," "The Hidden Hand," "Lucretia Borgia," "Romeo and Juliet," with Miss Kate Denin as *Juliet*; "Macbeth," "Pizarro;" Mr. McCullough as *Pizarro*, Mrs. Buckland as *Elvira*, and Miss Denin as *Rolla*. Miss Denin closed her engagement 16th July in "Katherine and Petruchio." Sam Ryan was also in the company. Miss Madeline Henriques appeared 18th July in "Clari, Maid of Milan," followed by "The Youthful Queen," "The Love Chase," "The Hunchback" and "Ticket-of-Leave Man." The Webb Sisters opened 1st August in "The Rose of Killarney," and closed 13th, the most notable of their productions having been "The Lady of Lyons," "Bride of Lammermoor," and "The Wandering Boys" for the close. Barton Hill came 15th, in Tom Taylor's "Ticket-of-Leave Man," "Our American Cousin," and closed 20th with "The Corsican Brothers" and "The Idiot Witness." Emily Thorne appeared, 22nd August, in "An Unequal Match." The season closed 5th September, but the theatre was kept open during September by a French repertoire company. Italian opera was also heard 14th, 15th and 16th November.

THE WEBB SISTERS, Emma and Ada, were born at New Orleans, the former on the 18th June, 1843, and the latter on the 18th Sept., 1845. They starred with but qualified success for some years, and later the elder took to the lecture platform in 1868. Ada married W. M. Connor, of Brooklyn, N.Y., and retired from the stage.

MADELINE HENRIQUES, born in New York, of Jewish parents, made her stage *debut*, Wallacks' Theatre, in 1860. She remained there until 1867, when she married Louis J. Jennings, of London, sailing on the same day.

JOHN EDWARD McCULLOUGH was one of the most genial and hearty of American actors. He made friends wherever he went and he owed his tremendous success as much to his personal popularity as to his talents.

McCullough was born at Blakes, near Coleraine, Londonderry, on the seacoast of Ireland, November 14, 1832. His father, James McCullough, was a "small farmer." His mother, Mary, died in 1844, leaving her son John, then a lad of 12, and three daughters. Their father was unable to provide for these children, and shortly after the mother's death they were obliged to seek their fortune in America. In the spring of 1847 John and his sister Jane came to this country, and, having a cousin named John McCullough in Philadelphia, they proceeded to that city. This cousin was a chairmaker, and in the business of chairmaking John McCullough was employed. His father and the sisters, Mary and Elizabeth, followed to America shortly after. The father died at Moorestown, N.J., in 1878. He is remembered as a small, thin man, who spoke with a heavy brogue. He did not maintain intimate relations with his children. He was a faithful worker and an honest man, but he had no ambition, and he was of a reticent and inoperative character.

When John McCullough, a youth of fifteen, came to America, he could read, but he could not write. He had received no education, and he was in ignorance of literature and art. Dying thirty-eight years later, he had become a man of large and varied mental acquirements, a considerable scholar in the dramatic profession, and the most conspicuous heroic actor of his time on the American stage. No ancestor of his was ever upon the stage. Dramatic faculty, however, is one of the peculiar attributes of the Irish race. In McCullough it was developed by the accident of his meeting with a "stage-struck" work-man in the shop of the Philadelphia chairmaker. This person made him acquainted with the tragedy of "Richard the Third," and stimulated in him a taste for reading Shakespeare. One of his first steps toward the stage taken at this period was his affiliation with "The Boothenian Dramatic Association." His experience at this time led him to branches of learning apart from the stage. One of the books that he read was "Chamber's Encyclopedia of English Literature," and in less than a month he had absorbed the whole of it, becoming so familiar with its contents that he could descant on the British authors as if he had been trained for nothing else—so eager was his zeal for knowledge and so retentive was the memory in which he stored it. He early married Letitia McCain.

McCullough's theatrical career, beginning in 1857 and ending in

1834, covered a period of twenty-seven years. His first engagement
was made at the Arch Street Theatre, under the management of
Wheatley and Drew, and his first appearance there was made August
15, 1857, as *Thomas* in "The Belle's Stratagem." E. L. Davenport,
at that time manager of the Howard Athenaeum, in Boston, engaged
him at that theatre, where he remained for one season—that of 1860-61.
In the ensuing season he was back again in Philadelphia, engaged at
the Walnut Street Theatre. Here he was when presently he attracted
the notice of Edwin Forrest, who chanced to be in need of an actor to
play the parts second to his own, and who procured his release from
Mrs. Garretson and gave him an engagement for leading business.
This was "*the tide which taken at the flood leads on to fortune.*" McCullough's first appearance with Forrest was made at Boston in October,
1861, in the character of *Pythias*. From this time he had a clear field
and he advanced in the open sunshine of success.

For some years he and Lawrence Barrett were joint managers of
the California Theatre, and it was during this association that he
first acted *Virginius* and one by one added to his repertory the other
great parts to which he had formerly played seconds under the leadership of Forrest. It was not until May 4, 1874, that he made the first
appearance as a *star* in New York, presenting himself as *Spartacus* in
"The Gladiator." His first appearance as a *star* in Philadelphia was
in the Arch Street Theatre in the spring of 1876. Thenceforth, until
the end, his career was an uninterrupted success, and in prominent
cities leading citizens honored him with public banquets. In April
and May, 1881, he played a successful engagement in London at the
Drury Lane Theatre, where his *Virginius* and *Othello* won high
encomiums. In April, 1884 while playing in Williamburg, it became
apparent that his powers were broken.

In June 1884, he went to Carlsbad, Bohemia, for his health. He
had also shown signs of weakness in Cincinnati the month before
at the Dramatic Festival. His last appearance on any stage was 29th
Sept., 1884, at McVicker's Theatre, Chicago, as *Spartacus*. His acting
on the fatal night clearly showed his great physical and mental weakness. He required frequent prompting, and in the death scene he
nearly broke down. Some of the audience hissed and jeered. McCullough came before the curtain at the close, and looking around
ironically, and with a half dazed expression that would have moved
to pity a more intelligent gathering, faltered out: "*This is the best-
mannered audience I ever saw. If you had suffered as I have you would
not have done this.*" He died 8th Nov., 1885. A monument to his
memory stands in Mount Moriah Cemetery, Philadelphia. It re-
presents the tragedian in bronze as *Virginius*. The inscriptions on
the monument are as follows :

"His life was gentle, and the elements
So mixed in him that Nature might stand up
And say to all the world: 'This was a man.'

"Manliness and meekness in him were
so allied that they who judged him
by his strength or meekness
saw but a single side."

Here was returned to the clasp and kiss of the universal mother one of the noblest souls ever housed in human clay, one who like those effluent oriental rivers that come down from the eternal snows and wind luxuriantly amid palms and plumes and break dazzlingly into silver jets at every obstacle—this broad stream, bountifully laden with the gifts of heaven and richly tuned with the voice of earth, narrows and lingers, and, with sad silence, sinks into the sand.

THE SEASON OF 1865.

A remarkable feature in Montreal theatricals during 1865 is recorded by Mr. Henry Hogan, who writes me that John Wilkes Booth played a short engagement under the Buckland management, preliminary to the regular opening. Mr. Hogan says that after his performance was over Booth would hurry over to the "Hall" and down to Joe Dion's billiard rooms to play with the best in the city. He was here just a week or ten days before the assassination of Lincoln; in fact, when the news reached here it was recalled by the friends of Booth that, just before leaving Montreal, he told them that they would hear in a very short time of something which would startle the world. His act on 14th April, 1865, caused a terrible sensation in this city, more especially among his theatrical colleagues and friends from the South, whom he had met at the " Hall."

JOHN WILKES BOOTH—The appearance of John Wilkes Booth in Montreal during the year 1864 marked an interesting feature, although calling up memories of history that remain gloomy and sad. Mr. Fred Leclair, manager of the Theatre Royal, is in possession of a programme gotten up on the occasion of an entertain- ment consisting of a selection of readings given by Booth at the solicitation of a number of his citizen friends at Corby's Hall, St. Joseph, 5th January, 1864. In reply to the request for the readings, Booth wrote as follows:—

"Thomas Harbine, John L. Bittinger, P. L. McLaughlin':

"GENTLEMEN:—Your flattering request has just been received, and I endeavour to show my appreciation of it by the promptness of my compliance. I have gained some little reputation as an actor, but a dramatic reading I have never attempted. I know there is a wide distinction, as in the latter case it is impossible to identify one's self with any single character. But as I live to please my friends, I will do all in my power to please the kind ones I have met in St. Joseph. I will, therefore, designate Tuesday evening, 5th January, at Corby's Hall.

"I am, very respectfully,

JOHN WILKES BOOTH."

The selection of the readings consisted of "The Shandon Bells," the trial scene from "The Merchant of Venice," "Selections from Hamlet," "The Remorse of the Fallen One," or, "Beautiful Snow," and "The Charge of the Light Brigade."

Later in the season, Booth became for a few months a member of the Theatre Royal Stock Company, under the Buckland management. The late Henry Hogan records that, after his performance was over, Booth would hurry to Dion's billiard-rooms to play with the best in the city. "He was here just a week or ten days before the assassination of Lincoln," Mr. Hogan once wrote, "in fact when the news reached here it was recalled by the friends of Booth that just before leaving Montreal he told them that they would hear in a very short time of something which would startle the world. His act on 14th April, 1865, caused a terrible sensation in this city, more especially among his theatrical colleagues and friends from the South. John Wilkes Booth, youngest son of the tragic genius, Junius Brutus Booth, and brother of the greatly esteemed Edwin Booth, but for his insane act, might have become one of the greatest actors of his epoch. Gifted with unusual personal beauty, supple and graceful in form, dignified and attractive in his bearing, essentially dexterous in the use of the sword, with a dare-devil in his nature which subsequently led him to the commission of the greatest tragic act of the age,—he carried with a brain power a subtle intuition of Shakespearean character which made him an ideal Hamlet, although he never seemed to have his heart on the stage, saying that there could hardly be room for himself and his brother, Edwin. His natural genius was so great that under proper conditions any career was within his reach. His friends were unable to associate the man as they knew him, with his gentle, sympathetic ways,—his quick interest in what appealed to his charity, which was boundless as his pride,—with his terrible doom. As this phantom fades away, we recollect only what was human in this rash, hot-headed youth of twenty-six, as we throw a flower upon his grave in sorrow for his act and fate, with its appalling consequence to the gospel of liberty, to mankind, and to his distracted relatives. A glorious career was beckoning to him, but his last words summed up the fruit of his existence: 'useless!' 'useless!' "

The 1865 Company was again headed by John McCullough, supported by Vining Bowers, Jas. A. Herne, Keller, J. R.

Spackman, Clarke, S. J. Barthe, Holmes, Barton, Miss Georgie Reignold, J. Clarke, Lizzie Leigh, Annie Wood and Mrs. Hill. The season opened 13th May with " The Fate of a Coquette." The celebrated actress, Mary Gladstane, made her first appearance 15th in " The Hunchback," followed by "Lady Audley's Secret," "Averted Bride," "Lucretia Borgia," "The Wife." "Plot and Passion," "East Lynne," and " The Hidden Hand." Ida Vernon was seen 29th, opening her engagement in " The Fate of a Coquette." Then followed "The Robbers," " London Assurance," " The Iron Chest," "Hamlet," and "The Stranger." Julia Daly appeared 12th June, followed by productions of " Our Female American Cousin," " Ticket-of-Leave-Man," " Richard III." Helen Western made her appearance 3rd July, in "The Flowers of the Forest," then in " Don Caesar de Bazan," "Wept of the Wishton Wish," "The French Spy," and closed 22nd July. Frank Drew came 24th, and appeared in "Handy Andy," " Mazeppa," " Irish Emigrant," " Comedy of Errors," and closed 5th August with " Rory O'More." Barton Hill and McCullough were seen in "Othello," 8th August, and, later, in "The Marble Heart." The event of the season was the appearance of Mr. and Mrs. Charles Kean, from the 14th to the 18th of August, in "Henry VIII.," "Merchant of Venice," "Hamlet," "Much Ado About Nothing" and "Richard II." This is the only record of "Richard II." having been performed in this city. Admission to the boxes was $10; first gallery, $1.50; second, 75 cents; pit, 50 cents. Tremendous crowds sought to gain admittance at each performance. The pit entrance in those days was through a passage, since converted into the office, and on one occasion, as the crowd was struggling to get in, a small boy shouted "Fire!" There was no panic, however. It was a common sight to see as many as 1,400 soldiers crowded into the pit. The Keans were supported by John McCullough, J. F. Cathcart, Barton Hill, G. Everett and Miss Chapman. Speaking to me of this season, Mr. Hill said :—

«My engagement with Mr. Buckland was to have terminated on the eve of Charles Kean's opening, but at his request I was invited to remain over a week longer to participate in Mr. Kean's revivals. Mr. and Mrs. Kean were accompanied by J. F. Cathcart and G. Everett. There was the utmost harmony and good fellowship in accepting the distribution of the various roles. Mr. Kean was in poor health and failing memory, and was obliged to depend much on Messrs. Cathcart and Everett, who understood his business thoroughly. The opening was in "Henry VIII.," Mr. Kean as *Wolsey*, and myself as the *King*. In "Hamlet" Mr. Cathcart was *Laertes*; Mr. Everett, *Horatio*; Mr. McCullough, *First Player* and *Osric*; and myself, the *Ghost*."

John McCullough had a farewell benefit 19th in "Black-Eyed Susan," on which occasion J. F. Cathcart appeared by permission of Charles Kean. The favorite little comedienne, Lotta, made her first appearance here on the 21st of August in "Po-ca-hon-tas," followed by "Lola Montez" and "Betsey Baker."

The first performance of "Uncle Tom's Cabin" in Montreal was given on the 26th August. Col. T. Allston Brown, after a careful research, declares that the first " Uncle Tom's Cabin" play of which he can find any record was written by Prof. Hewett, of Baltimore, and was produced at the Museum in that city January 5, 1852. The season closed 31st August with Christine Zavistowski in "Massaniello," and other operas.

FRANK DREW was an excellent comedian of the old school and a brother to the elder John Drew, who died in 1862. The brothers resembled each other very much, and their performance of the two *Dromios* was capital. Frank appeared for some time at Philadelphia under the management of his sister-in-law, Mrs. John Drew. Frank Drew was born in Dublin, 29th October, 1831. He was brought to America by his parents in 1837, and first appeared on the boards in his eighth year. His first appearance at Philadelphia was in 1853. In 1850 he married Mrs. C. L. Stone.

JAMES A. HERNE made his *debut* as *George Shelby* in "Uncle Tom's Cabin" in 1859. He was born at Troy, 1st February, 1840. For the major portion of his stage career this man steadfastly pursued all that was best in his calling, and he long since reached a point sufficiently near his ideals to entitle him to the *bravos* of the critics and the salvos of the populace. And yet for years he had been quite outdistanced in the race for general favor and critical consideration. His well-known play of "Hearts of Oak" was the source of some revenue to him for several years, but latterly he could only produce it at the cheap theatres, until his star rose several seasons ago in his "Shore Acres," and he has acquired fame and fortune. He had a spiritual magnetism that drew to him souls of his kind, and without robe or sceptre he swayed an empire that had sworn no allegiance yet which gave its unconscious tribute of laughter and of tears wherever he raised the standard of his heart. He married Helen, sister of Lucille Western, during their sojourn in Montreal as members of the stock company of 1865, the event taking place at the old St. George's church, on St. Joseph

street, in August of that year. Helen Western had married a Bal_
timore lawyer, but was divorced. She died in Washington 11th
December, 1868, aged 24. Mr. Herne managed the theatre here
for a short time during 1870. Jas. A. Herne's last play in which he
starred during the season of 1900 is entitled "Sag Harbour." He
died 3rd June, 1901.

. **STRAWBERRY BLONDE LOTTA** (*nee* Charlotte Crabtree, born
in New York in 1847) first appeared as a vocalist at the age of six as a
member of a variety troupe, of which her father was at the head. She
romped and skipped, picked the banjo and danced the breakdown in
so lively a manner that she soon made a name. John Brougham,
who was one of her earliest managers, called her "a dramatic cock_
tail," and he was not far wrong. She was the incarnation of drollery,
of mischief and of broad farce, and as such became the most popular
of *soubrettes*. In comparing Lotta to Maggie Mitchell, who, until
their retirement, were the two oldest and best known song and dance
artists on our stage, a friend remarked, "they keep their youthful
appearance so well that they seem to be getting younger every year.
I expect any morning, looking over the newspapers, to find their
names among the births." Lotta Crabtree, once the pet of the public,
declares that she never so much as thinks of going upon the stage
again. She has taken up painting, and has become a very clever
amateur artist.

Under the management of Ben De Bar, the most important people to appear during

THE SEASON OF 1866

were Barton Hill, Vining Bowers, Chas. Dillon, James Carden, Geo. F. Rowe, C. J. Fyffe, S. J. Barthe, Mrs. F. W. Lander, Mary, Lizzie and Emma Maddern, Helen Western, Lucy
Rushton, Cecile Rush and Mad. Marie Celeste, who had appeared here as early as 1835 at the old Theatre Royal. The
season opened 2nd June with "Kate O'Shiel," "Jones' Baby,"
and "A Day Too Late." On 4th Barton Hill was seen as
Lord Dundreary, and Vining Bowers as *Asa Trenchard*, in a
production of "Our American Cousin." "The Stranger" was
given 7th, with Hill as the *Stranger*, and, on 11th, Mad. Celesté
appeared in "Green Bushes," followed by "Flowers of the
Forest," "The French Spy." "Woman in Red," closing her
engagement 23rd with "The House on the Bridge." Charles
Dillon made his reappearance, after an absence of two years.
25th, opening in "Richelieu," following in "Macbeth," "Belphegor," "Hamlet." "Richard III.." "Othello," "A New Way
to Pay Old Debts," "Artist of Florence," "Used Up," and

made his last appearance 7th July as *King Lear,* supported by George Fawcett Rowe, this being Mr. Rowe's first appearance in Montreal. On 9th July Helen Western appeared, and on 12th Lucy Rushton was seen in "Ogarita,' following in "Black Dominoes," "As You Like It' and '"Lady of Lyons." A notable feature of the season was the appearance of Mrs. F. W. Lander (*nee* Jean Margaret Davenport). She had appeared here in 1839 as a youthful prodigy. It is generally supposed that it was she whom Charles Dickens travestied in " Nicholas Nickleby " as the " infant phenomena," *Minetta Crummels.* Her engagement began 23rd July, when Knowles' "Love" was produced, followed by "Lady of Lyons," "Mesalliance," "The Hunchback," "Romeo and Juliet," and "Charlotte Corday" for the close. Cecile Rush began a short engagement 30th July, as *Fanchon* in " The Cricket on the Hearth," "Ida Lee," etc. On 6th August Barton Hill made his first appearance in "The Dead Heart," assuming the role of *Robert Landry.* "The Corsican Brothers" was staged 7th and 8th, and he again appeared 9th as *Caleb Plummer* in "The Cricket on the Hearth." Charles Reade's "Never Too Late To Mend " was first staged 13th and 14th, with Barton Hill as *Thomas Robinson,* James Carden as *George Fielding,* and Vining Bowers as *Peter Crawley.* Productions of "Lost in London," "Wallace," "Dundreary," "Ticket-of-Leave Man " and " Streets of New York" were presented successively; and on 20th Lucy Rushton was re-engaged, opening in "As You Like It," "She Stoops To Conquer," "The Brigand," Boucicault's "Duel in the Dark," "School for Scandal," "Satan in Paris," "Honeymoon," and closed with "Three Black Seals," 1st September. The Maddern Sisters (Mary and Lizzie) began a season 5th September in "The Fall of Robespierre." Mary Maddern had terminated an engagement under De Bar's management at his New Orleans and St. Louis Theatre Companies. James Carden benefiated, 7th, in "The Iron Mask," when Lily Wood Carden made her Montreal *debut.* "The Octoroon" was billed 8th, and "Never Too Late To Mend" was presented 10th, with C. J. Fyffe as *George Fielding.* This was followed by "The Three Guardsmen," 12th; "The Willow Copse," 14th; and Miss Braddon's "Henry Dunbar," 17th, with Barton Hill as *Dunbar,* Vining Bowers as *The Major,* and C. J. Fyffe as *Clement Austin*; "Rob Roy," 18th; "Our American Cousin " and "The Rough Diamond," 20th;

Lizzie Maddern as *Margery*, and S. J. Barth as *Cousin Joe*, in the latter piece. Barton Hill had a benefit, 20th, in "How She Loved Him," and "Robert Macaire," followed by two of Boucicault's plays, "The Colleen Bawn" and "The Life of An Actress," Money," "The Marble Heart," "Fan Fan La Tulipe," " Camille," in which Mary Maddern was seen as *Gauthier*, and Hill as *Duval*. "La Tour de Nesle" was followed by other pieces, chiefly repetitions, and the season closed 6th October with three pieces, "Not Such a Fool As He Seems," "Love in Livery " and "Toodles."

CHARLES J. FYFFE, born 16th Sept., 1830, had a stage career of exactly forty years. His first appearance, he informs me, was in 1852 at Memphis, Tenn., as the *Doctor* in Tobin's "Honeymoon." From small parts he gradually advanced, until in a few years he played leading business in the support of all the leading *stars* of the period. He has played in the West Indies and in South America, as well as all over the U. S. and Canada. His last appearance in Montreal was during his last season on the stage in support of Edward Vroom, at the Queen's Theatre, during the last week of Sept., 1892. After his long service, Mr. Fyffe has retired to that ideal little spot, Holmesburg, known as the Forrest home, where, in company with a few other veterans, the days pass but too quickly in the exchange of interesting reminiscence. Mr. Fyffe is the librarian of the home, and is an exceedingly entertaining gentleman, possessing a considerable fund of anecdotes, most of which relate to his own personal experience while in close association with the great actor whose memory will be forever kept green by the munificence of his bounty.

CECILE RUSH died 12th August, 1897, at Cornwall-on-the-Hudson, where she had lived for several years. She was sixty-three years of age. Her first appearance on the stage was at the Walnut Street Theatre, Philadelphia, March 17, 1856, when she acted *Bianca* in "Fazio." She played for one week. Her *debut* was most successful. She appeared as *Julia* in the "Hunchback," as "The Countess in Love," as *Margaret Elmore* in "Love's Sacrifice." She then went West, and in 1859 was touring the country, giving, with considerable success, dramatic readings. During the season of 1862-3 she was a full-fledged *star*, and appeared in the various stock theatres, opening February 16, 1863, in Cincinnati, as *Bianca*. Col. Brown says that at that time Mrs. Rush was considered one of the handsomest actresses on the American stage. Nature had been bounteous in her bestowals upon Cecile Rush, but all that nature could bestow would avail little in assisting her to attain her position as an artist had not stern and rigid study been accessory. She was possessed of all the requisites an actress should be blessed with, viz., a beautiful face and eyes, an expressive countenance and a splendid figure. Her talents won for her a handsome fortune, but she retained nothing. Genius is prone to be impulsive and cannot be methodical; and while she could create she could not control.

THE MADDERN SISTERS, Emma, Lizzie and Mary, enjoyed a considerable portion of public esteem. Emma, born in 1847, was brought out by Ben DeBar. , In 1866 she married James M. Nixon, but is now the wife of R. E. Stevens. For five seasons she has been a valued member of the "Grand Avenue Stock Company," Philadelphia. Lizzie married Thomas W. Davey, manager of the Detroit Opera House, and was the mother of Minnie, now the wife of the intrepid Harrison G. Fisk, proprietor of the "Dramatic Mirror," and herself one of America's representative actresses. Lizzie Maddern died in 1879. Mary never married. She is a member of her niece's company.

JAMES CARDEN played in nearly every country of the globe. He was born in Ireland in 1835, but his stage life began in America. When at the old Jenny Lind Theatre in San Francisco he played the servant in "The Iron Chest" to the *Mortimer* of the elder Booth. This was the occasion of Junius Brutus Booth's first appearance in California and of the first appearance as *Wilfred* of Edwin Booth. In 1858 he came East. In 1865 he was engaged by Mrs. John Drew as leading man of the Arch Street Theatre Stock in Philadelphia. Later he was a brilliant member of the famous Wallack-Davenport combination. After travelling for two more seasons with Lucille Western and with John McCullough he was engaged by George Coppin to go to Australia. He is said to have been paid the then almost unprecedented salary of $500 a week. Onward he went to India and thence to Africa. Then he received a fine offer from the Court Theatre in London, where he filled engagements under Charles Reade and Wilson Barrett. He married there Lucy M. Heraud, daughter of John Heraud, editor of the London *Athenæum*. He next went starring through the provinces of Great Britain, until Augustin Daly brought him from England for a leading part in "The Flash of Lightning." After playing some months in this melodrama Mr. Carden joined Madame Janauschek's company to play *Macbeth*, and other leading parts. Another trip to Australia followed, where he remained three years and then returned to San Francisco, where he delivered the closing address in the old California Theatre. Of late years Mr. Carden had played engagements with various legitimate combinations. He joined the Forepaugh Stock in Philadelphia, Jan. 20, 1896, and was a member of that organization at the time of his death, 23rd March, 1898. His wife died a year before.

THE COMPANY OF 1867

included Vining Bowers, Jas. Carden, C. Walcot, Jun., F. F. Mackay, S. S. Cline, J. Gobay, Chas. Hillyard, E. B. Denison, S. J. Barth, Mark Brook, Maitre Claude, Thos. Placide, Effie Germon, Celia Logan, Emma Cline, Nellie Stewart, Kate Browning, Mrs. C. Walcot, Jun., and Mrs. Barton Hill. F. Dickson was the scenic artist. The season opened 3rd June, with "Married Life," followed by "Everybody's Friend," "The Octoroon," "The Husband at Sight " and "Colleen Bawn." On 17th and 18th June, Parepa Rosa gave two operatic concerts, assisted by Theodore Hadleman, Sig. Feranti, Sig. Fortuna, Carl Rosa and S. Behren. The balance of the season passed without noteworthy incident, the principal productions by the stock company being "The Lost Will," "Kate O'Sheil," "Invisible Husband," "Time Tries All," "Money," " Waiting for the Verdict," " Ours," " Guy Mannering," "Ladies' Club," "Kathleen Mavourneen," and "Kenilworth," in which Lady Don appeared 1st July.

THE GALLANT ROSSHIRE BUFFS,

those splendid fellows of the 78th Regiment who relieved Lucknow, whom the people of Montreal had the honor of having among them from 1867 to 1869, were conspicuous in their support of the theatre.

PAREPA ROSA first came to this country in 1865. She was then Euphrosine Parepa, known as one of the most brilliant of the dramatic sopranos, who had created a furore in Europe by her superb voice as well as by her fine appearance. Parepa was a lyric-dramatic singer after the old Italian method, having been taught in that school by her mother, Mme. Parepa, who was a celebrated Italian prima-donna in the 40's and 50's. Her father, Signor Archibuchi, was an Italian impressario and musical agent. Euphrosine was born in London in 1840. At the age of seventeen she was engaged for the winter season at the Grand Theatre of Malta, where there was an English colony. She made her *debut* in "Somnambula," scoring an immediate success. She went to London, where she married an English officer, but continued to sing, and became one of the greatest oratorio singers in England as well as in America. Her husband after a few years died in Santiago, Chili. He left debts of several thousand dollars, which she paid from the earnings of her American tour. She married Carl Rosa in 1867. De Vivo arranged a tour of concerts and operas for New York, April and May, 1867, under the title of the Parepa and Brignoli Concert and Opera Company, with the result that Parepa's and Brignoli's shares of the profits were $12,000 each. The organization continued until Parepa Rosa's death in 1874, when she left a fortune of £80,000 to her husband, who carried on the Carl Rosa Opera Company until his death in 1890.

F. F. MACKAY has been a pedagogue, manager, painter and playwright, and is still all of these, although returning more and more to his first love as the years pass, and is more than all a teacher. He was born in New England in 1832, and was brought to New York in his early youth, where he gleaned his first knowledge of the stage from the Murdock Dramatic Society late in the forties. Among his associates in that Society were W. J. Florence, George Boniface, Jane Coombs, Emily Wilton and Maggie Mitchell. He adopted the stage as a profession in 1851-52, but shortly afterwards became a schoolteacher. He returned to the stage in 1857, appearing with various stock companies through the South and West until 1865, when he joined the forces of Mrs. John Drew at Philadelphia, where he remained until 1871. Mr. Mackay has played nearly a thousand character parts from *Shylock* to *Uncle Tom*, and in every dialect from Scotch to Chinese. His last engagement was in support of W. H. Crane 1896-97, since which he has been conducting a dramatic school in New York.

THE COMPANY OF 1868

included Charles H. Vandenhoff, Owen Fawcett, A. W. Young, H. A. Langdon, G. H. Griffith, Thomas Burns, Jane Cameron, Kate Ranoe, Mrs. Buckland and Jennie Gourlay. Maffit and Bartholomew's Spectacular Co. opened the season 20th July. Chas. Vandenhoff benefited in "Hamlet," 6th August, Miss Ranoe being the *Ophelia.* The *tragedienne,* Mary Gladstane, played a *star* engagement, as also did Vining Bowers. A French Opera Troupe appeared, also the Hanlon Bros., Fanny Herring in "The French Spy," Violet Campbell in "Leah," and, on 24th October, the tragedian, Edwin Adams, began a short engagement in "Hamlet," "Macbeth," "Wild Oats," "Richard III.," "Romeo and Juliet," and "The Marble Heart." The Hanlon Brothers made their first appearance at Montreal at Northeimer's Hall, 6th October, 1866.

CHARLES H. VANDENHOFF, an actor of intelligence and originality, was the son of George Vandenhoff, inheriting much of his histrionic talent. He was born in England in 1850, and was only in the outset of his career when he was first seen in Montreal as leading man of the stock company at the Royal in 1868 for a season of three months. His experience was a varied one in the support of various *stars.* In 1888 he acted *Jacques* in "As You Like It," with Modjeska, and supported her in other important roles. His acting

in "The Chouans" with her was also the subject of critical commenda_
tion. His last appearance in Montreal was in "Paul Kauvar," week
11th February, 1889, at the Academy of Music, when he played the
rôle of *Honore Albert Maxime.* He died at Seattle, Wash., April 30,
1890.

JAMES S. MAFFITT was to the present juvenile generation
famous principally as the impersonator of the *Lone Fisherman* in "Evan_
geline," with which extravaganza he had been identified since the
original production in 1870 at the Boston Museum. Another creation
of Maffitt's was the role of *Wahnotce,* the Indian, in Dion Bouci_
cault's original production of "The Octoroon." He was also the
original of comedy parts in "The Twelve Temptations" and "The
Devil's Auction." When George L. Fox revived the popularity
of pantomime, Maffitt entered the field against him with success. He
retired in 1894, and died at Baltimore, 16th April, 1897, aged 65.

OWEN FAWCETT was born in London, Nov. 21, 1838. When
but two years old he was brought to this country, and thenceforth
America was his home. The Fawcetts are a noted family on the English
stage. There were two John Fawcetts, father and son, the elder
a comedian of Garrick's day, who died in 1792, and the younger
a celebrated player of the early part of that century. He was
born in 1769, died in 1837, and was the cousin of Charles
Fawcett, grandfather of the subject of our sketch. Charles
Fawcett was a member of Macready's company for several years,
and a popular provincial actor; of his two brothers, John, came to
America in 1795, and acted in all our leading theatres, while William
remained in England, and after a career at the Surrey Theatre and as
an imitator of leading London actors, retired from the stage to keep
a small book shop in Radnorshire, Wales, where he died. Owen Fawcett's father, also named Charles, was an actor at Hull, England, in
1826, and gave up the stage on coming to America. He was born Oct.
13, 1805, in Stafford, and died in Philadelphia on 27th July, 1867.
In 1853 Owen Fawcett began his career as a professional actor,
making his *debut* on Dec. 7, at Norristown, Pa., as young *George
Shelby* in one of the earliest dramatizations of "Uncle Tom's Cabin."
On July 4. 1861. Mr. Fawcett made his first appearance in New
York at the Academy of Music, as *Mr. Wadd* in support of the
Florences and Mr. and Mrs. Barney Williams in "The Irish Lion."
He was at Winter Garden under Booth and Clarke in 1864. With
the season of 1871-72 began Mr. Fawcett's seven years' association
with Augustin Daly. Between these notable appearances the comedian
was also seen as a member of various Summer Stock Companies.
From January to August, 1886, he was with Modjeska, and for
the four subsequent seasons played low comedy roles in support of
Edwin Booth, Booth and Barrett, and Booth and Modjeska. In 1890-
91 he spent his first season in Sothern's company, and then, after a
five weeks' engagement in the fall of 1891, in support of Minna Gale,

took an extended vacation, and travelled through Great Britain and the principal countries of continental Europe. His home is in Detroit, and is a centre of delight to the lover of theatrical lore. The treasures it contains in the way of scrapbooks, old play bills, portraits and curiosities carry pleasure to every one interested in the stage, and prove that Mr. Fawcett is a skilful and cultured authority on the history of the American drama during the past forty years.

FANNY HERRING was born in London, 6th April, 1832. She was about ten years of age when she appeared on the boards. Her name, up to her retirement a few years ago, had always been associated with the sensational drama, in which she met with some success. She married in 1868. Miss Herring resides in a little cottage of her own in Connecticut. Her once jet black hair is now snowy white. Her sons, David and Frank, are both married and have large families. Miss Herring has six grandchildren, of whom she is very proud.

HENRY A. LANGDON, a native of Philadelphia, first appeared on the boards 18th August, 1849, at the Arch Street Theatre. His first wife, Emily Rosalie Reed, died in 1857, aged 25. His second wife, Annie Senter, died in 1867. Mr. Langdon was a useful stock company player, and is still before the public.

EDWIN ADAMS was one of the most promising and versatile actors of the American stage. He was born at Medford, Mass., 3rd February, 1834, and first appeared on the stage as *Stephen* in the "Hunchback," at the National Theatre, Boston, 1853. His first great success was in 1863, when he produced "Enoch Arden," appearing in the title role at Baltimore. His great roles were *Rover* in "Wild Oats," *Melnotte, Frank Hawthorne* in "Men of the Day," *Adrian* in "The Heretic," *William* in "Black-Eyed Susan," and as *Macbeth*. During his Australian tour he became a great favorite, but lost his health, and returning home died in Philadelphia, 28th October, 1877. Mr. Adams was a whole-souled and open-hearted man, who knew of no use for money except to spend it. It was a beautiful life prematurely ended. It was a brave strong spirit suddenly called out of the world.

The lease and management of the theatre passed into the hands of the well-known American tragedian, J. W. Albaugh, in 1869. Among the members of the company were Mary Mitchell Albaugh, Ada Harland, Nellie Mortimer, Mrs. Hill, Frank J. Evans, Robert Duncan and G. C. Davenport. The season was opened 3rd May by the Ixion Burlesque Co. "The Lady of Lyons," "After Dark," "East Lynne," "Kathleen Mavourneen," "Richard III.," "Fazio," "Hunchback," "Ingomar" and "The Stranger" were produced successively. Alice Marriott, a strong and capable actress, opened 21st May, playing the title role in "Hamlet," following in "Macbeth."

"Romeo and Juliet" and "Jeannie Deans." Joseph Proctor reappeared in Montreal 1st June, after several years, in Knowles' "Virginius." He was also seen in "Ambition" and "Nick of the Woods."

Harry and Rose Watkins followed in "Kathleen Mavourneen."

Madame Moreau was then seen in "The Romance of a Poor Young Man," followed by Oliver P. Doud in "Lady of Lyons," "Richard III.," "Fashion," "Macbeth," "Idiot Witness," "£100,000," and closed 26th June owing to the illness of Miss Marriott. From 1st to 14th July a French Company from Porte St. Martin Theatre, Paris and New Orleans, held the boards; and on 15th and 16th Signor P. Brignoli gave farewell concerts. Gregory's Vaudeville Co. opened 2nd August for one week, followed by the character actor, G. L. Davenport, with the Clodoche Company. The remainder of the season was taken up by the Morris Combination, Vining Bowers and Barton Hill, in "Rosedale," closing 18th September with "La Tour de Nesle." Several Minstrel Troupes appeared from time to time until the end of the year.

JOHN W. ALBAUGH was born in Baltimore, 30th Sept., 1837, and first appeared on its stage in his eighteenth year as *Brutus* in "The Fall of Tarquin." He appeared as *Hamlet* the following month, and was well received. A series of engagements followed, and in 1865 we find him supporting Chas. Kean in New York. He then went on a *starring* tour. During 1868 he was manager of the Olympic Theatre, St. Louis, Mo., and in 1869 manager in Montreal of the Theatre Royal. He married Mary Mitchell in 1866, became manager of Leland's Opera House, Albany, in 1873, and held its lease for several years. He and his wife undertook several *starring* tours, and in 1878 his work in "Louis XI.," at Daly's Theatre, New York, was highly praised. He afterwards managed the Lafayette Square Opera House, Washington, and the Lyceum Theatre, Baltimore. Mr. Albaugh retired from the stage after his performance of *Shylock* with the Lyceum company, Baltimore, 9th Dec., 1899.

ADA HARLAND, the daughter of an eminent English surgeon, was born in London, Eng., on the 22nd of December, 1847. She made her professional bow at the St. James' Theatre, 8th March, 1862, as *Theodore* in "Friends or Foes." She was one of the several accomplished young women who accompanied Lydia Thompson to America, the troupe opening at Wood's Museum, New York, 28th September, 1868, with Miss Harland as *Jupiter* in "Ixion." She was a good dancer and a very fair player.

ALICE MARRIOTT, one of the many clever artists sent from England, graduated from a provincial troupe, and first appeared in the English metropolis in 1855. She crossed over in 1869, making her American *debut* on the 29th of March, New York, in the character of *Hamlet*, supported by J. F. Cathcart and J. W. Albaugh. Miss Marriott subsequently married Robert Edgar, the London manager.

MARY MITCHELL ALBAUGH is a sister to Maggie Mitchell, and was born in New York, 12th Nov., 1834. She began *starring* in 1863, and three years later married John W. Albaugh. Her first husband was the late J. W. Collier, from whom she was divorced.

HARRY WATKINS was born in New York, 14th Jan., 1825, and made his first appearance on the stage in 1839. He married Rose Howard in 1860. During his lifetime he played with all the leading actors and actresses of the day. His last appearance was in Philadelphia in the autumn of 1893. He died 5th Feb., 1894.

The opening of

THE 1870 SEASON

was a remarkable one, marking the occasion of Prince Arthur's visit to Montreal, and patronage to a benefit performance given to J. W. Buckland by a company of amateurs, who performed "Follies of a Night," and "The Irish Lion," 3rd January, followed by the appearance of Ben De Bar in a short engagement. E. M. Leslie, of the Boston Theatre, opened the regular season on the 30th of April, as business manager for seven performances. The company included Kate Reignolds and W. F. Burroughs. The pieces produced were "Frou Frou" for the opening, "East Lynne" and "The Married Rake." A French company followed in an extended repertoire, running several weeks; and, on 25th May, Mr. and Mrs. Howard Paul, the well-known artists, made their first appearance here.

James A. Herne assumed the management of affairs 30th May, Miss Lucille Western opening in "East Lynne," and following in "Green Bushes," "Rip Van Winkle," etc., and closed the following month. Ella Wren and Chas. Waverley were in the support. Brignoli's Opera Company played an engagement during July, followed by the reappearance of the old favorites, Vining Bowers and Kate Reignolds in "The Lady of Lyons," "The Wonder," and other standard pieces. Marietta Ravel, sensational actress, was seen during the first week in August in "The French Spy." An interesting engagement was that of Kate Reignolds during the last week of August. Van Leer and Phillips began an engagement on the 19th of September in "All that Glitters is not Gold," after which a company of acrobatic Japanese held the boards, followed by Nellie Nelson in "Mazeppa," and "Living Female Groups from Berlin," 28th of October. Walhalla's Variety Troupe was seen in November, and Ida Leslie's Combination produced "Love's Sacrifice," "Camille," "Nell Gwynne," "Colleen Bawn," "Under the Gaslight," "Othello," etc. In the support were, besides the *star*, A. R. Phelps and Norman S. Leslie. They held the boards one week from the 14th of November.

M. D. B. St. Jean appeared in feats of magic during the week of the 26th December, closing one of the dullest seasons artistically as well as financially since the opening of the house. James Taylor, English comedian; Ada Alexandra, prima-dona; George Cline, baritone; and the Freeman Family, appeared at Mechanics' Hall during August.

BENEDICT DE BAR was born in 1812 in London. His father was French. He was given a good school education, after which he became a stroller. He came to America in 1834, making his *debut* at the Bowery Theatre, and in 1842 we find him managing the affairs of that house. From 1850 to 1854 he was lessee of the Chatham Street Theatre, New York, but abandoned it to go South, where he became an immense favorite. He became the acknowledged best interpreter of *Falstaff* in the South and West before the war, while the East and North preferred and proclaimed Hackett as their champion. He was at one time worth over half million dollars, but lost the greater part during the war. The curtain was rung down at St. Louis in 1877. His wife, Harriet E., died at the Forrest Home, 24th Aug., 1894.

Harry Lindley records that

MISS MARIETTA RAVEL was very handsome, shapely, and her stage presence magnetic. Her favorite role was in "The French Spy," but she also did good work in "The Wizard Skiff" and "Wept of the Wishton Wish" (from Fenimore Cooper). She imbued the impassible pantomimic dramas with so much volatility as to make them palatable to the public. She was also an adept tight-rope walker, and in one of these dramas used her skill in escaping from the villain by crossing over a river on a rope, accompanied by *pizzicato* music and a balancing pole. It is recorded that she only had one speaking part, that of *Cynthia* in Buckstone's "Flowers of the Forest." There was only one fault, and that was in her having been tutored in the part by Pat Connolly, a good swordsman, but deficient in the Queen's English. In that one speech she innocently revealed the parentage of her lingual instructor by saying *"fetthered and bound."* Marietta Ravel was born in 1847, and retired from the stage a number of years ago to become the wife of Martin W. Hanley, for many years manager of Harrigan's Theatre, New York, and now engaged in looking after the interests of R. B. Mantell.

HOWARD PAUL, a Philadelphian, who met with some success in England in 1852 as a comic writer, made his stage *debut* at Bath in 1854, in a vaudeville sketch. He married Miss Featherstone, who accompanied him on two American tours in 1866-69.

SIGNOR LUIGI BRIGNOLI is remembered as having been the favorite tenor on this continent for thirty years. He was a pupil of Joseph Pasquale Goldberg, of Paris, and made his first appearance in America in February, 1855, at the Academy of Music, New York, under the management of Ole Bull. He was under the management of the Strakoschs from 1858 to 1864, then went to the Theatre des Italiens, Paris. He supported Nillson in 1870 and 1871, when she first appeared in the United States, and also in 1875-76, and was with Mapleson in 1879. He died in 1884.

IDA LESLIE, born 18th March, 1844, first appeared on the stage in San Francisco under the management of A. R. Phelps. She married Norman S. Leslie in 1863.

THE SEASON OF 1871

brought more variety to our theatre-goers, and the deficiency of the previous year fully made up and amply recompensed at the bills of fare catered by various managers. The season opened 10th January by the Holman Opera Company, who held the boards until 28th, followed by a lull until 10th April, when E. M. Leslie and G. E. Locke assumed the management, opening with "Richelieu at Sixteen." The old favorite, Fanny Herring, played a week from 17th, followed by Fox and Denier's "Humpty-Dumpty," week of 24th. John W. and Mrs. Albaugh, supported by the St. Charles Theatre Company of New Orleans, came 1st May, and opened in "Eustache." This was their first appearance in two years. Mr. Albaugh represented Ben De Bar, who leased the theatre, as manager. The company was a powerful one, and included John W. Norton, John Davis, R. G. Wilson, John Hurst, Francis Kenny, T. McNally, T. Morton, H. W. Mitchell, Mark Quinlan, M. B. Curtis, Eugene Eberle, J. R. Grismer, C. Wildman, W. Lane, G. Moore, Miss Amelia Waugh, Hattie Vallee, A. Moore, Kate Quinten, Ida Raymond, Mrs. Vandeeren and Miss Winton. "The Hunchback" followed the opening bill, and productions of "The Ticket-of-Leave Man " and "The Robbers" were then seen, prior to the first appearance in Montreal of the celebrated Alice Oates in a repertoire of standard operas. Among the members of the Oates Company at this time was included William H. Crane. The famous comedian was then only at the outset of his successful career. In a recent letter Mr. Crane makes this characteristic remark, "I have not played in Montreal since, but hope to." Mr. Albaugh was seen as the *Dane* 29th May, and, on 30th, Mrs. D. P. Bowers, supported by her husband, J. C. McCollom, made her first appearance here in a short engagement, terminating 3rd June, in productions of "Lady Audley's Secret," "Marie Stuart" and "Macbeth." In the last mentioned production Mrs. Bowers was the *Lady Macbeth*, J. C. McCollom the *Thane*, and Albaugh *Macduff*. The appearance of John E. Owens 5th June was quite noteworthy, the great comedian being seen during a short engagement in "Solon Shingle," "Heir-at-Law" and "The Poor Gentleman." The engagement of Owens was followed by that of Frank Drew in "Temptation," and "Rip Van Winkle," week of 12th June. On 19th June, Dominick Murray made his first *star* appearance here in "Escaped from Sing-Sing." A production of "Othello," 3rd July, introduced J. W. Albaugh as the *Moor*, and J. W. Norton as *Iago*. The Chapman Sisters followed in opera, and on 10th July J. K. Emmett made his first *star* appearance here. A bright feature of the season was the return of Charles Mathews, 31st July, in a round of characters lasting one week. D. H. Harkins appeared as *Dazzle* in "London Assurance," and as *Macbeth* 19th August. The distinguished actor, Lawrence Barrett, opened a week's engagement, 28th August, in " The Man o' Airlie," following in "Julius Cæsar " and "Rosedale." This was his first appearance here, and his last in this City was at the Academy of Music, week of 18th May, 1885. Following Mr. Barrett's appearance was that of Lillie Eldridge, from 4th Sept., in repertoire; then Joseph Murphy, for the first time here on 2nd October, in F. G. Maeder's "Help." The last day of the De Bar-Albaugh season was 14th October, when the Coleman Children appeared at the matinee in "Love's Sacrifice," and in "The Rising Generation," and "Little Sentinel' for the closing performance in the evening. The season had certainly

been a record-breaker for excellence, and most notable in
introducing a number of most eminent *stars*.

The actress, Kate Ranoe, became sub-lessee of the theatre
from 16th October, inaugurating what became known as

THE RANOE SEASON.

A. R. Phelps was manager. The opening bills, "Kenilworth," and the farce of "The Clockmaker," introduced Julia
and Sallie Holman, both of whom subsequently became very
closely associated with the Montreal stage as members of the
celebrated Holman Opera Company. On the 30th of October
Lillie Lonsdale and J. A. Meade, as principals of the stock
company, were seen in "Under the Gaslight," followed by
"Jessie Brown," "The Golden Farmer," "The Man in the Iron
Mask," "Revolt of the Commons," and "Colleen Bawn." The
Ranoe season closed on the 27th of November with "Kathleen Mavourneen" as the bill, in a benefit to Miss Ranoe.

A. R. PHELPS was born at Granby, Conn., 19th February, 1824,
His *debut* was in the rôle *Othello* at the Greenwich Street Theatre,
New York, in 1845. In 1854 he accompanied the Denin sisters to
California, remaining until 1866. He was married to Frances R.
Bickford, a non-professional, in 1849.

ALICE OATES in those days had a sweet voice, a lovely figure
and a winsome way about her that went direct to the hearts of the
people. She made enormous sums of money, but she wasted it like
water, and it is on record that in 1875, after playing four straight
months in San Francisco to the capacity of the house, she had to
borrow money to carry herself and her company east. Her last appearance in Montreal was at the Royal in a two weeks' engagement
from 21st December, 1885. Her financial condition was said to be
lamentable, and physically she was a wreck. She deserved a better
ending, but it only goes to show how quickly a public favorite may
wane. She was for many years among the foremost exponents of
opera bouffe in America. She was born Sept. 22, 1849, in Nashville,
Tenn., and was put on the stage by James A. Oates in Cincinnati about
1865-6, at which period they became man and wife. He died July 14,
1871. When he married her she was Alice Merritt, and was one of
the four sisters. On Sept. 16, 1867, they opened at the new Nashville
Theatre, Tenn., in "A Tale of Enchantment," and in 1868 were travelling with the Oates-McManus "Undine" troupe. Meanwhile she
had sung at different points in the West in concert under the name
of Mlle. Orsini. When the Hess troupe produced "The Field of
Cloth of Gold" at the Opera House, Chicago, in February, 1869, she

MUSIC.

made a hit as Darnley. On November 23, 1872, she was married to Tracy W. Titus, her business manager, from whom she was granted a divorce in 1875. On May 17, 1879, she was wedded to Samuel P. Watkins, then a non-professional of Philadelphia, who afterwards was her business manager. A cold contracted in April, 1886, in a badly heated dressing room of a theatre compelled her to disband her company and return to Philadelphia, where she died, January 10, 1887.

DANIEL H. HARKINS is a native of Boston, where he was born 27th April, 1835. He made his professional *debut* in 1853. During the war he served on General Slocum's staff, and returned to the stage after five years' absence. Mr. Harkins is a capable and very interesting actor.

JOHN W. NORTON, a useful stock actor and manager, was well known in several parts of the country. For a short time in 1877 he managed the Academy of Music, Montreal, and was also closely associated with Ben De Bar as a manager of his Opera House in New Orleans. It was under Mr. Norton's direction that Mary Anderson made her first stage appearance. Suddenly and terribly his life was ended in railroad collision at Coatesville, Indiana, 29th Jan., 1895.

WILLIAM H. CRANE was born at Leicester, Mass., 30th April, 1845. He evinced decided musical taste at an early age, and in July, 1863, joined the Holman Opera Company, composed of young people. He remained with this company seven years, being possessed of a powerful baritone voice. His first salary was less than $10 a week, but at the end of the second season the offer of $15 from a rival organization deprived the Holmans of his efficient services, but he soon returned to them at a salary of $20 a week. The repertoire for each night consisted of acts from operas, burlesques and pantomimes. There was no falling into a rut with a rehearsal call that compelled the player to be up in the title role of the farce "Paddy Miles," as *Count Arnheim* in "The Bohemian Girl," as *Dr. Dulcamara* in "The Elixir of Love," and as the clown of the pantomime, all for one and the same evening, a task that not infrequently fell on young Crane's shoulders. His next connection (1870-74) was with Alice Oates' opera company. Here he was principal comedian, and was identified with the hit of "Ali Baba" at Niblo's Garden. Later, he was the very first *LeBlanc*, the notary in "Evangeline," and then he abandoned burlesque for comedy, appearing first with the Hooley stock company of Chicago. The stock exchange inspired Crane with the idea of hitting off the peculiarities of certain brokers, and here he struck a vein which he has since worked with great success. Returning east, he was seen in "Our Boarding House," 1876-77, and soon afterwards he and Stuart Robson went into partnership. Their two *Dromios*, in Shakespeare's "Comedy of Errors" became a household word, and

Bronson Howard's "Henrietta" was at first their joint property. Then Crane decided to strike out for himself (1889), and in "The Senator" won both fame and fortune. He lost some of the latter as *Falstaff* in "The Merry Wives of Windsor," but quickly retrieved his error of judgment by securing Martha Morton as his playwright in chief. His *Elisha Cunningham* in "A Fool of Fortune" was an artistic creation. Mr. Crane has also met with much success recently in a dramatization of Westcott's famous novel "David Harum." ⸱

DOMINICK MURRAY. Few members of the profession, whether as actors or managers, have had a wider or more varied experience than Dominick Murray. His impersonations have embraced every phase of stage character: *Othello, Richard, Romeo, Shylock, Harlequin, clown, pantaloon*, hornpipes, jigs and comic songs. After five years' probation in the English theatres, associated with such celebrities as Gustavus Brooke, Charles Dillon, the elder Vandenhoff, Chas. Mathews Charlotte Cushman, Helen Faucit and others equally eminent, Mr. Murray embarked for Melbourne, Aus., where he opened at Coppin's Olympic as *Paddy Murphy* in "The Happy Man." At the Antipodes, by acting and management, he quickly made money ; entered into partnership with Alexander Henderson in mining speculations, and quickly lost it, and returned to England, to succeed Dion Boucicault as *Myles na Coppaleen* at the Adelphi Theatre, London. Following this came a starring tour of the English provinces, beginning at Cambridge, in a version of "The Woman in White," in which Henry Irving, at that time a member of the stock company, played *Henry Hartright*. Eventually, after a few starring and managerial ventures, Mr. Murray's services were retained as principal comedian and character actor for the Princess' Theatre, where he opened in a serious leading role, and appeared during the same evening as *Paudeen O'Rafferty* in "Born to Good Luck," achieving immediate success and enviable popularity. At the Princess he continued three seasons creating many original types of characters notably *Michael Feeny* in "Arrah-na-Pogue," *Crawley* in Charles Reade's drama of "Never too Late to Mend," *Dicey Morris* in "After Dark," and the leading comedy parts in "A Cup of Tea," "No. 1 Around the Corner," and numerous other farces. Migrating for a single season to the Olympic, then under the management of Benjamin Webster, he appeared in several of the Burnand and Byron burlesques, singing and acting the female caricature roles in a falsetto voice. This rather unpleasant engagement terminated, he returned to the Princess to give an entirely new reading of *Shylock* in "The Merchant of Venice." Mr. Murray's reading of the character was subsequently adopted by tragedians who are now very eminent indeed. Notwithstanding his unequivocal success and popularity, Mr. Murray's highest salary in

London was £12 per week. So much for English managerial liberality. During the summer of 1867, being compelled by private business to visit New York, he was induced by Jarrett & Palmer to appear at Niblo's Garden, and at that theatre, in conjunction with Dan Bryant and Rose Eytinge, he made his American *debut*, October 2, as *Michael Feeny* in "Arrah-na-Pogue." Counselled by Joseph Jefferson, Mr. Murray soon after contracted with Spalding, Bidwell & MacDonough to visit St. Louis, Memphis and New Orleans. Then came engagements at McVicker's Theatre, Chicago; Macauley's, Cincinnati ; Ellsler's, Cleveland ; the Globe, Boston, and in various other cities, his repertory comprising Shylock, Monte Cristo, Mickey Free and two Irish dramas written by the author of "A Midnight Marriage." For the past fifteen years Mr. Murray has been among the recognized American *stars*. Occasionally he sought relief from the monotony and fatigue of travelling by playing certain stock engagements—notably one season at Booth's under Dion Boucicault, and three seasons at the Madison square, with Steele Mackaye. To join the latter gentleman he declined a leading position at Wallack's. In 1872 he translated and produced, under the title of "Escaped from Sing-Sing," Edouard Plouvier's "Mangeur de Fer." He is also responsible for translations of "Le Portefeuille Rouge," "Le Fou par Amour," "Les Rues de Paris," "Le Pere Lefeutre" and "Micael L'Esclave" (presented at Wood's Museum under the title of "Peril"), which title was afterwards used by Bartley Campbell and more recently by Mrs. Langtry. His latest success was in "Master and Man." The actor's real name is Morogh, by which he is known off the stage. Since retiring from his professional pursuits a few years ago, Mr. Morogh has lived on his farm at the Back River, a few miles out of this city, which property he acquired some years ago.

MRS. D. P. BOWERS' characterization of *Queen Elizabeth* was a marvellous one, was also her *Lady Macbeth;* and in her line had few equals and no superior. Her maiden name was Crocker, the daughter of the Rev. William A. Crocker, an eminent Episcopal clergyman of Stanford, Conn., where the actress was born 12th March, 1830. Her first stage appearance was at the Park Theatre, New York, 16th July, 1846. A year later she married David P. Bowers. After his death in 1857 she retired from the stage for a time, but married Dr. Brown, of Baltimore, in 1859. She made her *debut* at London in 1861, and in 1867 again became a widow. James C. McCollom became her leading support in 1863, and on 29th January, 1883, became her third husband as well. He died in the same year, and Mrs. Bowers did not re-marry. After a short retirement she resumed her professional inclinations and played *starring* engagements in all the principal cities of the United States with little interruption up to the time of her death, 6th November, 1895.

JAMES C. McCOLLOM was an accomplished actor and a pleasant gentleman. He was born at Buffalo in 1837, and made his first bow at Lockport, N.Y., in 1858. From 1863 until the time of his death in 1883 he *starred* with Mrs. D. P. Bowers in a legitimate repertoire, and, as already noted in Mrs. Bowers' sketch, was married to that lady. He had, at the time of his demise, won his way to the front rank of his profession, and was capable of holding that rank.

JOHN EDMOND OWENS was known in several parts, but the part with which his name is most prominently identified is *Solon Shingle*. He was born in Liverpool, 2nd April, 1823, and came to America with his parents when a mere child. First appeared on the stage at the National Theatre, Philadelphia, in 1845. In 1849 he was joint manager with Hann, and from that time, until his death, in 1886, he was a successful actor and manager. William Winter recalls him as one of the most lovable men that have graced and cheered the stage.

M. B. CURTIS attained much cheap fame and many dollars in "Samuel of Posen." His real name is Maurice B. Strelinger, and he was born at Detroit. During his sojourn at Montreal he married a French Canadian lady, Albina DeMer. He was never seen here in *Samuel,* but it was produced for the first and last time, week of 21st November, 1887, at the Theatre Royal, with Frank Howard in the title role.

The value of personal magnetism was never more pointedly illustrated than in the case of

JOSEPH K. EMMETT, an actor of the most limited range, who built up a reputation and a fortune on the flimsiest foundation of artistic merit. Born at St. Louis, Mo., 13th March, 1841, he graduated upon the stage of a variety theatre there in 1866. He made a specialty of those vulgar Teutonic eccentricities known upon the stage as "Dutch business." He possessed a good eye for character, a very sweet and flexible voice, and a redundant fund of natural humor of the coarse order. His creation of "Fritz" won the popular heart at once. He made the journey round the world, his popularity being as marked in the Antipodes as in America. The end came at Cornwall, N.Y., 15th June, 1891.

LAWRENCE PATRICK BARRETT died in New York, 20th March, 1891, aged 53. Here came the lowering of a curtain so unlike that to which Mr. Barrett was used. There was no gaudy flare of the footlights; the music of tuneful orchestra was unheard, and there was naught but the sobs of those who stood beside the couch of death. At that moment almost Mr. Booth was enacting *Macbeth's* death agony at the Broadway, wholly unaware of the passing away of his friend and partner. Mr. Booth survived his friend until 7th June, 1893, when he in turn passed away. Mr. Barrett had been happily married since Sept. 4, 1859 when he led to the altar of a Catholic church in Boston, Mary F. Mayor. From this union came three daughters—Mary Agnes, now the Baroness Von Roder, a resident of Stuttgart, Ger. ; Anna Gertrude, who married Joseph Anderson, brother of Mary Anderson, and Edith M. Barrett, who was married to Marshall Williams, of Boston. Lawrence Barrett was an actor of indomitable purpose, of high aim, of scholarly intellectuality and of courageous enterprise. It has been said, and said most truly, that censure or criticism is easier given by most people than just praise or encouragement. When alive, Lawrence Barrett moved among an army of critics, but he moved like a general among his recruits. Some never saw anything beyond his "mannerisms," and these characteristics of his individuality displeased men even more eccentric than he appeared to them. He may have "stalked" across the stage, but, by the gods, give me the triumphant walk of the elephant among the bulrushes rather than the soughing of an offensive wind. Who ever saw his *Jamie Harebell* that did not sit down and think, and dream of better things than dreamed of before ? Who could with perfunctory interest watch *Jamie's* touching caress of the flowers that so reminded him of the dead loved wife ? The whole was a sweet idyll, where tears were more good than laughter ; where human sorrow often seems more blessed than joy. Lawrence Barrett was loaded with a grand force that was not often shot off at random. There was no end to his intensity and depth of feeling, Perhaps he lacked judicious supervision, but I do not want to dwell on this any more than I would wish to muzzle the joyous energy of the first bird of spring. His *Hamlet* was an interpretation of Shakespeare that was full of flesh and blood and poetry; his *Cassius* was the best we have ever had ; his *Yorick* a piece of noble intensity ; his *Gringnoire* and his *Harebell* exquisite poems.

Subordinating copious declamation to intense feeling, Lawrence Barrett taught the mission of Wordsworth's fine precept.

> *"Keep, ever keep, as if by touch,*
> *Of self-restaining art,*
> *The modest charm of not too much—*
> *Part seen, imagined part."*

THE SEASON OF 1872

was opened by J. W. Buckland on the first day of January, with a French repertoire company, for two weeks. They were followed by the Holman Opera Company on the 15th of January, for a season of three months, the event marking the first of a long line of successes at this theatre. The principals were Sallie, Julia and Alfred D. Holman, together with their parents, George and Harriet Holman, H. C. Peaks, J. Brandisi and W. H. Crane. Harry Lindley made his first appearance in Montreal immediately following the Holman season, and was seen in "The Spitalfields Weavers" during a short season. On 16th April a company of amateurs tendered a benefit testimonial to J. W. Buckland in "Kate O'Sheil, or the Irish Brigand," and "A Morning Call." The cast included Harvey Bawtree, Major Woosley, F. W. Mackay Green, of 61st Regiment, F. Hart, Col. Hamilton Gray, Mrs. Buckland and Lillie Lonsdale. "The Veteran" was also presented 22nd. From this time Mr. Buckland's connection with the theatre ceased. He died 20th November of that year.

The regular season opened 6th May under the management of Ben De Bar. J. W. Wallack, Jun., was the leading man, and in the company were Miss Waugh, Oliver Wren, Alex. D'Orsay Fitzgerald, Ogden, Alexander, John Davis and P. Gleason. The opening attraction was "Henry Dunbar," followed on 8th by "Hamlet." Dominick Murray appeared 13th for one week, and Marietta Ravel opened 20th in "The French Spy."

Barton Hill produced "Rosedale," 24th, and Mr. and Mrs. Harry Watkins came 8th July in "Under Two Flags," "Kathleen Mavourneen," "Pioneers of America," "Hidden Hand," and "School for Scandal." Lillie Eldridge, 15th July, in "Mignon" and "Caste," followed by M. W. Leffingwell in "Hot Coals" and "Cinderella." Oliver D. Byron came, 5th August, for one week, in "Across the Continent," then J. W. Albaugh, 12th, in "Poverty Flats," and standard repertory. Ben De Bar produced "Henry IV.," 19th, and was also seen later in his engagement as "Paul Pry," "Toodles" and "Jack Sheppard." The popular actress, Charlotte Thompson, began for one week, 9th September, in "One Wife," subsequently appearing in "Madeline," and "Rich and Poor." Kate Fisher appeared in "Mazeppa," and "The French Spy," week 23rd, and on 30th J. W. Wallack, Jun., opened in "Hamlet," following with "The Merchant of Venice," "Still Waters Run Deep," "Henry Dunbar," "Don Cæsar de Bazan," and "Macbeth" for the close, 7th October. Hogan, Mudge and Muster came week 9th October, and the prodigy, Blind Tom, made his appearance 28th. The Holman Opera Company began a season 2nd December, which terminated with the year.

MR. AND MRS. GEORGE HOLMAN. Mr. Holman was born in New York city in 1814, and made his *debut* in 1836 at the Chestnut Street Theatre, Philadelphia, Pa., as a ballad singer. His first New York appearance was made at the Park Theatre as a tenor. He subsequently sang with the Cooper Opera Company at Palmo's Opera House, and with Mme. Anna Thillon at Niblo's Garden. He married Mrs. Harriet Phillips, an actress and singer of repute. After the death of his daughter, Sallie, he mourned and fretted, until eventually his grief was the cause of his death. His whole mind was centered in the hope that he would soon lay at rest beside her in Woodlands. George Holman died at his home, London, Canada, 13th October, 1888. In twenty years, his appearances on the stage had been few, confined almost to infrequent performances of "Fra Diavolo." In private life he was a most entertaining companion, a well-read student, fond of rare books and collections of curiosities. Mr. Holman was an enthusiastic fisherman, and devoted a good deal of attention to natural history, of which he was considered an authority. Mrs. Holman was born at Portsmouth, Eng., about 1824, Harriet Jackson being her maiden name. She came to this country in the thirties and married a Mr. Phillips. Her second husband was George Holman, with whom she first appeared in London, Can., in 1840. After playing in various companies they joined the stock at Burton's Chambers Street Theatre, New York city, September 3, 1849. They remained members of that company for seven years. Later they formed the Holman Opera Company, with which they toured the country. On May 23, 1864, they opened Mrs. Holman's Broadway Opera House, formerly Hope Chapel, with the opera "Cinderella," and the operetta of "Mrs. Partington." Toronto then became their headquarters, Mr. Holman leasing the Royal Lyceum of that place. In 1870 they returned to London, Canada, and took hold of the Music Hall, rebuilding the place. It was called the Holman Opera House, and in this place, which was torn down about sixteen years ago, was witnessed their productions of comic and grand opera. After this they toured the States and Canada, and eventually landed again in Toronto, leasing the Royal Opera House for two years. They toured again in 1883. In 1884 they met with great success in a Canadian tour. The last appearance of the Holman Company was in the spring of 1885. Among those who were in the Holman Company were W. H. Crane, Signor Perugini, William Davidge, jun., J. T. Dalton, Johnie O'Connor and Brookhouse Bowler. Mrs. Holman had superb musical talents, and was the instructor in all the productions during their career. The reputation of the company made the Holmans celebrated, especially in the Southern States. Sallie, Julia and Allie, their daughters, were all good singers, the first two named being among the brightest operatic stars the stage then knew. Besides the daughters, two sons were also members of the company, Benjamin and Alfred D. For several years prior to her death Mrs. Holman had lived in retirement. In the winter of 1896 she personally conducted the performance of "Cinderella" in London, by amateurs, and she then directed the entire performance without a printed note. This was her last appearance in public. The active time of her life was one of devotion to both her profession and family. She was a friend in need to many in distress. She loved to have visitors, and those who first learned their accomplishments under her supervision were the most welcome. Some three years ago a complimentary benefit was tendered to her by W. H. Crane in New York. Mrs. Holman died at the old homestead in London, Canada, 21st of May, 1897, leaving one brother, Abraham Jackson, of Detroit, Mich. A brother of her husband is living in London. James T. Dalton, her son-in-law by marriage to Sallie, is a teacher of music, living in London. The only remaining member of the Holman family now alive is Alfred D., who is living in London, Can.

SALLIE HOLMAN, who married J. T. Dalton, died on the 7th of June, 1888.

HARRY LINDLEY was well known throughout the Canadian provinces, having for some thirty-five years been almost altogether associated with Canadian theatrical ventures. The comedian was born at Dublin in 1836. Abandoning his first intention of following the surgical profession, he entered the British service at the age of eighteen. He eventually took to the stage, however, and in 1855 at Newcastle made his initial bow as an actor. Being left some means he retired five years later, but reappeared in 1863 in company with his wife, Florence Webster, with whom he came to America in 1866, first appearing together at Boston. They subsequently came to Canada, where they have appeared in every important town. Mr. Lindley has essayed the managership of theatres in every city, but his success has not been pronounced.

OLIVER DOUD BYRON first produced "Across the Continent," 12th September, 1870, at Albany, N.Y. It had had a dress rehearsal at Toronto a few days before. Byron went to Albany with fifty cents in his pocket, and left with '$600. He had at last found the vehicle to carry him on the road to wealth. Mr. Byron is a native of Baltimore, and has been indentified with the dramatic profession since 1859, and since 1870 has *starred* himself with modest artistic but financial success in the sensational drama. He is married to Kate Rehan (Crehan), sister to Ada Rehan.

CHARLOTTE THOMPSON was an accomplished actress and a good woman. She was born in 1843 at Bradford, Eng., and was the daughter of Lysander Thompson, an actor. She made her first regular appearance in New York as a member of Wallack's company in 1857 as *Phœbe* in "As You Like It," and meeting with much success shortly afterwards began *starring*. Later, she appeared in a drama. tization of Charlotte Bronte's well-known novel of "Jane Eyre," and her success in the title-role was so great that her name ever since has been identified with that play. Miss Thompson married Loraine Rogers, of California, in 1867, and for some years resided on her plantation, near Montgomery, Ala. Previously to the death of Mrs. D. P. Bowers, that excellent actress and Miss Thompson were joint *stars* for a season. Miss Thompson had been in practical retire. ment for five years previously to her death, which occurred 22nd April, 1898.

BLIND TOM. People have been asking: "Is Blind Tom dead ?" He lives in the wooded, sea girt acres of the Highlands of Navesink, where one can see the great ships go down to the sea, and watch the seasons grow and fade in leaf, bud and blossom of glorious woods. He sits in the open air and mimics bird and beast. When weary of nature, he goes back to his life's solitary star that rose in his heaven at his birth. For hours he sits at the piano playing his old'pieces, without technical knowledge of time or note, or harmony, yet remaining apart in his genius from all others—the untutored master of melody. The piano in the hallway is his resting place for hours. For years he has lived his public life over in daily private rehersal, makes his bow, goes to the instrument, plays the old tunes, and jumping up, bows and applauds and "bravoes" heartily. In the pleasant weather he tires of the piano, and sitting in the grounds plays an imaginary pianoforte in the air, imitating perfectly the sound. He bows his thanks to the birds and dogs—and incidentally scares the passer-by out of his senses and adds to the reputation of an already "hoodooed" house. Blind Tom was born at Columbus, Ga., in 1848. He was born in American slavery ; he was one of a numerous tribe who adored him : he was the awe of his masters, the admiration of his equals. The little blind negro was, of course, relieved from all field duty and allowed to hang familiarly about the great house. Here at 5 years of age he showed the wild desire to listen to music, then to vehemently insist upon handling the instrument. His art of imitation reached a perfect stage so rapidly that he was regarded with unabated fear by the negroes. "He was hoodooed, sure," was their verdict. He was brought North by his master, Col. Bethune (killed 1883), in 1860, and first appeared in New York City at the Hope Chapel, 15th January, 1861. In 1863 he went to Europe and on his return travelled all through the United States and Canada. He was the product of the plantation. While never a master of classical music he played to the people: that satisfied majority to whom Wagner is as sounding brass, and Chopin as tinkling cymbals. His melody was essentially sentimental. Every one remembers his performances. The crowded playhouse ; the audience hushed by admiration dashed with superstitious awe, the imbecile negro, robust, wholesome, hopelessly blind, who walked to the piano and played brilliantly the tunes of the people. Wild applause which he poor soul, echoed as he bowed. The manager stepping forward asks pianists to come up and play. One after another complies. Blind Tom listens without interruption. At the final chord he is led to the piano, and striking splendidly into the selection, imitates his predecessors with every shade of feeling reproduced, no delicate minor toning evaded.

MIRON WINSLOW LEFFINGWELL, born 21st March, 1828, died in New York, 10th June, 1879.

George Holman was the manager and lessee of the theatre during the early

SEASON OF 1873,

which opened up on the first day of the year with "The Lottery of Life." Kate Fisher came, 6th January, in " Mazeppa," for the week, followed by Winette Montague and James M. Ward, week of 13th, in "The Winning Hand." On 18th, the Holman Opera Company was heard for one week, and a stock company then held the boards. Among the members of the company were John H. Jack, Lillie Lonsdale, Annie Firmin (Mrs. Jack), Harry Amler, Spencer Pritchard, Allan Halford, Denman Thompson, Joseph Brandin, and George H. Barton, stage manager. The plays were "Under the Gaslight," " Guy Mannering," " Ticket-of-Leave Man," " The Long Strike," " Leah, the Forsaken," " Lancashire Lass," "The Octoroon " and "Uncle Tom's Cabin." The Holman season closed 8th March. Harry Lindley's combination began a season, 24th March, with "The Lady of Lyons," and other standard plays, closing 5th April. In this company the principals were E. H. Brink, Florence Webster (Mrs. Lindley), and Amy Stone. The regular season was then opened under the lesseeship of Mrs. J. W. Buckland, represented by Ben De Bar as manager, and Alexander Fitzgerald as stage manager. The initial bill was Joseph Murphy in Fred Maeder's "Help." He closed 16th April, and was followed by Harry Lindley, Dominick Murray, Joseph Proctor in "Nick of the Woods," 9th June, "Ambition " and "Richelieu." John Thompson, John Collins, the Coleman Sisters and Alex. Fitzgerald were also seen in "The Corsican Brothers," Oliver D. Byron in "Across the Continent," Baker and Farron in "Chris

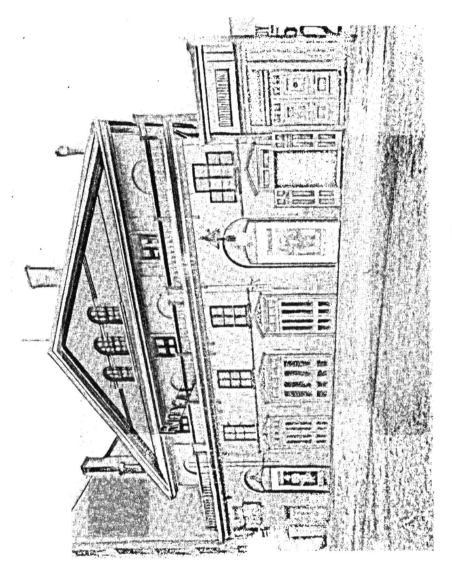

THEATRE ROYAL.

and Lena" (first appearance), and on 21st July the re-appearance of the favorite, John W. Albaugh, in " Watch and Wait," assuming the role of *Bert Bristow*; "Hamlet," "Poverty Flats" and "Macbeth." Ben De Bar was seen in "The Lancashire Lass," 28th, following in other plays. Winette Montague played the first act of "Hamlet," and "The Peep o' Day," 8th Aug., and was followed by Marion Mordaunt in "Hearts are Trumps" and "Family Jars." Ada Gray was also a *debutante* this season, in "The New Magdalen," a dramatization of Wilkie Collins' tale. Then came the Chapman Sisters and Lillie Eldridge in "Alma," "Mignon," etc. The tragedian, E. T. Stetson, came week 22nd September, in "Struck Blind," "Neck and Neck," etc. The season closed, 17th October, with "The Skeleton Hand" and "Black-Eyed Susan," but was subsequently extended by Harry Lindley's combination under Mrs. Buckland's and C. J. Miner & Co.'s management.

The passing of

WINNETTE MONTAGUE, at the Royal, during the season of 1873, deserves some notice, her career having been a most romantic one, and herself a Canadian. having been born in Cornwallis, N.S., February 1, 1851. Her real name was Bigelow. Her beauty and stage fame captivated Arnold W. Taylor, a Boston merchant, who married her when she was sixteen years of age. She subsequently fell in love with Walter Montgomery, a clever tragedian, whom she followed to England, and they were married in September, 1871. The honeymoon had not waned when each discovered that the other had not been free to wed—a stormy interview—a pistol shot, and the tragedian breathed no more. He was of a temperament that made suicide possible. The Montague attended the funeral wearing her bridal wreath, which she scattered in his grave. Subsequently, playing an act of "Hamlet" during her engagement here, it became known that she did so dressed in the dead actor's clothes. She then married the good-looking Irish comedian, James M. Ward, with whom she *starred* for a time. Afterwards there was some scandal about a Jersey City official, who fell a victim to the lures of the merry Montague ; but the end came, and she died in Brooklyn, N.Y., 3rd June, 1877, her beauty a wreck and her means exhausted. She was buried by the charity of the profession.

JAMES M. WARD died at Brighton, England, 10th March, 1892.

E. T. STETSON was born is Mamaronic, 8th October, 1836, and first appeared in public in 1855. He was successful as a leading man, but gave up tragedy for such sensational dramas as "Neck and Neck," "The Olive Branch" and "Struck Blind." His last *starring* engagement here was at the Lyceum Theatre, Beaver Hall Hill, week of the 17th January, 1887. He was in 1897-98 a member of the company playing "Shall We Forgive Her ?"

JOSEPH MURPHY, in the delineation of the rollicking heroes of Irish comedy, has never been surpassed. He began his professional career as a member of a minstrel troope, then took to Irish character parts, meeting with so much success that he began to *star*. His successes are "The Kerry Gow," "Sham Rhue" and "The Donah." His popularity has been the means of his accumulating a large fortune, but he is still before the public. Mr. Murphy was born in Brooklyn in 1839.

ADA GRAY was born in Boston, and first appeared on the stage at the age of fifteen· She soon became leading lady, and in 1863-4 was in the support of Edwin Adams, being the original *Annie Leigh* to his *Enoch Arden*. She supported nearly all the heavy *stars* of the time. She subsequently married Charles S. Watkins, but after two years of retirement returned to the stage, making a feature of "East Lynne" with a certain degree of success financially. Miss Gray, who was the wife of Charles F. Tingay, who has been an actor and a writer by turns, had been in the Home for Incurables at Fordham for seven years Ada Gray had asserted most emphatically that William Jennings Bryan certainly played *Sir Francis Levison* in "East Lynne" with her company in 1884, under the name of William Jennings. Miss Gray did not remember whether he was a good actor or a bad one. She died 27th August, 1902.

Mrs. J. W. Buckland was again lessee of the Theatre Royal during

THE SEASON OF 1874,

and Harry Lindley manager. The stock company was formed, which included, among others, E. H. Brink, Henry Gray, W. A. Greyston, Florence Webster, Carrie E. Martin, Lottie Ward and Zoe Gayton. The season opened early in January, and the first notable performance was on 26th January, when Zoe Gayton was tendered a benefit. Wybert Reeve appeared 2nd February, in "The Woman in White." The next important production was, "The Fireman," 5th March, for Harry Lindley's benefit, on which occasion William McRobie, Alfred Perry and fifty firemen appeared on the stage. William H. Otis made his appearance, 10th March, in *Lord Dundreary*. One of the features of the season was the appearance of Thos. C. King, the English tragedian, 18th March, in "Othello," following with "Hamlet," 19th; "Richelieu," 20th; "Ingomar," 21st; "Corsican Brothers," "William Tell," "The Hunchback of Notre Dame," "Virginius," and "Rob Roy." This engagement was followed by two more of ten days' duration, from the 6th of April, and a return engagement, 16th September to the 26th. He had been imported to New York with that gruesome drama of "The Hunchback of Notre Dame," which had proved to be a dire failure. His success in Montreal was great, and both Lindley and Chris. Atcheson, the veteran door-keeper, record that he always had full houses, his receipts never being less than $400 per night. The preliminary season was followed by the opening of the regular summer season on 4th May, Mrs. Buckland still being lessee. Dominick Murray in "The Gambler's Crime" was the opening bill. Kate Fisher came 1st June in "Mazeppa," and was followed week of 8th by Mr. and Mrs. Charles Walcot in "Pygmalion and Galatea," " Jane Eyre" etc. The well known actress Ada Gray then came in "Article 47" and "Led Astray." Joseph Murphy followed 28th. An interesting event of the season was the first appearance of Aimee, 20th October, in "La Fille de Madame Angot," for one week. The season was a remarkable one in representing a number of new and important stars, and closed as brilliantly as it opened. Neil Warner, who subsequently became so closely allied to Montreal theatricals, making his first bow to a Montreal audience 7th December, in the character of *Sir Giles Overreach*, in Massenger's "A New Way to Pay Old Debts." During his engagement he also appeared in "Hamlet," "Othello," "Richelieu" and "Macbeth," and his success was almost parallel to that of Thos. C. King. The season closed 19th December with "The Ticket of Leave Man."

THOMAS C. KING was the last of the old-time English tragedians, if we except James R. Anderson. He was born at Cheltenham, Eng., in 1823, and made his first professional appearance at the Theatre Royal, Birmingham. He afterwards joined the "York Theatrical Circuit," and played numerous roles in the Shakesperean and legitimate drama at York, Leeds and Hull. He first came prominently before the public at the Edinburgh Theatre, appearing principally in Shakespearean characters. It was there that his abilities attracted the attention of Charles Kean, who induced him to accept a three years' management at the Princess Theatre, London, where he made his *debut* 22nd July, 1857, as *Bassanio* to Kean's *Shylock*. He became extremely popular, and Kean's jealousy was at last revealed in the few and minor parts which he gave the young actor. King complained that it was hardly fair to keep him in the background after a successful *debut*, and Kean, thinking to crush the young actor by giving him a part which he believed was beyond his power, took him for *Iago* to his *Othello*. The result was that the old *star* was eclipsed by the new one. The London papers gave King the highest praise, while they treated Kean rather coldly. Then the latter resolved to keep' King in the shade, and for nearly a year the young actor was heard no more at the Princess Theatre. At the end of two years King, therefore, terminated his engagement at the Princess. He then went upon a *starring* tour in the principal theatres through the provinces. At Dublin he became a great favorite and the town went wild over his performances in "Hamlet," "Othello," ' Macbeth," "Merchant of Venice," "Richelieu," etc., which attracted large and appreciative audiences. The students nicknamed him "King Tom the Grand," and the gallery gods hailed him as the King they called their own. In 1868 King accepted an engagement from F. B. Chatterton, and in March in the year following again made his appearance on the Metropolitan stage at Drury Lane Theatre as *Richelieu*. During this engagement he also appeared as *Hamlet*, and subsequently alternated *Othello* and *Iago* with Charles Dillon. Later he appeared as *Macbeth*. During the season of 1870, at the same theatre, he played with much success the following parts, among others : *William Tell* and *Julian St. Pierre* in "The Wife," both pieces of James S. Knowles; and *Varney* on the occasion of the first performance on 24th Sept., 1870, of "Amy Robsart." He made his New York appearance in the character of *Quasimardo* in Hugo's "Hunchback of Notre Dame," in 1874. He was supported by a wretched company. The gruesome role which he assumed failed to please, and he was awaiting his salary and developments when he was engaged by Manager Lindley for a Montreal engagement, making his *debut* in this city 18th March, 1874, in *Othello*. He appeared in *Othello* six times, *Hamlet* six times, *Richelieu* eight times, *Richard III.*—thrice, and other plays in the same proportion. His success was great and on one occasion received the unusual compliment of a call in the middle of a scene in "Othello." His receipts during the engagement were never less than four hundred dollars nightly, and this success followed him for a year in every city in Canada. He had no idea of the value of money. At the Queens Hotel at Toronto his room did not suit his ideas, so the clerk remarked in tones of sarcasm, "Perhaps you would like the Dufferin *suite* ?" "Exactly what I want," the tragedian replied, and he got it. His temper was equable, and in stage business he would cover up any errors, excepting once when the *Lady Macbeth*, for whom he was looking on one side, entered the other. He glared for a moment, and then in deepest tones exclaimed. "Never more enter the rear portal !" Harry Lindley confesses that he quite disconcerted the actor at Kingston in a production of "Hamlet." It was warm and so was *Polonius* (Lindley) and when the cue came for the old courtier to go on, be left his beard in the dressing-room. It was the scene in the second act, after the player's long speech, when *Polonius* says, "This is too long." *Hamlet :* "It shall to the barber's with your beard," but as his eye caught sight of a smooth-faced *Polonius,* the actor lost his princely dignity and gasped, "Great Ceasar l he hasn't a beard on." His great liberality, his love for society and trust in his fellow men swallowed his immense earnings, and when he returned to England he did not carry much away with him. From this time his professional career practically closed, King losing his health and remaining in comparative obscurity in his native country, until his death, which occurred at King's Heath, Birmingham, 21st Oct, 1893. Mr. King possessed a tall and commanding figure, graceful and easy movements, an intelligent face, and a full-toned sonorous voice.

WILLIAM H. OTIS had a collection of thirty pairs of trousers, each of which were known by such cognomens as "In the Gloaming," "Shimmer in the Morning," "Moonlight on the Lake," etc. It was said that he invariably said a short prayer at the wings on making his first appearance.

ZOE GAYTON, whose real name is Zoreka Gazonia Laperero, is a Spaniard, and was born at Madrid in 1854. She first went on the stage in 1871. She has become more celebrated as a pedestrian than as an actress, having won world-wide celebrity by accomplishing the monotonous feat of walking all the way from San Francisco to New York for a wager at $12,000 covering 3,395 miles from 27th August, 1890, to 27th March, 1891.

Marie Aimee, must have been born for *opera bouffe.* She had the eye for it, the mouth for it, and the dash and *abandon.* One would have thought that she had never memorized her part, but that it was an improvisation, she was so natural. Her acting was in perfect sympathy with the spirit of the work she illustrated. She was undoubtedly the most brilliant soubrette ever seen in this country.

MARIE AIMEE (right name Frochon) was born in Algeria in 1852. She began to study music at an early age, and made her *debut* in 1866, at Rio Janeiro, S.A. She quickly gained a popularity, and was scarcely sixteen when the impressario Lindall, struck with the beauty of her voice and her astonishing execution, engaged her to create the role *Fliorella* in "Les Brigands." She performed in various countries and possessed souvenirs from the chief courts of Europe. During the Franco-Prussiau war she visited America, with a French opera bouffe troupe. She opened December 21, 1870, at the Grand Opera House, New York, and at once secured one of her greatest successes. After a tour of this country she returned to France. She made six more tours to America. Having accumulated quite a fortune, she finally determined to enter the managerial field, and leased the opera house in the Arcade, Brussels, as well as one

12

at Rouen, Fr. She expended a large sum of money in renovating
those houses, and in Brussels produced several operas for the first
time on the stage. "The Royal Middy" was the most successful,
but it took only two seasons for Aimee to lose over $85,000. She
died in Paris, France, 2nd October, 1887. The funeral of Mlle.
Aimee showed how very few friends an actress can count upon.
In spite of the fact that her will gave a very large amount to an
orphan asylum for the children of artists, and her well-known generosity during her active dramatic life, very few people found leisure
to go to the small church, and yet during the French war Aimee
sent from America 5,000 francs to these very comrades.

HENRY NEIL WARNER was born at Bury St. Edmonds, England, 5th April, 1831. He came of a family of clergymen, and his
right name is William Burton Lockwood. His mother died during
his earliest infancy and he was brought up by his aunt, the mother of
"Ouida." He went on the stage against the wishes of his relatives,
first at Brighton, Sussex, under Henry Farren's management in 1852.
His tastes and ambition were directed to the higher walks of the
drama, and being well qualified to undertake heavy work, in possessing a magnificent physique, a powerful voice, together with intelligence of a high order, he made rapid strides in his profession. In 1854
he went to Australia, where his success was only second to that of G.
V. Brooke. Returning to England he made his metropolitan *debut* in
May, 1865, at Sadlers Wells Theatre in his greatest role—*Othello*. In
an official list of famous London *debuts* the date of his first appearance
is given as 6th March, 1865, as *Hamlet* at the Marylebone Theatre,
but Mr. Warner does not corroborate this statement. He came
to America in 1869, making his *debut* at the old New York Theatre,
Broadway, 20th February, as   *Othello* to the *Iago* of McKean Buchanan.
When Palmer & Jarrett produced their great revival of "Richard III.,"
at Niblo's Garden, New York, 10th April, 1871, Warner was engaged
to appear as *Richmond* to the *Gloster* of James Bennett, the English
tragedian, who had been specially imported at a large salary. The
support included Milnes Levick, Edmund K. Collier, Mme. Ponisi
and Louise Hawthorne. The tragedy was mounted in a manner altogether unprecedented in New York, but at the end of the first week
Bennett was found to be so incompetent that Warner was substituted
in his stead, and the piece enjoyed a three weeks' run. After a short
starring tour through the country, Warner appeared at the Bowery
Theatre, November 4, in *Giles Overreach,* following in "Macbeth,"
"The Corsican Brothers," "The Honeymoon," "The Lady of Lyons,"
"The Iron Chest," and "Richard III." Mr. Warner married Belle
Chippendale, 16th March, 1874. Miss Chippendale is the daughter of
the veteran Frederick Chippendale, and the grand-daughter of the
famous comedian, the late Wm. H. Chippendale for many years a
member of Henry Irving's company. Mr. Warner made his Mont-

NEIL WARNER.

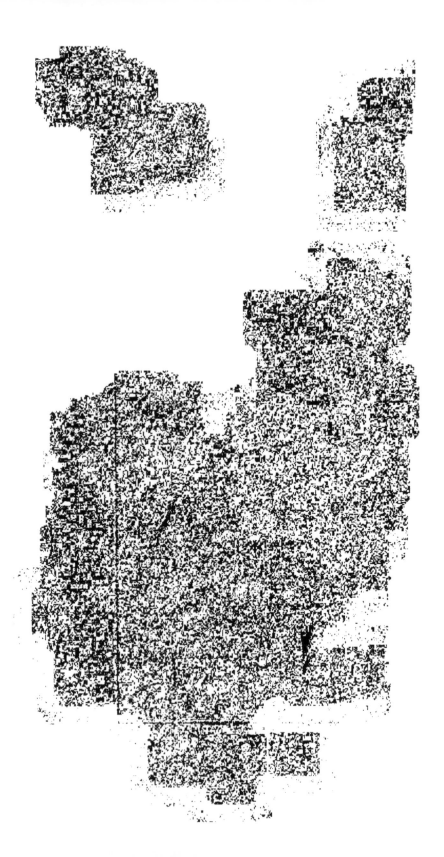

real *debut* 7th December, 1874, as *Sir Giles* at the Theatre Royal, and for the following fifteen years was a citizen of this city. He and his wife became great favorites here, and in later years opened a school of elocution, as well as directing innumerable amateur performances. In 1899 he went West at the head of a company in Shakespearean productions; but age had impaired his once robust constitution, and he returned after a year's absence. He then held the professorship of elocution at the High School for one year. His last professional appearance on the stage here was at the Academy of Music, 3rd October, 1891, when he played *Macbeth* to the *Lady Macbeth* of Modjeska, and his farewell appearance in Montreal was 19th September, 1892, when he appeared at the Windsor Hall in "Othello," supported by amateurs, including F. O. Hopkins. W. A. Tremayne, Fred A. Thomson and Mrs. Warner. Since that time he has been touring through the United States with various combinations. Two daughters, Affie and "Jack" (Lenore Lockwood), have also chosen stage life, and Mrs. Warner is still an active member of the profession.

Mr. Warner's great roles were *Sir Giles, Macbeth, Othello,* and *Shylock,* and had he been at all ambitious could have been a great actor.

"15th June 1901. Neil Warner has passed into his rest!" Such is the message that comes to me from the new to the old world. Although in the hurry and turmoil of theatrical affairs, the name of Neil Warner is well nigh forgotten by the public, it was not much more than a score of years ago that he had the distinction of being one of the foremost Shakespearean tragedians of the English speaking stage. He was a man of sound education, of thorough training in his art, and in his prime he was unusually handsome and of noble bearing. Six months ago I last held in mine the hands of Neil Warner, and for the last time looked upon his venerable and noble countenance, on the eve of my drifting further from the moorings of my youth. He suffered greatly, yet patiently, and in the full faculty of his old-time courtliness of thought as of manner. In his defiance of the inexorable malady, he leaned upon the prop of a noble woman's devotion, that never wearied—never faltered—as he welcomed the gathering of the shadows which lie beyond the patriarchal years. He was waiting for the end. To him the paling twilight came as sweet incense to break into the better life beyond.

THE 1875 SEASON

Mrs. Buckland, as lessee, and Harry Lindley, as manager, opened on 1st Jan., with Kate Mayhew, of the Union Square Theatre, New York, in "Valerie." The celebrated Hungarian artist, Ilma di Murska, appeared 11th and 12th. and on 19th G. M. Ciprico produced Dumas' play of

"Edmund Kean," followed by the engagement of Thos.
C. King in eleven representations from 25th January
to 5th February. Florence Webster was seen in "An
Unequal Match," 6th; "The Dead Heart" was given
8th; and the Holman Opera Company then held the
boards in comic opera from 9th to 20th. The Kiralfy
Sisters in "The Deluge," week of 22nd, followed by Julia Sea-
mon. A notable *debut* occurred 8th March, Edwin F. Thorne
appearing in "Don Cæsar de Bazan," "Jibbenainosay," "Damon and Pythias," etc. Frank Mordaunt came, week of 15th,
in "The Trail of the Serpent," Robert Butler's "Humpty-
Dumpty," week of 22nd, and O. D. Byron, week of 28th, in
"The Orange Girl," "Ben McCullough," "Donald Mackay,"
etc. Tom Hurst, a well-known local artist, was tendered a
benefit performance, 5th April, in "Masks and Faces," followed by the first appearance of the Worrell Sisters and
Sam B. Villa in burlesque, etc., preceding the first appearance here of the great *prima donna*, Clara Louise Kellogg,
whose subsequent appearances here became frequent. On
26th April, a trio of clever artists, Sara Jewett, Louis
James and D. H. Harkins, headed Daly's Company in
" A Big Bonanza," which proved so successful during
the week that the company extended its engagement one
night more in "Monsieur Alphonse." This was the first appearance here of Miss Jewett and Mr. James. N. C. Forrester, supported by his own company, in productions of "The
Two Orphans," and "Led Astray," played a short engagement
following the Daly Company, and was in turn followed by
James S. Maffitt's "Flick and Flock" Pantomime Company,
Maffit being tendered a benefit 14th May. The celebrated
English comedian, John L. Toole, made his first appearance
here, 17th May week, supported by Miss Johnstone and W.
Herbert, in "Off the Line," "The Weaver," and "Ici on Parle
Francais." Emily Soldene's English Opera Company ap-
peared week of 24th, and, on 31st May, Jarrett & Palmer's
famous "Black Crook" was first seen in Montreal. "The
Black Crook" was first produced at Niblo's Gardens, New
York, on Sept. 12, 1866. The text was written by Chas. M.
Barras. The music was composed by Thomas Baker. The
principal dancers were Marie Bonfanti, Rita Sangalli, Betty
Rigl and Rose Delval. "The Black Crook" on its original
production ran till January 4, 1868. It has frequently been

revived since then. John L. Toole played a return engagement, 14th June, giving three farewell performances.

The closest to Toole's in point of interest during the season was the engagement of the romantic tragedian, Charles A. Fechter, 21st June. He was supported by Frank C. Bangs, H. A. Langdon, Vining Bowers and Lizzie Prince (Mrs. Fechter?), all of whom were specially engaged to support the *star*. He opened in "Ruy Blas," following in "The Lady of Lyons," 22nd; "No Thoroughfare," 23rd; "Hamlet," 28th; "Don Cæsar," 29th; "Hamlet," 30th and 31st. On 5th July he appeared at the Mechanics' Hall for a benefit and farewell appearance, owing to a misunderstanding with Manager Lindley of the Theatre Royal, the tragedian having been found at fault. Mr. Fechter did not leave a favorable impression here with the management, and his engagement was not remunerative. His experience at Toronto was much the same, the engagement terminating in a deplorable *fiasco*. On one occasion "Hamlet" was billed, and a small audience assembled, but the support refused to appear. The curtain rose before the Castle of Elsinore, and *Bernardo* entered with the usual interrogation, "Who's there?" expecting to hear the cue followed up by the actor who played *Francisco*, but the latter was one of the dissatisfied, and could not be seen. The somewhat discomfited *Bernardo* repeated his line, and still no reply. Losing patience, the actor roared out for the third time, "Who's there?" when a voice was heard from the gallery, "Darned if I know; go on with the play." The curtain was rung down.

Daly's Company appeared 12th July for week, when the season closed until 11th August, when the theatre was re-opened by Neil Warner in "Money," supported by E. Randor. G. L. Greenwood, B. Ryan, H. Mitchell, W. Todd, Harry Lindley, Belle Chippendale (Mrs. Warner), Florence Webster and Mrs. W. Ayling. During his engagement, "Time and the Hour," "Loan of a Lover" and "Rob Roy" were produced. J. K. Keane was seen in "Rip Van Winkle," week of 16th. After another closing, Howard Clifton, the English and Scotch character singer, held the board three nights from 25th October, and Blind Tom made his appearance 15th, 16th and 17th November. The opening of the Academy of Music, on 15th November of this year, naturally transferred most of the public attention to the new house, and the annals of the Royal have now arrived at a much less interesting period in its history. With the close of the 1875 season, Mrs. Buckland's connection with the old theatre also closed.

We find George Holman lessee and manager of the house during the first part of

THE 1876 SEASON,

which began, 24th January, with the Holman Opera Company. On 25th May, E. A. Sothern made his Montreal *debut*, appearing in his great character of *Lord Dundreary*. He played the character over 1,600 times altogether.

GEORGE M. CIPRICO who made his *debut* 5th Nov., 1867, as *Hamlet*, at the Metropolitan Theatre, San Francisco, had but a short career as a *star*. He died 14th April, 1895.

EDWIN FORREST THORNE, son of Chas. R. Thorne, sen., and Maria Ann Mestayer, was born at New York in 1845 ; died 4th May, 1897. His first appearance was made as a child in San Francisco with his parents as *Eva* in "Uncle Tom's Cabin." His formal *debut* was made in the Winter Garden, in New York City, on November 20, 1860, when he played with Edwin Booth· He used the name of Mr. Edwin during this period of his stage career. In 1863 he returned to San Francisco, where he played for one season in the Metropolitan Theatre. As a member of his father's company, he then went on a tour to China, Japan and India. The season of 1869 he was in Quincy, Ill. The following year he played in the company at the Royal Opera House, Toronto. He was a member of stock companies in Washington, New Orleans, Philadelphia and Chicago at various times, and he travelled with E. L. Davenport. Early in the eighties he *starred* for several seasons in the English melodrama, "The Black Flag," by Henry Pettit. This play netted him a small fortune, which he subsequently lost in private speculations. Of late years he had been holding a clerkship in the postal service in New York City· His brother, Charles R. Thorne, jun., who died 10th February, 1883, aged 34, was considered to be the best leading man of his time.

FRANK MORDAUNT was born at Burlington, Vt., in 1841. He joined the Brougham Association in New York in 1853, and six years later made his regular professional appearance in that city. He has since been prominently before the public.

CLARA LOUISE KELLOGG STRAKOSCH was born of New England parents at Sumpterville, S. C., in 1842, but her parents went to New York in her early years. It is said that "she could sing before she could talk," so that her natural advantages were large and varied. She made her *debut* at New York in 1861, as *Gilda* in "Rigoletto." She appeared at London in 1867. She was gifted with a musical apprehension which even in infancy was looked upon as something marvellous. Her career has been marked by long series of distinct successes, but the tones of her once wonderful voice do not appear to have had the staying powers so remarkable in a few other song-birds, and she now appears but seldom in public. In November, 1887, she was married to Carl Strakosch, her manager.

LOUIS JAMES, one of the most versatile actors on the contemporary stage, was born at Fremont, Ill., in 1842. He began playing at Louiseville, Ky., in 1863, as a member of Macauley's Stock Company. He was for six years at Mrs. John Drew's Arch Street Theatre, Philadelphia, and in 1872 joined Daly's company, with which organization he remained until the end of the early season of 1875, after which he became leading man at McViker's Theatre, Chicago, and subsequently at Maguire's at San Francisco. From 1881 to 1886 he was leading man to Lawrence Barrett, after which he began an independent *starring* career in the legitimate, accompanied by Marie Wainwright whom he had wedded in 1879, and who had also been leading lady in their previous five years' engagement in support of Mr. Barrett. The talented couple visited Montreal, opening 18th November, 1886, at the Academy of Music in "Virginius," and appeared in three other representations. In 1889 Mr. and Mrs. James *starred* separately, and subsequently also separated as man and wife. Mr. James was married to Alphie Hendricks in 1892, and was for a few seasons joint *star* with Frederick Barham Warde, touring chiefly in the South and West, where he is a great favorite. Mr. James opened the new Winnipeg Theatre, 6th-9th September, 1897, in "Spartacus," and other classical plays. Mr. James ranks well forward in the first grade of the tragic walks, and his *Virginius*, *Spartacus* and *Othello* are performances difficult to improve on. He is also known to be as ardent a practical joker as he is a capable tragedian. Mr. James, during 1899, toured with Chas. B. Hanford and Katherine Kidder as associates, and recently as first *star* with Madame Modjeska.

JOHN LAWRENCE TOOLE was born at St. Mary Axe, London, Eng., March 12, 1832, and was the second son of the late John Toole who held the post of Civic Toastmaster in London for twenty-five years. He was educated at the City of London School, and at the expiration of his term there took a position in a wine merchant's office. His inclinations led him to abandon commercial life very early, for before he was of age he entered the dramatic profession. His first engagement was with Charles Dillon's company at the Queen's Theatre, Dublin, afterwards travelling to Belfast, Edinburgh, Glasgow and elsewhere. A notable event in Mr. Toole's career was his American tour in 1874-75. On his return from the United States, Mr. Toole reappeared at the London Gaiety, November 8, 1875. He continued playing there and elsewhere in London and the Provinces until November, 1879, when he took the management of what was then known as the Folly Theatre, but after his reconstruction was called Toole's Theatre. His rich and genial humor, never marred with any approach of vulgarity, made him, beyond question, the first English comedian of the day. His serious impersonations have ever been marked with pathetic intensity and tragic power, his admirers averring that, had he so wished, he could have attained conspicuous prominence as a tragedian. In private life his high qualities of heart and head, and his genial and buoyant disposition raised up for him a host of personal friends, among them many persons of high rank and position and names that are great in art and literature.

SARA JEWETT was the daughter of James A. Jewett, and was born in Buffalo. Few actresses were more popular, few names are better remembered by the elder generations of theatre-goers than that of Sara Jewett. Her beauty alone would have won her way on the stage, but aside from her mere physical grace, she had for her audiences the added charm of a refined and accomplished woman. Miss Jewett was a niece of Dr. Austin Flint, sen., and her family was highly connected in Boston. Her wish to become an actress was strongly opposed by her friends, and something of sensation was caused by her first appearance on the professional stage in autumn of 1872, in Bronson Howard's "Diamonds," with Mr. Augustin Daly's company, then at the old Fifth Avenue Theatre, in 24th Street. Her advancement was rapid, and when Miss Clara Morris suddenly resigned the position of leading lady, Miss Jewett was selected to replace her. Illness caused by over-work compelled her temporary retirement from the stage, and when she recovered she was engaged by Mr. A. M. Palmer for the Union Square company. She began her career there in 1879. During her stay at the Union Square, she created many roles. Her last appearance there was 1885. "All star" casts and triple star combinations were not as common fifteen years ago as they are now, and the announcement of the alliance formed by Sara Jewett and Geo. Edgar to make Shakespearean productions was a nine days' wonder in 1886, as many of the theatre-goers of the present day will remember. Curious that the deaths of these two once famous players should occur so close together. George Edgar died two days before. When she formed that alliance with Mr. Edgar, Miss Jewett was one of the most popular actresses on the stage. She had just closed a long and successful engagement as leading lady of the old Union Square Company, and was accounted a wealthy woman, with perhaps the best part of her career before her. But the alliance proved a failure and the actress lost nearly all her fortune in the venture. Other losses came and illness, too, and the brilliant promises for her future were never fulfilled. She passed away at Cambridge, Mass., 27th Feb., 1899, aged 54.

THE WORRELL SISTERS, Sophia, Irene, Jennie and Rosita, were daughters of William Worrell, one of the best known circus men in this country, who died 7th August, 1897. Their mother was the daughter of Emanuel and Sophia Judah, the former having been seen on the Montreal stage in 1824-25. The girls first appeared as dancers in California, and afterwards visited Australia, in which county their father was the first exhibitor of a circus. Returning to America, they came east in 1866. They made their first appearance before the footlights in America at a time when *stars* of the vaudeville were few. From the first night they became famous. Gay New York raved over their beauty. Night after night they entertained and captivated. The elder generation to-day remembers the golden tresses, the big sparkling blue eyes, the lithe and stately forms of the sisters. And to this generation Jennie was, by a few points, the most beautiful. By and by the three sisters were married. Sophie, the eldest, born (1848), became the wife of George S. Knight, the comedian. She helped him to achieve his brilliant successes, and yet in subsequent years he went to pieces. Jennie was married to a wealthy New York gambler and left the stage. The couple separated. Jennie returned to the stage, and her life, marred by her unhappy marriage, became one of pitiable dissipations. Irene was the wife of a Brooklyn merchant, but their love was short-lived, and they procured a divorce. In the flush of success the sisters once owned a theatre, where were presented brilliant spectacular pieces, which gave opportunities to the girls to display their own physical charms. Then, as their suns went down, the sisters drifted apart. A few years ago Jennie and Irene opened a vaudeville house at Coney Island. This they lost, and not long afterwards Irene died under sad circumstances; Jennie lingered at Coney Island. Occasionaly she would have an engagement in the music halls. The blonde tresses were tangled, the blue eyes had lost their lustre, the flush and beauty of youth were gone. In the midst of the salt marshes at Coney Island Jennie Worrell fought fire and death, and lost. She sank upon that field of fire, and her body, charred by the fierce flames, her hair gone, her face burned almost beyond recognition, was picked up and removed to the Hospital, where she died, 11th Aug., 1899.

FRANK C. BANGS was born in Virginia in October, 1837, and first studied law, but in Nov., 1852, he went on the stage, making his first appearance at the old National Theatre, Washington, D.C. He made successful studies, and in time became a capable tragedian. While playing in support of Edwin Booth, Mr. Bangs' *Antony* was conceded to be a masterpiece of dramatic effort. He was married tc Le Grove Singer, 4th June. 1883, from whom he was shortly after-wards divorced. In 1897 Mr. Bangs appeared as *James Ralston* in "Jim the Penman" and is at present playing in "The Christian·"

EDWARD ASKEW SOTHERN'S right name was Douglas Stewart. He was born in Liverpool in 1830, and was intended by his parents for the church, but about 1851 went on the stage and made his first appearance at the Boston National Theatre as *Dr. Pangloss* in "The Heir at Law." After a very up-hill struggle he succeeded in gaining a footing at Laura Keene's Theatre, New York, and in 1858 appeared in the character of *Lord Dundreary* in Tom Taylor's "Our American Cousin." This was originally one of the subordinate parts in the piece, but it was gradually elaborated by Mr. Sothern until he became one of the most celebrated creations of the century, full of fine and undemonstrative humor. He appeared in it for more than eleven hundred times in the United States, and then repeated the performance for four hundred and ninety-six nights at the Haymarket In 1864 he created the second great part with which his name is associated, *David Garrick*, in T. W. Robertson's adaptation from the French play, "Gullivar." He reappeared in England in 1874, but achieved no permanent success in any of the plays with which he was connected. In 1879 he returned to America. He declared that he was indebted for whatever position he attained in his profession to the Americans. On his last visit to America he appeared as *Fitzaltamont* in "The Crushed Tragedian·" and made a fair success. He returned to England in 1881 in broken health, and died in the same year. Three sons adopted the dramatic profession, Edward Lytton Sothern, Sam and Edward H· Sothern. The first mentioned died 11th March, 1887. E· H. Sothern, has met with some success as a *star* in romantic roles. Sam Sothern is a member of his company.

JAMES K. KEANE, born in Philadelphia in 1852, died 31st May, 1899. His first stage appearance was at the Walnut Street Theatre, with Lotta. He married Alice Roberts in 1883. For a number of years Mr. Keane was prominently featured in "Hazel Kirke," "Around the World in Eighty Days" and many other well-known plays acting principally with stock companies.

CHARLES ALBERT FECHTER, was born in London, 23rd October, 1824. He was of French parentage, although his father was descended from German stock. In 1836 the family returned to Paris, and Fechter, who was being brought up as a sculptor, soon developed such high talents for the stage that he secured engagements at some of the leading theatres, especially the vaudeville. In 1846 he visited Berlin, and two years later made his first appearance at London, together with a French company engaged at the St James Theatre. After rising to the highest position in his profession in Paris,

CHARLES ALBERT FECHTER.

he visited England again in 1860, acting at the Princess, where he astonished the critics by his impersonation of *Hamlet*. During the years that followed he frequently appeared at London, and in 1870 undertook a very successful professional tour of the United States, first appearing on the American stage at Niblo's Garden, 10th January, 1870, in "Ruy Blas," supported by Carlotta Leclercq. He there failed to satisfy his audiences. He assumed the management of the Globe Theatre, Boston, Sept 12, 1870, and retired from that management Jan. 14, 1871. Returning to Europe, on March 2, 1872, he appeared at the Adelphi Theatre, London, as *Ruy Blas*. He returned to New York in September. During the summer of 1871, Duncan and Sherman advanced Mr. Fechter a large sum of money to build the Lyceum Theatre, New York. He invested some $50,000 of his own money in the enterprise. His reckless expenditure caused a breach between Duncan, Sherman & Co., and himself, and they took the theatre from him by legal process of law before he opened. Consequently, what money he had invested of his own and borrowed from Carlotta Leclercq was lost. On April 28, 1873, Fechter resumed the practice of his profession by opening at the Grand Opera House, New York. His last engagement was at the Broadway Theatre (now Daly's), commencing Dec. 17, 1877, as *Edmond Dantes* in "Monte Cristo." He closed Jan. 26, 1878, impersonating *Ruy Blas*. His last engagement on any stage was to have commenced April 7, at the Howard Athenaeum, Boston, but he was suffering from a gastric attack. He appeared before the curtain, stated the cause of his illness, and dismissed the audience. He appeared 8th, as *Legardere* in "The Duke's Motto," and continued for the week. He was again too ill to act on 14th, but re-appeared 15th, in "Black and White" which ran until the close of the engagement, 19th, when he made his last appearance on any stage. Mr. Fechter went through the round of characters in which the reputation of Frederick Lemaitre had been achieved. Fechter had many gifts in common with Lemaitre, and no man on the English stage approached nearer to his level. In Shakespearean plays, certain passions were strikingly represented. In several cities the press wantonly and wickedly abused him. At Cincinnati, especially, they pelted him with the dirty gravel of the lowest Billingsgate. The result of this was that managers feared to give him again the terms he required, and he would not abate a jot. He refused to accept from Mr. Booth an engagement at the same terms given to Joseph Jefferson, the best drawing and best paying *star* in the world. He achieved triumphs in Paris, Berlin, London and New York in three languages. In the first-named city he was one of the foremost *jeunes premieres*, and created the leading male part in the well-known "Dame aux Camelias." In England his presence was hailed with great delight, the critics wrote rapturously of his finished natural style ; his name was heard at every dinner table, and the theatre was nightly crowded by his

thronging worshippers. The news that he was about to play
Hamlet after his success in *Ruy Blas* created a wonderful degree
of excitement, rumors sprang up in great clouds and travelled all
over the land, it was to be such a *Hamlet* as the English stage had
never seen; and when he did appear, oh ! what learning and research
did the historic wise bestow in commendation of his appearance in
a flaxen wig! Such was the rage for novelty that no one saw how
utterly incongruous suggestions of barbarous times were with character and surroundings of that polished gentleman, *Hamlet*. as Shakespeare created him. Despite his foreign accent, every word was clearly
and distinctly heard, and the sound he gave each blended to heighten
the finished effect of an entire speech with a subtlety of combination
artistic in the highest degree. No actor ever suited the action to the
word with more complete harmony. In melodrama Mr. Fechter
was decidedly at home. His *Ruy Blas* was a piece of acting intensely
romantic and burlesque. In the "Corsican Brothers" he strongly
defined the contrasting personal character of the twins with remarkable realistic skill, never confusing their individuality. In tragedy
Mr. Fechter's triumphs were less notable. His *Othello* was disfigured
by the introduction of ingenious little tricks and devices intended to
startle or surprise, which were altogether destructive of that calm
simplicity and grandeur of action which is characteristic of our great
poet's work. It lacked dignity, breadth and intellectual refinement.
There was much in it that was original in conception and effect,
many of the commonly recognized points received fresh force and
new meanings from delicate suggestiveness of sounds and gestures ;
he rendered the inner depths of feelings with great intensity, and gave
the more tender and pathetic phases of the part with a show of im-
pulse and emotion which was very touching. But as a whole his tragic
acting never rose to the poetic grandeur of Shakespeare's wonderful
creations. In *Hamlet* he came nearer to the lofty standard of a truly
great actor, clearing away much of that obscurity with which heavy
English tradition-holding tragedians had invested the character
simplifying some of the business in important scenes, and giving more
powerful coloring to *Hamlet's* awful reverence for his father's memory,
the deeply affectionate nature of his grief for him, and the irrepressible
tenderness and intensity of his love for *Ophelia*. Loving the country
ardently, he at last looked upon his artistic career chiefly as a means
of improving and enjoying his country home at Richland Centre. Pa.,
two hours' ride from Philadelphia. He retired there to read, study,
smoke and trace his triumphs over again in the scrap-books and
albums containing relics of his palmy days. Of all these relics those
pertaining to his long and intimate friendship with the late Charles
Dickens were most valued. There he passed a great deal of his time,
and there he died, a very poor man, 4th August, 1879. His remains lie

ın Mount Vernon Cemetery, Philadelphia, beneath a handsome stone, on which is a marble bust of the actor. On the base of the mcnument is the inscription :—

Genius hath taken its flight to God.

THE SEASON OF 1877

was also a short one, the Holmans opening up a season of comic opera in "Girofle-Girofla," 26th June, under the leadership and management of George Holman. The house was practically closed from the end of the opera season until 17th December, when Marie Aimee was advertised to make her last appearance before retiring from the stage. George Holman was again lessee, and Lucien Barnes manager, of the theatre during the first part of

THE 1878 SEASON,

which was a most important one in several respects to that of the preceding season. Kate Fisher was the first attraction, 4th January, in "Mazeppa," for the week, followed by the Holman Opera Company until 26th. M. A. Dawson assumed the lesseeship 28th January, opening with Robert Butler's Jack and Jill Pantomime Company. The Georgia Minstrels came week of 7th February, followed by Haverley's, 15th. The house then passed into the hands of Theresa Newcomb, who opened a season of French drama, 26th February, in "Marie Jaune." During the two weeks, "Le Doight de Dieu," and "La Fille du Paysan," were produced. "The Fatal Glass" was given 13th April, and on 22nd "La Dame Blanche," an opera, was staged, with Marietta Hassan in the cast. Happy Carl Wagner's Minstrels came 27th April. Texas Jack held the boards week of 13th May, followed, 20th, by Frank Mayo in "Davy Crockett." May Fiske's "Blondes" were seen for three nights from 27th May. During the month of June a French company produced a number of standard French plays, after which the house was entirely overhauled and renovated. Its lease passed into the hands of O'Brien & West, who inaugurated their season, 16th September, with the Foy Sisters' Specialty Combination. This class of attraction was catered to the public all through the fall.

KATE FISHER first appeared as a *danseuse* in New York, 6th October, 1852. She was born in Boston, Mass., 16th April, 1840. Her name has always been associated with such productions as "Mazeppa," "Cataract of the Ganges," etc. Her name in private life is Mrs. Gaines Clark.

FRANK MAYO (MAGUIRE), who died 8th June, 1896, *en route* from Denver to Omaha, was a strong actor of the sensational school, He was born in Boston, Mass., 19th April, 1839, and first appeared on the stage at the American Theatre, San Francisco, in 1856. He first played "Davy Crockett," in 1872, at Rochester, N. Y., after having had a Shakespearean flight, which 'resulted unsatisfactorily. His son, Edwin F. Mayo, also toured the country with the piece. In former years Mr. Mayo had enjoyed much prosperity, and was possessor of an elegant property at Canton, Pa., which he called "Crockett Lodge." The adjoining estates were owned by E. L. Davenport and Charles Fechter. Frank Mayo had not then entertained the ambitions which swamped him. He had not written "Nordeck"—had not formulated the notion that he could *star* in legitimate roles with success. He was then content to play honest *Davy Crockett* and big-hearted *Tom Badger.* He booked at the best and biggest theatres. What a royal princely, good fellow Frank Mayo was ! The summer sun never set upon a happier or more independent household that the Mayos'. Then came the fatal aspiration of the artistic nature of Frank Mayo. He had played "Davy Crockett" and "The Streets of New York" over three thousand times, and was tired of them. He knew his dramatic powers, and yearned to re-try the achievements of his youth, when he made his reputation on the Pacific Slope. Then he wrote "Nordeck"—failed! More outlay! The fortune was rapidly dwindling ! Then back to "Davy Crockett" - Finally he dramatized "Pudd'n-head Wilson." And a great success it was—until one night his tired head laid upon the sill of a window in a sleeping-car—his over-taxed discouraged heart, weakened and worn out; with his white hair blowing in the night-wind, and his pallid face turned up to the stars, the soul of the exhausted actor went forth into the prairie night—back to the Great Giver.

EDWIN F. MAYO, son of Frank Mayo, appeared at the Theatre Royal during his first *starring* tour in "Davy Crockett" in 1887. After the death of his father he became manager and principal actor of "Pudd'n-head Wilson." He dropped dead at the Chateau Frontenac, Quebec, 19th Feb., 1900. For him the *"strange eventful history"* came early to an end.

THE SEASON OF 1879

opened, 14th January, with Genevieve Ward, supported by Milnes Levick in " Jane Shore." Miss Ward began an engagement at the Academy of Music on the termination of her week at the Royal, appearing at the new house in "Henry the Eighth," 20th, and " Jane Shore," 21st. " Pinafore " was produced 24th, and James Green was seen, 28th and 29th, in

"Henry the Fifth." Tony Denier and Adams' "Humpty-Dumpty" opened 1st April for week. The next most important attraction was Shook and Collier's production of "A Celebrated Case," under the management of J. W. Collier. Edmund Kean Collier and Edward Lafayette Tilton appeared in the cast. Cool Burgess, Rice's "Evangeline," and the Criterion Comedy Company in "Our Boys," followed.

On the re-opening of the house, week 8th September, we first find the name of John B. Sparrow figuring as lessee and manager. The opening was with Haverley's Juvenile "Pinafore" Company. John A. Stevens' "Unknown," week of 15th, this being its first production here. Arnold Brothers' Minstrels next, followed by E. A. McDowell in "The Duke's Motto," 20th, 21st, 22nd. Duprez and Benedict's Minstrels were seen 21st and 22nd November, then Gus Williams, and on 28th "Uncle Tom's Cabin," with Grace Egerton. Charles L. Davis, in " Alvin Joslin," began an engagement 24th December, closing the year of 1879.

JOHN B. SPARROW was born in Cheltenham. England. in 1854. His parents shortly afterwards came to Canada settling at St· Catharines. Ont., whence he came when still a very young man, and found employment in the bill posting business with Mr. Vincent. He married a Miss Cater, and his subsequent career is well known. As a manager he has always shown wonderful enterprise. and has ever been ready to promote enterprises of merit. The fact of his having three theatres at present under his personal management is proof conclusive of his enterprising ability. He controls the Academy of Music and Theatre Royal, Montreal, and the Grand Opera House, Ottawa.

GENEVIEVE WARD (Lucia Genovera Teresa, Countess Guerbel), born in New York City in 1848, is the grand-daughter of Gideon Lee, who was mayor of New York ; her father was Samuel Ward, long in the consular service. At the age of fifteen she was introduced to Rosini, who charged himself with her musical education, and procured her lessons under Ranzi, director of the Opera at Florence. She sang first at La Scala Milan, in "Lucretia Borgia," under the name of Guerrabella, an Italianized form of her own name, for she was now the wife of Count Constantine Guerbel, a Russian officer. In her sixteenth year, while travelling in Europe with her mother, she met Lieutenant Constantine de Guerbel, a Russian nobleman, who fell desperately in love with her. Having satisfied herself that he was what he represented himself, Mrs. Ward, the prudent mother of the young girl, permitted the addresses of the young Russian, and a formal engagement was announced. Shortly afterward they were married in Paris by civil law, the binding ceremony of the Greek church being postponed because Lieutenant Guerbel declared that there was no priest of that order in Paris. Even then the two women did not suspect any dishonorable intention on the lieutenant's part. But Mrs. Ward and her daughter did not consider the civil service sufficient, and when the mother of the young American singer discovered that the young man could not legally marry without the permission of his parents, she hurried her daughter off, leaving an indignant letter for the young man, and forbidding him ever to see his bride of an hour. This matter assumed almost international importance. The young singer, convinced that Guerbel had not intended honorably by her, travelled to St. Petersburg, flung herself at the feet of the Czar and begged that the ceremony might for her honor's sake be completed. By the order of the Imperial Father of the Russians this was done. The young American went to the altar clad more like a widow than a bride, and at the church door she parted forever from the man she had learned to mistrust. I fancy they never met again. He died some years later, and Genevieve Ward has not re-married. She made her *debut* in English opera at the Concert Garden as *Maid Marion* in MacFarren's Opera, "Robin Hood.'" In the autumn she came to America, appearing in New York, Boston, Philadelphia and Havana. The great exertion she had undergone and the trying air of Cuba proved too much for her, and her voice gave way entirely. Rest and change proved ineffectual for its restoration. She determined to study for the stage, and on October 1, 1873, made her *debut* as *Lady Macbeth* at the Theatre Royal, Manchester, with great success. She made her first appearance on the London stage at the Adelphi, March 18, 1874, as *Unarita* in "The Prayer in the Storm," in which role she drew full houses for six months. In 1877 she went to Paris to study under Requier, of the Comedie Francaise, and, on February 11, played *Lady Macbeth* in French at the Porte St. Martin Theatre with such success that the Comedie Francaise would gladly have enrolled her as a member of their distinguished company. Returning to London in April, 1879, Miss Ward became lessee of the Lyceum Theatre during the temporary absence of Mr. Irving. On August 22, "Forget-me-not" was offered, and her impersonation was pronounced by the critics to be without an equal. In December she left for America and made a tour with "Forget-me-not" in the chief cities of the Union and the Provinces, beginning with Boston. At the end of 1882 she returned to England, and again played "Forget-me-not" in the Provinces and in London. On December 2, 1883, she sailed for India for a tour around the world. She again appeared in America and was seen in Montreal in November, 1886. She lives in London, and has appeared occasionally with Henry Irving. She was never divorced, as she had no desire to marry again, and although she enjoyed the respect of her husband's family, she declined, much to that family's astonishment, to take any share of his estates, not even her legal dower.

CHARLES S. DAVIS, as *Alvin Joslin*, was favorably known in all portions of this country. He came of a theatrical family, and was born in Baltimore, Md., October 21, 1852. When but four years old he faced the footlights. He had worked in every branch of his profession, having been connected with circus troupes. He played clown in the regular performances, and afterwards worked in the concerts. Having acquired some money, he made up his mind to start out on his own account. With a slight sketch for its basis, "Alvin Joslin" was started on its career. He made money, and except for gratifying an extravagant taste for diamonds, he was reasonably saving. With the money he made out of this piece he erected the Alvin Theatre in Pittsburg in 1891. Its noteworthy feature was the luxurious accommodations provided for the actors behind the scenes He died in Pittsburg, Pa., 1st March, 1900.

MILNES LEVICK, one of the ablest actors ever known to the American stage, was born at Boston, Lincolnshire, England, January 30, 1825, and appeared as an actor in the provinces before coming to this country in 1853. Many weary days after his arrival in New York he joined the cast of "Uncle Tom's Cabin" at P. T. Barnum's old museum at Broadway and Ann Street, playing *George Harris* at a salary of $15 a week, a compensation afterward increased by Mr. Barnum to $18 a week. Tours through the United States and Canada followed, Mr. Levick rapidly becoming recognized as one of the leading actors of the day. He appeared in New York in Laura Keene's famous company, including Joseph Jefferson, C. W. Couldock, E. A. Sothern and George Holland. After this engagement he returned to Barnum's Museum as leading man, remained until the place was burned, when he rejoined Laura Keene, and played afterward in a long list of memorable productions, among them the great revival of "Julius Ceasar" at Booth's Theatre, playing the title role. Later he appeared in support of all the great *stars*, his last engagement having been with Minna Gale Haynes, in 1892, at the Star Theatre in New York City, when he appeared in one of his best impersonations, *Master Walter* in "The Hunchback." He died in New York, 18th April, 1897.

Sallie Holman, at the head of the Holman Opera Company, began

THE YEAR OF 1880

12th January, followed by a troupe of Japs, 26th, 27th. The California Minstrels, with Cool Burgess, came 28-29th, and on 9th February the Holmans returned and opened a two weeks'

engagement.   John T. Hinds, in the " Groves of Blarney,"
came 30th March for week.   The event of the season was the
first appearance at this theatre of the great polyglot German
tragedian, Daniel E. Bandmann, accompanied by Mrs. Millicent Palmer-Bandmann.   They opened in " Hamlet," 5th
April; "Merchant of Venice," 6th; "School for Scandal," 7th;
"Richelieu," for the benefit of the Young Men's Hebrew
Society, 8th; "Narcisse," 9th; "Romeo and Juliet," 10th; and
"Arragh-na-Pogue."   This was Mr. Bandmann's second appearance in Montreal, his debut having been made at the Academy of Music, 17th November, 1879.   Mr. and Mrs Mc-
Dowell appeared for one night, 6th April, in "H. M. S. Parliament," followed by the English Opera Company for four
nights in " The Very Merry Mariner."   John T. Hinds returned, 12th, for week in " The Shaughran " and " Colleen
Bawn."   The Baldwin Baby Opera Company came week
19th in " Pinafore," then Haverley's Minstrels, 28th, for four
nights, and on 18th May the Hyer Sisters were seen in "Out
of Bondage," and "Uncle Tom's Cabin," followed by the Big
Four Minstrels, 27th, 28th, 29th.   Isidore Davidson, in "Be-
nighted," came week 14th June, this being his first *starring*
appearance in the city.   "Dr. Clyde" was given 21st, 22nd,
23rd, and W. H. Power, in "The Marble Heart," 25th, 26th;
"Lost in London." 28th; "Ticket-of-Leave Man," 29th; "A
Man of Mystery," 30th, repeated 1st July.   On 5th Oliver
D. Byron produced "Across The Continent," and "Ten Thousand Miles Away" was also given during that week.   Dominick Murray, in repertoire of standard drama, held the boards
for three weeks from 12th.   On 2nd August, "Under the Gaslight" was the attraction for week, and the summer season
closed 14th with Sidney C. France in " Marked for Life."
which engagement he began 9th August.   The fall season
opened 1st September with J. Franklin Warner's Comedy
Company in "Speculation." Herne's "Hearts of Oak" came
week 5th September, with James A. Herne and Fred Chippendale.   A dramatization of Jules Verne's "Around the World
in Eighty Days"   held the boards from 14th to 25th.   Anthony and Ellis' "Uncle Tom's Cabin" was the next attraction, week 4th October, giving place to "The Galley Slave,"
followed by John A. Stevens and Lottie Church in the former's play " Unknown."   George H. Adams in " Humpty-
Dumpty" came week 28th October.   Mrs. Scott Siddons first

appeared as a *star* at this house week 1st November, supported by Luigi Lablanche. During the engagement she produced "Romeo and Juliet," "School for Scandal," "As You Like It," "Much Ado About Nothing," "King Rene's Daughters," "The Honeymoon," and "Macbeth." The French Opera Bouffe Co. appeared in repertoire week 8th November, which extended to a second week, after which the Charles Drew Opera Co. came for a week from 6th December. This closed the year's annals.

MARY FRANCES SCOTT - SIDDONS was the great-granddaughter of the famous Mrs. Sara Siddons, whose memory is so closely allied to that of the Kembles, the elder Kean, Young and Macready. Mrs. Siddons had three sons, one of whom, George, held a high civil appointment in India. His youngest son, William Young Siddons, became a military officer and married the daughter of Col. Earl. The issue of this marriage was four children, one of whom is the subject of this sketch, born in 1844. After the death of Mr. Siddons the widow took her children to England and afterwards to Germany, where they were educated. Mary had met with some success as a public reader in the provinces of England before making her metropolitan *debut* on April 1, 1867, at the Hanover Square Rooms. Such was her success as a reader that she appeared on the regular stage 8th April at the Haymarket Theatre as *Rosalind* in "As you Like it." Her first professional appearance on any stage, however, was in the spring of 1866 at Glasgow as *Juliet.* She subsequently came to America, where she has been alternately seen as a reader and as an actress, but she is better known as a reader. Mrs. Siddons was married to a naval officer named Scott, from whom she separated. In person she had well been called one of the loveliest women on the stage. An actress of little force, her intelligence and beauty did much to win her the position she enjoyed as an interpreter of classical poetry. She died in Paris, France, 19th November, 1896.

A French company in repertoire began

THE YEAR OF 1881

10th January, followed by Harry Weber, week 17th, in "Nip and Tuck." Whitmore and Clarke's Minstrels, 3rd February, for three nights, and a return engagement of the French company, 7th, for a season of several weeks. Nick Roberts' Pantomime Combination came, 14th February, for four nights. An interesting event was the first production here of J. W. Collier's "Banker's Daughter," week of 22nd February, with Frank C. Bangs, E. L. Tilton and Mrs. C. Walcot, Jun., in

the cast.   The French Co. reappeared week of 28th, followed
by the Union Square Company in Sardou's "Daniel Rochat."
Malin's Grand English Opera Company, including Janet
Edmonson (Mrs. Fred Warde), began an engagement 11th,
followed, 18th, by the first appearance of that remarkably
strong aggregation, Barlow, Wilson, Primrose and West's
Minstrels.   The Malin Opera Company returned 21st, for
three nights, and on 29th-30th the Holman Company was
heard.   The great *tragedienne*, Mad. Janauschek, was first
seen here, week 9th May, in "Mary Stuart," "Bleak House,"
"Mother and Son," "Medea," and "Macbeth."   A summer
season of French Opera was inaugurated, 16th May, under
the management of Ed. Bageard.   The Vokes Family of
comedians appeared at this house, week 5th July, in a selection of chip comedies.   "Hazel Kirke" was produced here
week 11th July, 1881, with J. K. Keane as *Dunstan Kirke*,
and Helen Blythe as *Hazel.*   Healey's Hibernian Minstrels
came, 9th August, for one week, followed by Kate Glassford
in "Led Astray," "East Lynne," and "Camille."   "Florence
Gillette opened, 5th September, in "Romeo and Juliet," following in " Ingomar," " East Lynne," " Camille," " Frou
Frou," and " Adrienne Lecouvreur."   From the sublime
came the ridiculous in "The Jollities," week 12th.   James
O'Neill and Benjamin Maginley made their first appearance
here as *stars* in "Deacon Crankett," week 19th September.
Following O'Neill and Maginley came Minnie Palmer in "My
Sweetheart," 26th September, this being her first appearance
here.   Baker and Farron came week 3rd October, followed
by the Harrisons in "Photos," week 10th.   Bartley Campbell's "Galley Slave" was seen week 17th, after which the
same author's play of "My Geraldine" was produced.
Barney McAuley, as *Uncle Daniel* in " A Messenger from
Jarvis Station," appeared week 31st.   George Clarke in
"Connie Oogah" was seen week 7th November, the house
remaining dark until week of 5th December, when Wren's
"Uncle Tom's Cabin" held the boards.   Joseph Wheelock
and Rose Keene appeared in "The Planter's Wife," week
12th; Helen E. Jennings in "The Two Orphans," and "East
Lynne," week 19th; and Kraemer's Burlesque Co., week
26th December, closing the year.   Barlow, Wilson, Primrose and West started in a modest way from Wilmington
in 1877.   Milt G. Barlow and George Wilson were the
end men, while George Primrose and "Billy" West

"filled up" in the first part and did a song and dance in the olio. Barlow is from Lexington, and went into minstrelsy as an end man in 1870. Wilson was born in London, and became a minstrel in 1867 at San Francisco. Primrose is a Canadian, and first "blacked up" in 1867, when he used to be announced on the bills as "Master George, the infant clog dancer." West was born in Syracuse, and made his minstrel *debut* in 1870. He died in 1902.

BENJAMIN MAGINLEY was the most genial of men, with a soft spot in his heart for his fellow creature ; firm in his friendship, but relentless in his enmity ; honest and upright in his dealings, and conscientious in the performance of the most trival affairs of life. His faults were few, virtues many, and hundreds of sturdy friends and thousands of public admirers lament the abrupt termination of so valuable and exemplary a life. Mr. Maginley was born in Philadelphia in 1832, of well-to-do parents, but he conceived an early passion for the stage, and began life for himself by joining the stock company in Pittsburg, where he did utility business. Always ready to relieve the neccessities of others, he imprudently loaned a large sum of money to a circus company, and in order to liquidate the debt, he was made a member of the firm, under the title of Melville, Maginley and Co.'s Great Eastern Circus. His spirit of mirth asserted itself in the ring as clown, and many are living to-day who laughed at his antics and jests. He continued in the circus business until 1875, when he married Miss Carroll, a celebrated *equestrienne* of that time, by whom he had one child, Mrs. Buckel, at whose house he died; his wife died in 1876. He was also interested in other circus organizations. Mr. Maginley resumed the theatrical profession after leaving his circus life, and appeared with Lester Wallack in "Rosedale," Dion Boucicault, McKee Rankin and others. For nearly five years he was a member of the Madison Square company, playing with success in "Esmerelda" and "May Blossom." He last appeared in Montreal at the Theatre Royal, week 6th July, 1886, in "May Blossom." He died 3rd June, 1888.

STEELE MACKAYE, author of "Hazel Kirke," "Paul Kauvar," "Money Mad," etc., was pronounced by Henry Ward Beecher to have been the best equipped young man he had ever met. Born in Buffalo, N.Y., in 1842, Mackaye showed an early taste for art, and studied under Delsarte in Paris. Joseph Jefferson and John McCullough were among his pupils in a school which he opened in New York. In 1873 he played *Hamlet* in London, and also toured the provinces. A genius in art, Mackaye was as princely in his expenses as in his schemes. After writing "Hazel Kirke," Nate Salisbury told him he would make $500,000 for him in three years if he would wait six months, but Mackaye, who never waited, disposed of the play for $10,000. The crowning achievement of his career would have been his Spectatorium scheme at the World's Fair, Chicago, had not his subscribers withdrawn their influence. Mackaye had expended on this conception the energy of his entire vital forces. He had called science and song and poetry into his stupendous frescoes. No Roman spectacle of Vespasian was to have been so elaborate, but there he stood alone by the bleak, grey shores, anticipating the chill of unsuccessful age, while behind him lay strewn the wrecks of his mighty imagination. Some disappointments rob us even of our recuperative strength—to Mackaye the sun had set, the aurora was out. Hoping to rekindle the flickering embers, his friends placed him on a train bound for California. It flew westward in the face of a storm. The snow whirled in wild dervish dances after it. There were interminable wastes ahead, storm-ravished, but the train plunged on. Somewhere in a far region it slowed up gradually, then it stopped. No use going any further ! Steele Mackaye, actor, author, philosopher, prince of men, had gone on ahead, 3rd March, 1894.

EDWARD LAFAYETTE TILTON died in 1887. He was born at Ashland, Mass., 13th June, 1824, and from the time of his *debut* in 1845 at Palmo's Opera House, he experienced a long and interesting stage career, supporting all the contemporary *stars* of note.

EDMUND KEAN COLLIER some years ago gave promise of a coming tragedian, but his ambition was not sufficient to inspire him. He came of a theatrical family, being nephew to J. W. Collier and Maggie Mitchell, and began on the lowest rung of the ladder of tradition. After having been in the support of John McCullough, he began a *starring* tour in the late tragedian's chief roles, also reviving Forrest's great character of *Metamora*. His New York *debut* as a *star* was at the People's Theatre, 30th August, 1886. After three seasons Mr. Collier returned to melodrama, and appeared in "Paul Kauvar." He was afterwards with Mad. Janauschek in "The Sporting Duchess," and lastly "Ben Hur." His daughter, Helen, is Mrs. Thomas E. Garrick, and his son, Willie Collier, is becoming a recognized *star* in comedy lines. Mr. Collier died 27th Dec., 1900.

MINNIE PALMER was born in Philadelphia in 1865. She was partly educated in Vienna, and having shown a decided histrionic bent was encouraged to appear in a juvenile piece in her eleventh year at Brooklyn. Her first real work was at Booth's Theatre at New York in 1877, when her uncle, Henry Palmer, had her cast for *Little Dorothy* in "Daniel Druce." She has since made a distinct success in light comedy roles, not only in the United States and Canada, but also

JAMES O'NEILL.
(D'Artagnan.)
Photo Morrison. Engraved by the Weeks Co.

in England. Much of her success has been attributed to John R. Rodgers, her husband and former manager, from whom she separated a few years ago. Her father was a captain and shipowner. She is still before the public.

JAMES O'NEILL came to America in his early boyhood from Kilkenny, Ireland, where he was born 15th Nov., 1849. He was first with John Ellsler's stock company at Cleveland, and about 1870 became comedian at McVicker's Theatre, Chicago, remaining three seasons. He then joined Hooley's company there. Here is a little romance of an actor's life : Do you remember the tragic end of Miss Hawthorne, the leading lady of Richard Hooley's stock company at the time of the rage about the handsome young O'Neill ? Oh, it was pitiful ! She took that terrible leap in the dark which all men have feared since the world began. Miss Hawthorne was living at the old Tremont House at the time. She was popular, talented and beautiful. Her figure was lissome, willowy and graceful like Juno's. Her face—ah, well! let that pass. She was worthy of love, and it is said that young O'Neill loved her. Other admirers she had in great numbers, but he was the favored one. One day he called on her at the Tremont. They had an interview in her apartments. It must have been a stormy, a heart-breaking, life-crushing interview. Five minutes after Mr. O'Neill bade Miss Hawthorne adieu she leaped out of a fifth story window and fell on the pavement below a lifeless bundle of clothes. There are some events which murder a man's ambition. After a year of highly successful work in California, whence his fame spread to New York, the rapidly rising young player was engaged by A. M. Palmer for his Union Square company. Here he was the American creator of the cripple *Pierre* in "The Two Orphans," and became one of the renowned members of a renowned troupe. After a time he went back to San Francisco, and three years later played a part that no regular actor had ever before attempted. This was the *Messiah* in Salmi Morse's production of "The Passion Play." O'Neill, who is of a deeply religious nature, after having at first refused pointblank to accept the role, brought to it the deepest reverence of which he was capable. As one critic said, "to him it was not acting. it was devotion." But the public feeling was so strongly against the play that, after a few weeks, it was taken off by order of the authorities. O'Neill came back to New York, where he was engaged by John Stetson to play *Edmond Dantes* in "Monte Cristo." In this story of Dumas', dramatized by Fechter, O'Neill found his *metier*. He purchased the rights from Stetson, and won a fortune. Although he has added a few classical plays to his repertoire of late years, he is still seen in the old role from time to time. He stands to-day as a representative of the most admirable of the methods of the older school of actors, while his work describes the best arts of the newer school.

FRANCESCA ROMANA MAGDALENA JANAUSCHEK, born in Prague, Bohemia, 20th July, 1832, was one of nine children, and her father was a merchant. She very early developed remarkable musical ability, but the dramatic vein was soon displayed. At sixteen she went on the stage at Prague and soon after joined a travelling company at a salary of $14 per month. She was favored in having a good education, and rapidly advanced. She became a *star* in her twenty-ninth year, and in 1867 came to America with her own company. Opening at the Academy of Music, New York, 9th October, as *Medea*, in German, the English-speaking public also recognized her power, and encouraged it as they had Rachel's before her, and as they did Bernhardt's and Duse's after. Mad. Janauschek began the study of English, appearing in English performances of *Lady Macbeth, Marie Stuart, Medea*, etc., during the season 1873-74. She has since appeared in all the principal cities of the United States and Canada. She has co-*starred* with Kate Claxton in "The Two Orphans," and later with Stuart Robson, but Janauschek should have retired from the stage twenty years ago. Then she had fame and fortune ; her diamonds, the gifts of emperors, kings and other potentates, were the envy of her coevals. Where are all of these now ? But Janauschek, until recently stricken by paralysis, continued to be a great and finished actress. In private life this lady is Mrs. J. W. Pillot.

JOSEPH F. WHEELOCK is one of the few legitimate actors of the drama who are now left to us, and is an artist of the highest merit. He was born in 1838, and began his theatrical career at the Boston Museum in 1855. In 1865 he gave the first production in this country of "Enoch Arden." He was leading man at Booth's Theatre during 1873 and 1874, after having acted at McVicker's, Chicago, as leading man. Since that time Mr. Wheelock has supported a number of leading *stars* and to-day is still meeting with success. Mr. Wheelock was in 1897 elected President of the Actors' Society of America.

THE YEAR OF 1882

was opened 2nd January, with Fanny Louise Buckingham in "Mazeppa." This was the first appearance here of the equestrienne actress. The Amy Lee Opera Company came for three nights, 12th January, 1882, followed by Helen Blythe, week of 16th, in "Pique" and "Divorce." This was that lady's *stellar debut* in Montreal. Healey's Hibernian Minstrels were seen for four nights from 1st February, and on 9th Helen Blythe played a return engagement in "East

Lynne," "Pique," "Camille," and "Divorce." "A Noble Purpose" followed, week 20th; Anthony and Ellis' "Uncle Tom's
Cabin," with Minnie Foster as *Topsy*, week 27th; followed
by the German Opera Company in "Patience," for eight
nights from 6th March. Neil Burgess in "Widow Bedott,"
supported by G. W. Stoddart, was the next attraction, week
20th. Tony Denier's Pantomime Company, with Alfred
Miaco, came 30th March; the Daly Company, in the "Passing
Regiment," 10th April; Rentz Santley Burlesque Company,
24th, for three nights ; Baird's Minstrels, 27th, for three
nights; and Barry & Fay's "Muldoon's Picnic," 1st May, for
three nights. The theatre was closed until 4th and 5th August, when Tony Pastor's Vaudeville Company first appeared
here, followed by Julia A. Hunt in "Florinell." Barney
McAuley appeared for the second time here, week 28th, in
"Uncle Daniel" and "The Jerseyman." Atkinson's "Jollities" were seen week 11th September, and, on 19th, Baker
and Farron; followed by Topsy Venn, 27th, for four nights
in "Furnished Rooms"; Maffitt and Bartholomew's "Ma-
zulme, the Night Owl," 2nd October, for week; M. B. Leavitt's Minstrels, 9th, for three nights; Minnie Foster's "Uncle
Tom's Cabin," 16th, for week ; Harry Weber's " Nip and
Tuck," 23rd, for week; Hyde and Behman's "Two Johns,"
9th November, for three nights; Harrigan's "Squatter Sover-
eignty," 14th, for three nights; Davis' "Alvin Joslin," 23rd,
for three nights; Minnie Hauk in grand opera, 30th, for three
nights; and W. J. Scanlan in Bartley Campbell's "Friend and
Foe," 4th December, for week, followed by "The Jolly Path-
finders," week 18th, and Davene's Vaudeville, week 25th
December.

FANNY LOUISE BUCKINGHAM had a short but active stage
career, dating from 1877 to 1890. Born at Chestnut Grove, Ward's
Farm, Md., 1st March, 1852, Sally Ward was brought up in a manner
not likely to encourage histrionic tendencies, but circumstances eventually decided the lady to gratify early ambitions, and her first appearance on any stage was at the Broadway Theatre, New York (now
Daly's), in the character in which she became famous, *Mazeppa*, 2nd
July, 1877. Dashing and spirited, as well as possessing a magnificent
stage appearance, the young lady made a pronounced hit. Her engagement ran for two weeks at the Broadway, and was extended two
weeks longer at the Bowery Theatre. James Melville, the celebrated
equestrian, was her first fencing master, and Miss Buckingham subsequently gave that gentleman's name to her famous grey steed. Miss

Buckingham tells me that her horse died 25th May, 1895. After her successful *debut* the actress appeared in all the principal cities of the United States and Canada with great *eclat*, not only in "Mazeppa," but also in all the equestrian dramas as well as in "East Lynne," "Lady Audley's Secret," and "Green Bushes," Miss Buckingham was married 8th May, 1880, to William B. Pettit, who managed her professional work until her retirement in February, 1890, her last appearance being at the Third Avenue Theatre, New York.

"So Much for Buckingham."

HELEN BLYTHE'S dramatic instinct was precociously developed. At the age of five she was introduced to the public in children's roles by Clara Morris at Norwalk, Ohio, and six years later made her appearance as *Richard III.* She was born at Fairfield, Ohio, 10th August, 1861, and had made quite a reputation when she secured her first regular engagement at the Cincinnati Grand Opera House. Her real name is Blye, but an early mistake in the play bills to Blythe was never changed. She made steady headway, and became a great favorite in all the principal cities of the United States and Canada. Her dramatic methods are of the newer school, and her real strength lies in those more human impersonations which the genius of the modern playwright and the favor of the public have given a prominent position on our stage. Her husband is Joseph F. Brien. They were married in 1880.

BERNARD McAULEY was born in New York, 19th Sept., 1837. He made his professional *debut* at the Metropolitan Theatre in the same city in April, 1853. He managed Wood's Theatre, Philadelphia, from 1868 to 1877, and is said to have realized over $100,000 during his career at that theatre. After unprofitable managerial speculations, he began touring in "A Messenger from Jarvis Station" and "The Jerseyman," but he was not a money-maker, and had been left almost penniless. He was known as a most honorable man and kind friend. He died 28th March, 1886.

TOPSY VENN (*nee* Elizabeth Ann Reynolds) was born at London in 1857, and first appeared on the boards as a dancer in 1864. Her American *debut* was made in Philadelphia, 30th April, 1874. She married A. H. Steer in 1875, but was divorced in 1882, when she married H. S. Cornell, who shortly afterwards disappeared.

MINNIE HAUK, one of the most gifted of the many bright ornaments which America has contributed to the operatic stage, is on record as having been born 16th Nov., 1852, in New York city, of German parents. After European study she made her operatic *debut* in Vienna, subsequently appearing with pronounced success throughout the continent, England and America. She is the wife of Chevalier Hesse Von Wartegg. Minnie Hauk is still singing. During a recent pleasure tour through the East Indian tropics she gave a few concerts in Batavia, Soerabaja, Singapore, etc. The prima-donna was most enthusiastically received by English and Dutch alike and won flattening triumphs.

GEORGE WILLIAM STODDART was born at Lancaster, Eng., March 31, 1826. He was the eldest of five brothers, all actors, as were also his father and mother. J. H. Stoddart is his brother. After playing in the principal cities of England, Ireland and Scotland, he came to this country in 1853, appearing at the National Theatre, New York, as *Harold Skimpole* in a dramatization of "Bleak House." He afterwards played in all the principal stock companies in this country, including those of the Boston Museum under Thos. Barry, Laura Keene, and with Mrs. John Drew at Philadelphia. He was considered one of the best light comedians of his time, having supported Macready, Forrest, the elder Booth, Charlotte Cushman, Mathews, Charles Kean, etc. Of late years he played old men, his *Elder Shadrach Sniffles* in the "Widow Bedott" with Neil Burgess being fully as prominent as Mr. Burgess' *Widow*. In 1885 Mr. Stoddart retired from the stage on account of illness, and died 9th July, 1888. His daughter is Mrs. Neil Burgess.

HUGH FAY died in 1894. He had been a well-known *droll* in that absurd risibility "Muldoon's Picnic" for twelve years, associated with William Barry.

WILLIAM BARRY died in Brooklyn, 15th April, 1898. He began stage life as an end man and later served in the war. He always was a popular vaudeville comedian, and for a time had Harry Kernell as his stage partner. In 1882 he became associated with Hugh Fay, and both became favorites with that class of theatre-goers who thronged to see their skit "Muldoon's Picnic." After Fay's death he *starred* alone, and with "The Rising Generation" he made $70,000.

THOMAS ALFRED MIACO (*nee* Alfred Frisboe), a clever pantomimist frequently seen here, died 16th April, 1893.

THE SEASON OF 1883

was opened by Leavitt's Minstrels, 26th January. Miaco's "Humpty-Dumpty" came 19th February, followed by the first *star* appearance here of Pat Rooney. Fostelle, in "Mrs. Partington," came week 10th April; Rentz-Santley Burlesque Company, 19th, for three nights; the Guy Family, 23rd, for three nights, in "A Carnival of Fun"; Gorman's Irish Specialty Company, week of 26th; and Lizzie May Ulmer in "'49," week 30th April. The enormous individuals, General and

Mrs. Tom Thumb, were the feature of the season, commencing a week's engagement 7th May. On 11th June "The Veteran" was produced, and on 18th, for three nights, "The Danicheffs," followed by "The Banker's Daughter" for three nights; Tony Pastor's Company in vaudeville for three nights 27th; Topsy Venn in "Furnished Rooms," week 2nd July; "Ten Mile Crossing," 27th July, for week; Charlotte Thompson in "The Romanoffs," and "Jane Eyre," week 3rd September; Milton and Dollie Nobles, week 10th, in "The Phœnix" and "Interviews." Prof. E. C. Taylor, the magician, opened week 17th September, followed, week 22nd, by J. J. Dowling in "Nobody's Claim"; Kelly and Ryan's "Zanfrettas," 1st October for week; E. T. Gooderich in "Monte; or, a Double Life," week 15th; Girard Eyer's English Novelty Company, week 22nd; Ravel's "Drawing Room Circus," 5th November, for two weeks; Helen Jennings' "An American Marriage," week 19th; "Two Johns," week 26th; Vaudeville, week 2nd December; Rentz-Santley Burlesque Company, week 10th; Hyde and Behman's "Derby Day," week 17th; Miner's Comedy Four, 24th, for three nights; and Smith's Hand Bell Ringers, 27th, for three nights. It was in the early summer of 1883 that H. R. Jacobs opened the tent show at the corner of University and St. Catherine streets, and laid the foundation to a fortune. On 19th November of that year the Mechanics' Hall was also opened for a long season of Vaudeville at 10, 20 and 30 cents.

TOM THUMB died 15th July, 1883. He and his wife were at the time visiting friends at Cincinnati. The General was born at Bridgeport, Conn., 4th Jan., 1838, and his right name was Charles Sherwood Stratton. He was first exhibited by Barnum, 8th Dec., 1842. He then stood 24 inches and weighed 16 lbs. In 1862 he met Lavinia Warren, while on exhibiton at Barnum's museum. The diminutive couple fell in love and were married at Grace Church, New York, 10th Feb., 1863. After a two weeks' wedding tour, Mrs. Tom Thumb retired to private life, but returned to the public view a few months later. Mr. Barnum then arranged a three years' tour around the world for the little folks. They left New York, June 21, 1869. In Great Britain they exhibited in two hundred and eight towns, and left Liverpool for this country June 12, 1872, arriving here three years from the time of their departure, having in that period travelled 55,487 miles and given 1,471 performances, in 587 different cities and towns. Afterwards they toured this country up to the time of Tom Thumb's death.

MRS. GENERAL TOM THUMB, afterwards Countess Magri, and whose maiden name was Mercy Lavinia Bump, was born in Middleboro, Mass., Oct. 31, 1842. After she became a year old she grew very slowly, and ceased entirely at the age of ten. She attended school regularly with the other children of the neighborhood, and found no trouble in keeping up with them in her studies, as she was considered very bright. At home she was taught to do all kinds of household work. In 1862 she was engaged by P. T. Barnum for his Museum, New York City, at which place Tom Thumb was then on exhibition, and they were married, as already noted, in 1863. It was during her first engagement that she assumed the name of Lavinia Warren. Both were forty inches in height. In 1884 Mrs. Tom Thumb organized a company for the road (Gen. Tom Thumb having died July 15, 1883), among whom were the Magri Bros. Count Magri and Mrs. Gen. Tom Thumb were married April 6, 1885.

COUNT PRIMO MAGRI was born in Bologna, Italy, in 1850, and was one of a family of thirteen children, three of whom are small, while the other ten are of ordinary height, as were both the parents. Count Primo is thirty-seven inches tall and weighs fifty-two pounds. His brother, Baron Ernest Magri is thirty-eight and one-half inches in height, and weighs fifty-four pounds. In company with his brother. the Count began travelling in 1865. In 1878 they came to this country and made a tour of the States, remaining in California and Oregon about three years. In 1882 they were engaged to travel with Mr. and Mrs. Gen. Tom Thumb.

PAT ROONEY, the well-known Irish comedian, was always a favorite with a certain class of play-goers, and since his death, 28th March, 1892, his place has not been filled. He was born in Ireland in 1844, and at the age of fourteen was already a clever dancer. He did Irish character work for twelve years in the English music halls, and came to America in 1871.

MR. AND MRS. NOBLES. Milton Nobles (real name Tamey) is a graduate of the old stock system, and an actor of ability. He was born in Cincinnati in 1847. He *starred* in his own plays for nearly 20 years, and has been fairly successful. Dolly Woolwine-Nobles was born at Lebanon, O., in the sixties, and was educated in Cincinnati. Her first professional experience was as a member of the Summer Stock Company at the Dayton Soldiers' Home, where she attracted much attention as *Louise* in "The Two Orphans" and similar characters. Mr. Nobles, then playing "The Phœnix" and "A Man of the People," was looking about for a young and attractive *soubrette*. A member of his company, who had been in the company with Miss Woolwine at Dayton, sang her praises so incessantly that they entered into a professional engagement in Jan., 1881, and in the following June they were married. Of recent years they have been appearing in vaudeville.

THE SEASON OF 1884

was opened by a vaudeville company from 31st December, 1883, followed by Ada Gray in "East Lynne," this being the last attraction to play at this house under the old prices. The fortunes of the old Royal had been at a very low ebb for some time, and Mr. Sparrow at this time entered into a partnership with H. R. Jacobs to carry on the lesseeship and management at popular rates of 10 and 20 cents, subsequently raised from time to time until the present admission price of 10, 20 30 and 40 cents has been reached. The theatre was for a couple of seasons styled the Royal Theatre Museum, but the old style was afterwards resumed. Vaudeville held the boards throughout most of the season. Bonnie Runnels, who had appeared under Jacob's tent show, and whose popularity had no little to do with making that venture the success it achieved, reappeared at this house, 11th Feb., in conjunction with the Hollywood Family. They put on "Cinderella" for two weeks from 3rd March. Partington's Comedy Company, in "Rooms for Rent," appeared week 26th Sept.; "Capers," week 13th; Pauline Markham, in "Two Orphans," and "Ticket-of-Leave Man," week 20th; J. H. Gilmour, in "Monte Cristo," week 10th November ; "Under the Gaslight," and "The Governor," week 17th; and Daniel E. Bandmann for two weeks from 24th November in "Hamlet," "Lady of Lyons," "Merchant of Venice," "Called Back," during first week, and "Called Back," "Narcisse," "Hunchback," and "Richard III.," during the second week. He was supported by Louise Beaudet and Chas. Thornton. J. H. Gilmour, in "Rosedale," week 15th December; "Enoch Arden," "Leah, the Forsaken," and "Oliver Twist," week 22nd; and Lottie Church and Charles Barringer, in "Unknown," week 29th December. The other dates were filled up by vaudeville combinations. During the summer season the Tent Show was again catering to cheap patronage. A new theatre was also opened on Beaver Hall Hill under the lesseeship of Beaucleigh & Co., opening for a few weeks from 3rd May. It was also during the same season that Roland G. I. Barnett opened the Crystal Palace Opera House with "Iolanthe," 24th May.

LOUISE BEAUDET will long be remembered as one of the most versatile artists of her generation. She has won unstinted applause in a range of roles varying from *Lady Macbeth* to *M'lle Fifi* and dancing *soubrette*. Born in France about 1860 Louise was brought to America as a child and received most of her education in the convents of Montreal. Her first stage appearances were in opera *bouffe*. It was in San Francisco twenty years ago that she attracted the attention of Bandmann, the tragedian, who conceived the idea of transforming *la petite* Louise into ,a Shakespearean *artiste*. She accompanied him on his great eastern tour which termminated in 1884, after which they toured in America for several seasons. The association between the two was dissolved upon the retirement of Bandmann from the mimic scene. Ten years ago Miss Beaudet returned to the field of comic opera.

PAULINE MARKHAM began her stage career in England at an early age, first appearing at the Princess Theatre, Manchester, thence to the Queen's Theatre in London in 1867. She was one of the several handsome young women who accompanied Lydia Thompson to America, opening at Wood's Museum, New York, 28th September, 1868, in the burlesque in "Ixion," with Miss Markman as *Venus*. The charming young women of the company were much in evidence that night ; so much in evidence that some of the audience hissed and others laughed loudly at what seemed the audacity of the performance. But much transpires in thirty years. Conditions and view points change. The performances which electrified New York in '68 would seem a bread-and-milk affair to the burlesque audience of to-day. The burlesque of those days has long since been laid upon the shelf as too tame and out of date to be useful. All the planets that revolved and twinkled about the sun, the dazzling Lydia, are forgotten or buried in the memories of old men. The clergy thundered forth its denunciations and some of the ,papers said harsh things of the representation, particularly the *Chicago Times*, and for this editor Story received a whipping at the hands of Lydia Thompson, assisted by Miss Markham. Pauline became very popular in burlesque, and subsequently appeared in the "emotional" at the cheap theatres, supported by her second husband, Randolph Murray. She was first married to Col. MacMahon.

BONNIE RUNNELLS was a very droll comedian of German eccentricities and first appeared in Montreal during June, 1883, at Jacob's Royal Museum and Theatorium. Thousands were attracted to the resort to see the work of that merry son of Momus. His engagement lasted throughout the summer season. He was born at Edinburgh, Scotland, in 1844, and died of paralysis at Chicago, 16th August, 1884.

THE SEASON OF 1885

was opened by Jennie Calif, in "M'liss." 5th January, followed by "The World," in which Charles Barringer and W. H. Lytell appeared; "The Miner's Daughter," week 19th; Fanny L.

Buckingham, in "Mazeppa," week 26th; Corinne, in opera, week 2nd February; Daniel E. Bandmann, supported by Louise Beaudet, week 9th, in "Othello," "Romeo and Juliet," "East Lynne," "Don Cæsar de Bazan," and "Richelieu," evening of 14th, which was Mr. Bandmann's last appearance in Montreal. "Fun on the Bristol" came week 16th; Miaco's "Humpty-Dumpty," 23rd; "Sawyer's Mine," 30th; Dowling's "Nobody's Claim," 9th March; "Ten Mile Crossing," 17th; "Octoroon," and "Christine Johnston," by Tayleur's Company, 23rd; Frances Bishop, in "Mugg's Landing," 30th; Jas. A. Herne, in "Hearts of Oak," 6th April; "Uncle Tom's Cabin," 13th; Pauline Markham, in "The Two Orphans," and "The New Magdalen," 20th; "Ranch 10," 27th; Helen Blythe and Joseph F. Brien, in "The Silver King," 4th May. Lawrence Hanley appearing as the *Spider*. This was his first professional engagement, he tells me. "Our Strategists," 11th; Wilbur Opera Company, 18th; "Zozo," 25th; "Hoop of Gold," 1st June; J. H. Gilmour, in "My Partner," 8th; "Stranglers of Paris," 15th; Janet Edmonson, in "Pirates of Penzance," 22nd. During the second week of her engagement was produced, for the first time in Montreal, Gilbert and Sullivan's "Princess Ida." "Iolanthe" was put on during the third. Miss Edmonson closed her four weeks' engagement 18th. The attaches of the theatre were given a benefit 27th, when the theatre was closed for the summer. The terrible epidemic of smallpox which raged during the summer of 1885 delayed the fall opening until 5th October, when Bennett Matlack, supported by Stella Rees, appeared in "A Celebrated Case," "Hamlet," and "Damon and Pythias." "The Danites" followed, week 12th; "After Dark," 19th; "Only a Farmer's Daughter," and "Only a Woman's Heart,' 26th; Jos. Proctor, in "Nick of the Woods," 2nd November. This was the veteran's last appearance in this city. The boards of the Royal were held by a company in "The Streets of New York," and "Jessie Brown," week 9th November. Two weeks of vaudeville followed; then Gustavus Clark, in "Monte Cristo," week 23rd November ; "The Silver King," and "Lucky Ranch," week 30th; Phosa McAllister and Robt. E. Graham, in "The Pavements of Paris," week 7th December; "Jolly Argonauts," week 14th; and Alice Oates in burlesque opera for two weeks from 21st December, presenting "Robin Hood" and "The Field of the Cloth of Gold." She did not reappear in this city.

BENNETT MATLACK was born at Wilmington, Del., 4th Oct·,
1842 ; died in Brooklyn, N.Y., 19th Aug., 1898. We find him first as
an amateur in Wheatley's Association, during which time he played
Hamlet in Philadelpnia. His first important engagement was at
Booth's Theatre in a production of Sardanapalus in 1876. In
ran 160 nights. During his career he played with Anna Dickinson,
F. B. Warde, Roland Reed and T. W. Keene. He *starred* two
seasons in "A Celebrated Case," "Hamlet" and "Virginius," and
had latterly been teaching elocution.

THE CENTURY YEAR

of Montreal theatricals was opened in 1886 by Dominick
Murray in "Escape from Sing Sing," week 4th January, followed by the *stellar debut* here of Edwin Arden, in " Eagle's
Nest," week 11th. Frederick Bock came week 18th in "The
Power of Money"; Gibson & Ryan, in "Irish Aristocracy,"
week of 25th ; James Hardie and Von Leer, in "A Brave Woman" week Feb. 1 ; Miss Buckingham, in "Mazeppa," week
8th February; Jos. J. Dowling and Sadie Hasson, in "No-
body's Claim," week 15th; "Argonauts of 49," week 22nd;
J. Z. Little, in "The World," week 1st March; Lilly Clay's
"Adamless Eden," week 8th; Geo. C. Boniface, in "Streets of
New York," week 15th; Pauline Markham, in "The Two
Orphans," "Led Astray," "Camille," and "East Lynne," week
22nd; Austin's Novelty Co., including the Austin Sisters,
week 29th; Frances Bishop, in "Mugg's Landing," week 5th
April. Leavitt's Vaudeville Co. came week 12th April; and
Louise Pomeroy, supported by her husband, Arthur Elliott,
began week 9th April in Shakespearean repertory, including
"Hamlet," "As You Like It," "Romeo and Juliet," "Richard
III.," and a few standard dramas. The opening bill, "Engaged," was performed under the disadvantages of the flood
filling the entire orchestral portion of the house, which was
illuminated by oil lamps. The engagement was, nevertheless, a financial, as well as an artistic success, Miss Pomeroy
being greatly praised for her characterization of the melancholy
Prince, as well as for her other assumptions. This was her
first and last engagement here. The Rentz-Santley Combination followed week 26th; and Nicholas S. Wood, the "Bov
Actor," came week 3rd May, being seen in "The Boy Detective," and "The Boy Scout." Edwin Arden, in "Eagle's
Nest," returned week 10th May; Grav and Stevens, in "Saved
from the Storm," week 17th; O. D. Byron's "Across the Con-

14

tinent," week 24th; "Zozo, the Magic Queen," week 31st;
H. P. Chanfrau, in "Kit, the Arkansas Traveller," week 7th
June; Billy Kersand's Minstrels, week 14th; and Corinne, in
extensive comic opera repertoire, two weeks from 21st. The
Company remained over until 5th July, on which date was
tendered a benefit to the attaches of the house, which closed
until 9th August, when the season was reopened by Clap-
ham's Minstrels, followed by George H. Adams, in "Humpty-
Dumpty," week 16th; "A Cold Day," week 23rd; James C.
Padgett (died 16th February, 1896), in "The Long Strike,"
supported by Emily Fairchild, week 30th; Ben Maginley, in
"May Blossoms," week 6th September; Horace Lewis, in
"Monte Cristo," and "Two Nights in Rome," week 13th;
Harry Lacy and Edna Carey, in "The Planter's Wife," week
20th ; Gray and Stephens, in " Storm Beaten," week 27th ;
Phosa McAllister, in "Taken from Life," week 4th October.
During the Saturday matinee performance a small panic was
caused by the noise of a small boy being rushed down the
back stairs by a stalwart "bouncer." No person was hurt,
and, after a few minutes of interruption, the play proceeded.
The Wilbur Opera Co. was heard in standard repertoire week
11th; King Hedley, in "Youth," week 18th; Victory Bateman and John Burke, in "Romany Rye," week 25th; Murray,
in "Escaped from Sing Sing," and "From Palace to Prison,"
week 1st November ; Gray and Stephens, in " Without a
Home," and "Saved from the Storm," week 9th; Austin's
Novelty Co., week 15th; "A Prisoner for Life," week 22nd;
"The World," week 29th; Edwin F. Thorne, in "The Black
Flag," week 6th December; Neil Burgess in "Vim," week
13th; "The Pulse of New York," week 20th; and "Blackmail,"
week 27th, introduced the reputed Brooklyn bridge jumper,
Steve Brodie. This attraction closed the year, as well as the
annals of the theatre so far as the compass of this compila-
tion is concerned. Inasmuch as the list of subsequent attractions have varied little from year to year, the task of reading the events would necessarily be as monotonous to the
reader as recording them would be laborious to the compiler.
The partnership existing between Sparrow and Jacobs was
dissolved in 1898, when Mr. Sparrow became sole lessee.

MINNIE OSCAR GRAY made her first appearance in John T.
Raymond's company at Savannah, Ga., in 1870. In 1878 she began
starring with her husband, William T. Stephens, at Baltimore, Md.,
and by a strange coincidence she made her last stage appearance

also in that city in 1893, retiring for a few years. She has since returned to the boards, however, and is at present touring in the English provinces.

LOUISE POMEROY-ELLIOTT was the daugter of Col. Ryder, of Cleveland, O., and was in her fortieth year when she died, 7th January, 1893. Her first husband, whom she wedded in 1871, was Mark M ("Brick") Pomeroy. She had been a pupil of the old-time tragedian, J. B. Roberts, and on her wedding day her husband gave her, as a gift, an Opera House in the West, valued at $75,000. Her first professional appearance on the stage was 16th October, 1876, when she appeared as *Juliet* at the Lyceum Theatre, New York. Her inclination for the stage resulted in a choice in 1877, and in 1885 she visited Australia, where she met Arthur Elliott, a tragedian, whom she married in 1883. Mr. and Mrs. Elliott came to America in 1884, and began *starring* on their own account, as well as appearing in leading support to other *stars*. Mrs. Elliott possessed good literary ability and had played nearly all of Shakespeare's heroines as well as portraying a very strong and intelligent characterization of *Hamlet*. Arthur Elliott during the fall of 1900 was the leading man of Mr. Grose's Montreal Stock Company.

JOHN Z. LITTLE, a native of Philadelphia, was at one time manager of a theatre in Chicago. He toured the country in "The World," in which production he played the leading part, and was financially successful. He died 9th March, 1900, aged 62.

GEORGE C. BONIFACE, born in New York city in 1833, first appeared on the amateur stage as a member of the Olympic Theatre company, and subsequently joined the stock company of the Holiday Street Theatre, Baltimore, making his first professional appearance as *Capt Blenheim* in "The Rough Diamond." After three months he became a member of the Pittsburg Company, and in 1851 he appeared at the Richmond Hill Theatre, New York, with Mr· and Mrs. John Drew. After gaining some experience in other large cities, Mr. Boniface opened at the Bowery Theatre as a joint *star* with George Arnold, playing *Iago* to his *Othello*. I quote the following from his own narrative: "This was a very few years after I left New York a fledgeling, and when my old friends all came to see me and made a little tin god of me· I was quite proud of myself, you may be sure. I next went to Richmond, playing opposite parts to James H. Taylor, and was next in support of Junius Brutus Booth as *Ratcliff* in 'Richard III.' I was not given the part until the night before I was to play it. and was nervous at the prospect. I thought that I had it pretty well, however, until *King Richard* said to *Ratcliff: How now ? What news ?* I should have answered *'My gracious sovereign. upon the western coast there rideth a puissant navy,'* etc. But my memory had deserted me ; all I could say was : *'There's a big fleet coming up the bay.'* " Mr Boniface was afterwards seen in the support of such *stars* as Forrest, Cushman, Heron, and in 1864 toured through the West in a round of Shakespearean roles. Mr. Boniface continues as follows : "Then I came back to New York, and played the leading juvenile part in 'The Black Crook,' and afterward did the same kind of work in "The Twelve Temptations.' The Boston Globe Theatre was my next field of activity. I was leading juvenile and chief support of Edwin Forrest during his engagement there. One day Mr. Forrest was taken suddenly ill and at 6 o'clock in the evening I was asked if I would play *Richelieu* in Forrest's place that night. I played the role. Then I went on a *starring* tour to Dublin, came back and opened about 1870 at Wallack's Theatre in the original production of 'Pygmalion and Galatea,' originating the role of *Pygmalion.* I was also the original *Micawber* at Niblo's Garden in 1869, and the original *David Garrick* at the Broadway Theatre, New York. Of recent years I have *starred* in 'Soldiers of Trust,' 'Micawber,' 'David Garrick, 'The Streets of New York.' 'Under Cover' and 'Rosedale.' For three seasons, from 1889 to 1892, I was a member of the Boston Museum stock company, and was in the original cast of 'All the Comforts of Home.' And this brings us pretty nearly up to date."

NICHOLAS S. WOOD was born at Bingen on the Rhine in 1861, and first appeared on the stage at Booth's Theatre in 1871 as a page in "Romeo and Juliet." When he was only fourteen he made his appearance as a *star* as "Poor Joe" at the same theatre. During the engagement he played "Hamlet," and subsequently enacted "The Boy Detective" at the Old Bowery Theatre. He has also appeared in the following dramas: "Fool's Revenge," "Richard III.," "Jack Sheppard" "Boy Scout," "Dick, the Newsboy," "Jack Harkaway." He has also appeared with Lester Wallack in the comedy of "A Scrap of Paper" and "My Awful Dad" in New York city for a period of eleven weeks. The newsboys and bootblacks are especially fond of him, and the Philadelphia newsboys at one time showed their appreciation of him by presenting him with an elegant gold medal, which he now wears.

EDWIN ARDEN (real name Edwin Smith), a capable young actor, proved to be a strong drawing card for several seasons in "Eagle's Nest," which he wrote in collaboration with his father, Arden Smith. They were also the joint authors of "Raglan's Way," also the dramatization of "Louis XI.," from Sir Walter Scott's "Quinten Durward," for Thos. W. Keene, the tragedian. Mr. Arden is married to Mr. Keene's daughter. His father, Arden Smith, died in Oct., 1897. Edwin Arden was born in 1861, and first appeared on the stage in Chicago in 1882, as *Tyrrel* in "Richard III." He *starred* for six years in "Eagle's Nest," following which he was for two seasons in support of W. H. Crane and one season with Julia Arthur.

Among the prominent people who have had the curtain rung down on them for the last time are:

FRANK I. FRAYNE, who appeared at the Theatre Royal, week of 28th April, 1887, died 16th March, 1891. He was born in 1836, and first appeared on the stage in 1862. He was featuring as an expert shooter in "Si Slocum," and by an unfortunate miss caused the death of his leading lady, Annie Von Behren, 30th November, 1882.

JAMES L. EDWARDS, last seen here week of 9th October, 1888, as *Jack Herne* in "The Romany Rye," died 14th June, 1891, in his thirty-eighth year. At the time of his death he was a member of H. R. Jacob's company playing "The Way of the World" at Havlin's The-atre, Chicago, and was found dead in his room. Mr. Edwards was a vigorous actor, and had of late years played leads in numerous travelling companies and in support of well-known *stars*.

DAN McCARTHY, so popular in "True Irish Hearts," in which he *starred* from 1886 to 1892, died 15th Jan., 1899, aged 39. He and his wife, Kittie Coleman, first appeared in the varieties.

GEORGE T. ULMER, frequently seen here, died at Juneau (Klondike), 1st March, 1899, aged 51. He had been a drummer in the Civil war, and his first stage efforts were as a member of the Selwyn stock company in Boston, 1868. He was the husband of Lizzie May Ulmer.

THE DOMINION THEATRE,

situated on Gosford Hill, between St. Louis and Champ de Mars streets, was Montreal's eleventh theatre. It was the original Trinity Church, and, later, the "Garrison Chapel." The place was afterwards used as militia offices, and in time purchased by the Catholic diocese of Montreal. In 1870 the property passed into the hands of John A. Rafter, the pur-chase price amounting to $11,000, and several thousand dol-lars more were expended in fitting up the place for theatrical purposes. It had one gallery, and altogether had a seating capacity for 1,000 or 1,200. The property was held by Mr. Rafter until 1878, when it was purchased by Michel Lefebvre for a vinegar factory. Andrew Brissett & Fils are its present occupants. Melvin (Diamond) Smith was its first lessee; then McLeish and Fortin assumed control. During a short season, commencing 21st September, Hartley Neuville was the manager. The house was then known as the Palace Musi-cale. Neuville was fairly successful, but was under rather high rental, having a sublease from Fortin. During the month of November the name of the theatre changed to Neuville's Variety Theatre. The principal attraction was

Miss Sophie Neuville at the head of vaudeville performances. "George Pogey" was a favorite production, and in its cast appeared the leading people attached to the house, viz.: Hartley Neuville, Albert Smith, J. Elseman, G. Esmond, Jacob Nibbs, Sophie Neuville and Annie Hindle. It continued under the same management until the spring, when, after a short close, it reopened as the New Dominion Theatre, 4th August, 1873, under the management and lesseeship of A. Macfarlane, with the Zanfretta Ravel Troupe, which included at the time Jessie Macfarlane and Jennie Kimball, then a serio-comic artist.

MRS. JENNIE KIMBALL, the well-known manageress, died March 23, 1896, in St. Paul, Minn. She was born in New Orleans, La., June 23, 1848. Her first public appearance was as *Obeda* in "Bluebeard" at the Boston Theatre, in 1855. On the completion of her studies she was engaged for leading *soubrette* business at the Continental Theatre, Boston, in 1868, appearing as *Cinderella* in Byron's Burlesque and *Stalacta* in "The Black Crook." In 1881 Miss Kimball commenced her career as a manageress, organizing an opera company of juveniles, of which Corinne was the *star*. They continued uninterruptedly successful until the interference of the Society for the Prevention of Cruelty to Children, of New York city. After the celebrated trial, which gave Mrs. Kimball and Corinne much notoriety, they played throughout the United States and Canada, meeting with considerable success. Mrs. Kimball had a capacity for work that was something marvellous, and had by her untiring energy and executive ability brought Corinne to the front rank as a *star*. Mrs. Kimball, who was a widow, was married to Arling Schaefer, October 1, 1893, at Milwaukee, Wis.

The management of the house changed hands in November, George J. Deagle assuming control and continuing in vaudeville features until the spring of 1874, when E. M. Hall became manager under the lesseeship of Gonghier and Mallette. In April we find the style changed to the Royal Opera House. On 10th November Shoemaker and Leslie became its managers, and among its principal attractions was Annie Hindle, the well-known male impersonator.

ANNIE HINDLE. In Jersey City, N.J., in 1892, occurred one of the strangest funeral spectacles ever witnessed in this or in any other country. Annie Ryan, the wife, was dead, and Annie Hindle, the husband, was burying her. Beside Annie Hindle being a woman's widower she was also a man's widow. What wonder that the funeral was unique. About 1852, Annie Hindle, then 5 years old, was adopted by a woman in England and went on the London stage. She was popular as a singer from the start, and as she grew older her popularity increased. Her forte was as a "male impersonator." In 1867 she came to New York, and her accuracy of mimicry reaped fame and dollars. At the same time Charles Vivian, an English actor and founder of the Order of Elks, was in this country, and he and Annie fell in love. In 1868 they were married in Philadelphia, Pa., and a few months later separated forever at Denver, Col. In 1880 Vivian died at Leadville. Annie continued on the stage, gaining fame, making friends and winning money. One of those who waited upon her in her character as "male impersonator" was Annie Ryan They were much attached to each other, and one night in June, 1886, the couple were married by a minister at Grand Rapids, Mich. For four or five years Annie Hindle and her wife, Annie Ryan, lived happily on Jersey City Heights, in a neat little house which Hindle had built years before. The neighbors respected them; the world did not disturb them with its gossip; fortune was kind to them. There were many mourners over the bier of Annie, but the deepest sorrower was Annie Hindle. A strange fate has overtaken Annie Hindle, who has passed her life impersonating men on the variety stage. She has grown a moustache, and believes at times that she is a man. In male dress she presents all the appearance of an ordinary man. Annie Hindle was originally a rather pretty girl, very thick set and sturdy in physique. A faint line of black hair adorned her upper lip. Then she shaved the lip, with the result that the hair came out thicker than before. When she took to impersonating men on the stage she shaved regularly, and eventually succeeded in raising a fine moustache. She also shaved her chin, and that part of her face presents the customary appearance of a shaven surface. Her voice became masculine in tone, and recently it appears that her mind has become somewhat unhinged on the subject of her sex.

Gerty Granville was also a favorite during this time, her song of "Down in a Coal Mine" being very popular, as was also Iona Lang. The Ben De Bar season of 1875 was the most notable in the history of the theatre, which again changed its name to De Bar's Opera House on 3rd May, under Mr. De Bar's management, with Baker and Farron in "Chris and Lena." The tragedian, T. C. King, appeared, 17th, in " Macbeth' ; " Richelieu," 18th ; "Hamlet," 19th ; "Othello," 20th; "Pizarro," 21st; and "Ingomar," 22nd, when he closed. Dominick Murray came week 24th; Ada Gray week 31st; J. J. Wallace, in "The Man from America," week 7th June; George L. Fox, in "Humpty Dumpty," week 14th; Rose Wood and Lewis Morrison, in "A Bit o' Ash," week

21st, this being Mr. Morrison's first *star* appearance in Montreal.   P. E. Sullivan, in "Kathleen Mavourneen," was seen 28th June.   Thomas G. Riggs and W. F. Harris appeared week 29th; and Daly's Company, which had been fulfilling an engagement at the Theatre Royal during the previous week, opened in "A Big Bonanza," 5th July, for week.   Following came Lizzie Pierson and Charlotte M. Stanley in "The Marble Heart." Tony Pastor, Belvil Ryan, Troupe of Japs, Lizzie Wilkinson and John Thompson *starred* successively, and on 23rd August Rena and Fred. G. Maeder appeared in "Hazel Eye," and "Kit Carson."   Augusta L. Dargon, in "Camille," and "Lucretia Borgia," came week 30th; Miss J. Vandyke week 6th September; John Dillon week 14th; and a return engagement, 20th, of Thos. C. King in Shakespearean repertoire.   The season closed 27th, with "Belphegor," in a benefit performance to Henry W. Mitchell; King was *Belphegor* and Lizzie Pierson the *Madeline.*

AUGUSTA L. DARGON, the Irish *tragedienne*, was the daughter of a physician, whose father was General Dargon, a well-known Irish patriot.   Miss   Dargon's mother was Scotch.   Augusta came to America at an early age, and it was at the suggestion of Horace Greeley that she first gave a series of readings.   Meeting with some success she adopted the stage as a profession.   She was fulfilling an engagement in Chicago on the night of the great fire, 8th October 1871, and was the victim of serious injuries, which obliged her to go to Paris for treatment, and interrupted her career for a time.   Her record in America was not a brilliant one, but in Australia she was more enthusiastically received.

LEWIS MORRISON was born in Jamaica, W.I., 4th September, 1844. He had scarcely attained his majority when he became an officer in the U. S. army, in which he served three years and six months.   He was one of the forlorn hope of Port Hudson.   In 1863 he entered the dramatic profession at New Orleans, under Barrett's management.   He made rapid progress and soon rose to be a recognized leading man, his work in that capacity being well received at the Walnut Street Theatre.   He subsequently supported Salvini, playing *Iago* to the Italian's *Othello,* etc.   Since commencing an independent *starring* career some ten years ago this actor has met with considerable success, both artistically as well as financially.   His principal production has been "Faust," but he has of late years also appeared with deserved approbation in revivals of Howell's "Yorick's Love," made familiar to us by Lawrence Barrett.   Richelieu" was played by Mr. Morrison for the first time on 24th September, 1892, at the Queen's Theatre, Montreal.   He has of late added two new plays to his repertoire, "The Master of Ceremonies," and "Frederick the Great." His second wife is Florence Roberts. The actor first married Rose Wood, daughter of Wm. A. Wood, 28th August, 1865. Florence Roberts' first husband was Walter Gale, whom she married 15th April, 1882.

THOMAS GRATTAN RIGGS was an exceedingly droll comedian, who for many years entertained delightful audiences. He was born at Buffalo, N.Y., in 1835, and was best known in vaudeville features of Irish parts. He went to Australia in the seventies and played there for many years. He died in Tasmania 15th June, 1899.

GEORGE L. FOX, probably the most celebrated pantomimist since the days of Grimaldi, was born in Boston in 1825. He first appeared on the boards in his fifth year at the Tremont Theatre in a benefit performance to Chas. Kean, and in New York in 1850, in the "Demon of the Forest." He served in the war and was at Bull Run. Returning to the stage in July, 1861, he subsequently became manager of the old Bowery Theatre. It was at the Olympia in 1867-68 that he made his great hit in "Humpty Dumpty." His flight was not high as an artist, but within it he was unsurpassed, his humor being a most spontaneous and irresistible drollery. He died in Cambridge, Mass., 24th October, 1877.

JOHN DILLON (John Daily Marum), born in Ireland, 1831, came to America at the age of seventeen. He was early doing stock work under Laura Keene and others, and later *starred* in "The Crucible," and "State's Attorney."

During the 1876 season the style was once more changed, the theatre being called the Champ de Mars Theatre. Chas. L. Howard was the manager. A season of vaudeville ensued, and on 17th August, Denman Thompson appeared in the first draft of "The Old Homestead," then known as "Joshua Whitcomb." The year following was without interest, and in 1878, which was the last in the history of the house as a theatre, it became known again as the Dominion Theatre. The opening was on 3rd June, with Mlle. Lefavre's Burlesque Troupe, which continued for a few weeks. Wood and West became its managers and lessees 6th August, when the house was called Wood and West's Varieties. John B. Sparrow was the next, and last recorded, lessee, opening a three weeks' season with May Fisk's British Blondes. Capt. Bogardus and others also appeared during the short season. The theatre was never a money-maker for its lessees, and at odd times during its two last years of existence some of the most objectionable scenes were represented within its walls, of which "Bathing in the Nile," and kindred attractions, may be remembered as fair specimens of the prevailing taste of our play-goers. An interesting diversion of the pit was "tossing." A boy on a back bench would say, "Toss me," and two or three of his companions would pick him up and swing him over the head of those in front. The latter, upon whose heads he had landed, would forward him with another swing, and, finally, he would arrive at the front bench, where he was privileged to stay as a reward for the hardships of his flight. The building has scarcely changed its appearance during the past twenty years, still being in a good state of preservation.

THE ACADEMY OF MUSIC.

This structure, which is situated on the east side of Victoria street, a few doors above St. Catherine street, was commenced early in 1875, the late Mr. Taft being the architect. It has a neat exterior, and is built of brick with a stone frontage. The interior consists of four boxes, four stalls, two galleries, and has a seating capacity of about 2,000. It was erected by a company composed of the late Sir Hugh Allan as president; Chas. D. Tylee, secretary; Harrison Stephens, Boswell Fisher and others. The late Eugene A. McDowell was the first manager, and its opening took place on the 15th November, 1875, with Lester Wallack's military drama, "Rosedale," McDowell appearing as *Col. Eliot Gray*, and Miss Fanny Reeves as *Rosa Leigh*. Chief in the supporting stock company were Mr. and Mrs. Charles Loveday, Jos. Alfred Smith, Affie Weaver, Felix J. Morris, Fred. Bryton (then known as Fred. O. Smith), Victoria Cameron and Florence Vincent. G. B. Greene was the business manager. On the 4th of June, 1877, the reins of office passed into the hands of John W. Norton, who was in turn succeeded by F. J. Morris & Co. in August. William Nannary assumed affairs in December, continuing until September, 1878, when Lucien Barnes ventured his chances. After a very short season he left for parts unknown, and it is said that some of his creditors are still looking for him. He is now living in Chicago, and reputed to be quite wealthy. Barnes' successor was George Wallace, the journalist, who met with better success. In 1880 Henry Thomas became lessee and manager. He was closely assisted by Mrs. Thomas, who continued to conduct the affairs of the theatre after her husband's death in 1893. This clever woman faced the ordeal of opposition and business depression single-handed, and with success up to the occasion of her marriage with Mr. Frank Murphy, when the labors became divided. The Allan family, who had in time acquired all the shares of the theatre, sold the property after the death of Henry Thomas, in March, 1894, to David Walker, for $60,000. In the first week of January, 1877, during a performance of "The Naiad Queen," the building suddenly settled, the top gallery sinking fully five inches. Matters grew worse and worse, until March, 1896, when the building was officially condemned. The Murphys retired from the management and leased the Monument National Auditorium, where was produced, week of 16th March, Palmer Cox's "Brownies." Since then the work of reconstructing the theatre has been well done, three of the walls having been entirely rebuilt. Messrs. Sparrow and Jacobs, already lessees of the Theatre Royal and Queen's Theatre, assumed control of the new Academy, which was reopened 7th September, 1896, with De Wolf Hopper in "El Capitan." Sparrow and Jacobs continued together until early in 1898, when, after some litigation, Mr. Jacobs retired. W. A. Edwards became Mr. Sparrow's representative in 1896. This is the brief outline of the Theatre's twenty-five years' history.

Following the opening bill of "Rosedale," 15th November, 1875 (first produced at Wallack's Theatre, New York, 30th September, 1863), came "Saratoga," and Gertrude Kellogg appeared, week 22nd, in "Mary Warner." The stock company appeared in the following pieces successively until the end of the year : the Fifth Avenue successes, "Divorce," "Pique," "A Big Bonanza," "Saratoga," and "Under the Gaslight"; the Union Square pieces, "The Two Orphans," "The Geneva Cross," and "Rose Michel"; also "Ticket-of-Leave Man," "Arrah na Pogue," "Married Life," "My Uncle's Will," "Turn Him Out," "Cinderella," and, 14th and 15th December, the prima-donna, Clara Fisher, appeared in "The Rose of Castile."

Writing of this period, Felix Morris says: "The opening night of the new theatre in Montreal came, and with it a packed house and splendid audience. 'Rosedale' was the attraction, and the verdict was unanimously a great 'go.' My popularity was quickly at the full, our receipts were very large, and the harvest never-ending.

And yet I had the utmost difficulty in getting my salary. Our business manager had a knack of vanishing behind doors and of disappearing around corners, and, as for excuses, he was a perfect master in the art. My salary was very small considering the position I held and the popularity I enjoyed. I was urged by my fellow actors, Frederic Bryton among the number, to insist upon an increase. This I hesitated to do, for I was happy in the enjoyment of my extraordinary popularity, and in the knowledge that my name was a household word. Numberless considerations influenced me in my hesitation about asking for adequate compensation, but at last I summoned up courage and approached my manager. An opportunity to attack him offered at his hotel, and I lured him into the smooking-room, which happened to be vacant. He was unsuspicious of my motive, and slapped me on the back, and in pleasant tones assured me of his esteem. I hummed and hawed a little, and then ejaculated the words, 'Increase my salary!' With a broken, disgusted look, and a smothered groan, he sank into a chair like a man striken with disease, and actually wept. 'My boy,' said he, between sobs, 'after all my kindness, after all I've done for you! Why, Felix, I've made you, and this is your gratitude?' I never felt so guilty in all my life, and vainly tried to comfort him. The scene ended in my being almost as much affected as he was, and away I went, loathing myself for having caused his gentle heart such pain. On comparing notes with my fellow actors, I found my account of the interview was received with the utmost hilarity, and that the whole scene was simply a chesnut."

EUGENE A. McDOWELL was a conscientious actor and a painstaking manager, never grumbling at the cost of mounting a play properly. He was a favorite with every one, being most affable and courteous, and was a staunch friend. He was born at South River. New Jersey, in 1845. He went on the stage at an early age and very soon became known in theatrical circles as a very promising actor and capital stage manager. It was at the outset of his career that he was engaged to manage the affairs of Montreal's new temple of art as well as to play leading business in the lighter parts of standard drama. It has been well said that not only did Mr. McDowell and Miss Fanny Reeves capture their audience by their charming acting, but that they also became susceptible to each other's charms and from making love to each other in fun, it became real, with the result that they were married, the event taking place at the church of St. James the Apostle, the bride being given away by Sir Hugh Allan, who had taken a fancy to the young couple. This event occurred 30th January, 1877. on the eve of his resigning the management of the house, after considerable hard work and very little financial success. It was not the time of *star* touring combinations, and although excellent performances were given by the stock company the system met with less support from the fickle public. After retiring from the management of the theatre here, Mr. and Mrs. McDowell engaged a company of their own and started out on a *starring* tour. They went all over Canada, playing in all the leading cities to good business for years, but would lose what they made in Canada in the United States. This always worried poor McDowell a great deal, and he finally broke down under the strain in 1892, dying of paresis at Bloomingdale, 21st February, 1893. His wife and daughter survive him. The patrons of the Academy and Victoria Rifles will remember how beautifully he mounted "Our Regiment," in which the late Major Short, R.C.A. took the leading role, and McDowell played the *Chaplain* in 1889. The entertainment was for the Victoria Rifles Armony building fund, and was a financial and artistic success. In 1891 Mr. McDowell and his wife last appeared at the Academy, supported by an excellent company. He was in good health and spirits then, and he would say, laughingly, to his friends, "Going through Canada once more for another fortune."

FANNY REEVES is a daughter of W. H. Reeves and a niece to the great Sims Reeves. She was born in 1852, and first played on the stage with her mother and brother at Laura Keene's Theatre when still a mere child. Fanny Reeves' father was a prominent tenor, at one time with the Seguin Operatic Troupe, who died in 1859. Her mother, Jane C. Porter, died 24th Dec., 1898, aged 78. Her father was Christopher Webster, an English actor.

Neil Warner opened the year of 1876 on 1st January as *Sir Giles Overreach* in "A New Way to Pay Old Debts," and "Robert Macaire," this being his first appearance at the Academy. Mr. Warner was engaged by the management for leading heavies, and after productions of "Simpson & Co.," "Pocahontas," and "The Shaughran," he appeared as *Shylock* and *Macbeth*, when the regular season closed.

THE YEAR 1876.

Productions of "Simpson & Co.," "Pocahontas," "Caste," " Merchant of Venice," " Shaughran," and " Macbeth," followed to the end of January, when the season closed until 17th April, opening with "Uncle Tom's Cabin," first produced at the Chatham Street Theatre, New York, 24th August, 1852. Geo. Kunkel appeared in this Montreal production, supported by the regular stock company, consisting of Connie Thompson, Carlotta Evelyn, Florence Chippendale (Mrs. Neil Warner), Victoria Cameron, Isabel Waldron, and others.

Following a series of standard productions came Edwin F.
Thorne, as *D'Artagnan* in Dumas' story, 14th June; then Geo.
F. Rowe in "Brass"; the Vokes Family, consisting of Rosina,
Victoria, Jessie, Fred and Fawdon, their Montreal *debut*, 24th
July, in "Belles of the Kitchen," and "Delicate Ground."
Isabel Morris, sister of Felix, began 11th August in "Lan-
cers," this being her first appearance here. Joseph Murphy,
in "Kerry Gow," made his first appearance at this house 14th
August. The season closed 26th August with "The Shaugh-
ran." Sir Randall Howland Roberts was seen in " Don
Cæsar," and "King O'Neil," 13th October.

THE VOKES FAMILY were all born at London, Eng. The four
eldest made their appearance in America in 1868. They subsequently
became scattered. Fred. M. was born in 1846. Jessie and Victoria
appeared on the stage at the ages of four and two years respectively.
Victoria was not only a *comedienne* and singer, but attempted higher
walks in her earlier days, when she appeared as *Amy Robsart* at Drury
Lane Theatre. Her last appearance as a *star* in Montreal was
at the Academy of Music, week 2nd October, 1889. Her tour was not
a success. She died in London, 2nd of December, 1894. Fawden
(who was a Vokes by profession only) made his *debut* at the Lyceum
Theatre, London, in 1868, in "Humpty Dumpty." Poor Rosina !
How well we remember her high spirits, her impetuous laugh and
that saucy toss of the head. Her husband, Cecil Clay, had been an
attorney, and after their marriage Rosina retired from the stage,
but reverses brought her back in 1884, under the management of her
husband. We shall not soon forget her clever work on the boards
of the Academy, when so ably supported by our late lamented friend,
Felix J. Morris. She died of consumption 1st of January, 1894.

"Her 'art was true to Poll."

FELIX JAMES MORRIS was born in England, 25th April, 1850,
and first studied medicine. His father attempted to dissuade the
boy from going on the stage, but without success, and, after considerable privations after coming to America, was encouraged by J. W.
Albaugh, where at Albany he was given speaking parts. In 1875
he came to Montreal, remaining two seasons as a member of the
Academy stock, and during a part of the third season was joint
manager and lessee with Neil Warner. Following an engagement with

Lotta, he went with Boucicault, and then into the production of the stage version of "Michael Strogoff" in Booth's Theatre in the metropolis, scoring heavily as one of the comic correspondents. Going to London, he made a hit there in "On Change." It was following his return from England that he became associated with the late Rosina Vokes, in whose company he first became known to the general theatre-goer as a player of fine intelligence, considerable versatility, and a genius for detail that mounted to a positive defect. Miss Vokes had not been too successful in her effort to establish herself as a *star* in bills consisting of three pieces in the course of a single evening although her vehicles were clever and her company composed of players of skill and ability. Morris succeeded Weedon Grossmith in the genre-roles of the repertoire. He was co-*starred*, or, rather, featured with Regina Vokes. The scheme of arrangement put him for ward as the *star* of the first play of each evening. The second had Miss Vokes in the principal role. The third would give both players equal opportunities. Morris gave us some excellent acting during his association with the English *comedienne*. His best work was in the roles in short plays permitting of elaborate characterization. His picture of the old aristocrat in "A Game of Cards" marked his very best achievement. In a character calling for sustained impersonation throughout an entire evening, Morris usually grew monotonous; for he didn't possess the "voice various," and his work was generally all in one key. After leaving Miss Vokes, Morris tried *starring*, but the venture was quite unsuccessful. He played for a short period in London, and then returned. joining the Daniel Frohman "stock." He was a member of the company at the time of his death, although his arrangement with the management permitted him to appear in the varieties when not wanted for the play in course of presentment. Mr. Morris married Mary B. Schoot, who is better known by her stage name, Florence Wood. They first met at Halifax and were married at San Francisco. The popular comedian died at New York city, 13th January, 1900, being survived by his widow, a son and two daughters, Felice and Mildred.

SIR RANDALL H. ROBERTS, actor and dramatist, died 10th October, 1899, aged 62.

E. A. McDowell reopened the house as lessee, with Charles Arnold as business manager, on the 13th of December, in a benefit performance for the Brooklyn fire sufferers, but it closed again and was not reopened until 1st January, 1877.

THE SEASON OF 1877

was opened 1st January, by "The Naiad Queen," with Clara
Fisher and the St. Felix Sisters as the principals.   It was
during one of these performances that week that the top gallery of the theatre sank fully five inches, the building settling
considerably.   "Uncle Tom's Cabin" was produced week of
8th, with Alice Kemp as *Topsy*, E. A. McDowell as *George
Harris*, and Felix Morris as *Marks*.   O. D. Byron, in "Across
the Continent," week 15th, and "The Mystery of Edwin
Drood," week 22nd, Neil Warner as *John Jasper*, in W. H.
Young's dramatization of Dickens' novel.   This was followed by a revival of "Rosedale," and on 29th Ida Savory
began an engagement in "As You Like It," "Romeo and
Juliet," "Pygmalion and Galatea," and "Led Astray."   Dominick Murray came week 5th February, after which the stock
appeared in "After Dark," and "Rob Roy."   The great event
of the season, the appearance of the brightest *star* of them
all, Lilian Adelaide Neilson, under the management of Max
Strokosch, in five representations, supported by Neil Warner,
Eben Plympton, and the regular stock company.   The opening was, 27th February, in "Romeo and Juliet," Miss Neil-
son as *Juliet*, Plympton as *Romeo*, Warner as *Mercutio*, Felix
Morris as *Benvolio*, and Florence Vincent as the *Nurse*.   "As
You Like It" was given 28th; "Lady of Lyons," 1st March;
"Twelfth Night," 2nd March; and "The Hunchback," 3rd.
This was Miss Neilson's *debut* here.   Her last appearance
here was 31st January, 1880.   The stock company appeared
5th March in "The Shaughran," etc., until 12th, when
"Daniel Druce," with J. B. Studley, under the management of
Jarrett & Palmer, was produced. . George Fawcett Rowe
came week 19th, in "Little Em'ly," etc., followed, 2nd April,
by Maffit & Bartholomew's "Robinson Crusoe," and "Robert
Macaire."   "Uncle Tom's Cabin" was revived week 9th,
when George Kunkel reappeared.   Rose Eytinge came 16th
April in "Miss Multon," and "Love's Sacrifice," supported by
the Academy stock company.   It will be interesting to note
that it was during this engagement of Miss Eytinge that
Annie Russell, the clever *comedienne*, made her first appearance on the boards.   Miss Russell tells the story as follows:

" I remember very vividly my first appearance.   It was when I was
about ten years old, in Montreal.   It wasn't accident—it was grim
necessity that led me to make the attempt.   My mother saw an ad-

WILLIAM CHARLES MACREADY.

vertisement in a newspaper for a little girl, and holding me, a small and fragile looking tot, by the hand, she answered it at the stage door oi the theatre. It was my first experience with those humble en_ trances on a side street that I now know so well, and I was awe_ struck. Fear and trembling filled my small soul· Nor did our re_ ception allay these feelings. We were told abruptly that I was much too little and puny, and my mother and I turned away disheartened. But we heard that Rose Eytinge was coming to Montreal and wanted a child for the play, "Miss Multou." We applied to her advance man, and he said I might learn the part. I was in the seventh heaven of delight at first, and then I settled down to study. Oh, how I studied and practiced those lines ! At last came the fateful day when Miss Eytinge was to arrive in town, and I was to know whether or not I could have the part. I was a very timid little girl, and I looked for_ ward with terror toward the meeting. When Miss Eytinge saw me, shrinking and infantile, she exclaimed in a tone of much annoyance:

" 'Who ever thought that little thing could play the part ? Get me somebody at once—a woman who can play a child's part.—anybody.'

" 'Just let the child repeat the lines, Miss Eytinge,' exclaimed the gentleman who said I might try the part.

" 'Oh, very well, but I know it's useless. Go on, little one.'

" And then I began to speak the lines that I had conned over until I could have said them in my sleep. Miss Eytinge listened atten- tively until I had finished, and then exclaimed in a tone of satisfaction and relief:

" 'Why, this little girl will do very nicely indeed.' Thus it was that I made my first appearance."

Annie Russell, was born in Liverpool, England, in 1865. In early childhood, however, her parents decided that their fortunes would be bettered by migration to Canada, and in 1869 were living in Montreal.

John T. Raymond first appeared, week April 24, in "The Gilded Age," and "Col. Sellars." W. H. Lytell was a pro- minent figure, 30th April, in "Our Boarding-House," and during the following week, which was the last of the regular season. He was seen as *Passpartout* in "Around the World in Eighty Days." Jehin Prume and Calixa Lavallee, both a credit to Montreal as representative musicians, produced their musical piece, "Joan of Arc," week 14th May, followed 21st by E. A. Sothern in "Our American Cousin"; "Dundreary's Brother Sam," 22nd; "The Hornet's Nest," 23rd; "David Garrick," 24th; "The Crushed Tragedian," 25th, which was repeated 26th. John W. Norton reopened the theatre 4th June with Lotta, supported by C. W. Butler and John Ellsler's dramatic club, under the management of Max Strakosch, in "Musette," and "Bip." Her first appearance here was at the Theatre Royal, 21st August, 1865. H. J. Montague, in "False Shame," "Society," etc., came week 11th June, and George Rignold came week 18th June in a grand production of

"Henry V." Kate Claxton came 26th June in "The Two
Orphans," and "Conscience." Jennie Hughes, in "Love
Among the Roses," and "Caste," came 2nd July, followed by
Alice Oates in operatic burlesques.

This again closed the season, which was reopened by Felix
J. Morris & Co. as lessees and managers (Morris & Warner),
20th August, with a return of George Rignold in "Henry V."
Miss Isabel Morris was the *Katherine*; Mr. Orvey as *Bar-
dolphe*; Mr. Meade the *Pistol*; and Mr. Morris as *Fluellen.*
During the week of 28th Mr. Rignold produced "Amos
Clark," "Alme," and subsequently "Romeo and Juliet," he as
Romeo, and Marie Wainwright, who had been one of his
Juliets already mentioned, as the *Capulet* maiden. This was
Miss Wainwright's *debut* here. Mr and Mrs. Albaugh came
3rd September in "Louis XI.," and "Victor of Rhe," sup-
ported by the Leland Opera House Company. On 7th
"Othello" was produced with Albaugh as *Iago*, and Neil War-
ner as the *Moor*. The engagement closed with "Eustache."
Rice's "Evangeline," headed by Eliza Weathersby and Nat
C. Goodwin, Jun., opened week 10th September. They also
produced "Le Petit Corsair." Joseph Murphy, in "Kerry
Gow," "Help," etc., was seen week 17th September, followed
by Neil Warner and Gertrude Kellog in "The New Magdalen," and in turn by productions of "Jo," "The Two Roses,"
"Ticket-of-Leave Man," "Guy Mannering," "The Taming
of the Shrew," "Pink Dominoes," "Kathleen Mavourneen,"
"Colleen Bawn," "East Lynne," "Still Waters Run Deep,"
and 26th November Harvey Bawtree, a well-known elocutionist, appeared as *John Mildmay* in a benefit performance
to Warner, closing the season. William Nannary became the
next lessee and manager, opening the house 31st December
with the Anna Granger-Dow English Opera Company,
which included Joseph Maas, tenor, and W. T. Carleton,
baritone.

OF THE 1877 SEASON

Mr. Morris writes :—" We supported, during the course of
the season, George Fawcett Rowe, in his unrivalled performance of *Micawber*, and the incomparable Adelaide
Neilson. We had been waiting about at the theatre for hours
one day, expecting her arrival. Trains were delayed, and
it was three o'clock before she put in an appearance. At

that hour she bustled on to the stage in travelling ulster and soft-crowned hat. She was very tired, and evidently out of sorts. She was accompanied by Eben Plympton for leading support. 'And this is the great Neilson,' I told myself· The reverie into which I disappointedly had fallen was disturbed by the sound of a gruff voice, accompanied by an angry push. 'Clear the stage, you supers,' said the voice. 'One moment,' I explained, 'I'm the super who plays *Touchstone.*' Plympton understood his mistake, and made amends by introducing me to Miss Neilson. At night what a transformation we witnessed in this remarkable woman ! As she sailed on she was nothing short of a vision, and her performance of *Rosalind* was a revelation. She was very gracious to me; sent for me to come to her dressing-room, and complimented me in the most flattering terms on my *Touchstone.* The success of my Shakespearean comedy characters I attribute very largely to the kindly interest of Mr. T. D. King, of Montreal. He was an enthusiast, and had accumulated a valuable Shakespearean library. Together we made researches, compared notes, verified certain readings, and the results were unusually satisfactory. When Mr. King died his valuable collection became the property of McGill College. As the season drew to a close, my name was put up for a benefit. I was the recipient of a handsome testimonial from the company, in the form of Knight's edition of Shakespeare, and an overflowing house greeted my appearance. I played *Bob Sackett* in Bronson Howard's ' Saratoga.' A tremendous call brought me before the curtain, and after a shower of bouquets, I was allowed to return thanks, which I did in a few carefully prepared remarks. I was somewhat disappointed, however, at the reception of my words."

HENRY J. MONTAGUE (Mann), the idol of the matinee girl, was a most pleasing *jeune premier*, who came to this country from England in 1874 to repeat unqualified successes in a limited range of parts. He died in San Francisco, 11th August, 1878, aged thirty-five.

CALIXA LAVALLEE, after a short but very brilliant career as a musician, died 21st January, 1891.

FRANTZ HENRY JEHIN-PRUME was a noted Belgian violinist, who, after brilliant achievements in Europe, Mexico, Cuba and the United States, settled in Montreal in 1865. He died 29th May, 1899, aged sixty-nine.

CHARLES ARNOLD was born in Lucerne, his father being a captain in the Swiss Legion, who rendered such good service to the British during the Crimean war that the Government rewarded him by giving him a grant of land in Canada. Charles Arnold served five years in the study of law. His first appearance on the dramatic stage was as an amateur, and while playing at Hoboken, N.J., in a burlesque of "Romeo and Juliet," he was engaged by the manager of Mrs. Conway's Brooklyn Theatre. That was in 1875. After remaining there one season he came to Montreal, Can., and became manager of the Academy of Music. From here he went to Winnipeg with his company—the first which ever appeared in that place. Winnipeg at that time was merely a village, principally inhabited by Indians and half-breeds, the English population being very limited. They next visited Emerson, the population of which numbered about one thousand, and they had never had a theatrical performance before. The "theatre" was an old warehouse full of farming implements and boxes. The place had but two exits, one of which was from the platform to the prairie, where tents had been rigged up for the company. There was not a house nearer than a mile, and, as everybody came on horseback, the outside was like a horse fair. Soap and candle boxes formed the back seats, champagne and brandy cases being in front. The inhabitants were anxious for the company to remain a second night, which they could not do on account of being booked elsewhere, so another performance was given that same night at 11.15. A Canadian political burlesque, "H.M.S. Parliament," written to "Pinafore" music, was given. The orchestra consisted of a church organ. Mr. Arnold has been all over the world during the last twenty years. His "Hans the Boatman" was played for forty-six weeks in the English provinces with success. He made his London *debut* July 4, 1887, at the Grand Theatre, Islington. Having played at Terry's Theatre, Strand, London, and met with considerable success, in February, 1888, Mr. Arnold sailed from England for Australia, and for a season of ten months made a tour of the colonies. After visiting Adelaide he went to New Zealand. He seldom acted in a theatre, but appeared in halls and drill sheds. No orchestra of any description could be had in any of these towns, and the only music was a violin solo by the leader that he carried with him, Mr. Arnold having to sing his songs as Hans to a single violin accompaniment. After a brief stay in England Mr. Arnold came to America for a three years' tour. He is now playing in Australia.

JOHN B. STUDLEY was born in Boston, Mass., in 1831. He first appeared on the professional stage in 1848 at Columbia, S. C. He became leading man at the National Theatre, Boston, 1853-54, and subsequently *starred* with Sallie St. Clair through the South and West, later supporting Charlotte Cushman. An able critic wrote of

JOHN T. RAYMOND.

him during a Bowery Theatre engagement: "I may remark that I have seen an actor of leading business, who is not only one of the best performers in New York, but could not be easily surpassed in London." Mr. Studley was last seen in Montreal as a *star* at the Theatre Royal in "A Great Wrong," week of 20th February, 1888.

EBEN PLYMPTON, one of the most talented men on the stage, has long been known as a capable leading man. He was born in Boston in 1853, and began his stage career at an early age. He has supported all the great contemporary *stars*, including Booth, Barrett, Neilson and Mary Anderson. His best work has been done in the Shakespearean drama, in which he has shown an artistic and intelligent conception of the great roles, in which he has so ably supported the most famous actors.

ROSE EYTINGE has experienced a most eventful career, and her beauty and talents begot her crowds of admirers. She was born in Philadelphia in 1835, and at the age of 17 made her first appearance at a Brooklyn theatre. In 1855 she married Mr. David Barnes, from whom she was subsequently divorced, and in 1868 married Geo. H. Butler, nephew of General Butler, and went with him to Egypt. She obtained a divorce from him before his death, and afterwards played successfully in England and America. John T. Raymond subsequently married her daughter, Miss Barnes.

JOHN T. RAYMOND, whose real name was O'Brien, was born in Buffalo, April 5, 1836, and made his *debut* June 27, 1853, in Rochester, N. Y., as *Lopez* in "The Honeymoon." His first appearance in England was made in July, 1867, at the Haymarket, London, as *Asa Trenchard*. His best known characters—which indeed were world-wide—were *Fresh, the American and Colonel Sellars*. Mr. Raymond was a great favorite in Montreal and was billed to appear at the Academy of Music the week following his death, which occurred 27th April, 1887, at Evansville, Ind., and the message was speeding over the wires that was to bring anguish worse than death to a young widow and her little one. and tears of sympathy to the eyes of hundreds of thousands, whom in his lifetime the dead actor had helped to make happy. Raymond divided with W. J. Florence the honor of being the first comedian in America. His sunny nature was to the people as an open book. They laughed with him in his spontaneous flights of humor; they wept with him in scenes of pathos. He played upon their emotions with a master hand and touched at will the springs that govern men's sympathies. Every play-goer entertains feelings of respect and admiration for a great tragedian like Booth or Keene, but the comedian is closer to our daily life. He becomes like one of ourselves, and the more we see of him the more we learn to love him.

So it was with Raymond. Raymond, Florence and Sothern made up a trio of practical jokers who earned a reputation. Raymond was fond of "matching" for anything, from pennies up to hundreds of dollars. Once in the California Theatre he and John McCullough matched for the house receipts and McCullogh won. On another occasion when he wanted to go to Europe the habit was so strong on him that he went into a steamship office and offered to match for the passage ticket. Mr. Raymond was twice married. His first wife was Mary Gordon, of Baltimore, a very beautiful woman, whom he married in 1868. He was divorced from her in 1880. His second wife was Rose Courtney Barnes, the daughter of Rose Eytinge and David Barnes. They were married April 11, 1881, and enjoyed a very happy life together. Mr. Raymond was of a very domestic nature and fairly idolized his only child, a boy then four years old. His marriage to Miss Barnes was two days before he had legally changed his name to Raymond. It was a very strange coincidence that he should have followed his future mother-in-law's engagement at Montreal the following week and that the sketches of both should now follow so closely. The original manuscript of the play in which John T. Raymond made his mark as *Colonel Sellars* was at one time stolen, and, in spite of the actor's efforts to get it back, remained out of his possession for months. When it was finally restored to Mr. Raymond, it came mysteriously, with the following note :

"*Dere Col i send you bak your play i seen you on the theatre and i see you are in want all the time, so i send you bak the play and i wish you luk for i dont want to take no poor man's property.*"

The thief had evidently been so impressed by Mr. Raymond's acting of *Sellars* that he took him seriously.

GEORGE RIGNOLD first attracted notice on the London stage by praiseworthy work in 1870, and was for several years closely connected with the Bath and Bristol Theatres. During 1872 he sustained the part of *Posthumus* in "Cymbeline"; of *Icilius* in "Virginius," and several other efforts. He twice visited America and on one occasion played *Romeo* to six *Juliets* at Booth's Theatre, New York, 31st May, 1877. These were Fanny Davenport, Ada Dyas, Maud Granger, Marie Wainwright, Minnie Cummings, and Grace d'Urfey. He is at this writing in Australia, which country now claims him as her own.

KATE CLAXTON was the daughter of Col. Spencer W. Cone, whose father had been a clergyman. Miss Claxton first appeared on the stage at Chicago, but made her regular *debut* at Daly's, where, after playing minor roles, she first made a great hit in "Led Astray." 5th December , 1873, as *Mathilde*, and renewed her success subsequently as *Louise* in "The Two Orphans," and it was while performing that part at the Brooklyn Theatre, 5th December, 1876, that it took fire, and, out of an audience of 1,000, 291 lost their lives, including two actors, H.S. Murdoch and Claude Burroughs· This sad event gave her a great advertisement. She was twice married, first to Isidore Lyons, from whom she was divorced, and in 1878 married Charles A. Stevenson. Her latest efforts have been jointly associated with Mad. Janauschek in a revival of "The Two Orphans·" As an actress she displays little variety or power from the characters with which accident has fitted her.

MARIE WAINWRIGHT is the granddaughter of Bishop Wainwright of the Protestant Episcopal Church and the daughter of Commodore J. M. Wainwright, who was killed during the Rebellion. She is a native of Philadelphia, where she was born May 8, 1855, and was educated at a convent just outside of Paris, Fr· A reverse of fortune, I believe, was directly responsible for turning her thoughts to the stage. She had the advantage of Fanny Morant's professional counsel, and it was largely through that actress's efforts that Miss Wainwright was enabled to make her *debut* as one of the *Juliets* who played for the benefit of George Rignold at Booth's Theatre, May 31, 1877. Her success on that notable occasion brought her into prominence, and her path was thenceforth a comparatively smooth one. The following season she joined the stock of the Boston Museum. There she was the original *Josephine* in the first American performance of "Pinafore." She was quite as successful in that opera as she had been in *Juliet's* robes. Eventually she, with Louis James, went to join Lawrence Barrett as his leading support. Her excellent work with Mr. Barrett need not now be recalled. She was with him five years, and then, the situation seeming ripe, she made her first formal venture as a *star*, acting jointly with Mr. James· This was at the opening of the season of 1886-87. Miss Wainwright has been thrice married. Her first husband was Henry W. Slaughter, an actor, who died in Australia. In August, 1879, she was wedded to Mr. James, with whom she appeared in Montreal in 1886 as a joint *star*. Three years later they separated. Miss Wainwright then made a *starring* feature of *Viola* in "Twelfth Night," etc. In 1899 she married Franklyn Roberts, who had been her leading man the season before in "Shall We Forgive Her?"

ELIZA WEATHERSBY (Mrs. N.C. Goodwin, jun.) was a native of London, Eng., and was born in 1846. Her family name was Smith. Her professional career began at the Alexandria theatre, Brantford, during the sixties, and before coming to America she was for two seasons at the Strand Theatre, where she made her London *debut*. She arrived in New York, April 28, 1869, to join the Elise Holt Burlesque Troupe, with which, on May 12, she made her American *debut* at the Chestnut Street Theatre, Philadelphia, in burlesque, but without attracting marked attention. The Holt Troupe disbanded in the following June, and Miss Weathersby joined the Lydia Thompson Troupe, with which, at Niblo's Garden, June 14, 1869, she made her metropolitan *debut*, playing *Hafiz* in "Sinbad the Sailor," and soon becoming prominent by assuming the title role in the place of Miss Thompson, who was ill.   Col. T. Allston Brown organized a rival party, called the British Blondes, in which were Miss Weathersby, the late Harry Beckett and other seceders from the Thompson Troupe.   Maguire brought them out in San Francisco ahead of Lydia Thompson's artists, and for a time there was strong rivalry. The business of both troupes was affected, but the British Blondes had to quit the field first.   On Nov. 14 Miss Weathersby rejoined the Thompson Troupe.   On June 24, 1877, she was wedded to N. C Goodwin, jun.   They last appeared with the "Evangeline" party, Nov. 10, 1877, in Chicago, and on Dec. 24 following the twain began their first professional engagement together on the joint stock basis, appearing in "Pippins" at the Globe Theatre, Boston.   In the following January, they organized the Weathersby-Goodwin Froliques, which started out Feb. 4, 1878, and in one form or another, presenting "Cruets,"."Hobbies," "The Ramblers," "Those Bells," "A Member from Slocum" and "Warranted," kept the road for several years, Jennie and Emie Weathersby being of the company.   Emie died in 1884.   Eliza last appeared on the stage about 1884, and died at New York 24th March 1887.

NATHANIEL C. GOODWIN, JR., is one of our best comedians. He was born in Boston in 1857.   In 1876 he went to New York at a salary of $50 a week, which was soon advanced to $500.   His imitations were the craze of the city, and he played several successful engagements.   His career from that time was associated with Miss Weathersby, and fully noted in her sketch.   After her death he went back to legitimate comedy, in which line he is still catering to a delighted public, his most successful productions of recent date being, "An American Citizen," and "When we were Twenty-One." Goodwin has been thrice married, his present wife being the charming Maxine Elliott, to whom he was wedded in 1898.

LILIAN ADELAIDE NEILSON. The greatest representative of Shakespeare's heroines of this century is remembered as a shooting meteor, a creature of goodness and beauty, possessing the rare combination of imaginative power, dramatic fire, emotion, tenderness and grace.   Her voice was musical and impressive capable of great modulation, with a most artistic command of what may be called the material of elocution—the inflections.   The actress's story is one of early hardship and sorrow.   Lizzie Ann Browne

LILIAN ADELAIDE NEILSON (Juliet).

was torn out of wedlock at 35 St. Peters Square, Leeds, Yorkshire, England, 3rd March, 1846. She did not have Spanish or gipsy blood in her veins as was claimed, but was the daughter of Miss Browne, an obscure actress, who subsequently became Mrs. Bland. Her father's name is not revealed. As a child she lived at Skipton and later in the village of Guiseley near Leeds, where she afterwards worked in a factory. She had attended the parochial school, and her teacher, Mr. Frizell, remembers her as an earnest and studious pupil, possessing a great memory with an unusual talent or recitation. Her early pastime was in studying the chief feminine characters she was destined to portray. When fourteen years of age she accidentally discovered the secret of her birth. There never had been sympathy between mother and child, and becoming discontented with her lot, Lizzie, by one account, went to service for a long time, eventually becoming a member of a strolling company. Accounts of her early life differ, and Colonel Brown says that when twelve years of age "she coaxed her old uncle to let her ride in the market wagon that was going to London. When the old gentleman had crossed London Bridge Lizzie could not be found, and her parents heard nothing more of her for five years, when they discovered her to be Adelaide Neilson. Only five years had passed between the time that the barefooted country girl, who spoke with a strong Yorkshire accent, had dropped from the back of the cart and the time when she appeared as *Juliet*." Her earliest stage experience is said to have been at Margate, Eng., at the Theatre Royal in her fifteenth year, as *Julia* in "The Hunchback." Her first stage name was Lilian Adelaide Lessont, which she soon changed to Neilson. Her London *debut* was in July, 1865, at the New Royalty Theatre as *Juliet*, without attracting attention, but she persisted, and her first genuine success was when she played *Victorine* at the Adelphi Theatre in November, 1866. In that year she married Philip Henry Lee, the son of a clergyman of Stoke Bruerne, who accompanied her on her first visit to America in 1872. They were divorced in 1877. He died 29th October, 1886. On 18th November, 1872, she opened at Booth's Theatre, New York, as *Juliet*. The critics generally agreed that her *Juliet* was the best that had graced the New York stage for many years, and her success was assured. During the ensuing tour of the United States and Canada, her repertoire, in addition to *Juliet*, included *Beatrice, Pauline, Lady Teazle, Julia, Isabella* in "Measure for Measure," and *Viola*. In May, 1873, Miss Neilson made her first appearance in this country as *Amy Robsart*, having first appeared in that character at the Drury Lane Theatre of London in 1870. In April, 1875, she began a long engagement at Booth's Theatre, New York, with a remarkably successful run of "Amy Robsart." Her last season in America was in the autumn and winter of 1879 and spring and summer of 1880. Her tour proved an ovation from start to finish. Her farewell to New York was 24th May, 1880. at Booth's Theatre. In the course of an address before the curtain the actress said: "*It seems to me that I am not only leaving friends, but happiness itself ; that the skies can never again be as bright as they have been to me here, nor flowers bloom so beautifully, nor music sound so sweet any more.*" Her last appearance on the stage was at Baldwin's Theatre, San Francisco, 17th July, 1880, when she acted *Juliet* in the balcony scene of ":Romeo and Juliet" and "Amy Robsart." She had been playing there from June 8. Returning to New York. she sailed for Europe July 28. In eighteen days she was dead. Miss Neilson suffered from dyspepsia, combined with neuralgia of the stomach. Any undue excitement or mental depression was favorable to the attacks. During the violent recurrence of pain after drinking a glass of iced milk in the Bois de Boulogne she fell into a state of syncope, and died while in that condition in Paris, August 15, 1880. She passed from the world with all the radiance of her glory about her like sunset from a mountain peak that vanishes at once into the heavens. She was buried in Brompton cemetery, London, where a white marble cross marks the grave, inscribed with the words :

"Gifted and Beautiful—Resting."

THE YEAR OF 1878

was opened 7th January by Alfred Dampier and May Howard in "Battling for Life," and "The Lyons' Courier." "London Assurance," "New Magdalen," and "Baby," followed until 4th February, when Dominick Murray came. Frederic Robinson was seen, week 11th, in "The Fool's Revenge," "Not Guilty," and "Dora." Alice Dunning and William Horace Lingard, at the head of their own company. came 25th February in "Heart and Crown." The stock company then produced "Pink Dominoes," and on 11th March, for Mr. Nannary's benefit, was presented "Led Astray." Mr. and Miss Morris benefited 27th March in "Tom Cob," making this their farewell appearance. On 29th April a company from Wallack's Theatre, headed by Charlotte Thompson, appeared in "Jane Eyre," "Miss Multon," followed by the re-engagement of Eliza Weathersby and N. C. Goodwin, Jun., in "Hobbies." 6th May. Butler's "Jack and Jill" Pantomine Company came 11th, and on 13th our local artists. Prume and Lavallee, presented M. Hassian in "La Dame Blanche." The Union Square Theatre Company came 22nd, and played in repertoire for four nights. On 10th June a French company came up town from the Theatre Royal and played dur-

JOHN McCULLOCH.

ing a short season. Ilma Di Murska, the Hungarian artist, came 9th August for two nights at the head of a concert company, as also did Clara L. Kellogg and Annie L. Cary for one night, 30th September. Di Murska died at Munich, 18th January, 1889. Lucien Barnes, at one time manager of the Theatre Royal (1878), and having the reputation of being a most skilful and successful manager, next tried his fortune as lessee of the Academy, the fortunes of which had been at a very low ebb from the earliest times of its history. The opening of the new season was 25th September, when Fanny Davenport, supported by F. F. Mackay, appeared in *"Olivia,"* she in the title role and Mr. Mackay as the *Vicar*. This was her Montreal *debut*. Thorne and Chrisdi's "Jack and Jill" followed; then came Helen Blythe and Joseph B. Brien in "Romeo and Juliet," "Ingomar," "Camille," and "The Lady of Lyons." "Magia, the Water Queen," was next seen, followed by productions of "Uncle Tom," Stetson's "Evangeline," "Babes in the Wood," Marie Roze Mapleson in operatic concert, August, Wilhelmj and Carreno in concert, and Blind Tom. Mr. and Mrs. McDowell came 23rd December in "Beauty and the Beast," and on 31st December, for eight nights, came Frederick Warde and Maurice Barrymore in a grand production of "Diplomacy."

MR. AND MRS. LINGARD Alice Dunning Lingard was the first artificial blonde to visit America. She was a beautiful woman, and the yellow hair, tied with blue ribbons, that hung on her shoulders always created a sensation along Broadway in those somewhat remote days. She was followed soon by Lydia Thompson and her canaries, and then the novelty wore off. She was born in London in 1847, and her *debut* was made there at the Grecian Theatre, after which she appeared as a music hall singer, and then in burlesque. Having won fame for herself at home, Miss Dunning came abroad in 1868 to garner the more substantial reward all artists crave, making her American *debut* at the Brooklyn Academy of Music as the *Widow White* in "Mr. and Mrs. Peter White." She married William Horace Lingard, at whose Broadway Theatre she became a favorite. Later Mr. and Mrs. Lingard made a tour of the globe in "Ixion" and other burlesques. They ended their tour around the world richly rewarded for the perils they had braved and the inconveniences they had suffered. Returning to America, 22nd March, 1880, they toured through the principal cities of the United States and Canada. Mrs. Lingard became at length leading lady of a San Francisco Stock Company. In 1881 she reappeared in New York, originating in this country the role of *Cyprienne* in Sardou's "Divorcons," playing also *Frou-Frou* and *Camille.* Later she appeared occasionally in melodrama at Drury Lane Theatre, London. She was a woman of extraordinary physical beauty, which constituted a charm so potent that her audiences overlooked her meagre ability as an actress. She died in London, where she had resided in retirement for some years, 25th June, 1897.

FREDERICK BARHAM WARDE, one of our prominent tragedians, was born in the small village of Wardington, in Oxfordshire, February 23, 1851. His father was the schoolmaster of the village and died when Frederick was quite a child. His family removing to London, young Warde was educated in the City of London School, a large public institution founded by Edward VI., and at the age of fourteen, choosing the law as a profession, the lad was articled to a firm of attorneys in London for five years, as required by the legal practice there. After having served three years of his allotted term, he became dissatisfied with his prospects as a lawyer, and, obtaining an engagement through a friend from a dramatic agent, made his first appearance on the stage in the part of the *Second Murderer* in "Macbeth," at the Lyceum Theatre, Sunderland, September 4, 1867. After an extensive experience in both cities and provinces he left England and came to this country, making his American *debut* August 10, 1874, at Booth's Theatre as *Capt. Pike* in "Belle Lamar." He remained in the stock of that house several seasons, and toured in the support of various prominent *stars.* For several years he has *starred* on his own account, visiting all sections of the country. Warde *starred* jointly with Louis James for two seasons, and in 1896-97 made a feature of "King Lear."

MAURICE BARRYMORE, who is easily in the first flight of leading men of the present day, was born in Calcutta, India, in 1854. He took his degree at Cambridge University, and studied for the Indian Civil Service. He gave up the idea of going to India, and was called to the bar, but gave up the law for the stage. He has been on the American stage since 1874. He wrote "Nadjesda" for Modjeska, and the libretto for the comic opera, "The Robber of the Rhine." In 1876 he married Georgie Drew, who died 2nd July, 1893, leaving two children, Lionel and Ethel, both of whom are on the stage. Ethel was born in August, 1879, and first appeared as a member of John Drew's company. The actor married Mary Floyd in 1894. Maurice Barrymore, or rather Herbert Blythe, for that is his real name, has appeared in a long list of plays, and has been several times seen in Montreal in support of Lily Langtry, Mrs. John Drew and Olga Nethersole. His work in "Captain Swift" was very commendable. His career in England, were he was the hero of a number of personal encounters, added to his very brilliant success on the stage He fell in with a dramatic writer of some prominence, became a famous athlete, finally winning the middleweight championship of boxing at Oxford, and wound up with a more or less sensational tour of this country, which was brought to a close by a desparate assault upon an actor in Texas, in which Barrymore, at the risk of his life, apprehended the murderer. There were many episodes in his early career on the stage which lifted him above the ordinary rank of humdrum humanity. His clever daughter, Ethel, promises to become as popular a *star* as was her gifted father. Poor Barrymore is now ending his career in illness and distress.

FANNY DAVENPORT was the daughter of the eminent actor whose name she bore, and was born in London, 1st April, 1849. Her first appearance on the stage was 4th July, 1858, at Boston. She began her career by waving the "Star Spangled Banner." Although a successful interpreter of Shakespeare's heroines, Miss Davenport had been mostly distinguished as an interpreter of Sardou's queens of tragedy, her *Fedora, Cleopatra, Tosca* and *Gismonda* having been most prominently before the public in late years. She was an actress of considerable emotional power, the result of certain natural gifts of passion trained to usefulness by her extensive experience of the possibilities of the stage, but her acting lacked delicacy, without a compensating spontaneity of human fire ; hence her success in Sardou over Shakespeare. After her divorce from her first manager, Edwin H. Price, 8th June, 1888, whom she first married in 1879, she married her leading man, Melbourne McDowell, in 1889, a brother to the former lessee of the Academy here. Melbourne may be remembered as a ticket-seller at the box office. His is a case where physique has done much to make an actor. Miss Davenport again visited Montreal week of 4th January, 1892, in Sardou's "Cleopatra," a production to be long remembered as powerfully magnificent from a scenic as well as artistic point of view. Her last appearance here was at the Academy of Music, week of 15th November, 1897, in "The Saint and the Fool." Fanny Davenport's career was eminently that of a successful artist, which must be attributed in no small part to the fact that she was not only a good actress but a good business woman. Miss Davenport was one of the best paying *stars* in the country. It is said that in one season she cleared $90,000 from "La Tosca." Miss Davenport died 26th Sept., 1898.

ALFRED DAMPIER, an English actor of ability, came to this country, with his daughters Rose and Lily, making his *debut* at the California Theatre, San Francisco, 12th Nov., 1877. His first New York appearance was 28th Jan., 1878. For many years his labors have been in Australia.

THE YEAR 1879

was opened by the Martinez Opera Company, 13th January, for one week. Genevieve Ward came, 20th, for two nights in "Henry VIII.," and "Jane Shore." Following Miss Ward came the Lilliputian Opera Company in "Jack the Giant Killer," 30th, for three nights, and on the 3rd and 5th February Herman Linde was announced as "the greatest living tragedian," in readings from "Macbeth."—"A towering giant among a company of forests"—*Boston Gazette.* The Union Square Company came, 11th, in "Mother and Son"; then successively Italian Opera; G. F. Rowe, supported by McDowell's Company, in "Little Em'ly," and "Brass"; Salsbury's Troubadours, with Nellie M'Henry (first appearance here); "Pinafore." Mr. Rowe returned 28th April, in farewell performances to Canada in "Brass." The notable feature of the season was the first appearance here of Mary Anderson, supported by John W. Norton, week 13th May, in "Ingomar," "Evadne," "Romeo and Juliet," "The Hunchback," and "The Lady of Lyons." Maggie Mitchell came 27th May, opening in "Fanchon," playing a week's repertoire. Tony Pastor and "Pinafore" preceded the reappearance of Miss Mary Anderson, 16th September, supported by Milnes Levick and Atkins Lawrence, in a week of repertoire, followed by Joseph Murphy in "Shaun Rhue," and, on 20th, by the Weathersby-Goodwin Company in "Hobbies." Mr. and Mrs. Majeroni came 6th October in "Camille," "Diplomacy," etc.; "Our Daughters," by the N. Y. Criterion Company, 20th; and on 10th November the first appearance here of the prima-donna, Emma Abbott, in " Paul and Virginia," ·etc. Daniel E. Bandmann, supported by Miss Benison, made his first appearance 17th November, opening in his great role of *Hamlet*, following in " Merchant of Venice," " Narcisse," " Othello," "Macbeth," "Richard III.," and "The Lady of Lyons." Then came "Pinafore," "Uncle Tom's Cabin," and, on 22nd December, the Standard Opera Company in "Fatinitza," etc.

MARY ANDERSON-NAVARRO was born at Sacramento, California, 28th July, 1859, shortly before the outbreak of the Civil war. Her father, Charles Joseph Anderson, died three years later in

MARY ANDERSON-NAVARRO.

his 29th year fighting under the Confederate flag before Mobile on the Gulf of Mexico. Her mother, Marie Antoinette Lengers, was a native of Philadelphia. Mary was brought up at Louisville, Ky., where her stepfather practiced medicine. Her dramatic taste developed in her early childhood. When she was about thirteen she saw Booth in "Richard III," and her imagination was instantly fired. Three years later she made her *debut* at Louisville. She acted all over the States and Canada, and also met with success in Great Britain in the roles of *Juliet, Parthenia, Pauline and Galatea,* during her engagements at the Lyceum in 1884-85. In 1889 she returned to America, but her health broke down. She went to England,where she has since lived in retirement. She married Antonio Ferdinand Navarro de Viana 17th June, 1890. Her brother Joseph is married to Anna Gertrude Barrett, daughter of the late Lawrence Barrett.

EMMA ABBOTT was born in Chicago in 1850; her father was a professor of music. She was taken an interest in by a church congregation, and through the kind offices of Mr. and Mrs. Lake in 1872 was sent to Europe to study. She subsequently married Mr. Wetherell, and after returning to America in 1879 formed an opera company which up to the time of her death proved a genuine success. Emma Abbott died in Salt Lake city, January 5, 1891. She was last heard in Montreal, week of 14th April, 1890.

MARGARET JULIA MITCHELL. No actress on the American stage was more widely known than this lady before her retirement. Born in New York in 1832, she appeared as a mere tot at the old Bowery and from the humble station of ballet girl made her way to public favor. In 1868 she married Henry Paddock, who became her very efficient manager, but from whom she was divorced, and married Charles Abbott, the former husband of Nellie Taylor. Happy in her domestic relations as she has been prosperous in her professional ones, this lady now wears the crown of a life of honorable labor without a thorn to mar its enjoyment. Her mission was to make the masses happy, and our lives are much as we try to make them. No fortune was ever won with greater credit or more deserved than hers.

NELLIE M'HENRY had been on the stage a year or two before she joined the original Salsbury's Troubadors, but it was as the bright particular *star* of that organization that she became a prominent public favorite, now about fifteen years ago. Miss M'Henry is still before the public and as popular as ever. In private life she is Mrs. John Webster, and has a son, Jack,who is also a member of the profession. John Webster disappeared in Nov., 1899. It is supposed that he went over the falls of Niagara.

DANIEL EDWARD BANDMANN was born in that beautiful Hessian city, Cassel, 1st November, 1839. He came to America for the first time when but a lad, and first appeared on the stage as a member of a company of German amateurs at Turn Hall, New York. Returning to his fatherland he entered the dramatic profession at the age of eighteen, making his professional *debut* at the Court Theatre of ' New Strelitz. He early attracted the attention of the great Duchess of Mecklenburg, who took him under her protection. A series of brilliant and rapid successes in various towns in Germany and Prussia and in Vienna, chiefly in Shakespearean work, established for him a very flattering reputation. Subsequently coming to America, Mr. Bandmann acted for the first time in English, 15th January, 1863, at Niblo's Garden; New York, where he created a very favorable impression as *Shylock*. His *Hamlet* also attracted considerable attention, he introducing much *business* that was new here, but well known in his fatherland, bringing his *Ghost* from beneath the stage, introducing a manuscript copy of the speeches of the actors in the play scene, and turning its leaves back and forth in a nervous way to hide the nervousness of *Hamlet*. This was subsequently noticed in the performances of Fechter. Bandmann also drew from his pouch tablets upon which he set down the some *"dozen or sixteen lines"* to be introduced by the *First Actor* in the incident of the murder of *Gonzago*, and at the end of the scene he fell back into the arms of *Horatio* in a state of complete collapse. His acting throughout was effective and powerful. On September 1, 1863, was presented for the first time in New York, John Guido Methua's adaptation from the German of Brachvogel, entitled "Narcisse.; or, The Last of the Pompadours." Mr. Bandmann was first married to Anne Herschel, of Davenport. Iowa, 22nd June, 1865. So great was his success that he made a five years' tour through the country, acting *Hamlet, Shylock, Othello, Iago, Gloster, Macbeth,* *Benedick* and *Narcisse.* At Philadelphia, where his tragic powers attracted the attention of Edwin Forrest, he was selected to play "Hamlet" at the commemorative celebration of the tercentenary birthday of Shakespeare. He performed the part at San Francisco during a run of the play, which lasted a month. He then crossed to London, when he made his first appearance on the British stage at the Lyceum Theatre, 17th February, 1868, in "Narcisse." Miss Millicent Palmer, who had just previously scored a great hit as *Juliet*, was engaged to appear in "Narcisse." and in February, 1869, she became Mrs. Bandmann. The newly married couple, uniting business with pleasure, went for their honeymoon to the antipodes, where (at Melbourne), appropriately enough, the bride made her *debut* as *Juliet*. At Melbourne, Sydney, Adelaide and other places Mr. and Mrs. Bandmann were received with immense favor, winning *golden* opinions from all

DANIEL E. BANDMANN.

classes of play-goers. We find Mrs. Bandmann's name chiefly as.
sociated there with *Ophelia, Juliet, Beatrice, Pauline, Rosalind, Desdemona*,
etc. Returning the pair made their appearance and were abidingly
successful in New Zealand, and at Honolulu in the Sandwich Islands.
There they gave two state performances by command and in the
presence of King Kameamea and his court. Mr. and Mrs. Bandmann subsequently played in the different cities and towns of America,
including Salt Lake City, where they made the acquaintance of and
acted before the late Brigham Young. They returned to London in
the summer of 1872, and reappeared in London at the Queen's in
"Narcisse." In the following spring they acted at the Princess in
"Hamlet," "Merchant of Venice" and Macbeth," Mrs. Bandmann
making her first appearance as *Lady Macbeth*. Returning to America,
they *starred* through the principal cities of the United States and
Canada. About this time they separated as artists, and also as man
and wife. Mrs. Bandmann has since lived in England with her son
and daughter, and in 1896 made her 150th appearance in the character
of *Hamlet*. After a long engagement at the Baldwin Theatre, San
Francisco, Mr. Bandmann undertook another eastern tour, which
lasted three years and a half, returning to America in January, 1884.
He was supported by Louise Beaudet. The tour in the far east was
in every way a remarkable one. Opening at Sydney, he travelled
through Australia, New Zealand, Tasmania, India, China, the Malay
peninsula, and back again through India, Australia, the Hawaiian
Islands to San Francisco, the whole covering 70,000 miles. Received
on friendly terms by governors-general and their ladies, making
everywhere a host of friends, the journey reads more like a romance
than a citation of facts. At Calcultta he played *Othello* and *Shylock*
before an audience of 3,000 natives. Mr. Bandmann, on his return,
began touring through the principal cities of America at popular
prices. Whatever may have induced him to appear under the auspices
of dime museums, this may be safely affirmed, that he did as much
to extend the influence of Shakespearean literature as the most
cultured critic or the highest priced actor. In addressing a turbulent
top gallery at the Theatre Royal, Montreal, on 14th February, 1885,
during a performance of "Othello," Mr. Bandmann pointedly put it
when he said: "*I am not here for your filthy lucre, but to educate you—
to bring Shakespeare before you.*" In 1888 Mr. Bandmann appeared as
Dr. Jekyl and Mr. Hyde, in London, England, but the production was
not a success. He then produced "Austerlitz" at Niblo's, New York,
and shortly afterwards retired to his cattle ranch at Missoula, Montana.
In May, 1892, he married Mary Kelly, a California actress. His
favorite role is *Hamlet*, which he played so well as to rank as one
of the great *Hamlets*.

THE NEW YEAR OF 1880

presented Kate Girard in Elliott Dawson's "Prejudice."
Adelaide Neilson, supported by Messrs. Compton, Frank
Sanger, H. A. Weaver, Mrs. Tannahill and Nellie Morant,
played a series of farewell performances commencing 26th
January, in "Romeo and Juliet"; "Twelfth Night," 27th; "As
You Like It," 28th; "Lady of Lyons," 29th; "Twelfth Night,"
30th; and "The Hunchback," 31st, this being her last appearance here. She died in the following August. The house
remained dark until 16th February, when "H.M.S. Parliament" had a five nights' season, followed by E. F. Thorne
and Charlotta Evelyn in Daly's "An Arabian Night." Mrs.
Scott-Siddons 11th March for three nights; "The Tragedian
of Kalamazoo," and Sid Rosenfeld's "Our School Days,"
week 15th, with Gertie Granville, Nellie Larkelle, Gus. J.
Bruno, etc.; M. Grau's French Opera Company in "Mignon,"
etc., 23rd; Felix J. Morris in "Our Girls," 13th April, for
three nights; Marie Gordon in "Delicate Ground," 16th; and
then Mr. and Mrs. Florence in "The Mighty Dollar," and
"Ticket-of-Leave Man," week 21st April, this being Mr. Florence's first appearance here as a *star*, and his second appearance in the city since the opening of the Royal in 1852.
Mr. and Mrs. Daniel E. Bandmann came up from the Theatre
Royal 19th April, and played a farewell performance in "The
Stranger," and "The Happy Pair," previous to Mr. B.'s departure on his great eastern tour. Joseph Jefferson made his
first appearance in Montreal 11th and 12th May in the play
that has made him most famous, "Rip Van Winkle." It was
our fortune to see a third celebrated comedian, within very
short time of each appearance this season, in E. A. Sothern,
13th, for three nights in "Our American Cousin," "Brother
Sam," and "David Garrick." The Montreal Operatic Society,
assisted by Marie Stone, of Emma Abbott's Company, week
17th, in "The Chimes of Normandy," followed for three
nights by the D'Oyly Carte Opera Company in "The Pirates
of Penzance," "The Queen's Shilling," week 1st June. This
closed the season. Contrary to what has already been
stated of Mr. Lucien Barnes' administration of affairs, he
seems to have catered some good morsels to Montreal's play-
goers, even if he was obliged to leave the city suddenly.
Henry Thomas, formerly ticket-seller, became lessee of the
house, which he reopened for the regular fall and winter

season, 6th August, with Kate Claxton, supported by Charles A. Stevenson, in the "Two Orphans," "The Double Marriage," and "Frou Frou." Joseph Murphy came week 14th September; Lotta, 20th, for four nights; Tagliapietra Italian Opera Company, 5th October, for week; Pond's Musical Combination, 18th, for three nights; D'Oyly Carte Opera Company, in "Pirates of Penzance," 21st, for three nights; Minnie Palmer, in "Our Boarding School," 25th, for week; Jarrett & Rice's "Fun on the Bristol," 1st Nov., for week, followed by the first appearance in Montreal of the little favorite, Corinne, in "The Magic Slipper." This charming and clever little *comedienne* has since been a frequent visitor to the city. A French opera company came week of 22nd November, followed by the Soldene Opera Company, week 29th. "A Celebrated Case," with Mrs. Thos. Barry and Sir Randall Roberts as the principals, opened week 13th December, and on 17th Sir Randall was tendered a benefit. Sara Bernhardt made her first appearance in this city, 23rd December, in "Adrienne Lecouvreur"; "Frou Frou," 24th; "Hernani," 25th; and "Camille," at the matinee. Her second engagement in Montreal was at the same house week 6th April, 1891, and her last, week of 24th February, 1896, in "Gismonda," when the theatre was so crowded that the attention of the building inspector was directed to its condition, resulting in its being almost altogether reconstructed.

MR. AND MRS. W. J. FLORENCE. It was in 1876 that Florence made his first hit as the *Hon. Bardwell Slote.* in "The Mighty Dollar." That character soon became as closely allied to him as *Rip* is to Jefferson, *Sellars* to Raymond or *Sol Shingle* to Owens. Williams Jermyn Florence (family name Conlin) was born in Albany, 26th July, 1831. His theatrical career began in 1849 at Richmond, Va. After undergoing the vicissitudes of a young player, he became a member of various stock companies, notably that of John Nickinson, of Toronto and Quebec—the famous Havresack of his period. Florence married Malvina Pray, a sister of Mrs. Barney Williams, in 1853. Three years later they toured in England. Returning to the United States, Mr. and Mrs. Florence renewed their triumphs, appearing all over the country. Florence joined forces with Jefferson in 1889-90, but this interesting combination was interrupted by death, the comedian being called away 19th Nov., 1891. Then died one of the most cultured character comedians of the century ; a genial companion, and a well-informed man of much versatility and charm, whose gentleness, modesty, affectionate fidelity and fine talents.

united with his spontaneous drollery, to enshrine him in tender affection. For a number of years the comedian had been in the habit of resorting to the Restigouche, and on the St. Andrew's Day preceding his demise had been distributing heather to the *sons o' auld Scotia* in the store of Messrs. Fraser, Viger & Co. On 10th June, 1893, Mrs. Florence married an actor named George Howard Covenay. In her application for a divorce in 1900, Mrs. Covenay said that she knew her husband for only one month when she married him; that three years ago he demanded $10,000, which she gave him, and then he left her. Mrs. Florence recently said : "My last appearance as an actress was in "Heart of Hearts" in Brooklyn several years ago. I love the stage, but I am content now to view it from just without the active working circle, and with a feeling that I have earned my rest."

JOSEPH JEFFERSON, the dean of the American stage, was born in Philadelphia, 20th February, 1829, and is a descendant of an old theatrical family, his father and grandfather (Thomas) both being actors, and the latter a contemporary of David Garrick. Mr. Jefferson is the second "Joe," and was a half-brother to the celebrated prodigy, Charles Burke. His early career was marked by much discomfort and privation, and his managerial efforts in the south were not all triumphs, as his own story (Autobiography of Joseph Jefferson) tells it. He first met with decided success in England, where Boucicault rewrote "Rip Van Winkle" for him, and the piece ran to packed houses for 150 nights. Returning to the United States in 1872 after an absence of seven years, he recommenced there the career which has since become familiar to all play-goers. It is a question if his impersonation of *Bob Acres* has ever been equalled. The ease of his manner and the simple perfection of his methods render him capable of handling the most extravagant farcical roles with a delicacy that redeems them from the stigma of burlesque. Mr. Jefferson lives much on his Louisiana plantation, passing hours of repose in sketching, etc., and still occasionally favors the rising generation with the opportunity of witnessing his great histrionic genius. Mr. Jefferson's infatuation for painting and acting were contemporaneous. In his daily life both are simply different expressions of the same truths. He could no better live without one than the other. Passion for the theatre is but part of his heritage. His certificate of admission to the great guild of the world's famous actors and artists is engrossed with many vouchers, for it is a long flight from the Jefferson of to-day to the Yorkshire farmer, Thomas Jefferson, who appeared at Drury Lane in 1746. Words are but the mere shadows of all that was, the mirror of all that is. His fame is secure. He has laid the foundations of it deep in the human heart.

HENRY THOMAS, lessee and manager of the Academy of Music, died Nov. 28, 1893, after a lengthy illness. Mr. Thomas was fifty years of age, and had been connected with the theatrical profession during nearly all of his adult life. He was first connected with the

JOSEPH JEFFERSON.

Theatre Royal, Montreal. He afterwards became treasurer of the Academy of Music, and assumed the management of that house in 1880. He was well known throughout Canada and the United States as one of the most popular theatrical managers on the continent. He left a widow, who is now Mrs. Frank Murphy.

CORINNE. Born in Boston, Mass., December 25, 1873, Corinne has been on the stage almost from the cradle. She is the daughter of the late Mrs. Jennie Kimball, who was at the time a popular vocalist and comedienne. Mrs. Kimball became her daughter's sole manager, and the girl's successful career, from a financial point of view, is due almost entirely to the remarkable managerial work of the mother, Corinne's first appearance was at the National Baby Show in Boston, October 22, 1877, when she created a sensation as a musical prodigy, and received the prize of a gold chain and locket studded with diamonds. She made her *debut* as *Little Buttercup* in Juvenile "Pinafore" company at the Boston Museum, May 12, 1879, and was the central figure of the company. Her impersonation of the character revealed her as an astonishing example of precocity, and no person of her age ever made a greater triumph than Corinne did at that time. She captured the audience the moment she came upon the stage by her rippling voice and graceful movements. During the season of 1880-1, she visited the principal Canadian cities and almost every American city, receiving marked attention everywhere. Her tours continued until the interference of the Society for the Prevention of Cruelty to Children. The tearing of the child from its mother, the abduction, the arrest and the incarceration and the climax in the decision of Judge Donohue, the return of Corinne to her friends—all these things are, no doubt, familiar to my readers. Corinne is not yet married, and is a very wealthy young woman, boys, even if her name is Flaherty.

EDWARD H. COMPTON. The son of Henry Compton, a famous comedian and one of the favorites of the old Haymarket Theatre, the actor may be said to have been born on the stage. He had been in harness since he was a child, and his success from an artistic viewpoint was unquestioned. He was one of the actors in the company of Adelaide Neilson, whose husband he was generally thought to have been by their friends. Later he appeared at the head of a company which he himself organized, and which was devoted to the presentation of high-class plays, both classic and modern. In a series of Shakespearean revivals, he came into comparison with Irving, while his high comedy impersonations were praised without stint. Mr. Compton married Virginia, one of the famous Bateman sisters. A brother, Chas. Compton, died 16th August, 1897.

SARA BERNHARDT. Mdme. Damala, *nee* Rosine Bernhardt, called Sara, was born in Paris, Oct. 22, 1844. She is a Jewess, of French and Dutch parentage, and spent the early part of her life in Holland. In 1858, she entered the Paris Conservatoire, became a pupil of M.M. Prevost and Samson, professors of elocution, gained a second prize for tragedy in 1861, and a second prize for comedy in 1862. She made her first public appearance on the stage at the Theatre Francais, in Racine's "Iphigenie" and the "Valerie" of Scribe. She attracted hardly any notice, and after a brief withdrawful from the stage, reappeared at the Gymnase and the Porte Saint Martin in burlesque parts. In January, 1867, she returned to high art at the Odeon, playing several minor parts with much applause, till she achieved a notable success as *Marie de Neuborg* in "Ruy Blas." She was thereupon recalled to the Theatre Francais, and first showed her higher power in *Andromaque* and *Junie* ; but it was as *Berthe de Sauigne* in the play of "Le Sphinxe," performed in March, 1874, that she won greatest laurels. In 1879, she visited London, with the other members of the Comedie Francaise. In the following year, Mme. Bernhardt returned alone to the Gaiety. About this time she severed her connection with the Comedie Francais and was condemned to pay £4000 costs and damages for the breach of her engagement. In June, 1881, she again appeared in London at the Gaiety Theatre in "La Dame aux Camilias" for a short series of performances, and afterwards made a successful tour, from a money point of view, in the United States. She revisited London in 1885, and played Fedora for the first time in England at the Gaiety Theatre. In 1890 she played a long season in "Cleopatra." She is the authoress of the one-act play, "L'Aveu," produced in 1888, and a few years ago had the order of the French Academy conferred upon her. In April, 1882, she was married in the church of St. Andrew, Well street, London, to M. Damala, a Greek actor, from whom she was shortly afterwards divorced. He died in August, 1889.

THE SEASON OF 1881

was heralded by Tomasso Salvini, supported by Marie Prescott, Lewis Morrison and H. A. Weaver. The powerful Italian tragedian began his first and only Montreal engagement, 17th January, in "The Gladiator," and "Othello," 19th, the intervening night having been filled by the Union Square Company in "French Flats." Gus Williams, in "Our German Senator," came week 3rd February ; Haverly's Minstrels 11th and 12th March; Daly's "Needles and Pins," 1st and 2nd April; Sol Smith Russell in "Edgewood Folks," week 18th April; Louis Aldrich and Charles T. Parsloe, in "My Partner," week 28th; and Mr. and Mrs. McKee Rankin, in "The Danites," week 2nd May. The Holman Opera Company appeared two nights from 29th April, and Mrs. J. W. Buckland appeared in a benefit performance, 17th May, in "Little Treasure" and "Married Life." Genevieve Ward, in

SARAH BERNHARDT.

"Forget-Me-Not," 18th, for four nights; Norcross Comic Opera Co., week 7th July; French Comedy Company, week 11th; Haverly s Minstrels, 11th August, three nights; "The World," 15th August, week; Rose Eytinge, in "Felicia," 31st, four nights; Ada Gray, in "East Lynne," week 5th September; John P. Smith and Wm. Metayer's "Tourists," 12th, week; Lotta, 19th, for four nights; L. O. David's "One Hundred Years Ago," translated by John Lesperance from the author's French. Both these gentlemen were prominent Montrealers, and the former is the present city clerk. The company which presented the piece was a poor one, and did not do justice to the very laudable and clever effort of Mr. David. C. W. Couldock and Effie Ellsler, the original *Dunstan* and *Hazel Kirke*, appeared week 19th September in "Hazel Kirke"; Mr. and Mrs. W. J. Florence, 13th, for three nights; Mrs. Burnett's "Esmeralda," from Madison Square Theatre, week 18th, including Agnes Booth, Kate Denin, Eben Plympton and E. A. McDowell. Frank Mordaunt, in "Old Shipmates," came 31st October. A very strong feature of the season was the appearance of the Wallack Company, 7th November, opening in "School for Scandal"; "Money," 8th; "She Stoops to Conquer," 9th; and "London Assurance," 10th. The *personnel* of the company is shown in the following cast of "The School for Scandal": *Sir Peter Teazle*, Mr. John Gilbert; *Sir Oliver Surface*, Mr. Henry Edwards; *Sir Benjamin Backbite*, Mr. Wilmot Eyre; *Charles Surface*, Mr. Osmond Tearle; *Joseph Surface*, Mr. Gerald Eyre; *Careless*, Mr. Herbert Ayling; *Moses*, Mr. William Elton; *Trip*, Mr. C. Edwin; *Crabtree*, Mr. Dan Leeson; *Rowley*, Mr. Harry Gwynette; *Joseph's Servant*, Mr. H. Pierson; *Snake*, Mr. J. Bishop; *Lady Teazle*, Miss Rose Coghlan; *Lady Sneerwell*, Miss Agnes Elliot; *Mrs. Candour*, Madame Ponisi; *Maria*, Miss Stella Boniface. This was unquestionably the strongest company that ever appeared in the piece in Montreal, and marked the first and last engagement here of John Gilbert and Henry Edwards. Sam Hague's Minstrels came 10th for four nights; Alex. Caufman in "Lazare," week of 14th; and Eric Bayley's Comedy Company, week of 21st, in "The Colonel," a play based on the æsthetic verse by F. C. Burnand, editor of *Punch.* Ernesto Rossi, the great Italian tragedian, made his first and last appearance in Montreal 31st November for three nights, commencing in "King Lear," "Hamlet" and "Othello." No actor has since played "King Lear" in this city. The tragedian was supported by Milnes Levick. Following

Rossi came "Rooms for Rent," week 5th December, and the Boston Museum Company in "Patience," week of 26th December, closing a very bright and eventful theatrical year.

TOMASSO SALVINI was born in Milan, Italy, 21st Dec., 1833. His parents were strolling players, but their son was educated at the best schools in Florence, where the most beautiful works of art abound, and where the Italian language is spoken in its purity.   While here it became evident that he had inherited a taste for dramatic performances and talent for acting.   There was a small theatre connected with the school, and while playing here with his companions he played such precocious abilities as to attract the attention of his teachers and his parents. It was then determined to educate the youth for the stage, and his father assumed the direction of his studies. When only 14 years of age he was engaged in a well-known theatre, and assigned to important characters.   It should be borne in mind by the reader that the human form matures more rapidly in the sunny clime of Italy than in colder latitudes.   In 1848 Salvini became a pupil of the celebrated actor, Gustavo Modena, whose training bore immediate fruits ; and in the subsequent engagements which he obtained he acted *David* in "Saul," *Carlo* in "Il Fillipo," *Nemours* in "Luigi XI" (Louis XI), and numerous other characters more successfully, it is said, than they had been previously interpreted by any other actor so young in years.   At the age of 15, by the death of his father (his mother having died sometime previously), he was left very poor.   Ristori at that time was making a tour of the Italian cities.   Salvini successfully applied for an engagement.   He played the leading opposite roles to this distinguished artist: shared with her the laurels of many great performances.   This troupe was known as the Roman company, because at certain fixed periods it appeared in Rome. While playing there in 1849, during the progress of the French invasion, and when the city was seiged by the forces of Napoleon, Salvini shouldered a musket, and took his place in the ranks of the patriots.   When the Roman Republic succumbed, Salvini, with other patriots, escaped from the capitol, and fled toward Florence: but, being forbidden to land at Leghorn, he proceeded to Genoa where he was arrested and lodged in prison.   Subsequently a relative procured his release, and upon his arrival in Florence he was again seized and imprisoned, and at last set free only upon the condition that he should at once leave the country. Going to his native city, then in possession of the Austrians, he was banished from Milan, and for a long time thereafter he was kept under rigid police surveillance, owing to his attachment to the cause of Italian freedom.   These persecutions caused him to retire from the stage for a time, and he went to Florence, where, in the home of some near relatives of his mother, he lived for one year sequestered from society and police observation.   He

TOMASSO SALVINI.

occupied this time by studying *Othello, Saul* and *Orosmano* in Voltaire's "Zaire," and when he resumed his profession he made some of the greatest successes of his life in these roles. He subsequently added to his repertory the character of *Edipo*, and in it gained an artistic fame, which spread throughout Italy. Salvini's reputation being now thoroughly established in his native land, he desired to go abroad, and first tempted fortune in Paris, where he played in "Zaire," "Oreste," "Saul," and "Othello," with marked success. Returning to Italy, he pursued his profession and won the special friendship of Giacometti, who wrote for him the tragedy of "La Morte Civile," in which Salvini afterwards roused the wildest excitement by his superb acting. During this time he organized the Mutual Protective Society of Actors, of which he was elected president. When in 1865 the six hundredth anniversary of the birth of Dante was celebrated in Florence, he participated in the festival upon invitation of the government of that city, and recited portions of that poet's "Divine Comedy," and walked in the procession, under the banner of the society of artists above referred to, as the representative of the dramatic profession. Upon that occasion he was decorated by the King, Victor Emanuel, with the Order of St. Mauritius and Lazarus. At this time, both Ristori and Rossi being in Florence, a representation of "Francesca di Rimini" was projected, and to strengthen the cast Salvini acted the small part of *Lanciotto*, and made a great impression in it. He was presented by the Government of Florence with a statuette of Dante and a costly watch in recognition of his services. He next went to Spain and Portugal, and while playing in Lisbon he received from King Louis the Order of St. Iago. In 1870, he received an offer to play in South America, which he accepted, and sailed with a large theatrical company for that country, in 1871. He played in Montevideo, Buenos Ayres and Rio de Janeiro. During the period of this visit the Emperor of Brazil was travelling in Europe, and when Salvini returned to Rome to fill an engagement, he was notified by the Brazilian Ambassador that Dom Pedro, the Emperor of Brazil, on his return to his kingdom had conferred upon Salvini the Order of the Rose, with the insignia of which he was subsequently duly invested. September 10, 1873, Salvini and an Italian company arrived in New York from Havre, France, and made their first appearance in America in the Academy of Music, acting "Othello," Salvini playing the title character, and demonstrating that he was one of the greatest exponents of that role that ever trod the stage. After concluding a tour of this country he sailed for England, where his performances in London elicited the highest encomiums of approval, and where during his sojourn he wooed and won an English wife. Together they returned to Florence, where they have since resided, much of the time in retirement, although he has since returned to America on three more distinct tours—1880-1, 1884-5, and 1887-8

His son Alexandro met with success here in the romantic roles in English. He was a promising young actor, but his career was soon cut off, dying 15th December, 1896, aged 35. Another son Gustavo, has, however, taken up the mantle of the sire and has already been proclaimed a great actor.

GUS WILLIAMS is one of the best delineators of Dutch business of the century. He was born in New York city, 19th July, 1848, and his real name is Gustave Wilhelm Leweck. He enlisted in 1862, serving until the close of the war, when he joined Ashton's company at Huntsville. He was with Tony Pastor from 1868 to 1878, since which time he has starred in various pieces calculated to bring out his particular talents. Recently he has returned to the vaudeville stage.

SOL SMITH RUSSELL was a western product of 1848—15th June, at Brunswick, Mo. He first appeared on the stage at the age of fourteen. His father had never seen a play, but his mother was a sister-in-law to Sol Smith, a well-known actor in that day. His first regular salary was $6 a week. His star began to glimmer about 1866, when he was in Ben De Bar's Theatre in St. Louis. He did not appear in New York city until 1871, and began *starring* in "Edgewood Folks" in 1880, a piece that permitted of songs and sketches and some character work. He later appeared in "A Poor Relation," "The Tale of a Coat," "A Bachelor's Romance," and lastly "Hon. John Grigsby." His home was in Minneapolis, where his widow and two children, Robert and Lillian, reside. At Chicago, on 18th Dec., 1899, Mr. Russell broke down, and died 28th April, 1902.

ARTHUR M'KEE RANKIN is a Canadian, having been born in 1844, at Sandwich, Ont. His theatrical *debut* was made in Rochester, N. Y., in 1861. He married Kitty Blanchard, the actress, 11th December, 1869. Her mother, who thought herself dying, expressed a wish that she should be married. Mr. Rankin, who was fulfiling an engagement in Canada, was telegraphed for. He arrived in good time, for his mother in-law rallied and lived to bless him for five years. In 1877 he bought the right to dramatize "The Danites," from Joaquin Miller, for $5000, and it was first produced 22nd August, at the Broadway Theatre. It was very successful here, but failed in Great Britain. His next effort was a grand production of "Macbeth" in San Francisco. To us he is most familiarly remembered as *Jean Baptiste Cadieux* in "The Canuck," a character which he played to the life, and in which he appeared at the Academy of Music, week 13th October, 1890. Mr. and Mrs. Rankin separated as artists, and also as man and wife, some time prior to this. His last appearance in Montreal was during the week of 22nd May, 1893, in association with the Drews, Barrymore and E. J. Lyons, in a revival of "The Rivals." His daughter, Phyllis, also appeared in the cast, and is a prominent stage figure at this writing. His eldest daughter, Gladys, is Mrs. Sidney Drew. Mr. Rankin's latest efforts have been in the production of several standard dramas, in association with Nance O'Neil.

KITTY BLANCHARD RANKIN was born in 1847 in Philadelphia. Her father, Loring Blanchard, died when she was four years of age, and she made her first appearance on the stage as a dancer, when not quite ten years of age, at the old National Theatre, under the management of John Drew the elder. She has acted in all the principal female roles of the Shakespearean repertoire except *Juliet* and *Lady Macbeth*, and competent critics have pronounced her *Nancy Sykes* to be one of the most finished impersonations of the character ever presented on the American stage. Thousands of theatre-goers all over the country have enjoyed her acting in the dual role of *Nancy Williams* and *Billy Piper* in "The Danites" and her roguish delineation of *Carrots* in '49.

LOUIS ALDRICH (right name Salma Lyon) had the distinction of being born in mid-ocean, 1st October, 1843. His boyhood, which was spent in Cleveland, was filled with hardship and sorrow. When he was but little more than ten years old he was thrown upon his own resources, and, forturately for the theatrical profession, he elected to earn his living on the stage. In school he had been noted among his fellows as a declaimer and recitationist. His talent in that direction was remarkable. He sought the theatre, therefore, as the natural and most promising field for his bread-winning. It happened that, when he was about eleven, a benefit performance to Mrs. John Ellsler was arranged at the Cleveland Theatre. The boy begged John Ellsler to let him appear in it, and Mr. Ellsler, after testing him, agreed to let him appear as Richard III. in two acts of that tragedy. So extraordinary was the acting of the youngster that the management engaged him for the following week to play the entire tragedy, and billed him as "the Ohio Roscius." He repeated his first success and was immediately taken on the road through the West as a boy star. In May, 1863, he went to New Zealand returning to America in the following October. His first appearance at New York was on the occasion of a farewell performance of Charles Kean in America, in "Louis XI.," Aldrich appearing as *Coitier.* Mr. Aldrich rose to fame with Bartley Campbell's play of "My Partner." As an officer of the Actors' Fund he accomplished more in the way of philanthropy than any actor of the time. He was among the earliest active members of the Fund; he served as first vice-president for eleven years, and from June, 1897, to June, 1901, he was president of the Fund. During that period he labored in the cause of charity with a devotion rarely equalled. his enthusiasm never for an instant cooled, his purpose never faltered. The Fund became his very life, as he, truly, became the presiding spirit of the Fund. His last and greatest work in behalf of the institution was the raising of money to build the Actors' Fund Home. He died 17th June, 1901.

MRS. AGNES BOOTH (*nee* Agnes Land Rookes) was born in Australia in 1843. She arrived at San Francisco in company with her sister, Belle, in 1858, and shortly afterwards married Harry Perry, an able, but too jovial actor, who died in 1861. Coming east she became a strong star, and in 1866 married Junius Brutus Booth, son to the elder of the same name and brother to Edwin and John W. Booth. J. B. Booth died in 1883, leaving her $200,000. After a year of widowhood she married Mr. John Schoeffel, the partner of the late Mr. Abbey. Mrs. Booth retained her stage name, and only recently retired. She is to the American stage what Mrs. Kendall is to the English boards.

JOHN GIBBS GILBERT probably never had an equal in such parts as *Sir Anthony Absolute, Sir Peter Teazle* and similar roles of the old comedies. John Gilbert was born 27th February, 1810. After leaving school he measured calico for five years, and finally trod the boards for the first time 28th November 1828, as *Jaffier* in "Venice Preserved" at the Tremont Theatre, Boston. He was successful from the start, and rose rung by rung on the ladder of fame until around this splendid actor some of the proudest memories of the stage entwine themselves. The veteran died 17th June, 1889.

GEORGE OSMOND TEARLE, who was known in America through his memorable work some years ago as leading man of the late Lester Wallack's company, died at Newcastle-on-Tyne, England, Sept. 6, 1901. Osmond Tearle was born in Plymouth, in County Devon, in 1852. At the age of fifteen he was articled in a law office in Liverpool, since it was the desire of his parents as well as himself that he should become an attorney. For two years he devoted himself to his legal studies, attending, when occasion offered, elocutionary classes, public readings and theatrical performances. He soon gained some reputation among his fellows as an elocutionist, and as a result he was invited to take part in an amateur performance of Julius Cæsar. In the character of Trebonius, upon that occasion, he gave so creditable a performance, and was so highly complimented upon it, that he decided to abandon the law in favor of the stage. He had little difficulty, it appears, in finding an opportunity to enter the profession, for on March 29, 1869, when he was but seventeen years old, he made his debut on the stage of the Adelphi Theatre, Liverpool, in the role of Guildenstern in Hamlet. Mr. Tearle's fame eventually reached America, and several American managers sought to bring him to this country. Among them was Lester Wallack, who finally secured him for the position of leading man of his company. In September, 1880, Mr. Tearle made his first appearance in this country at the Star Theatre, under the management of Mr. Wallack. He quickly sprang into public favor and became one of the most popular leading men that New York has ever known. When Henry E. Abbey took over the management of Wallack's in 1887, Mr. Tearle was engaged as leading man of the company. He acted there and on the road in America for several seasons, and about twelve years ago he returned to England, to remain permanently. In 1889, and again in 1890, Mr. Tearle managed and acted in the Shakespeare commemoration performances at Stratford, producing upon the first occasion Julius Caesar and the first part of "Henry Sixth," and upon the second "Two Gentlemen of Verona" and "King John." Since leaving this country Mr. Tearle has toured steadily at the head of his own company in England. He was highly popular with the public, and was regarded by critics as one of the best Shakespearean actors of his time. Mr. Tearle was twice married. After being divorced from his first wife, he married Minnie Conway, the American actress—formerly the wife of Jules Levy, the cornetist—in Denver, Col., in 1883.

HARRY EDWARDS was one of the soundest actors of the modern stage, and it was in the line of "old men" that he chiefly excelled, associated with the names of Wm. Warren, Wm. Davidge, John Gilbert and Chippendale. He was born at Ross, England, 23rd September, 1824. He was a clerk in his young manhood, and an ambitious amateur actor in company with J. L. Toole and Walter Montgomery. In 1853 he went to Australia, where he remained many years. He married Avonia Jones-Brooke, widow of Gustavus V. Brooke, the tragedian, and the daughter to Mrs. Melinda Jones, at one time lessee of the old Theatre Royal on St. Paul Street. In 1866 he went to San Francisco, and in 1878 first appeared in the East as *Master Walter* to the *Julia* of Mary Anderson. He joined Wallack's company 8th December, 1878. His last engagement was as the *Earl* in "Fauntleroy," in Australia, returning to New York a year before his death, which occurred 9th June, 1891. Mr. Edward was a man of refined and cultured tastes, scientific as well as literary, and an orator of great power. He had great interest in entomology, his collection of moths and butterflies containing more than 300,000 specimens.

CHARLES THOMAS PARSLOE died in New York city, 22nd January, 1898. He was born in New York, October 1, 1836. His father, Charles Parsloe, was an English actor, and managed the second dramatic agency in this country. He was identified chiefly with the role of the *Chinaman* in "My Partner," and was *co-star* with Louis Aldrich in that melodrama during its great vogue of fifteen years ago. His portrayal of *Wing Lee* was in accordance with Bret Harte's descriptions rather than with any results of actual study and observation of such "Chinks" as had made the West their abiding place in those days; but the public accepted the impersonation as a triumph of character acting. In other roles Parsloe was not so successful, although he was a fair actor of comic character. His tours with Mr. Aldrich netted him $65,000, yet he died poor. He was last seen in Montreal as a *star* at the Academy in 1887 in "A Grass Widow." He lost $5,000 on that tour.

ERNESTO ROSSI was born 27th Aug., 1829, at Leghorn, Italy,
which is not far from Pisa, where he was educated at the university,
to fit himself for the legal profession. Much to his parent's disappointment, he found that his son evinced no predilection for that
pursuit, and that his declaiming propensity was histrionic rather
than forensic. He read plays, recited passages from them, and
frequented theatres, instead of poring over the musty tomes of
Justinian, etc. He joined an amateur company, and, having once
felt the inspiration of playing before an audience, he could not be
brought back to the routine of the university. In 1846 he ran off,
joining a strolling company, and made his regular *debut* at Fogano,
Tuscany. His salary was 15 centissimi per day—3 cents. His father
having abandoned all hope of seeing his son a conspicuous advocate,
and his kinsmen and friends having failed to draw him from the
avocation which had fascinated him, he was permitted to follow the
bent of his own desires. He enrolled himself as a member of a professional dramatic company managed by Signor Marchi, and speedily
gave indication that nature had intended him for the stage. Possessing youth, personal comeliness, a slight, graceful figure, and a melodious voice, he was especially fitted for the impersonation of lovers,
in which roles he made a signal success. After leaving Marchi he
entered a dramatic school, then recently founded by Gustavo Modena,
under whose instruction he vastly improved. He subsequently
appeared at the Carcano theatre, Milan, and later at the Carignano,
Turin, being cordially received at both. After performing in many
other Italian cities, he first visited Paris, France, in 1855, as a
member of the company supporting Ristori, he then being 26 years
of age. He was highly complimented by the critics for the delicacy
and finish of his impersonations. From Paris, Rossi went
to Vienna and introduced to the Austrian public many of the
comedies of Goldoni, the Molière of the Italian stage. In 1866 he
made his second professional visit to Paris, and was cordially received.
While playing at the Italian theatre there he presented many of the
pieces of Goldoni, who passed the last thirty years of his life there,
during which time he wrote his best known comedy, entitled "The
Benevolent Grumbler." On the anniversary of Corneille, Rossi appeared by invitation at the Theatre Francais, impersonating the hero
in "The Cid" in the Italian translation of the French poet's masterpiece. The Parisians were so favorably impressed with his art that
they proclaimed him the Italian Talma. Rossi began to study Shakespeare, and achieved distinction as *Hamlet, Lear, Romeo, Coriolanus,
Macbeth* and *Othello*. These delineations were witnessed in Madrid,
Lisbon, Paris, London and other European capitals, and elicited
very favorable criticism. *Hamlet* was Rossi's favorite role, and in
it he made his first appearance on the English stage in Drury Lane
theatre, London, April 19, 1876. The success achieved here by
Salvini, who was a personal friend of Rossi, induced him to visit us.

ERNESTO ROSSI (as Hamlet).

He arrived September 30, 1881, in which year he published a book: "Forty Years of an Artist's Life." He practically retired in 1889, but reappeared, occasionally playing, in Russia chiefly, where he was very well liked. Signor Rossi, rich with honor, and revered by the world, passed through the sunset gates, 4th June, 1896.

THE YEAR OF 1882

was opened by Anna Graham, week 2nd January. She was supported by Forrest Robinson in a production of " The Legion of Honour." Hermann, the magician, first appeared here week 9th January. Haverly's Minstrels came for three nights from 26th January; the Hoey-Hardie Company, in Geo. Hoey's "A Child of the State," 14th to 16th, when "Diplomacy" was staged for three nights, and Brookes & Dickson's "The World," week 20th January, after which the house was dark until 6th and 7th March, when Barlow, Wilson, Primrose & West's Minstrels appeared, followed by Haverly's Opera Company in "Patience" and "The Mascot," week 13th March. Genevieve Ward in "Forget Me Not," 20th and 21st, and the second engagement here of Mary Anderson, supported by William Harris, J. B. Studley, Robert L. Downing and Mrs. M. A. Pennoyer, opening 22nd March with "Romeo and Juliet," Mary Anderson as *Juliet*, Wm. Harris as *Romeo*, J. B. Studley as *Mercutio*, Robert Downing as *Friar Lawrence*, and Mrs. Pennoyer as the *Nurse*. Then followed "Ingomar," "The Hunchback," "Lady of Lyons" (matinee), and closing 25th with "Pygmalion and Galatea." This was Mr. Downing's first appearance here. His last engagement was at the same house, week of 23rd October, 1893, in classical repertoire, supported by Edmund K. Collier and Eugenia Blair (Mrs. Dowing). W. H. Gillette, in "The Professor," was the next attraction, week 10th April ; J. T. Raymond, in "Fresh," and Col. Sellars," 17th, 18th, 19th; Helen Coleman in "Widow Bedott," 20th, 21st, 22nd; Gus Williams, in "Our German Senator," and "Prof. Keiser," 27th, 28th; and J. W. Collier's " Banker's Daughter," with Joseph Whiting and Adele Belgarde, 2nd May, for five nights. Montreal's most popular tragedian, Thomas W. Keene, made his first bow week 8th May in this city as a *star*, and a bright one too. George Learock was in the leading support. The opening was in "Richard III.," 8th; "Richelieu," 9th; "Othello," 10th; "Hamlet," 11th; "Macbeth," 12th; "Fool's Revenge," 13th (matinee); and "Richard" for the closing performance. Mr. Keene reappeared here week 12th March, 1883; 18th February, 1884; 19th January, 1885; 29th February, 1892; 10th April, 1893; 25th March, 1895; and lastly, 10th May, 1897. He had always been Montreal's favorite Shakespearean actor. Maurice Grau's French Opera Co. followed, 16th, for eight nights; Kate Claxton, in "Two Orphans," "Double Marriage," and "Frou Frou," 25th, for three nights; Charles Wheatleigh and Sydney Cowell, in "Hazel Kirke," 29th, for three nights. Miss Cowell was the original *Dolly Dutton* in the piece. The season closed until 14th August, when "Youth" was produced for the first time here; "Michael Strogoff," 21st, for one week; also first production Gorge S. Knignt in "Baron Rudolphe," 28th, for one week; Hermann came 4th September, for four nights; Helen Blythe, in "Only a Farmer's Daughter," 8th, for two nights; Alex. Caufman, in "Called to Account," supported by D. H. Harkins and Lottie Church (Mrs. J. A. Stevens), 11th September, for one week; Lotta, in "Bob," etc., week 19th; Laura Don, in "A Daughter of the Nile," week 25th; Collier's "Lights o' London," 2nd October, for week; Edwin F. Thorne; Nat C. Goodwin, Jun., and Eliza Weathersby, week 9th October. Lawrence Barrett made his second *star* appearance here 25th October, appearing four nights, supported by Louis James and Marie Wainwright. He opened in "Richelieu"; "Hamlet," 26th; "Shylock" and "David Garrick," 27th; "Marble Heart" (matinee), and "Yorick's Love," 28th. The following was the cast of the opening night in "Richelieu": *Cardinal Richelieu*, Lawrence Barrett ; *King Louis XIII.*, Charles Rolfe ; *Duke of Orleans*, Erroll Dunbar; *Count de Baracas*, F. C. Mosley; *Adrian de Mauprat*, Louis James; *Sieur de Berenghen*, Chas. Plunkett; *Huguet*, Homer Cope; *Father Joseph*, B. G. Rogers; *Francois*, Albert T. Riddle; *Clermont*, Percy Winter; *Captain of the Guard*, Louis Lyon; *First Secretary*, Garrie Davidson; *Second Secretary*, George Vail; *Third Secretary*, Robert Sutton; *Julie de Mortimer*, Marie Wainwright; *Marion de Lorme*, Josie Batchelder. This was the tragedian's first visit to the city since 28th August, 1872, at Theatre Royal. His last appearance was at the Academy week 18th May, 1885. Maud Granger and Harry Lacy came week of 30th October in Tillotson's "The Planter's Wife." M'lle. Rhea, supported by William Harris, made her Montreal *debut*, week 6th November, appearing in "Adrienne Lecouvreur," "Camille," and "Much Ado About Nothing." Following Rhea came Snyder and Grau's Opera Co. for three nights from 13th November; Fanny Reeves (Mrs. McDowell), week of 20th, in repertoire; Sam Hague's Minstrels, 27th; "The Rose of Yuba Dam," with Hattie Grinnell, week 4th December; Haverly's Opera Co., week 11th, in "The Merry War"; Boston Ideal "Uncle Tom" Double Co., week 18th; and Lillian Cleues, supported by Richard Foote, week 25th, in "The New Magdalen," closing the year.

ANNA GRAHAM was born in Philadelphia about 1837. She and her sister, Lillie, made their appearance on the stage at the City Museum in 1855 as *Julia* and *Helen* in "The Hunchback." She was for several years a favorite leading lady under the management of J. S. Clarke at the Walnut. She married Frank L. Gardner, and several years ago retired from the stage, now living in Philadelphia.

ALEXANDER HERMANN was born in Paris, 1844. He followed in the footsteps of his father, S. Hermann, who was also a well-known magician in his time. He left a widow, but no children. He made his first appearance in America at the Academy of Music in New York city in 1861, where he played 75 nights. Then, with his brother, he made the tour of the world. In 1867 his partnership with his brother was dissolved, and Alexander started out for himself, making another tour of the world. He returned to this country in 1874, and remained until his death, 17th December, 1896.

MAUD GRANGER (*nee* Annie E. Brainard) was born in Connecticut in 1846. She made her *debut* from the class of a New York teacher of elocution at the Union Square theatre, 1st October, 1873, as *Fraisette* in "The Geneva Cross." She made good headway, and subsequently was one of the six *Juliets* whom Rignold made love to in his historic performance of "Romeo and Juliet" at Booth's Theatre. She afterwards supported McCullough. In 1880 she married Alfred Follen, under whose management she toured for some time. She is now Mrs. Wm. R. Baxter. She is an actress of no profundity of emotion or variety of power, appealing altogether for endorsement to the senses alone, and has little trace of vital intelligence about it.

HARRY LACY has created roles in a number of modern dramas and has been *starring* since about 1880, "The Planter's Wife" being among his earlier successes. He has since appeared in "The Still Alarm." He is thorough in all his work, and his fine stage presence makes him particularly fitted for heroic work. He was last seen in the Vaudeville theatres.

GEORGE S. KNIGHT was a welcome feature for several seasons. His real name was Sloan, and he was born in Philadelphia in 1850. He was a graduate of the vaudeville, where he attained celebrity as a dialect singer and comedian. In 1875 he married Sophie Worrell (born in 1848 in New Orleans), with whom he subsequently *starred*, meeting with considerable success. They appeared in London, Eng., in 1880 in "Otto," but their most pronounced hit was in "Over the Garden Wall." They afterwards appeared in "Baron Rudolph," and had made preparations for an Australian tour, but death prevented, Mr. Knight having the curtain rung down on him 14th January, 1892.

JOSEPH F. WHITING is a son of the late David Whiting, and brother of the late Virginia Whiting Loring, both known and esteemed in American theatrical circles, Joseph E. Whiting was born in Boston, Mass., but was educated in New York city, at Trinity School. His first public appearance was as a chorister in Trinity Church, where he sang during two years. As a youth Mr. Whiting naturally breathed a dramatic atmosphere, and it is not surprising that, as soon as he had finished his studies, he went on the stage, about 1858, at Washington, D.C. He became a favorite leading man in the best stock companies of the day. Mr. Palmer engaged him to play the leading part in "Jim the Penman," and he played nothing else until he did *Abbe Latour* in "The Dead Heart," with James O'Neill, and then with Margaret Mather, playing *Mercutio, Rolando, La Hire* in "Joan of Arc," etc. He married Lillie Brandon, who obtained a divorce from him.

ADELE BELGARGE (*nee* Adelaide Levy) has been on the stage since 14th February, 1879, when she appeared in "Romeo and Juliet" in Newark, N.J.

ROBERT L. DOWNING. The history of the American stage records few instances where an actor has so suddenly sprung into prominence as has Robert L. Downing. Mr. Downing was born in Washington, D.C., October 28, 1857. At a very early age he evinced a decided liking for the Thespian art, and at eighteen he became a member of the stock company at Ford's Theatre, Baltimore. His parents were averse to his adopting the stage as a profession, but, when they observed how strongly the twig was bent, very sensibly allowed their son to follow his inclination. After a prosperous season with Mr. Fechter, he was engaged as leading support to Edwin Booth, and afterward played in that capacity with Charlotte Cushman, Dion Boucicault, Joseph Jefferson and other stars. In 1881 he made his New York *debut* with Miss Anderson as *Claude Melnotte* at the Fifth Avenue Theatre, remaining with her until she left to fulfil her engagement in England. During his engagement with Miss Anderson and other stars, his career had been carefully watched by Joseph H. Mack, who had taken a friendly interest in the young actor, and who, after McCullough's death, conceived the idea of bringing Downing out as *Spartacus* in an elaborate production of "The Gladiator." His wife, Eugenia Blair (*nee* Wren), first married Forrest Robinson in 1881. They have lived more or less apart for the last five years. Downing is a very fair representative of the school that had its last modern representative in John McCullough. A decade ago Downing could pack any theatre when he appeared in "The Gladiator," and many of you remember the effective posters that announced him, and to which no little of his prosperity in those days was due. Of late years he has known very little of good fortune, and has not been a very conspicuous figure in the theatre of the hour.

HORTENSE BARBE-LORET, called **RHEA,** was born in Brussels 4th September, 1844, and, in accordance with the custom of that country, was placed by her father, a wealthy manufacturer, in a convent, where she remained until she was fifteen years of age, being recalled home by the death of her mother. Not long after her mother's death, Melle. Rhea's father lost his fortune, and soon after died, leaving his three daughters with but a small sum of money with which to struggle against adversity. Luckily, the elder daughters married early, and the future actress endeavored to turn her musical accomplishments to profit by giving lessons, but the tax upon her strength proved too severe, and she was forced to abandon this mode of earning a living. She then determined to try her luck upon the stage, and, having studied "Athalid's Dream," she presented herself to Charles Fechter, who encouraged her to continue her studies. In Brussels she played for some time with success, but returning to Paris, and finding it almost impossible to obtain an opening at any of the Paris theatres, she formed a company and played "L'Etrangere" through the Provinces. Eventually she was offered an engagement in St. Petersburg, Russia. The disturbed state of the empire and the assassination of the Czar closed the theatre, whereupon Melle. Rhea visited England and began to study the English language, of which she already had considerable knowledge, placed herself under the dramatic guidance of John Ryder, and made her *debut* on the English stage a month later. She appeared at a matinee performance in the Gaiety theatre, London, Eng., June 21, 1881, playing *Beatrice* in "Much Ado About Nothing," speaking English. She made her American *debut* at Haverly's Theatre, Brooklyn, N. Y., and her New York *debut* at Booth's theatre in the fall of 1881. Melle. Rhea had an intelligent face and exuberant vivacity, but her voice, as I remember it, was far above concert pitch, and her English very difficult to follow, nevertheless her *Josephine* was well liked here. Her last engagement here was at the Academy week of 6th December, 1897. She retired from the stage in 1898, to Montmorency, France, where she died 9th May, 1899. She was personally a woman of great beauty, but of little real artistic quality. Her managers used her reputation, which was purely artificial, to give her an eminence she never deserved. She was a hard working woman, an indifferent actress and had public successes, which were created

by good advertisements which gave importance to her interest and
do not belong to her death.

WILLIAM HARRIS was born in New York, 25th October, 1839,
and made his *debut* at the National Theatre in that city in July, 1854,
as the *First Soldier* in "Pizarro." He subsequently travelled with
Crisp's company through the South. In 1860 he enlisted in the 34th
Ohio Regiment at Cincinnati and rose to the rank of captain. He
was with Sheridan through the campaign in Shenandoah Valley, and
was wounded 25th July, 1865, at Martinsburg, shortly afterwards
returning to the stage, first appearing at the Boston Museum. His
best work has been done in support of Hortense Rhea for many
seasons. More recently he has been in the support of Julia Arthur. ·

SYDNEY COWELL on or off the stage is the same blithe
being. For her it is no task to simulate gayety or high spirits; she is
by nature a genuine comedienne with a rare fund of good humor and
inherent fun. Miss Cowell tells us her story as follows: "I was
born within the sound of Bow Bells, but my grandfather, Joseph
Leathley Cowell, was a naturalized citizen of America, and my father,
'Sam' Cowell, was raised and reared here. Both my father and
grandfather were famous comedians in their day, and my father's
sister was Sydney Cowell before me. She was the mother of the
celebrated Bateman children. Miss Bateman was renowned for her
performance of *Leah.* Isabel Bateman and Mrs. Edward Compton
are my first cousins." I had accepted an engagement with the late
J. B. Buckstone for the Haymarket Theatre, London, when Charles
Wyndham offered me substantial inducements to come to New York
with his famous comedy company. Since then I have played only in
this country. *Dolly Dutton* in Hazel Kirke was my next success· I
played it for twelve months at the Madison Square Theatre, and
afterwards in almost every city in the Union· In 1890 I retired from
the stage, and for five succeeding years was a confirmed invalid,
never dreaming that I should 'ever be able to play again. But in
1895 I accepted an offer from Mr. Hilliard for the character part,
Mrs. Churchill, in 'Lost-Twenty-Four Hours.' I have also appeared
with Mrs. Fiske in 'Tess of the d'Urbervilles,' and at present I
am playing the amorous widow in 'Love Finds the Way.''

MRS. SARAH A. BAKER, so frequently seen here with T. W.
Keene, died in the Forrest Home, 1st Sept., 1899. She was the oldest actress in America, having been born in Philadelphia in 1818.
Her first stage appearance was at the Walnut Street Theatre December 15, 1837, as *Virginia.* Her second regular season was played
at W. E. Burton's theatre, and among her associates was Charlotte
Cushman. In March, 1853, Mrs. Baker was married to J. S· Baker,
an actor. Mrs. Baker's last appearance as a member of a stock
company was in Philadelphia during the Centennial. Since that time

THOMAS W. KEENE (*Hamlet*).

she has been attached to various combinations, and travelled all over the country. Mr. Baker died in Atlanta, Ga., in 1864. Mrs. Baker joined Keene's forces at the outset of that actor's starring career, he promising that she should continue with him as long as she cared to, after which she could retire a member of his family. The tender care which the old lady received up to the time of Mr. Keene's death in 1898, was the constant subject of the veteran actress's conversation. In 1887 she celebrated the fiftieth aniversary of her *debut*.

THOMAS WALLACE KEENE probably did more to popularize Shakespeare in America than any other actor. He went about with *"his wild harp strung behind him"* like the minstrels and historians of old carrying the echoes of Shakespeare into the fastnesses of the wilderness; he sang in caves, and waved his garish banner through the darkness. Mr. Keene rose from the foundation of dramatic apprenticeship to be recognized as a competent impersonator of characters so complex and elevated as *Gloster* and *Othello.* He was not a genius, but he was a diligent and ambitious man of alert intellect, who had mastered the technical difficulties of his profession, and used its symbols in such a way as to make his conception of a part perfectly clear to a miscellaneous audience. In San Francisco I have heard of an audience turning from McCullough, and rise to its feet in wild cheers for Keene, because of the splendor of his voice and the tremendous fire and magnetism of the man. His art lacked the last degree of refinement, but all his faults accumulated were most forgivable. To Mr. Keene I owe many moments of artistic qualification at the theatre, and I should like to add one *immortelle* to the wreath that will preserve the memory of a robust and conscientious actor of truly manly qualities. The tragedian was born in New York city, 26th Oct., 1840. It was with J. H. Hackett that he secured his first regular engagement in 1863, and he was eminently successful from the outset. At Marylebone, he opened the theatre, where Charlotte Cushman, the Wallacks, Mrs. Mowatt and E. L. Davenport achieved their successes, and was himself spoken of in the most favorable manner by press and public. Early in life Mr. Keene married Margaret Creighton, by whom he had two children, Agnes and Claude, the former being Mrs. Edwin Arden. After a brilliant career in the support of the first stars of the day, Keene himself was firmly placed in the stellar firmament by W. S. Cole in 1880. Season after season this actor crossed and recrossed the continent. He had a large and loyal following of admirers, who ranked the name of Keene only after that of Booth, and for eighteen years these tours invariably yielded profit. He had played *Richard* 2,525 times. Nature had peculiarly fitted him for that character, he having that quick, nervous impetuosity of manner and mobility of countenance so necessary to simulate the swiftly changing emotions of the crafty monarch. In later years he had also given a truly great performance of

Louis XI., in which characterization he was aided by advancing years. Mr. Keene, or rather Thomas R. Eagleson, for that was his original name, died at his home, at Castleton Corners, S.I., 1st June, 1898. His last appearance on the stage had been at Hamilton, Ont., 23rd May, as *Richelieu*. It was there that the actor was striken. Then fell a rugged oak, over whose prostrate trunk the sunshine was gleaming broadly through the vista of a beautiful life.

"Strive to remember that the realization is very oft a bitter disappointment, and that the expectation is the buoyant hope which is part and parcel of happiness."—THOS. W. KEENE.

THE YEAR OF 1883

was theatrically summoned in with sweet symphonies by the Emma Abbott Opera Co., January 1, for week; Haverly's Minstrels, week 8th; Eugenie Le Grand, in "Camille," "Lady of Lyons," and "Black Sheep," week 15th. This was a very feeble effort, and did not receive much encouragement. Louis Aldrich and Chas. T. Parsloe, Jr., came carnival week in "My Partner," from 22nd January. Montreal's first Carnival began on that date. Jeffreys Lewis and J. Newton Gotthold followed in Belasco's "La Belle Cerisse," week 29th. Collier and Rice's "Iolanthe" Co. sang week 5th February; Willie Edouin, in "Dreams," and "A Bunch of Keys," week 12th; Ella Stockton, in a dramatization of Black's "Madcap Violet," week 19th; Salsbury's Troubadours, in "Greenroom Fun," four nights from 26th; C. B. Bishop, in "Strictly Business," week 6th March; and the second appearance of T. W. Keene, week 12th, in Shakespearean repertory. Charles Wyndham, supported by Miss Kate Rorke (Mrs. Gardiner), and the Criterion Theatre Company of London, England, made his Montreal *debut*, week 26th March, in "Brighton," and "Fourteen Days." The Hanlon Bros., in "Voyage en Suisse," came for four nights, 2nd April, followed by the first appearance here of the celebrated "Jersey Lily," Mrs. Langtry, week 6th April, in "An Unequal Match." She appeared in "Pygmalion and Galatea" at the matinee, and closed in "As You Like It." Mr. and Mrs. Florence were seen in "The Mighty Dollar," and "Ticket-of-Leave Man," four nights from 18th April; Collier and Rice's "Iolanthe," week 23rd; Mr. Grau's French Opera Company, 30th, for nine nights; Barlow, Wilson, Primrose and West's Minstrels, three nights from 10th May; Boston Ideal Opera Company, three nights from 16th; C. W. Couldock, E. J. Buckley and W. H. Crompton, in "Hazel Kirke," week 23rd; Raymond in "Paradise," week

29th; and J. K. Emmett, in "Fritz in Ireland," week 5th June, which closed the season until 14th October, when W. H. Lytell came in " Around the World " and " The White Slave," followed by the Italian Opera Company week 20th and 27th with Sig. Brignoli. "Romany Rye" was produced 3rd September; Grau's English Opera Company, week of 11th; Shook & Collier's "Lights o' London," week 17th; Baker and Farron, week 22nd; Joseph Murphy, in "Kerry Gow," week 2nd October; Lytell's "Galley Slave," week 8th; and on 15th was produced, for first time here, "The Silver King," with the following principals in the cast: *Wilfred Denver*, Carl A. Haswin; *Nellie Denver*, Etelka Wardell; *Spider*, William Morris; *Eliah Combe*, Perkins Fisher; *Jakes*, Harry Rich. "Young Mrs. Winthrop" followed, 22nd, for week; Lily Langtry, in "School for Scandal" and "She Stoops to Conquer," week 29th; Rhea, in "Adrienne," "Frou Frou," "An Equal Match" and "Richelieu's Wager," four nights from 12th; Her Majesty's Colored Minstrels, week 19th; "7-20-8," week 6th December; and Etelka Gerster, week 10th, with Patterson's New York Opera Company in Strauss' "Queen's Lace Handkerchief." Richard Mansfield made his initial bow here week 17th December in "A Parisian Romance." Cast of characters : *Baron Chevrial*, Richard Mansfield; *Henri de Targy*, Leonard S. Outram; *Dr. Chesnel*, H. B. Phillips; *M. Tirandel*, Clinton Stuart; *Signor Juliani*, F. de Vernon; *M. Laubaniere*, Harold Russell; *M. Vaumartin*, W. F. Blande ; *Ambroise*, F. Sullivan; *Pierre*, T. Barrett; *Marcelle De Targay*, Miss May Brooklyn ; *Madame De Targay*, Mrs. Sol Smith, jun.; *Baroness Chevrial*, Mrs. Chas. Watson; *Madame De Valmery*, Miss Mary R. Perkins; *Madame De Luce*, Miss Helen Windsor; *Maria*, Miss Jessie Glassford; *Gillette I.*, Miss M. Barbour; *Gillette II.*, Miss E. S. Tarr; *Bertholdi*, Miss Nellie Whiting; *Rosa Guerin*, Miss Isabelle Evesson. Her Majesty's Opera Co., with Etelka Gerster, came week 24th December, closing the year.

ETELKA GERSTER was born at Kaschau, in Hungary, on June 16, 1857. She studied singing with Madame Marchesi, from 1873-76. She made her *debut* at Venice in *Rigoletto* with pronounced success. She next appeared in Berlin and created a furore. After becoming famous in all the large cities of Europe, she came to America in 1878, and was hailed as a second Jenny Lind. She lost her voice some years ago and retired to private life.

J. NEWTON GOTTHOLD (born Isaac Gotthold), was a good actor, and at one time *starred* in the legitimate. He died in 1888.

CHARLES WYNDHAM is one of England's best comedians, but is of American birth (1839), and his first stage appearance was on the boards of the Olympic Theatre, New York city, in 1861. During the Civil War he acted as a surgeon in the South, and in 1866 he made his first London appearance. He has paid us several visits, and his career has, up to the present, been a most satisfactory one. His *David Garrick* is quite popular, and among his most recent successes was his production of "Rosemary."

RICHARD MANSFIELD (Rudersdorff) is one of two sons of the late Erminia Rudersdorff, a famous singer, who came here from Europe about 1869. He was born in Heligoland, 24th May, 1857. His father was an Englishman of culture. He inherited from his gifted mother the nervous and delicate temperament of the true artist. Much of his earlier life was passed in Boston, Mass., where he was carefully educated, and where, for a time, he was employed variously in commercial pursuits in journalism, etc. He then visit-ed Europe and travelled considerably. Long before he had decided on adopting the stage as a profession, he was *perzona grata* at the pleasant evening meetings of the Savage Club, in London, from his skill both as a vocalist and musician, and as a clever imitator of most of the well-known actors. His natural bent at last asserted itself, and he joined the German Reeds, and subsequently played with success at some of the principal London theatres, doing *Sir Joseph* in "Pinafore" among other roles. He soon determined to visit America, and made his *debut* in his native land, Sept. 26, 1879, as *Dromez* in "Les Manteaux Noirs" at the (old) Standard theatre, New York. His subsequent career hardly needs recalling. It may be said briefly, however, that he soon joined the Union Square theatre stock, and that, after a round of unimportant roles, he found one that revealed his real power in the *Baron Chevrial* of "A Parisian Romance." His creation of that character for American play-goers (1883) gave him instant and wide recognition as an actor of deep intelligence and singular power. His earlier *starring* tours (preceded by versatile work in light opera and serious drama) netted him much profit, and the esteem entertained for him by Irving led directly to his last English engagement (1888), when he produced "Richard III," in grand effect, also producing that nightmare, "Dr. Jekyl and Mr. Hyde." The actor's production of Clyde Fitch's drama-tization of "Beau Brummel" has been in every sense successful. His *Richard* has some clever bits in it, and is acknowledged to be superior to his *Shylock*. Mr. Mansfield is married to Beatrice Cam-eron (Susan Hageman), formerly his leading lady. Mansfield is the very type of man about whom long eulogies will be written when he is dead. His versatility will be pointed to as one of the most re-markable attributes of a marvellous capacity for projecting himself in-to the character of others. The dual role of sharpest contrast in *Jekyl*

RICHARD MANSFIELD.

and *Hyde*, the pink of perfection *Beau Brummel*, the dashing *Prince Karl*, the wicked old *Baron Chevrial*, the matter of fact *Bluntschli*—that one man should have gained a distinction in all of these that inseparably links his name with each will serve as the capsheaf to his fame. He sings well, speaks six languages with fluency, exclusive of that which he uses when the rattling of steam pipes irritates him and leading women are an aggravation, plays on a dozen instruments, can dance well when necessary, and is capable of a range of acting from the highest emotional to the comically grotesque. Several years ago he announced his ambition to have a theatre in New York. "I feel sure," he said, "the moment I have a theatre of my own, my difficulties will disappear from my path." His ambition was realized. In the Garrick he possessed one of the prettiest play-houses in the metropolis; but troubles thickened on his pathway instead of disappearing from it, and after less than a year's tenancy the management of the Garrick was handed over to Charles Frohman. Mansfield has since toured the country, presenting his various characterizations of human monstrosities, including that of *Cyrano de Bergerac*. His most recent effort was "Henry V.," a really praiseworthy production.

EMILY CHARLOTTE LE BRETON LANGTRY-DE-BATHE.

the best advertised actress of the century, is the daughter of Dean W. C. Le Breton, an Episcopalian clergyman of St. Heliers, where she was born in 1854. She first met Edward Langtry in 1873. He was then a gay young widower. His father, although a Quaker of orthodox principles, was not averse to the enjoyment of life by his son, and when the latter came of age he settled a fortune upon him, bought him a yacht and sent him off to enter the lists at Cowes. It is said that on his way thither his yacht was driven out of her course by stress of weather, and the young sailor found himself one stormy night among the Channel Islands. He made the harbor of St. Heliers safely, and went ashore until the storm should abate. He was invited to the deanery by Dean Le Breton, the most important man on the Island of Jersey, and was asked to remain at his house instead of at the inn. The dean introduced him to his two beautiful daughters, and before Mr. Langtry left the island he was betrothed to one of them. After a courtship of five months they were wedded, her father officiating in his own beautiful church of St. Saviour's. The ceremony was performed 12th March, 1874, at the rather unusual hour of 3 a. m. After living on the Island of Jersey for some years, they removed to Southampton; but the wife, leaning instinctively toward the glitter of smart society, induced her husband to take a handsome house near Belgrave square, and they began to entertain. The time was short before she developed into a woman of extreme fashion, and the fame of her beauty spread. It reached the ears of John Millais, a painter, subsequently baroneted at the recommendation of Mr. Gladstone for the excellence of his art. Mr. Millais sought the beauty, and the following spring, at the Royal Academy, exhibited a portrait, which he had labelled "A Jersey Lily." The label stuck. All London went to see that picture, asked who was the original, learned that it was Mrs. Edward Langtry, and the fame of the *Jersey Lily* began. The Prince of Wales saw the face, craved an introduction, and from that time until the crash that followed Mrs. Langtry was the most conspicuous figure in London's social whirl. At Grosvenor House, at a dance given by the Duchess of Westminster, she stood in the centre of the great reception room, hated by every peeress that was there ; hated, it may be, by the duchess herself, but radiating loveliness, unapproachable, semi-circled by four men, of whom one was a crown prince and the other three were kings. When supper was served it was at the royal table that she sat. The honor—for such it is regarded—was unprecedented. But so, too, was her success. That night her first ambition was achieved. Meanwhile there had come another. To be properly admired a woman must be properly frocked. To go to dances means traps. To be entertained means entertaining, and by the same token to be Queen of Mayfair means coin. Given a few years in Belgravia a man can squander an earldon—a woman can squander two. Mr. Langtry was in what is called comfortable circumstances—for the reason, perhaps, that they lie between the devil and the deep blue sea. Expenses became such that when Mr. Langtry was not interviewing the one he was up to his neck in the other. It was at this juncture that Mrs. Langtry took matters in hand. She had conquered one world—she determined to conquer another. After society, finance. With a business tact that has since developed into genius the Lily went on the stage, and, with an appropriateness which, when you consider it, is delightful, appeared in "She Stoops to Conquer." That event occurred on December 15, 1881. In the autumn following she came to this country under the guidance and management of the late Henry E. Abbey. But a few hours before the time set for her first appearance, on the night of October 30, 1882, the Park Theatre, at Broadway, near Twenty-Second street, burned to the ground. At 6 o'clock that evening love and money could not have bought a stall. At 7 the theatre was on fire. By 9 it was glowing embers and circling smoke—in short, a brilliant advertisement. She appeared at Wallack's, 6th Nov., instead. The house, packed to the doors, admired her gowns, but not her art. and it would have been difficult for the house to have done so. She had none. Splendid in beauty, artistically she was null. Her charm was that of the gentlewoman. It belonged to the drawing-room, not to the stage. But Mrs. Langtry had not stooped to conquer for nothing. If artistically she failed, commercially she succeeded. To express it discreetly, she allowed herself to be insulted into fame. She owed her *debut* on the stage to Mrs. Henry Labouchere, who was herself an actress, and to Marie Wilton, now Lady Bancroft. What her profits were she and her business manager alone could state. That, however, is a side issue. Such results as she achieved in this country she is reported to have accentuated abroad. but ultimately less through the box office than through the stable. And now the plot thickens. In 1882 Freddie Gebhard came into her life, and a memorable sleigh-ride was had one night after the play. and her chaperone, Mrs. Labouchere, went home in anger and confusion. Gebhard's subsequent successes on the turf are said to be due very largely to her advice. Then there was Sir Robert Peel, and Squire Abingdom Baird, the latter having been accused by Mrs. Langtry of having beaten her on more than one occasion. Baird alone. it is said, spent $500,000 on her. There was a story that the entire Marlborough family cut the Lily because in a playful mood she had slipped a piece of ice down the Prince's collar at a late and merry supper. From time to time she came again into the zone of gossip, and Sir George Chetwyn, he who was in a measure responsible for her original social introduction, had a first fight with the Marquis of Lonsdale over her. She was also coupled with Lord Rosslyn in a brief scandal. Numberless other men worshipped at her shrine, but met with no success. She was busy with the rich, who would dare anything for her, and the minor devotees failed in all things. It was Lord Rosslyn, to whom she owed her introduction to racing, he being her first racing partner. His money, however, soon gave out, and his entire string of horses passed into her possession, constituting the nucleus of what has since become one of the best known and most successful racing stables in England, its fair owner racing under the name of "Mr. Jersey." Lord Shrewsbury succeeded Lord Rosslyn as her racing partner, but they have since parted company, and the Lily is now alone on the turf. All over the United States she owns lands, and her name appears on the tax rolls of many Western States. After society, finance. After finance rehabilation. In that already the turf had been serviceable. On one of its green intervals she encountered Prince Esterhazy, an Hungarian and a great sportsman, incidentally a great noble, a descendant of Attila, who, where he passed, left the earth forever bare. And now the plot grows thicker. Her first attempt at divorce was in vain, but she made another and yet another, finally succeeding in a California court, May 14, 1897. Edward Langtry died in the Chester Lunatic Asylum, 15th October, 1897, while Mrs. Langtry was entertaining a select party of sporting friends at dinner at the Savoy House. They were celebrating her winning $200,000 in bets on her horse Merman, which won the Cesarewitch stakes. "A beautiful woman," said Epictetus, "is a disaster." And Epictetus, who was seldom wrong, was right. There is something in the gift of beauty which—speaking historically—renders the recipient perverse. And yet, who shall blame them. The divine cannot mate with mere man.

Edward Langtry was an Ulsterman and 52 years of age. He was the son of a wealthy shipping merchant, who was for a long time agent of the Guion Steamship line at Belfast, and a member of the Society of Friends. For some years back Edward Langtry had displayed unmistakable signs of the life of dissipation he had led. Originally he was good looking and gentlemanly. Many idle con. jectures as to who would be his successor were dispelled by the an. nouncement of the Lily's marriage, 27th July, 1899, to Hugo Gerald de Bathe, 28 years of age, the eldest son of Sir Henry Percival de Bathe, Bart., a retired general and Crimean veteran. The ceremony was private, the only witness being Mrs. Langtry's daughter. The Prince of Wales is said to have been in the confidence of the pair, and he sent them a telegram of congratulations. It is understood that young de Bathe was greatly shocked when he discovered that his wife was in the habit of mildly flirting with men friends. He had gathered, it is said, that she was the pink of propriety—in fact, she had told him so herself. The awakening came, and the callow youngster, who believed himself the object of a grand passion, had his hands held by his friends while he slept all night with ice on his head and gazed blankly into vacancy, pondering on what might have been. Sir Henry Percival de Bathe, the irate father of Mrs. Langtry's bridegroom, is a crusty old soldier. It is said that when the youth married he had his son's effects thrown out of the windows by servants. Then he went to his lawyers and made a new will, leaving out all reference in it to Hugo. It is asserted that after signing it he exclaimed : " I almost wish that I would die right now so that the will would take effect." Apparently young de Bathe lost not only his fortune, but his wife, and wishing to revenge himself on some one, proceeded to Africa to assist in the capture of Oom Paul. Mrs. Langtry returned to the stage 1st September, 1899, producing "The Degenerates" of the Haymarket Theatre in the presence of a fashionable audience, all on the *qui vive* to know how far she and Sydney Grundy, the author of the drama, had dared to go in depicting the incidents of her past. From London she came to New York, opening at the Garden Theatre, 15th January, 1900. The general verdict was that she had never acted better, that her beauty had worn splendidly, and that her dresses and jewels were superb. The Philadelphia press showed no courtesy in its reception, the dignitaries at the Capitol turned her down and throughout her reception was " frosty." Mrs. Langtry de Bathe appeared at Her Majesty's Theatre here, 17th May, for three nights, and matinee, and then returned to England.

MARY JEFFREYS LEWIS. Few actresses have filled the position of leading lady in a metropolitan stock company before they were out of their teens. Jeffreys Lewis is among the few who have had such an honor thrust upon them. Lester Wallack saw her play *Esmeralda* in "Notre Dame" at the Fourteenth Street Theatre, and without hesitation offered her the opportunity of playing the leading female roles in the famous Wallack Stock company, then performing at the theatre known to-day as the Star. Recently Jeffreys Lewis was playing *Cassy* in "Uncle Tom's Cabin" at the Star—on the same stage where twenty years ago her beauty and histrionic achievements were the talk of the town. Miss Lewis was born in Wales, England. She came to America with T. C. King. Following Wallack, she was with Daly's company. About that time she married Mr. Mainhall, and played an engagement in Australia. Returning to America she *starred* in the emotional drama. Lately Miss Lewis appeared with Stuart Robson.

THEATRICALS IN 1884

were opened by Harry Lacy in Tillotson's "The Planter's Wife," from 31st December, followed by "The Power of Money," week 7th January; Kate Claxton and Chas. A. Stevenson, in "The Sea of Ice," week 22nd; Aimee, in Mr. Grau's Opera Company, week 29th; J. T. Raymond, in "Paradise" and "Col. Sellars," 6th February for four nights; T. W. Keene, week of 18th, in Shakespearean repertoire, including "Julius Cæsar" and "Macbeth"; Wilbur Opera Company, 25th, 26th; Salsbury's Troubadours for balance of week; Rice's "Surprise Party," week 3rd March; and Lytton Sothern in "Dundreary," "A Regular Fix," "Brother Sam" and "David Garrick" made his *debut* here 10th March. Edwin F. Thorne, in "The Black Flag," was the next attraction, week 17th; Mr. and Mrs. Florence, in "Facts" and "The Mighty Dollar," week 14th; "The Devil's Auction," week 21st; Callendar's Minstrels, 28th, 29th and 30th, with whom appeared Billy Kersands; "In the Ranks," came week 12th May; "The Stranglers of Paris," week 19th; and Hanlon's "Voyage en Suisse," week 26th, closing the season, which reopened 1st September with "Lights o' London," and Mr. and Mrs. W. A. Mestayer in "The Tourists," 8th. "Romany Rye," week 16th, was followed by Salsbury's Troubadours, week 22nd. Henry Irving and Ellen Terry, supported by Wm. Terriss and the Lyceum Theatre Company, of London, made their first bow to a Montreal audience, 1st October, in "The Merchant of Venice," "Much Ado About Nothing," "Hamlet" and "Louis XI.," appearing four nights. This was the event of the season, and a large business was done. Lillian Lewis, in "Only a Farmer's Daughter," came week 6th October. Roland Reed, in "Cheek" and "Humbug," made his *stellar debut* here week beginning 13th October. The Boston Museum Co. came 20th October for week, in "The Rivals," "Angel of Midnight," "A Scrap of Paper," "Inquisitive Donkey," "She Stoops to Conquer," "London Assurance" and "The Poor Gentleman." The principals were Charles Barron, Mrs. Vincent and Annie Clarke. Cast of "The Rivals:" *Sir Anthony Absolute*, Alfred Hudson; *Mrs. Malaprop*, Mrs. Vincent; *Capt. Absolute*, Charles Barron ; *Lydia*, Annie Clarke ; *Bob Acres*, George W. Wilson; *Sir Lucius O'Trigger*, George R. Parks; *Faulkland*, A. R. Wytal; *David*, James Nolan; *Julia*, Elizabeth Robins; *Lucy*, Miss O'Leary. Charles Kent was also with the company. Barry and Fay, in "All Crazy," 27th, for three nights; Rhea balance of week; Jos. Murphy, in "Kerry Gow" and "Shaun Rhue," week 3rd November; "The Private Secretary," week 10th; James M. Hardie, in "Ivanhoff," 17th for week; Mr. and Mrs. Florence, in "The Mighty Dollar" and "Our Governor," week 24th; and the great Adelaide Ristori, for the first time in Montreal, played in English in " Marie Antoinette," 11th December ; " Elizabeth," 12th ; " Marie Stuart," matinee of 13th; her engagement closing in "Macbeth." Within as many years Montreal saw Italy's three great living artists—Salvini, Rossi and Ristori. One is now no more; the others in retirement. The next attraction was "Storm Beaten," week of 15th December, and "7-20-8" closed the year.

CHARLES BARRON (*nee* Brown) was born in Boston in 1838, and made his first stage appearance at the Athenaeum as *Huguet*. For a period of nearly twenty-five years Mr. Barron cast his fortunes with Wm. Warren at the Boston Museum, playing leading business in company with Miss Annie Clarke. On the death of Mr. Warren in 1888, Mr. Barron went in support of the then new star, Miss Julia Marlowe. His talent is of the finest order. and his elocution is remarkably fine. He plays Shakespeare's heroes of tragedy, and were it not for his modesty Mr. Barron would be known as a great actor.

MRS. MARY ANN VINCENT, known also as Mrs. Wilson, made her *debut* in England in 1832. Her work was always in stock companies· She was an intelligent actress, a true and sympathizing friend, and known in Boston as the mother of actors and actresses. She died in Boston 4th Sept., 1887.

LILLIAN LEWIS came of good Kentucky stock. She was married in 1879 to Julian J. Lewis, but they separated in 1884, when Mrs. Lewis went on the stage, first appearing on the stage as the

Queen in "Zozo." She then *starred* in "As in a Looking Glass" and "Donna Sol," and also toured in Sardou's "Odette," in which play a new act was written for her, that she might display her cleverness with the rapier. She was also seen in "L'Article 47," and "Cleo. patra." In private life she was Mrs. Lawrence Marston, wife of the playwright, and author of "Therese Raquin," "Lady Lil," and "For Liberty and Love," a play written on the sympathies of Cuba, in which Mrs. Marston *starred* with indifferent success. She died 12th Aug., 1899.

ROLAND REED can be said to have been virtually born on the stage at Philadelphia, 18th June, 1852, his first appearance on the boards having been when six months old. The infantile Reed was stage-door tender at the Walnut, and usher and call-boy at the Arch before he again came before the footlights. "I was promoted to prompter," he has said of his life in those days, "and used to read the plays to the actors, standing beside Mrs. Drew, who corrected me when I made mistakes. While I was still call-boy Lotta came to play her first *star* engagement in Philadelphia. One day 'Bob' Craig. the comedian, fell ill, and I sang the songs with Lotta, and made a hit. Then I applied for the position of comedian for the next season, but Mrs. Drew had already engaged another. I left the Arch, my father exclaiming 'My boy, you've ruined yourself.'" Reed then shifted to the Walnut, where he scored his first pronounced success as the *Jew* in "The World." After that he *starred* in Mardsden's "Cheek" and "Humbug," and in 1887 produced "Lend Me Your Wife," an adaptation from the farce which formed the basis for "Jane." His work in "The Club Friend." "Innocent as a Lamb." "The Politician" and "The Wrong Mr. Wright " is well known to play-goers. In 1885 he created, in Chicago, the character of *Ko-Ko* in "The Mikado." It was one of the most humorous portrayals of Gilbert's executioner ever seen. He died 30th March, 1901.

LYTTON EDWARD SOTHERN, eldest son of E. A. Sothern, died in London, Eng., March 11, 1887. He was born in this country June 27, 1856, and went on the stage as a child, appearing, billed as Master Sothern, in his father's company, about 1862. Probably his first part of prominence was *Capt. Vernon* in "Our American Cousin," July 24, 1872, in London, Eng. September 16 following he played *Bertie* in "Home" at the Walnut Street theatre, Philadelphia. About 1878 he began to star in Australia, and after his father's death he toured England in the latter's repertory. In the fall of 1883 he came to America, appearing here as *Dundreary, Sam, Garrick*, etc., and returning to Engaud during 1884. Eva is his sister, and Edward H. and Sam. Sothern are his brothers.

ADELAIDE RISTORI was born at Friuli in 1821. She was the child of strolling players, and her grandmother, Teresa Ristori, was her first instructress. Her first appearance on the stage was when she was but two months old. Her regular *debut* was as *Francesca di Rimini* in 1835, after which she joined the Royal Sardinian Company, where Carlotta Marchioni, perceiving the genius of the young Adelaide, trained her as her successor in the leading parts. A romantic love affair, followed by her marriage in 1847 with the young Marquis del Grillo, caused Ristori to relinquish her profession until the objections of her "hubby" were overcome, when she returned to the stage. In 1851 she went to Paris, where, despite the fact that Rachel was then in her zenith, her genius conquered, nor was she less successful in England in 1858. Fresh laurels were gained in every European capital from Moscow to Dublin, and from Egypt to Constantinople. After her first visit to America she returned to England in 1873, and since that time twice revisited America, visiting thirty cities on her last visit in 1886, without any diminution of her powers of pleasing the cultured public.

MISS VAUGHAN was born Teresa Ott, and her early years were passed at the Highlands, Boston, Mass. There she sang in the choir of one of the Catholic churches, and we believe occasion. ally appeared in concerts. As a graceful actress and cultivated singer she has acquired an unenviable reputation. She married Wm. A. Mestayer, the comedian, who died 21st November, 1896, aged 52.

WILLIAM TERRISS (real name William Charles James Lewin), was born in London, 20th February, 1847, and came of an excellent family belonging to the Earl of Zetland's family, and was the son of an English barrister and nephew of George Grote, the historian. He commenced life in the Royal Navy, became a banker's clerk, then went into the wine trade, from which he sought relief as a practical engineer in the great Penn workshops. His next experience was on an Indian tea plantation, and finally he reached the stage at the age of twenty years, making his first appearance in 1870 at a provincial theatre at eighteen shillings a week. His next move was to Kentucky (1873), where he engaged with Percy Tattersall in the horse breeding business, the net result of which was a return home in the steerage of a ship. After a short interval on the stage at Drury Lane, he took to sheep farming on the Falkland Islands. This soon gave out, and so he returned home and to the stage once more. His first hit was under the management of John Hare at the Court in "Olivia" as *Squire Thornhill*. After a varied experience at the London theatres, he settled down under Henry Irving. When the French melodrama of "Roger la Honte" was translated, Terriss undertook to *star* in this country, and began his tour at Niblo's, New York city, in the fall of 1889. When Irving revisited us in the

ADELAIDE RISTORI.

ELLEN TERRY.

season of 1893-94, Terriss came with him, appearing as *Henry II.* in Tennyson's "Becket," and was *Thornhill* in a revival of "The Vicar of Wakefield." Once back in London, he resumed his position as leading man at the Adelphi, and remained there continuously since that time, although he occasionally appeared in productions at other theatres. When Gillette and his American company concluded their London engagement at the Adelphi in "Secret Service," and an English cast was put into the melodrama, Terriss succeeded Gillette as *Dumont*, the spy. Of his work, I always regarded *Henry II.* in "Becket" as his best portrayal, although he had no superior of contemporary activity in the roles of *Bassanio*, *Nemours*, and *Cromwell* in "Charles I." Born William Lewin, he adopted "Terriss" as *nom-de-theatre*, because of its similarity to Terry, he being a great admirer of the actress. Mr. Terriss was assassinated 16th Dec., 1897, being stabbed as he was entering the stage door of the Adelphi theatre for the performance of " Secret Service." His assassin was a mad supernumerary.

ELLEN ALICE TERRY was born at Coventry on February 27, 1848. She made her first appearance on the stage at the Princess theatre under Charles Kean's *regime*, April 28, 1856, playing a child's part, that of *Namillius* in "The Winter's Tale." In 1858 she appear. ed at the Princess as *Arthur* in the second revival of "King John." It was not until March, 1863, that she made what might be termed her real professional *debut*, when she played the part of *Gertrude* in "The Little Treasure" at the Haymarket theatre. On October 24, 1867, she was cast for the part of *Rose de Beaurepaire* in " The Double Marriage" on the opening of the New Queen's theatre in London. After that she lived in retirement till 1874, making her reappearance on February 28 of that year at the Queen's theatre as *Philippa Chester* in "The Wandering Heir." In April, 1875, she made a great hit as *Portia* in the revival of "The Merchant of Venice" at the Prince of Wales' theatre, and subsequently played *Clara Douglas* in "Money," *Pauline* in "The Lady of Lyons," *Mabel Vane* in "Masksand Faces," etaoin hrdlu shrdlu shrdlu hrdluu theatre. In 1875 she joined the company of the Royal Court theatre, and appeared there in November in a revival of "New Men and Old Acres." At the same theatre, on March 30, 1878, she acted the title role of *Olivia* in Will's dramatization of the "Vicar of Wakefield." On December 30, 1878, she appeared in *Ophelia* to Irving's *Hamlet* on the opening night of the Lyceum theatre under Irving's management, and has since shared in all his triumphs and few failures. She has also accompanied the great actor in all his American tours. During the last Montreal engagement, however, illness prevented her appearance in this city. Ellen Terry has thrice been married (Watts, Craig and Kelly-Wardell), and her son and daughter. Gordon and Ailsa Craig, have also appeared on the stage. Al

though greatly gifted, Ellen Terry never permits her art to over-
shadow the enchantment of a winning personality; and yet so
cleverly are the two elements blended, that while one is conscious of
the complete sinking of the woman in whatever character she
depicts, the depiction takes on a new grace because there is Ellen
Terry behind it. The dominant note in Miss Terry's stage presence
is ease, and yet her memory is very treacherous. One of the many
things for which she will .be remembered is her perennial youth-
fulness, for, like Swedenborg's fabled angels, she seems to become
more winsome as time creeps in its pace from day to day.

SIR HENRY IRVING (John Henry Brodribb) was born 6th
Feb., 1838, at Keinton, near Glastonbury, England. The history of the
eminent actor's later years is too well known to the English-speaking
world to need more than a passing notice, and, like most other men
who have attained success, the chief interest in his life lies in its
beginning, and in the romance that surrounds the opening of his
career. Irving's father, Samuel Brodribb, took to wife Mary
Behenna, a-woman of considerable personal beauty and of a very
sweet disposition. The actor's childish days were spent principally
with an aunt at Helston, near the Lizard Point. The future actor
was still a child in years when the monetary exigencies of his family
forced him into a clerkship with a firm of booksellers, and he found
himself earning his own living in a congenial way. His access to
standard works and all the best new books fostered his studious
disposition, while his evenings were free for worship at theatrical
shrines. When he was 17 his employers wished to send him out
to their branch establishment in Bombay, but by that time the youth
had cast the die of his life in favor of the stage, and he declined
the offer. Two years later he made the plunge, left his desk and
trod the boards; from which rumor has it that he was hissed. If so,
it was the Disraeli incident over again. For nine years Henry
Irving worked " in the provinces," founding life-long friendships,
gaining a measure of popularity in Edinburgh, Glasgow, Manchester
and Liverpool, but always struggling to attain London, the actor's
Mecca. The chance came at last, in 1856, when he was engaged to
support Kate Terry in Boucicault's "Hunted Down," in which he
acted so well that a London appearance followed. At the Gaiety,
Drury Lane, the St. James' and the Haymarket he acted a long
round of characters, generally being cast for the villain, who, in
those days, was a necessity in every play. During 1869, Irving
married Florence, daughter of Daniel J. O'Callaghan, a surgeon-
general of the Indian Army. In 1870 he created *Digby Grant* in
"The Two Roses." His performance aroused interest and curiosity
respecting the "new actor." He next moved to the Lyceum, then
under Colonel Bateman, and here his *Mathias* in "The Bells," played
triumphantly to an audience that was at first languid, clinched the

HENRY IRVING.
(1884.)

SIR HENRY IRVING.

matter forever. The morning after that memorable first night, after fifteen years of heart-breaking labor, Henry Irving woke to find himself famous. From that hour he has never looked back, and fame and fortune have keep pace with him. Colonel Bateman was sufficiently astute to turn the temporary engagement into a permancy. Then came a series of Shakespearean efforts, with more or less applause, but it was in character work of a heavy nature that brought the actor to the front, notably in *Louis, Mephisto, Shylock* and *Mathias*. His association with Ellen Terry began in 1878. With an analytic mind, a comprehensive grasp of detail and an unwavering integrity of purpose, his efforts culminated in successful consummation. In 1883 Irving first seized the American continent, starting on his tour with the most extraordinary banquet in all the history of English society, and carrying with him the whole nation's wishes for success. Since that time he has deservedly made huge fortunes in America, where he is as genuinely admired as in England. Irving was honored by his Sovereign, Victoria, in 1895, by being knighted, the first instance of an actor being thus favored. In Feb., 1899, the University of Glasgow conferred the degree of Doctor of Laws upon the eminent actor; Scotland thus followed the lead of England, and Ireland, Sir Henry Irving having already received similar degrees from Cambridge and Dublin Universities. Such a tribute to an actor's talent was unprecedented in the annals of the British stage. Lady Irving lives in retirement, but two sons are achieving social success in the walks of their illustrious sire. The elder, Henry B. (born 1870), who married Dorothea Baird, the original of du Maurier's drawings of Trilby, is an author of scholarly temperament and an actor of increasing power. Laurence (born 1871), is an impulsive, excitable actor, but a dramatist of no mean merit. He was seen in the support of Sir Henry during the last American tour. Sir Henry's second visit to Montreal was 22-23-24 Feb., 1894; his third, week September 16, 1895, when he opened his fifth American tour. Following a production of "Peter the Great" Sir Henry presented Sardou's "Robespierre," which he featured during his last American tour of 1899-1900, and in which he was seen on the opening of a three nights' engagement at the Academy of Music, Montreal beginning 8th March, 1900, with *Shylock* 9th, and in "The Bells" and "Waterloo," 10th. The tour of twenty-nine weeks in this country, which closed May 18, is said to have earned about $200,000 for Sir Henry. Before sailing Sir Henry sent to Col. Baden Powell, the hero of Mafeking, the following cablegram: "*Great Glamis; worthy Cawdor.*" Irving and Terry have visited America six times, their first tour being in the season of 1883-84 and the others in 1884-85, 1887-88, 1893-94, 1895-96 and 1899-1900. Irving has played 22 parts in these tours and Miss Terry has played 16. Irving is admired for the delight and instruction he has rendered with so lavish a hand, and those whose privilege it is to know him love him for his gentle, kindly qualities and unostentatious generosity. When this most conspicuous and talented figure of our stage retires from the mimic scene, let us hope that it will be with a generous fortune. He has crowned the heights which now decline gently into the vale of years, and has all

"That which should accompany old age,
As honor, love, obedience, troops of friends."

THE YEAR OF 1885

ushered in Lotta, 6th January, for three nights, followed by E. F. Thorne in "The Black Flag"; Thos. W. Keene, in Shakespearean repertory, week 19th; Bride and Frear's "Bunch of Keys," week 26th; and, week 2nd February, Marie Prescott, in "The Wages of Sin," made her *stellar debut* here in presenting, also for the first time in Montreal, that very moral and strong play. She was supported by Charles E. Manbury and Charles Overton. Her first appearance here was in support of Salvini, week 17th January, 1881. "The Pavements of Paris" was seen week 23rd February, and during the week 9th March "In the Ranks," headed by E. J. Buckley, held the boards. The Thompson Opera Company was heard in "The Beggar Student," week 17th March; "A Bunch of Keys," week 23rd; Mr. and Mrs. Neil Warner, in "Man and Wife," 10th April; George S. Knight, in "Over the Garden Wall," week 13th April; French Opera Company for five nights from 20th April; E. A. McDowell's Comedy Co., 25th; Jacques Kruger, in "Dreams," week 27th; and Theo, in repertoire, week 4th May. Lawrence Barrett, supported by Louis James and Marie Wainwright, opened 18th May in " Richelieu," following in " Francesca di Rimini," " Julius Cæsar," and "Much Ado About Nothing." This was the tragedian's third and last visit here. Margaret Mather, supported by Milnes Levick, made her first appearance here week 25th May in "Romeo and Juliet," "Leah the Forsaken," "The Honeymoon," "The Hunchback," "The Lady of Lyons," and "Macbeth." Grau's French Opera Company came week 8th June, extending their engagement three weeks, after which the house was closed for the season. Owing to the epidemic of smallpox, which continued during the summer and early fall of 1885, the theatre was not reopened until 30th November, when George S. Knight began a week's engagement in "Over the Garden Wall." Following him came Rose Coghlan, for two weeks from 21st December, in "Our Joan," this being the lady's *stellar debut* here. During her second week she appeared in "Victor Durand" and "Idol of the Hour"

MARIE VICTOR PRESCOTT was one of those women whom nature had gifted for the stage, her figure being graceful and commanding, her features beautiful and capable of a great variety of expression. Her support of Salvini developed her powers which her best friends never dreamed of, and, without being an ideal classical artist, she possessed a fund of passion and emotion which instantly found sympathetic recognition from the most exacting audiences. Miss Prescott was born at Paris, Ky., in 1853 (*nee* Victor), and her *debut* on the stage was made at Cincinnati in 1876, as *Lady Macbeth* to the *Thane* of Frank Roche. Her success was so signal that she was engaged for the rest of the week. After supporting John McCullough and Daniel Bandmann, she went with Salvini, as noted. She was married first to Mr. Perzel, from whom she was divorced in 1891; then married R. D. (Shepard) MacLean, the tragedian, in June, 1892. Miss Prescott died in New York city, 28th August, 1893,

EDWARD J. BUCKLEY died of paralysis 27th December, 1897, at his home in New York city. Born in Australia in 1843, he came when an infant to America, and made his first public appearance in 1864, at Victoria, B.C., as *William*, in an amateur production of "Black-Eyed Susan." His professional *debut* was made soon after as *Etienne* in "Fanchon," with a stock company at Stockton, Cal., Amy Stone being the *star*. He advanced rapidly and soon joined John McCullough's San Francisco Co., as "walking gentleman." In 1869 he was a member of the famous company which opened the California theatre. As a member of the Booth and Barrett Co., and as *Sir Lucius O'Trigger* in Jefferson's production of "The Rivals," he made distinctive hits. His last appearance in New York was with Nat C. Goodwin in the "Gold Mine." His last engagement in Montreal was in support of Maude Banks in "Igomar," at the Academy, week 8th October, 1888.

ROSE COGHLAN, by superior intelligence and power, rose from one of the witches in "Macbeth" to be one of America's most brilliant leading ladies. In such characters as *Lady Teazle* she was unapproachable. Her humor was racy, spontaneous and abundant, her art having been essentially that of the comedienne, as she never appeared to the same advantage in sentimental roles. Miss Coghlan was born in Peterboro, Eng., in 1853, and, like Garrick, Irish and French blood flows in her veins. Her father was a *literateur* and her mother of a devotional turn of mind, wishing that Rose should become a nun; but through the influence of her brother Charles, who had abandoned the bar for the stage, his action confirmed his sister in her choice of a future, and in 1868 she made her *debut* in Greenock, Scotland. In 1871 she came to America, and for some years divided her work between the two countries, supporting several *stars*, including Barry Sullivan. Her best efforts were in the Wallack stock company. She married Clinton Edgerly in 1885, but, after being divorced, married her leading man, John T. Sullivan, with whom she *starred* for several seasons. Of late years they played separately. The exceptionally bright career that opened up to her in the summer of her triumphs has now been shaded by the grey clouds of a chilly autumn. This actress, during the past few years, has had less of good fortune than her talents entitle her to; and I am not alone in my desire to see Miss Coghlan once more as *Lady Gay*, as *Peg Woffington*, as *Stephanie*, as *Zicka* and as *Lady Teazle*. She has adorned our stage with honor in the past, and belongs among the *stars*.

MARGARET MATHER was born Oct. 21, 1859, at Tilbury, Can., but her childhood was spent in Detroit, Mich. She was the daughter of John Finlayson, a mechanic, who, being out of work, set her to selling newspapers when she was ten years. Margaret passed her childhood among squalid surroundings, not in any way tending to divert her attention toward the stage. After she left home, a half-grown girl, she engaged as dish-washer in the Russell House. When about nineteen years of age, under the name of Margaret Bloomer, she entered the profession as a member of a road company. In 1879 she was a member of the George Edgar combination, playing leading roles in Shakespearean repertory. She was next engaged by J. M. Hill, and, after undergoing several months of study, she made her stellar *debut* Aug. 28, 1882, at McVicker's Theatre, Chicago, Ill., as *Juliet*, in "Romeo and Juliet." Public curiosity had been previously aroused in consequence of the many private readings Miss Mather had given before critics and friends in the various cities throughout the United States, and a representative audience witnessed and gave the verdict of success to her *debut*. A tour of the larger cities followed, and in Cincinnati, St. Louis and Boston she shortly became well known. For three years following she travelled on the various circuits West and East. Oct. 13, 1885, her metropolitan *debut* occurred at the Union Square Theatre, as *Juliet*. At that house she remained until Feb. 6, 1886, playing in that interval but three characters—*Juliet*, *Juliana* and *Leah*. The "Romeo and Juliet" run—eighty-four consecutive representations—goes on record as the longest run of that play in this country. She then went on the road again, and continued under Mr. Hill's management until the spring of 1887. On Feb. 15 of that year Miss Mather and Emil Haberkorn were married at Buffalo, N. Y. Mr. Hill was not informed of the marriage until two weeks later, when Mr. Haberkorn told him, and also demanded to see Mr. Hill's account with Miss Mather. Manager Hill denied Mr. Haberkorn's authority to interfere, and litigation followed, which resulted in the court releasing Miss Mather from her contract with Mr. Hill (which had still sometime to run), and she went on a *starring* tour with her husband as manager. This arrangement continued for four years, during which time she made several large productions. On Sept. 16, 1889, she made her first appearance in the title role of "Gretchen" at the new California Theatre, San Francisco, Cal. On December 8, 1890, she produced at the Fifth Avenue Theatre, New York, and for the first time in this country, Wm. Young's English adaptation of Jules Barbier's "Joan of Arc." In 1891 she separated from her husband and became her own manager. On July 2, 1892, she was divorced from Mr. Haberkorn, and on the 26th of the same month she was married to Gustave Pabst, a son of the rich Milwaukee, Wis., brewer of that name. On her marriage to Mr. Pabst, Miss Mather retired from the stage. They did not live happily together, and on one occasion, in October, 1895, she horsewhipped him in a Milwaukee street. Mr. Pabst sued later for a divorce, alleging cruelty, and it was reported that he gave his wife $100,000 not to defend the suit. On Oct 19, 1896, they were divorced, and Miss Mather returned to the stage, her first production being a revival, on a grand scale, of "Cymbeline," at Wallack's, New York. She then went on the road for the remainder of the season. The next season she added "Romeo and Juliet" and other plays to her repertory. Margaret Mather died April 7, 1898, at Charleston, West Virginia. The night before, during the performances of "Cymbeline," she was suddenly prostrated. She was carried off the stage in an unconscious condition, and never regained consciousness. Miss Mather thrice visited Montreal, her second engagement having been week 8th Sept., 1890, in repertoire, supported by Otis Skinner, and her last appearance here was week 24th May, 1897, supported by E. J. Henley, Wm. Courtleigh, Wm. Redmund and Mrs. Thos. Barry, in "Cymbeline," this being the first production of the piece in Montreal. During this engagement, on the evening 27th May, one of the most remarkable pieces of acting was that of Miss Mather's, when, just as she came on the scene and stood before the cave of *Belarius*, a shock of earthquake shook the Academy as though it were a reed. Midst great excitement she, one of the few, kept calm, and ere the gallery had ceased its shouting, she went on with her lines:

"I see a man's life is a tedious one;
I have tir'd myself; and for two nights together
Have made the ground my bed."

It was a great effort, and one which will be long remembered by those who witnessed it.

THE OPENING OF 1886 SEASON

marked the century anniversary of Montreal theatricals. Janish was the attraction, week 4th January, in "Princess Andrea." The Haymarket Theatre Company, of London, headed by Emily Sheridan and Felix Pitt, appeared, week 11th, in

"Dark Days," followed by the first representation here of Gilbert and Sullivan's most popular comic opera, "The Mikado," by John Stetson's Company, week 21st. The Daly's in "Vacation," held the boards week 28th; and Haverly's Minstrels four nights from 4th February. The Cragg Family of acrobats appeared during this engagement. Lizzie May Ulmer, in "Dad's Girl," followed week 8th; John Stetson's "Mikado" returned week 15th; Rosina Vokes, week 22nd; the Madison Square Theatre Company, in "The Rajah," week 1st March; Cornell's Imperial Japanese Troupe, week 8th; and Mme. Judic in repertory of comic operas during week 22nd March. Following Judic came Bartley Campbell's spectacular play, "Clio," week 29th, with 100 people in the company, headed by Mlle. Adele Cornalba and Atkins Lawrence. Joseph Murphy, in "Kerry Gow" and "Shaun Rhue," appeared week 5th April; Lotta, in "Mlle. Nitouche" and "An Old Trick," for four nights from 13th April; Stetson's "Mikado," week 3rd May; Haverly's Minstrels, week 10th; and then Joseph Jefferson made his second appearance in this city, week 17th, in "Rip," "Cricket on the Hearth" and "Lend me Five Shillings." Annie Ward Tiffany and Nelson Wheatcroft, at the head of L. R. Shewell's "Shadows of a Great City," appeared week 24th May. The Fay Templeton Opera Company, minus the *star*, appeared in "The Mikado," week 9th August, when the house closed for a few weeks. The regular opening of the fall season was week 6th September, with Frank Harvey's "Wages of Sin," headed by Chas E. Maubury. Then followed Hanlon's "Fantasma," week 13th; Arthur Rehan's "Nancy & Co.," week 20th; John Templeton's Company in "The Mikado," week 27th, and Rose Coghlan, week 4th October, presenting "School for Scandal," "London Assurance," "As You Like It," "A Scrap of Paper," and "The Lady of Lyons." Miss Coghlan was supported by Frederick De Belleville, A. S. Lipman, Charles Walcot, Verner Clarges, Mrs. Walcot and Maud Peters. George W. Monroe, in "My Aunt Bridget," came week 11th October, followed by Hortense Rhea, week 18th, in "A Dangerous Game," "Pygmalion and Galatea," "Romance of a Poor Young Man" and "The Country Girl." Lilian Olcott, supported by J. H. Gilmour, was seen, week 25th October, in Sardou's "Theodora." Edmund Collier made his *stellar debut* here week 2nd November, opening in John A. Stone's great Indian tragedy, "Metamora," this being its first representation in this city. It was one of Edwin Forrest's greatest successes. The following was the cast: *Lord Fitz Arnold*, Lawrence Hanley ; *Sir Arthur Vaughn*, Henry Hanscombe; *Mordaunt*, Saml. C. Du Bois; *Errington*, Joseph P. Winter ; *Walter*, Wm. Wilson ; *Capt. Church*, Marcus Moriarty; *Wolfe*, Jerome Stansil; *Tramp*, Fred Kent; ; *Officer*, Thos. W. Hudson ; *Oceana*, Henrietta Crossman ; *Metamora*, Edmund Collier ; *Otah*, Wm. Bowers ; *Anahwand*, John Bell ; *Kaneshine*, Sedley Brown ; *Kahmao-kee*, Sara Neville ; *Child*, Little Etta. "Metamora" was repeated 3rd ; "Jack Cade" 4th and 5th ; "Virginius" 6th and 7th ; and " Damon and Pythias," matinee 7th. Genevieve Ward, supported by W. H. Vernon, appeared week 9th November in "The Queen's Favorite," "Nance Oldfield," "His Last Legs" and "Forget-Me-Not." Mrs. Chas. Watson gave a dramatic reading 17th. Louis James and Marie Wainwright began a three nights' engagement 18th November, opening in "Virginius." with the cast as follows : *Virginius*, Louis James; *Appius Claudius*, F. C. Huebner; *Caius Claudius*, John W. Thompson ; *Dentatus*, E. L. Tilton ; *Icilius*, F. C. Mosely ; *Numitorius*, Geo. D. Fawcett ; *Lucius*, Percy Brooke ; *Titus*, Ed. N. Hoyt ; *Marcus*, Chas. D. Mackay; *First Soldier*, F. W. Cline; *Servia*, Kate Meek; *Female Slave*, Aurelia Sarner; *Virginia*, Marie Wainwright. This was the *stellar debut* here of this talented couple. "Hamlet" was produced 19th; "Romeo and Juliet," matinee, 20th ; closing that evening with a double bill, " Shylock " and "Katherine and Petruchio." Charles Erin Verner, in "Shamus O'Brien," was the next attraction week 25th Nov. Joseph Haworth appeared in Montreal for the first time, week 30th November, as a feature in the production of " Hoodman Blind." Sydney Armstrong and Augustus Cook were also in the cast. May Fortescue, a late importation from England, was seen here week of 6th December in " Frou Frou," "Gretchen and Moths." Dion Boucicault and Louise Thornedyke (Mrs. Boucicault) appeared, week 20th December in the former's own play, " The Jilt." This was his last appearance here, dying 18th September, 1890. He first appeared here in 1853. "The Main Line" closed the season's annals, week 27th December, as well as the theatre's detailed record, for what from this date has been subsequent is already familiar to my readers, and space will scarcely permit further mention.

IDA LILIAN OLCOTT, the popular actress, was the daughter of Dr. Cornelius Olcott, a Brooklyn physician. She was born in 1861. She became a prominent amateur actress. In 1882 she played *Juliet* with the Williamsburg Amateur League, and shortly afterward went on the road for a few weeks professionally, making an appearance at the Brooklyn Theatre as *Juliet.* She made preparations in 1887 for an extended tour, which was abandoned on account of her father's illness. In 1884 she *starred* in "Dark Days." The next year she went to Paris and purchased the American rights to "Theodora" from Sardou, in which drama she played with artistic success for two seasons. Litigation with the Franco-American agency caused her to disband her company in Chicago very shortly before her death, which occurred 8th April, 1888, from a cold contracted during a blizzard in New York.

JOHN H. GILMOUR (our Jack) has always been a favorite here, not only for the fact of being a Canadian. but also owing to his histrionic capabilities. He was born at Ottawa, 1st August, 1858. His father took up his residence at Montreal two years later. As a boy Mr. Gilmour developed dramatic tendencies, and made his *debut* under very favorable auspices as *Valentine* in "Twelfth Night." 2nd March, 1877, at the Academy of Music, in company with Adelaide Neilson, Eben Plympton and Neil Warner. In 1880 he joined McDowell's company and went to the West Indies, returning in the spring of 1881, when he joined Wallack's company in the "Veteran")n tour, again appearing here. He next undertook the management of the Ottawa and Quebec theatres. and in 1885 and 1886 was seen at the Lyceum Theatre on Beaver Hall Hill. After a season with Lilian Olcott, he was with Rose Coghlan for a short time, after which he appeared in and created the leading role of "Mr. Barnes of New York" at the Broadway Theatre, New York, subsequently also creating the part of the old *Earl* in "Little Lord Fauntleroy" at the same house. After a few seasons of stock company work, he was this season leading man for Julia Marlowe. Mr. Gilmour is still in his prime, and we look to him for great things in the near future. About 1881 he married Caroline Vinton, and is the happy sire of two boys and a girl. His home is at Larchmont, N. Y., where he finds time during the summer months to enjoy merited recreation in the circle of his family, as well as to profit in the exercise of athletic sports, of which he is very fond.

GEORGE W. MUNROE, first seen here as *Bridget* with George S. Knight in "Over the Garden Wall," is a graduate of the varieties, although his first appearance was in a regular play at Philadelphia, where he was born in 1859. After being with Mr. Knight two seasons, he secured "My Aunt Bridget," and embarked on a joint *starring* tour with John C. Rice, which continued for five years.

JOSEPH HAWORTH.

They separated, Munroe appearing for two seasons in a sequel. called "Aunt Bridget's Baby." For three seasons he toured in "A Happy Little Home."

NELSON WHEATCROFT, one of the cleverest exponents of the modern stage villains, was born in London, 15th February, 1852. He first appeared as an actor in 1873 at Swansea, in South Wales. Later he went to Sadler's Wells Theatre, London, where he supported Miss Bateman in "Leah," "Mary Warner," and also in some Shakespearean revivals. After joining the New York Lyceum theatre company, he made a notable success as *Martin Culver* in "The Wife," and also as *Dick Van Buren* in "The Charity Ball." He later became leading man of Charles Frohman's new Empire Theatre Company. His last engagement was at the Knickerbocker Theatre, New York, as *D'Aubenas*, in Sardou's short-lived play, "Spiritism," staged a few days prior to his death, which occurred rather suddenly 3rd March, 1897, from pneumonia. His wife, Adelaide Stanhope, is conducting a school of dramatic instruction in New York.

ANNIE WARD TIFFANY has played all lines from *Topsy* to *Lady Macbeth*. Of late she has been identified with Irish character parts. Miss Tiffany was born in Limerick, Ireland. When a child she was brought to Syracuse, N. Y., where she made an early appearance on the stage. Soubrette work followed in Philadelphia under Mrs. Drew, and in 1867 she became enrolled at Wallack's, remaining two years. The season of 1884-85 she engaged for the part of *Biddy Nolan* in "Shadows of a Great City," and played it for eight consecutive seasons. The season of 1892-93 she produced Alfred Kennedy's play, "Lady Blarney," then went *starring* in "Lady Blarney" and "The Step-Daughter." In private life she is Mrs. Charles H. Greene.

MME. JUDIC, the once famous artist, made her *debut* at Wallack's Theatre, New York, September, 1885, in "Mlle. Nitouche." She used her voice, both in singing and talking, very skillfully. but her tour could scarcely be called successful. On her return to France she found that her popularity had waned.

JOSEPH S. HAWORTH was born at Providence, R. I.; April 7, 1858, and made his *debut* with his tutor, Charlotte Crampton, in May, 1873, as the *Duke of Birmingham* in "Richard III." at the Academy of Music, Cleveland, O., Miss Crampton playing *Richard*. The following season he joined John Ellsler's stock company at Cleveland, playing his first part as a member of a stock company in "Aladdin," upon the same stage where a year previous he had made his *debut*. Three years later he took his farewell of Cleveland in the character of *Hamlet*. Mr. Haworth then joined the Boston Museum company, where he remained four seasons, playing a round of leading parts in comedy, tragedy, drama and comic opera. Incidentally he played *Romeo* to Mary Anderson's *Juliet*, at the Boston Theatre, with success. He was offered, but declined, the position of leading man at the Boston Museum, having arranged to join the late John McCullough's company, in which he played *Iago, Julius Cassius, Ingomar*, etc., Since that time he has played in "Demise," with Clara Morris; in J. M. Hill's "Moral Crime" company, and later in French & Sanger's "Hoodman Blind" Company, appearing here as noted. He has since been a frequent visitor here, having been seen in "Paul Kauvar," "Rosedale," "Aunt Jack," and during his last *starring* engagement here, in the spring of 1895, was seen in the classical roles of tragedy. He was, in 1896-97, a feature in Bret Harte's play of "Sue." A *co-starring* tour with Modjeska (1898) was followed by his metropolitan engagement to play *John Storm* in support of Viola Allen in "The Christian." This season he was the *Vicinius* in the Whitney production of "Quo Vadis." In the roles of *Storm* and *Vicinius* Mr. Haworth was profoundly true and beautifully sympathetic, embracing into these interpretations the marked reverence which renders his *Hamlet* so exquisitely filial and ideal. Mr. Haworth lacks few of the essential qualities to place him as the representative American actor of to-day. He has not the full intellectual influence of Edwin Booth, nor can he make the icy scholarly appeal which marked the acting of Lawrence Barrett. He is not fiercely robust like John McCullough, nor romantically beautiful like H. J. Montague, but he has some quality of all these men, and adds to that a voice of sonorous eloquence and solemn music, with a native grace of action that must have been the inheritance of Edwin Adams.

SYDNEY ARMSTRONG has had a theatrical career dating since 1884. She was born in Memphis, Tenn., and in 1884 made her *debut* among amateurs. Being successful, the young lady was advised to go East, and try her fortunes, and eventually became a member of a touring company. While playing in "Forgiven," at McVicker's, Chicago, she was noticed and engaged by F. W. Sanger to create the leading role in "Harbor Lights." She was afterwards with "Hoodman Blind," "The Burglar," and then engaged by C. Frohman. Her's has been a notable instance of success won on artistic merit, without recourse to the aid of notoriety. She is now Mrs. W. H. Smyth.

MAY FORTESCUE had large audiences. The majority were attracted out of the celebrated Garmoyle breach of promise suit. They found a girl, pretty, it is true, but not strikingly so ; slight of figure, and of medium height, with nut brown hair, and large expressive eyes. The face bore a rather sad expression, and the voice was full and musical. As an actress Miss Fortescue cannot be judged by comparisons with any one. She confined her talents—and she had considerable—to such roles as were not too heavy for her to grapple with, and by so doing shielded herself from harsh criticism. Miss Fortescue's surname is Finney, and her father is a coal merchant in England.

FREDERICK DE BELLEVILLE is a native of Belgium, and was born in 1853. He served in the army before he became an actor. His stage *debut* was made in England, and, after playing in farce, tragedy, melodrama, pantomime, comedy and extravaganza for several years, he came to America via Australia, and soon reached New York city, where he joined the Palmer forces at the Union Square. He was leading man for Clara Morris during a series of important matinees, and then took to starring, appearing in "The Corsican Brothers," "Monte Cristo," "The Silver King," and "Paquita," the latter one of Bartley Campbell's plays, and the failure of which is alleged to have caused a disappointment so acute as to be responsible for the mental derangement that overtook the playwright shortly before his demise. He was leading man for Rose Coghlan for a season, was identified with the premier of Steele Mackaye's "Paul Kauvar," with Viola Allen in "Hoodman Blind," supported Clara Morris for a couple of seasons, appeared in "Men and Women," "Diplomacy," and "Thermilor," under Charles Frohman, joined Rose and Charles Coghlan for their big revival of "Diplomacy," and assisted W. H. Crane in a reproduction of "The Senator." This is but a slight *resume* of the productions in which De Belleville has appeared ; and he frequently has been called upon to create in special productions. Later he appeared in support of Mrs. Fiske in "Tess of the d'Ubervilles."

EMMA (LAJEUNESSE) ALBANI-GYE. The annals of the Academy cannot be passed over without a special mention of our own Albani, who appeared on its boards from time to time, her last appearance in regular opera having been week of 25th January, 1902. Madame Albani is the eldest of three children of Joseph de St. Louis *dit* Lajeunesse, and was born at Chambly in 1850. She received her early education at the Sacred Heart Convent, at Montreal, and, under the management of her father, first appeared at a concert in her eighth year at Mechanics' Hall. When the father decided that she should receive all the advantages of a musical education, the religious bodies did their utmost to dissuade him, but without avail. In 1864 the family settled at Albany, N. Y., and it was from this city that she chose her stage name. It was also here that she attracted the attention of Brignoli, whose influence brought her before responsible authorities. She subsequently realized $1,800 from a benefit concert, which, together with her savings, enabled her to visit Paris, then to Milan, where she soon developed those exquisite and wonderful talents which have since edified the musical world. Her operatic *debut* was as *Amina* in "La Somnambula," at Messina, in 1871, appearing in the same role at Covent Garden Theatre, London, 2nd April, 1872, and a year later in New York. Her first regular appearance in Montreal was during Carnival week, 1883, and her last appearance was in concert features at the Windsor Hall, 7th December, 1895. During 1897-98 she was heard in Australia. Albani became Mrs. Ernest Gye in 1878, having married the son of her first London manager. She has a son who has also developed considerable musical talent as an instrumentalist. Her father is still living at Chambly, and a brother, Adelard, is *cure* of St Calixte.

CRYSTAL PALACE OPERA HOUSE.

When those superstitiously inclined will note that this was Montreal's thirteenth play-house, not taking into consideration the Mechanics' and Nordheimer's Halls (which were only intended for concert purposes and magical entertainments), they will at once attribute its ill-luck to that fact. This house of amusement occupied the present site of the new Young Men's Christian Association, on Dominion Square, and was originally a skating-rink. It was a large wooden structure with an arched roof. In 1884 it was neatly fitted up for theatrical representations, with a seating capacity of from 1,200 to 1,500. It was opened up by Manager Roland Gideon Israel Barnett, 24th May, 1884, with a company of comic opera artists in "Iolanthe." The company included Janet Edmonson, Fanny Wentworth, Perle Dudley, Lillian Greer, Signor Brocolini (*nee* John Clark), W. H. Seymour, Henry Molton, Frank Barnes, James H. Finn and Frank Moulten. Prices of admission were: boxes, $5; reserved seats, 75c; 50c and 25c. General admission, 15c. A number of standard comic operas were well staged, and during the season W. T. Carleton, the talented baritone, was specially engaged, appearing frequently, but the season was unprofitable. Louis McGowan became lessee at the end of the opera season, opening, 1st October, with Haworth's Comedy Co., for one week, but the effort was not remunerative. The second and last season opened, 25th May, 1885, with "The Merry War." J. H. Gilmour produced Tillotson's drama, "Lynwood," week of 29th June, followed by the Standish Grand English Opera Company, 6th July, in "Martha"; extending the engagement until the production of "Ixion," which was advertised as the initial feature of the "grand reopening" under the Barnett management. The season was short and again unprofitable, the doors of the theatre closing, to reopen no more. Barnett left some creditors behind, as well as the regrets of our music loving population. Probably few men have had an experience so varied as that of Barnett. During his life he has been a theatrical manager, a diamond broker, a stock broker and money-lender, a millionaire, and, at present, a convict.

No other Montreal theatre has had such varied annals as

THE LYCEUM THEATRE.

Situated on the northwest corner of Beaver Hall Hill and Latour Street, on the site of A. E. Small & Co.'s new warehouse, the building was erected by the Congregationalists in 1845, and called Zion church, Dr. Wilkes and Rev. Mr. Bray being prominent in its pulpit. In 1880 the property was sold to a syndicate for $20,600. Stores were added to its front and the hall turned into theatrical uses. John Stephen, editor of *Canada First*, was the first manager. It was then known as Albert Hall, and was the scene of variety performances as an advertising medium for the paper. It was then rented for synagogue purposes until the 28th April, 1884, when it became known as the Victoria Theatre, opening a short season of variety performances under the management of Beaucleigh & Co. On 12th May the San Francisco Minstrels opened a week's engagement. The principals were Weston, Bryant, Hanson, Saville, Petrie, Fish and Laird. The house was then closed until 10th November, when it changed its name to the Montreal Theatre Museum, with Coleman & Mooney as lessees and managers. Bennett Matlack, in "A Celebrated Case," was the opening bill. "The Danites" was produced week 17th, after which a series of vaudeville performances followed. Ed. Chrissie, in "Detected," for a week from December 29th, was followed by the St. Quinten Opera Company, week 12th January, 1885; then Foreman & Meredith's Combination Troupe, week 19th; the Bijou Minstrels, week 26th; Fanny Herring, in "Little Buck Shot," and Louise Hoyt, in "Sold"; week 9th February closed the Coleman & Mooney lesseeship, their successor being Wm. H. Lytell, who opened his season, 16th February, with "Youth." He surrounded himself with a very fair stock company and produced a number of standard plays. The company included Wm. Morris, O. B. Collins, Walter Walker, J. H. Gilmour, J. Bunney, H. C. Hartsell, Blanche Mortimer (Mrs. Lytell), Floride

Abell, Mrs. Savage, Helen Parr, Frederick Vroom, Horace Dawson and others.

WILLIAM MORRIS is a native of Boston, entering the dramatic profession at the age of fourteen. Mr. Morris has risen in the profession, having been in such companies as Daly's, Modjeska and the Frohmans. In October, 1891, he married Esta Hawkins, of Aurora, Ills. None of Mr. Frohman's company of excellent actors is more popular than he.

Following "Youth" was produced at this house successively: "The Shaughrahn," week 23rd February; "The Galley Slave," week 2nd March ; " The World," week 9th ; " Monte Cristo," week 16th; "Lights o' London," week 23rd; and, for the first time in Montreal, Bartley Campbell's "Separation," week 30th, with the following cast: *Brenton Blair*, J. H. Gilmour; *Felix*, J. Bunny; *Abner Day*, O. B. Collins; *Major Maxwell*, Harry Parker; *Duke Warren*, Ralph Bell; *Mais*, Walter Walker; *Meldrum*, Newton Dana; *Dora Blair*, Blanche Mortimer; *Mlle. Florinne*, Flori Abel; *Mabel Blair*, Susie Howard; *Fanny Maxwell*, Jenny Savage; *Abagail Day*, Nellie Sandford; *Mamie Maxwell*, Miss Richardson; *Milly*, Carrie Webster; *Mr. Swift*, Harry Hartwell ; *Lucy*, Laura Simon. The name of the theatre had been changed a short time previously to Lytell's Opera House. "The White Slave" was produced week of 6th April ; and, on 13th, the Dora Wiley Opera Co., including Richard Golden, opened a two weeks' engagement, followed by "Fairfax," week 27th; "Michael Strogoff," for two weeks from 4th May; "Romany Rye," week 18th; "Hazel Kirke," week 25th; "Banker's Daughter," week 1st June; and "Silver King," week 8th, which closed the Lytell season. On 20th June "L'Habitant" was produced, with Cyril Searle at the head of a company. This was the work of a Canadian, but failed to draw. John H. Gilmour opened the theatre, 6th July, as the Montreal Theatre, with "The Gov'nor" and "Esmeralda" during the first week; "pin_k Dominoes" was presented week 13th. W. H. Lytell resumed the lease, 12th October, opening with "The Galley Slave," and restoring the name of the house to Lytell's Opera House. Again followed "The Lights o' London," week 19th; "The Colleen Bawn," week 26th; "Streets of New York" and "Jessie Brown," week 2nd November; "The Corsican Brothers," week 9th; "Sea of Ice," week 16th; " The World," week 23rd; and " After the Ball" and "The Coming Member" (double bill) during the last week of the season, closing 5th December, 1885.

The house was opened week of 1st February, 1896, as the Lyceum Theatre, with " Youth," " A Box of Cash," with Edith Sinclair, week 8th ; " Lynwood," week 15th ; and " A Barber's Scrape," with Richard Golden, week 12th. This piece was written by a Canadian, and was backed by Erastus Wiman. The theatre remained closed until 21st March, when Lester and Allen's Minstrels, including the pugilist, John L. Sullivan, appeared for three nights. About this time was produced Clay M. Green's drama, "Louis Riel," the author appearing in the cast, which also included Arthur H. Forest, who assumed the title role, and Archie Boyd, who was subsequently seen here as *Joshua* in "The Old Homestead," in 1890. From this time the career of the house closed as a theatre. The premises were subsequently occupied by the "Montreal Herald" for a few years, but were badly gutted by fire, 27th March, 1893, torn down in 1896, and rebuilt for office and warehouse purposes.

BLANCHE MORTIMER-LYTELL, frequently seen here as leading lady, was a great favorite and a clever actress. She was the wife of William H. Lytell, comedian and stage manager. She died of consumption at Gilboa, N. Y., 30th January, 1897. Her husband and two sons survive her. Mrs. Lytell was of a cheerful and sprightly disposition, loving the flowers and sunshine of nature, and, grievous as her long malady had been, the little lady had ever confidence of ultimate recovery. In a letter to the writer some two weeks preceding her death, she expressed expectations of regaining strength in time to write a few recollections for this record, but in a few days she passed calmly into the dreamless sleep of the dead, and the story of her life will be told instead in loving tenderness by the immense circle of her personal friends.

THE QUEEN'S THEATRE

was situated on the north side of St. Catherine street in the Queen's Block, between University and Victoria streets, and is the property of the Ogilvy estate. It was situated on the second story, and was originally a concert hall known as the Queen's Hall. On 22nd June, 1891, an Opera Company, under the management of Messrs. Roth & Slocum, began an extended engagement in "The Mikado." The principals were Lily Post, N. S. Burnham, George Lyding and J. W. Herbert. The house was then known as the Queen's Opera House. In August of the same year Messrs. Sparrow & Jacobs became lessees and managers of the house, when it also assumed the name of Queen's Theatre. The interior was completely re-modelled, and was one of the prettiest in the country. The house opened 21st September, with R. E. Graham in "The Little Tycoon." A number of leading attractions were booked, including James O'Neill, who appeared here for the first time as a *star* in "Monte Cristo," week 5th October, 1891; first appearance in Montreal of Clara Morris, week 11th January, 1892, in "Odette"; and first appearance in Montreal of Wilson Barrett, week 2nd January, 1893, in "Pharaoh," "Silver King," "Claudian" and "Hamlet." Chief in his support were the late Franklin McLeay and Maud Jeffries. Robert Mantell was seen in repertoire, week 9th Jan., 1893. During July a stock company, including Tyrone Power and Edith Crane, presented several dramas. Lawrence Hanley came week 4th Sept., in "The Player," and the clever young tragedian, Walker Whiteside, made his first bow to Montrealers, week 2nd Oct., appearing in "Hamlet," "Richelieu," "Othello" and "Richard III."; Wilson Barrett reappeared, week 1st January, 1894, in "Virginius," "Othello," "Hamlet," and other plays. Harry Kellar, the wizard, first appeared in Montreal, week 8th January, 1894. In the early spring of 1894, the Geo. A. Baker Opera Co. played a long engagement. The foregoing were the leading attractions of many that appeared, space not permitting individual mention. At the opening of the autumn season of 1896, the prices of admission were made to suit popular tastes. Admission was further reduced, week of 7th December, to 10, 20 and 30 cents. A stock company was engaged, opening on that date in "The Two Orphans." The following were in the company : Nestor Lennon, Chas. R. Crolins, Basil West, Chas. E. Fisher, Clayton W. Legge, Grace Sherwood, Helen Robertson, Marion Clifton, Annie Mortland. A new feature was also inaugurated, of introducing vaudeville turns between the acts. Several dramas were produced, after which the plan of booking regular dramatic and operatic combinations at cheap rates was resorted to with but a qualified degree of success. About this time Mr. J. B. Sparrow became sole lessee of this theatre. A new stock company, under the direction of W. H. Wright, was organized, and opened its season, 21st February, 1898, with the drama "In Spite of All." A repertoire of standard plays was presented, including "The Amazons," "The Banker's Daughter," Lord Chumley,"

"Sweet Lavender" and "The Fatal Card." The company's roster was as follows : W. H. Wright, manager ; Sedley Brown, stage manager ; William Harkins, Harold Hartsell, A. C. Deltwyn, Stephen Wright, John C. Ince, Thomas Ince, Berryl Hope, Una Abell, Dickie Delaro and Clara Knott. Mr. and Mrs. W. H. Wright (Berryl Hope) were prominently connected with the Francais stock company the previous year and made many friends. The venture was not sufficiently profitable to warrant its continuance beyond 30th April. Combination companies filled irregular dates, comic opera being a feature. With this paragraph the annals of this theatre in all probability close, for on Sunday evening, 16th September, 1899, the University Street portion of the building suddenly collapsed, fortunately at an hour when there were few passers by, and no person was injured. The property was considerably wrecked and the theatre rendered untenable. The announcement of the death of the young Canadian actor, Franklyn McLeay, in London, Eng., was received with such genuine sorrow by his friends here, that an outline of his career may be deemed within the province of this book.

FRANKLIN McLEAY was a young Canadian, who a few years ago was playing minor roles in Wilson Barrett's company. His genius, however, was of that order which would not be kept down, and he soon rose to the position of leading man of the organization. His work as *Nero* in "The Sign of the Cross" and as the *Bat* in "Pharaoh" stamped him as an actor of remarkable power and versatility. His later triumphs as *Jediah* in "Daughters of Babylon," and as *Iago* in "Othello" attracted the attention of Beerbohm Tree, who promptly engaged him to play *Cassius* in "Julius Ceasar." McLeay fairly shared the honors with Mr. Tree in that production, as he afterward did in "Ragged Robin," with which the distinguished English actor entertained his patrons at Her Majesty's theatre, London, in 1898. Mr. Beerbohm Tree took such a fancy to McLeay that he made him the leading man of his company, and he began a notable career that has now been cut short at a time when he was in the way of winning great fame as a historian. McLeay was born at Watford, Ont. A brilliant university career was achieved in Toronto, and his dramatic training was under the guidance of the late James E. Murdoch, until he joined the forces of Wilson Barrett. The special trait of Mr. McLeay was his ambition. He took life with deep seriousness, and never ceased to analyze his work, his life, his opportunities and his possibilities. At the same time he was not egotistical. It was all pure ambition. While he was proud of his athletic record and accustomed to bicycle a great deal, he looked a very frail man and never had a good color, but his

face was so kind, and his manners so sweet, it was always a pleasure to see him. McLeay married Grace, daughter of Charles
Warner, 18th Dec., 1898. During June, 1900, he organized a benefit
performance at Drury Lane theatre in aid of the Ottawa fire sufferers, which netted $15,000. It is believed that overwork from this
great effort brought about the brain fever of which he died, 6th
July, 1900. Among those that took part were Sir Henry Irving
and his company, Beerbohm Tree and his company, George Alexander and his company, the American beauty company, and, in
fact, almost every actor, actress and singer of prominence in London. was there to help swell the splendidly planned charity. Queen
Victoria was the principal patron, and among the other patrons
were nearly all England's dukes and earls and lesser titled persons.
For this occasion Mr. Clement Scott wrote a special patriotic
poem, which I here append. It is called "Sister Canada," and was
written for Mrs. Leslie Carter, to recite at Mr. McLeay's monster
benefit.

Sister Canada! Safe at home
  We are no strangers ! Listen to me!
Often across Niagara's foam
  Kisses, America, blows to thee!
Take them again from these lips of mine,
  Here in old England, friend and guest!
Drink from a love cup! Toast, divine!
  England! America! Canada blest.
    Sister! lovely in snow or sun.
    This is the union—three in one !

Ottawa sister! tears were shed,
  Tears of sympathy rose and fell,
Pity from all, as you mourned your dead;
  Horror at clang of your tocsin bell !
Desolate Ottawa! Leagues away
  You have our sympathy, staunch and true.
Sisters in England kneel and pray,
  God in mercy will comfort you.
    Ottawa dream in your hearts and homes,
    After bitterness sunshine comes.

Loyalist Canada, let me twine
  Joyful laurel with mournful yew ;
Did you not head the colonial line ?
  Fight for the Queen and the Empire too?
Bravo, Canada ! loved at home,
  England's proud of your bone and back ;
Wherever we march in the days to come
  Canada carries the Union Jack!
    England, America, Canada free!
    We are the union—one in three !

THEATRE FRANCAIS.

THE THEATRE FRANCAIS,

the sixteenth to be chronicled, in only the second to have suffered destruction by fire, excluding the Nordheimer's Hall. The building was merely a whaleback shell erected in 1884 by W. W. Moore as a skating rink, on leased ground originally belonging to Peter Cavello. It was first opened 16th June, 1884, as the Grand Central Dime Museum, with the Harts, Al. Fostelle and Professor John Wingfield as the principals in a vaudeville entertainment. Coleman & Co. were its lessees. It was afterwards known as the Dominion Palace Opera House. In 1888 Mr. Moore strengthened the building considerably, and also lengthened it nearly thirty feet. In 1890 he altered it into a summer theatre. During the first summer, however, he made up his mind to continue both in summer and winter. The entrance was originally on St. Dominique street, near St. Catherine street. During the fall of 1890, a Wild West Show, headed by Rio Grande Bill and Col. Harry T. Murtha, began a short and unprofitable season. In 1891 the entrance was changed by tearing down the frontage of some store property on St. Catherine street. In the early summer of that year, W. W. Moore opened a season of comic opera, 1st June, with "Erminie." The principals were, the late Myra Morella, Mamie Taylor and Edgar Martin. The place was then called the Lyceum Opera House. The season was suddenly closed at the end of the same month. From this time on to 1893 the house was known as the Empire Theatre, and the class of attractions presented were third-rate variety shows. During the summer of 1893 a number of prominent French citizens formed a joint stock company, of which J. M. Fortier was the president. The interior of the house was entirely renovated, and a company of operatic artists were imported from France. The opening was on 2nd October, with "La Grande Duchesse," the principals being Madame de Goyon as *Stella*; Mad. Loys as *Claudine*; and Mr. Girard as *Monthabor*. For three seasons of grand as well as comic opera the Theatre d'Opera Francais was patronized by the *elite* of Montreal's French citizens. The power which the church influenced against the performances, however, had not a little to do with the unprofitable results of the venture, the directorate dissolving in the early part of 1896, with the final disbandment of the artists. The principals that time were: Adrien Barbe, Armand Mary, Mme. Bossy-Conti and Bennati. William E. Phillips

was the next lessee, opening the house as the Theatre Francais, 2nd March, 1896, with "The Black Flag," inaugurating a
series of standard dramatic and vaudeville representations in
continuous performances at popular prices.   The original
stock company included John B. Knight, Wm. Stuart, Richard
Baker, Hawley Francks, George Rose, Louise Arnott, Berryl
Hope (Mrs. W. H. Wright), Camille D'Elmar and Virginia
Ayer. Wm. S. Hartford, a capable young English actor,
previously seen here at the head of Sparrow's "Jack Harkaway" Company, was engaged as leading man for the opening
of the second week in "The Ticket-of-Leave Man." : From
season to season the attractions presented at this house were
duly appreciated by Mr. Phillips' patrons, who recognized
and rewarded his up-to-date efforts by filling the auditorium
to full capacity.   A long series of choice dramas were produced and interpreted by a generally capable company.   In
the mid-season of their activity the total destruction of the
building by fire on the morning of 26th February, 1900, most
rudely arrested their laudable efforts.   The company played
the same night at the Monument Nationale, but closed 28th
February.   Daniel Ford, owner of the property, and W. E.
Phillips, sustained considerable personal loss.   Coincident-
ally, the greater Theatre Francais, the dramatic monument
of France, was similarly destroyed within two weeks.

LE MONUMENT NATIONALE,

situated on St. Lawrence street, opposite to the old market
house, is the name of a building erected by the French Canadian National Society, known as L'Association de St. Jean
Baptiste, in 1890-91.   Judge Loranger, F. L. Beique, Hon.
Senator A. A. Thibaudeau and J. C. Beauchamp are members
of the finance committee directing its affairs.   The building,
which is extensive and substantially constructed, contains a
second floor theatre of large capacity, while the ground floor
consists of several stores.   Experts value the property at
$300,000.   During 1895-96 the Grand Opera Company from
the Theatre Francais rendered several operas as well as concerts. Mr. and Mrs. Frank Murphy, after retiring from the
management of the Academy of Music, leased the hall and
opened a short season, 16th March, 1896, with Palmer Cox's
"Brownies," for one week.   Of the several attractions which
followed, that of "Rob Roy" was the most successful.   A season of grand opera by a French Company, under other man-

agement, was inaugurated 6th October, 1899, the opening being in "La Juive." The artists included Mlles. Talexis and Badilia, Mmes. Laffon and Bergs, Messrs. Anseldi, Grommen, Javia, Defly and Salvator.

A number of amusement resorts have not been fully noted in these pages, from the days of GUILBAULT'S GARDENS to those of SOHMER PARK. The latter resort, established in 1889 at Panet and Notre Dame streets, has been closely identified with band concerts, vaudeville turns and some pretence at comic opera. The BONAVENTURE HALL flourished for a very short period twenty-five years ago under Mr. Vilbon's direction, and during the '70's and '80's the MECHANICS' and NORDHEIMER HALLS occasionally catered to the public in minstrel and vaudeville performances. The principal minstrel features of the country appeared during that period at the Mechanics' Hall, Christy's and Cool Burgess's being very popular. There is also a record of the appearance of the famous but erratic tragic genius, Fechter, at this house in 1875, while George Vandenhoff rendered frequent readings. Neither can we give more than passing notice to the BIJOU at Chaboillez square and St. Maurice streets, opened 27th February, 1899, with "The Parisian Belles," followed by other belles, for a season terminating the same spring. This house was under the management of Charles H. Laberge and Frederick Thomas, and was situated in the old St. Maurice Skating Rink. The GRAND CENTRAL THEATRE and MUSEE, corner St. Gabriel and Commissioners streets, has flourished since March, 1899, in a similarly modest manner, giving two variety performances daily. Thomas Burdette, proprietor; Louis Payette, manager. At the ARENA SUMMER GARDEN (on the site of the old Shamrock Grounds), a season of comic opera was begun 24th July, 1899, in "Said Pasha," by the Robinson Opera Company, the principals being Lizzie Gonzalez, Ethel Vincent, Clayton Ferguson and Ben Lodge. A second season of opera was inaugurated 18th June, 1900, Frank V. French being manager and lessee.

HER MAJESTY'S THEATRE.

This beautiful temple of Thespis takes rank with the finest in America. It was built in 1898 by a chartered company, which included among others : Senator A. A. Thibaudeau, Mayor Prefontaine, K.C., M.P.; Mr. William Mann, the contractor; Messrs. William Barclay Stephens, William Strachan,

Beaumont Shepherd and David Russell, all of Montreal. The capital stock of the company is $100,000, divided into one thousand shares at a par value of one hundred dollars. The corporate style of the Company is, "The West End Theatre Co" (Limited). It is situated on Guy street, east side, above St. Catherine street. The ground dimensions of the building are 171 feet in depth by 170 in width. There is an 18-ft. lane on the south and a 10-ft. alley on the north. Both are paved in asphalt. There are in all twenty-one exits, and the house can be completely emptied in three minutes. The building is constructed in the style of architecture known as the Italian Renaissance, with a mixture of Rococo. The front is of pressed brick, relieved with Ohio buff, the walls possessing a solid limestone foundation. The main lobby is eighteen feet wide and thirty feet deep. Surrounding it are the manager's office, the box office, an apartment for advance agents, the ladies' toilet room and a smoking parlor for gentlemen. The lobby itself is floored in Mosaic tiling of very chaste design. On the second floor is located the café, which is accessible from all parts of the house. There are two galleries, the upper one of which is divided, and contains the family circle and the "gods." There are ten boxes on each side of the stage, six of which are a part of the procenium arch. Precautions have been taken against fire. A solid fire-wall of brick, three feet thick, separates the stage from the auditorium; another of equal strength separates the auditorium from the lobby. The division walls between the lobbies in the front of the building and the dressing-rooms at the side of the stage are also of brick. The doors leading from the stage to the auditorium are of iron, and can be automically closed in half a minute. There is also an asbestos drop curtain, which would confine a fire, if such occurred, exclusively to the stage. The walls and ceilings of the auditorium, lobbies and toilet rooms, are finished in asbestic plastering. Messrs. McElpatrick, the architects of Her Majesty's, have built upwards of 200 theatres, and in their large experience not an accident of any kind has happened in one of their buildings. The decorations are beautiful and in excellent taste. The lobby, with its warm tints of maroon and richly frescoed ceiling, prepares one for the brilliant scenic display within the auditorium. Mr. Toomey was the scenic artist. Mr. and Mrs. Frank Murphy secured the lease of the theatre, which opened Monday, 7th November, 1898, with E. E. Rice's " The Ballet Girl : a pro-

PROCTOR'S THEATRE.

duction of scenic splendour, introducing sixty artists, the principals being Gus Bruno, David Lythgoe, Edgar Halstead, James Lindsay, Jacques Kruger, Solomon Violette, Violet Deane and Christine Anderson. The performance was preceded by a short address by Mayor Prefontaine. "We are proud of the theatre," said His Worship, "and we are proud of the name, for nowhere in those broad dominions, over which the sun never sets, is there a community more devoted to the person and the pure and noble throne of Queen Victoria than our good population of Her Majesty's devotedly loyal city of Montreal. I have great pleasure, therefore, to dedicate this theatre to the art which ' ———*holds, as 'twere, the mirror up to nature,*' that answers and educates, and that makes a really useful and valuable contribution to the material progress of the world by affording the relaxation that worn-out humanity justly requires." As His Worship finished reading, the audience applauded tumultuously, and, a minute or two later, Mr. Murphy again appeared before the curtain, this time introducing Miss May Reynolds, who recited a prologue, which had been prepared for the occasion by Dr. George Murray. This was as follows :

> Ladies and Gentlemen, we hail to-night
> Your friendly presence with unfeigned delight,
> And let me say it as I have the floor,
> Your future patronage will charm us more.
> Lend me your ear three minutes for some verse ;
> It might be better, and it might be worse!
>
> Here, months ago, a weed-encumbered spot
> Shrank from publicity—a vacant lot—
> Now, gaze around ; survey in every part
> This stately temple of dramatic art,
> Stage, drop-scene, orchestra, box, stall, parterre."
> And the twin galleries that bridge the air.
> No cheap gilt gingerbread offends the eye,
> No tawdry tinsel makes us almost cry ;
> Good taste, throughout, the victory has won,
> And all that money can do has been done.
> Are you content ? If so, the fact confess,
> And answer with a sympathetic "Yes."
> Thanks ! and as crowds of bright-eyed French I see,
> "Je vous remercie bien, mes cheres amis !"
>
> You wish no doubt, to hear the bill of fare
> That for the public palate we prepare ;
> Well, since variety's the spice of life,
> We'll furnish that, for man and maid and wife.

You shall have dramas fit for youth or age,
Played by the best performers on the stage,
Plays of all kinds—farce, opera, burlesque,
Plays, grave and gay, romantic and grotesque—
And we are mindful that at Christmas time
Those darling children cry for pantomime.
One thing remember, you may rest secure
That all we offer shall be clean and pure ;
"Immodest scenes admit of no defence,
For want of decency is want of sense.".

Watch our career ; some venial faults forgive,
And aid the "Servants of the Queen" to live.

My time is up. So once again I say,
Watch us impartially from day to day,
If we play fairly, we bespeak fair play.

All that we promise we will perform,
And strive to take Society by storm !

A few last words. Attention ! One and all !
And bless the name selected for our hall ;
It is the noblest that on earth is known;
It is "Her Majesty's," we proudly own.

Yes! There is one whose venerated name
We dare to borrow, and we dread to shame,
Who needs no Crown—no Sceptre in her hand—
The world's spontaneous homage to command,
Who, from sheer goodness plays a gracious part,
And when she speaks is prompted by her heart;
Long may she linger, loved upon the scene,
Long may we listen to "God Save the Queen !"

Then the audience arose, and the orchestra, under Professor
Zimmerman, rendered "God Save the Queen."

It may be interesting to future generations to note a few
of those in attendance :

In Box A were Mr. and Mrs. Hector Mackenzie, Mr. and
Miss Mackenzie.

In Box B—Mayor Prefontaine and Mrs. Prefontaine, Dr.
and Mrs. Foucher and Mr. P. D. Roland.

In Box C—Mr. and Mrs. H. Vincent Meredith, Mr. and
Mrs. Wanklyn, Mr. Justice Hall and Mr. H. Allan.

In Box D—Mr. and Mrs. E. S. Clouston, Mr. and Mrs.
Charles Meredith and Miss Margaret Angus.

In Box E—Comtesse des Étange, Miss Thibaudeau and
Miss Rodier.

In Box F—Mr. and Mrs. Vere Goold, Miss Skinner, Mr.
Douglass Plye and Miss Gendron.

In Box G—Mr. and Mrs. William Mann, Mr. and Mrs. J. A. Mann, Miss McLean and Mr. S. McLean.

In Box H—Mrs. Donald Macmaster, Mrs. Peterson, Miss Roddick and Miss Redpath.

In Box I—Mr. and Mrs. John Russell, jun., Miss Russell, Mr. David Russell, of St. John, N.B.; Dr. and Mrs. Allison, New York ; Mr. D. Pottinger and Mr. T. B. Blair.

It was a representative audience of Montreal's best society, and, although a more appropriate choice in the class of attraction should have been made, there was not standing room left for late comers. The view from the galleries was picturesque in the extreme. Nearly all the ladies wore evening dresses of exquisite design and shade, contrasting vividly with the prescribed black and white of the men, who, in their turn, did what was possible to add to the poetry of colour—if it may be permissible to ascribe poetry to colour as well as to motion.

How different the scene ninety-four years before ! when, during the same month, our forefathers gathered in humble array at the corner of St. Sulpice and St. Paul streets to be entertained by Ormsby and his troupe of poor, half-fed, half-clothed itinerants, whose social standing was considered scarcely better than wandering gypsies or vagabonds, without accoustic effects or adequate stage wardrobe, interpreting Centlivre's "Busybody," an obsolete comedy by a forgotten playwright, and directed by an actor-manager whose name has no place in the list of *biographia dramatica*. And still this primitive effort was the event of the day in dear, staid, old Montreal, the performance being followed with unflagging interest by those whose memory and deeds we hold in such sacred esteem—from whose being the every-day events of a century have gathered together the legacy of splendour and comfort we now enjoy.

Geographically unfortunate is Montreal in its pretensions to recognition from managers of the more important attractions in comparison to the advantages of American cities of even lesser population. The close grouping of cities on the well-beaten tracks of commercial highways in the United States afford facilities and inducements that Montreal cannot hope to enjoy for many years in its isolation and annoying customs' formalities. Nevertheless, Montreal is occasionally favored by modern attention, sometimes accidentally, oftentimes as a last resource. It is only fair to say, however, that results from a financial point of view have been reasonably felicitous in the aggregate. At the present writing, the subject of the drama in Montreal, with its paucity of supporters and overplus of theatres, presents a question worthy of parliamentary debate and force of ordinance. Thousands of dollars will be expended in futile experiments until the public decides what it will have. In the meantime, the leaven of experience will extend towards that attainment, when, within a decade, Montreal will permanently support an English and French stock company on a paying basis, also a first-class combination house of untramelled and free jurisdiction.

Those of you who are familiar with the methods and scope of the theatrical trust or "syndicate" will readily realize what obstacles were to be surmounted by the experienced but handicapped Murphys over such a combination, the Academy of Music being the "syndicate" house in Montreal. What good attractions were to be had outside of the "trust" were secured, but only on conditions entirely inadequate for the maintenance of such a house. After two seasons of uncrowned effort in the administration of this theatre, "Her Majesty's servants" surrendered their trust to the patentees, this being in turn handed over, 28th April, 1900, to John A. Grose, a man of keen perception and varied business experience, of whom much was expected in handling the managerial reins. His initial offering was Frank Daniels in the comic opera, "The Ameer," week of 30th April.

Mr. Grose subsequently went to England for the purpose of recruiting a special company of players for "stock" work, but after a short and unprofitable season, he in turn withdrew from theatrical management. The lease of the house was then assumed by the enterprising New York manager, F. F. Proctor, who inaugurated a season of continuous vaudeville, from 4th March, 1901, which gave way in the following June to the presentation of dramas by a stock company. To date, Mr. Proctor holds a fair clientele through the excellent work of his company. The Proctor Stock Company is a big organization, divided into six sections, one appearing at each of the half dozen Proctor theatres each week. The companies are transferred from one theatre to another, so that all the theatre are equally well supplied. There are 150 people employed the six sections of the company, and the supervision of the entire scheme is in the hands of Frederic Bond.

EPILOGUE.

"Thus far with rough and all unable pen,
  Our bending author hath pursued the story,
In little room confining mighty men,
  Mangling by starts the full course of their glory."

In glancing over the careers of the many men and women preceding these lines, how startling is the thought of the strange mutations which attend our fleeting lives—the errors of which afflict us here, and in the memory of our acquaintances live after us. Our good apportionment of humanity, and all have some, is often forgotten and interred with our dust.

"We are such stuff
As dreams are made of, and our little life
Is rounded with a sleep."

How often in the silence of our meditations are we carried back to incidents witnessed behind the glare of the footlights, often so impressively parallel to our own personal experiences of joys and sorrows. Then must we realize the reflective force of that great mirror of humanity, and, like the remembrance of an intensely human sermon, regret the often unheeded passing of its vivid and prophetic appeal, but ephemerally felt on the emotional cords of our sympathetic natures.

I discovered, a good many years ago, when the skies seemed to be a brighter blue, and the fields a lovelier green than they are now, and when the birds sang twice as well, that fun was the most cheerful thing on earth, and that people preferred laughing to crying. Some of our happiest hours have been passed in following the frolicsome and eccentric methods of a favorite comedian, for variety is the spice of life, and no person can afford to confine his taste in one narrow groove, either as a student of the drama, or in the regular walks of life, after allowing for some little intelligent discrimination in choosing the plays to be patronized, for no reasonable authority can exist to gauge the standard of what a few may have pronounced ideas upon. If a man prefers seeing "Harris from Paris" to "Hamlet," he certainly has a right to follow his inclination as much as his neighbour, who, probably having to fight less hard for the daily necessities of life, has more time to reflect on the divinity of art. So it is with the lover of harmony in music when he steals off to listen to Sousa's marches in preference to what he considers the "boiler shop" symphonies of the late lamented Wagner. Our preference and ambition should, of course, incline to the cultured in the drama as in music, but the individual who goes to the theatre to be entertained has a right to indignation if snarled at by a set of classical dudes who whine over the degeneracy of the drama.

William Winter says that "*the stage of the present is always 'degenerate.' Persons who seek the golden age invariably find that it retires as they advance.*" Notwithstanding the fact that in our day the stage is being adorned and beautified by such artists as Henry Irving, T. W. Keene, Haworth, Miller, Crane, Mansfield, Beerbohm Tree, Joseph Jefferson, Ada Rehan, Olga Nethersole, Ellen Terry, Duse, Mrs. Fiske and Bernhardt, the cry is heard bewailing the loss of the lights of two decades ago, when shone Edwin Booth, Lawrence Barrett, Wm. Warren, John Gilbert, Charlotte Cushman, Clara Morris, John McCullough and Adelaide Neilson.

Richard Mansfield, who most fortunately is seldom taken seriously off the stage, has recently asserted to the press that the stage of to-day is degenerate. His opinion has not been endorsed by other players of equal experience and ability.

In 1845 James Rees described the genius of the drama as an "*owl sitting in gloom and eternal night upon the wreck of the stage*"—yet that was the time of Junius Brutus Booth, Edwin Forrest, Thomas Hamblin, Charles Kean, Macready, Helen Faucit and G. V. Brooke.   In 1811, Mary Godfrey, one of the intimate friends of the poet Moore, writing to him about the theatre in London, said that "*an author who hopes for success on the stage must fall in with popular taste, which is now at the last gasp and past all cure.*"   Yet at that moment Kean, Young, Cooke, the Kembles, Fawcett, Munden and Eliza O'Neil were in full career.   Macklin, when an old man, used to ask disdainfully, "*Where are your actors?*"   Yet Macklin, who lived in the period of Doggett, Mrs. Barry, Barton Booth, Thos. Elrington, Mrs. Oldfield and Mrs. Pritchard, might, even as he spoke, have seen Kemble, Shuter, King and Mrs. Siddons.

Cibber, in his last years, could see little or no merit in contemporary players. Yet that was the time of Garrick, Mrs. Cibber, Mrs. Bellamy, Mossop, Henderson and Barry. Meres, in "Wit's Treasury" (1598), complimenting the poet Drayton, speaks of "*these declining and corrupt times when there is no-thing but roguery in villainous man.*" The stage was compre-hended in that censure, yet that was the time of Shakespeare, Ben Jonson and Burbage, and so it goes back perpetually to the earliest origin of the drama.

It has been estimated that our theatre-going public pays $70,000,000 a year for its entertainment. The calculated at-tendance is 1,500,000 persons a week in the various play-houses of the country. On January 1st, 1900, there were 574 amusement enterprises before the public, of which 427 were dramatic companies.

We are not degenerating. We have more theatres than were in existence in previous times. We have more good plays than our ancestors were blessed with, and we have more bad ones than they were ever afflicted with. We have more good actors than they ever admired in any past period of time, and we have more bad ones than any past period of time was ever burdened with. There must be an abundance of both in order to balance the scales of existence, for just as science teaches us that there must be death in order that there shall be life, so does the light of dramatic experience teach us that there must be bad plays in order that there shall be good ones; that there must be bad actors in order that we may more fully appreciate the good ones.

> "Use every man after his own honor and dignity ;
> The less they deserve, the more merit is in your bounty."

And now, patient reader, the chronicle for the present has ended. If the compiler has succeeded, in his humble way, of awakening pleasant recollections in the minds of his senior readers, or to have excited the envy of juniors in wishing they had lived earlier in order to have seen the celebrities of past decades, his task has not been altogether without fruition.

> You remember what old Omar says :
>
> Yon rising moon that looks for us again—
>   How oft hereafter will she wax and wane ;
> How oft hereafter rising look for us
>   Through this same Garden—and in vain !
>
> And when like her, oh Saki, you shall pass
>   Among the Guests-scatter'd on the Grass.
> And in your joyous errand reach the spot
>   Where I made One—turn down an empty glass !

CURTAIN.

Illustrations

✦ ✦ ✦

For Biographical Sketches, see Index.

INDEX.

INDEX.

Prologue

✣ ✣ ✣

"Shall this speech be spoke for our excuse; or shall we on without apology ?
                              Romeo and Juliet, Act 1, Sc. 4.

The study of Shakespeare is the study of life, and without the aid of the actor there are thousands who never would have dipped into that intellectual ocean, *whose waves touch all the shores of thought,*" remaining unfamiliar with the most sublime and moral sentiments that ever adorned a language.

Through the factor-ship of the theatre, thousands have also become better acquainted with the more imposing drama, so skillful and multifarious in plot, as time has wrought. The humblest auditor, from the seats of the mighty exalted among the gods, or from his almost royal divan in the lower arena, may summon before him the glittering pageant of monarchs, statesmen, conquerors or philosophers—no poet, however godlike his imagination, but all will play their parts.

Realizing that the annals of a temple, wherein is enacted the muse of genius in portraying the achievements of nations in war, politics, and literature, as well as the grand aim of mankind in social ethics, should be a record of much interest, the compiler has been induced to rescue from oblivion such facts relative to the drama of Montreal as can now be collected, and herewith presents this volume to the public.

The idea of compiling this work was conceived in 1896 (just after the writer had disposed of his entire dramatic and general library), being first undertaken in a very humble way, and merely for distraction.

Inasmuch as records and newspaper files in Montreal are deplorably incomplete, opportunity was afforded the writer of obtaining data from sources somewhat removed from the general reader, on tours, which have extended through nineteen or more countries, including over one hundred and fifty cities, the most valuable notes being found in Ottawa, Quebec, Chicago, Washington, New York, Boston and Philadelphia, while much important biographical matter was gleaned in the libraries of the British Museum, Trinity College. Dublin, the Memorial Theatre of Stratford-on-Avon, at Birmingham, and at Edinburgh. A certain portion of the work was also facilitated by condensing matter from the writer's initial effort, "Kings of Tragedy," published in 1888. The history has, therefore, the unique distinction of being decidedly international in its contribution matter.

The first edition was published in serial by the "Metropolitan," of Montreal, from May, 1897, to March, 1898. Gross, although unavoidable, typographical errors in the first, have been rectified in this edition, while a careful revision of the text has, in a large measure, remodelled the original draft.

A paragraph of thanks is due to the following friends, who have given me much assistance :

Edwin Mason, Henry Mott and David Waters, of Montreal; J. F. Ash, Philadelphia; Walter Thorpe, Wm. F. Hartley, Wm. Winter and Col. T. Allston Brown, of New York. To the last mentioned, I am specially indebted. Col. Brown's interest in this edition has extended so far as to read the proofs, and scrutinize the data. When it is recalled that he has for over forty years had a personal acquaintance with nine-tenths of the members of the dramatic profession, the reader will share all due appreciation of his courtesy to us.

My regards are also tendered to the reverend librarians of Laval University, Quebec, and Richard Savage, antiquary of Stratford-on-Avon, *that hallowed ground where began and ended the life that knew, and felt, and uttered all.*

"So on your patience ever more· attending."

THE COMPILER.

ADDENDA.

In order to complete our record to date, mention may be made of the passing away of several familiar names since our forms were closed·

ROSE OSBORN, once noted through the country as an emotional actress, died 23rd April, 1902, aged forty years. She was in her youth a woman of great beauty and exceptional accomplishments.

DAVID HANCHETT, one of the oldest of American actors, died 20th April, 1902. In the height of his career he played with Edwin Forrest, Charlotte Cushman, and other distinguished stars· In recent years he taught the dramatic art in various cities. His last public appearance was in "The Penitent."

MRS· GEORGE HOLLAND (Catherine de Luce), widow of the elder George Holland and mother of E· M. Joseph and George Holland, died 25th April, 1902, aged sixty-nine years·

MISS ANNIE CLARKE, formerly a well-known member of the Boston Museum Stock Company, died 22nd May, 1902.

DANIEL H. HARKINS, after a stage career of forty-nine years, died 7th Dec., 1902. His last appearance was on the 14th April, 1902, in "The Last Appeal," at Wallack's, when he broke down. His training in his profession was thorough, and whatever he undertook to do was thoroughly well done. In character, he was notable for sturdy manliness, integrity, simplicity, and truth· He had a laborious life without much reward for all his toil, but he never lost his faith in the nobility of his calling or the fidelity of his friends.

JAMES F· CATHCART, seen here in support of Charles Kean, died in December, 1902. He was a prominent actor of the old school, and for many years had made his home in Australasia. He died in Sydney, N·S.W., in December, 1902, in his seventy-fourth year· Apart from his sterling worth as an actor, he was greatly esteemed for his genial and earnest personality. His first engagement was with Charles Kean, with whom he first visited the Antipodes, afterward making with him a trip to San Francisco· On the death of Mr. Kean, Mr· Cathcart joined Barry Sullivan, appearing in England and America· After his return to Australasia in 1879, he appeared with George Rignold. Williams and Musgrove, Brough, Boucicault, and Charles Holloway, Mr· Cathcart's favorite roles were Sir Peter Teazle and Brutus in "Julius Caesar." He is survived by one sister, Fanny Cathcart, who went to Australasia with G. V· Brooke, and later married George Darrell.

AUGUSTA DARGON, who retired from the stage after her marriage with Dr. Percy, died at her country home near Sydney, N. S. W·, in December, 1902·

FREDERICK CHIPPENDALE, the father of Mrs. Neil Warner, died 23rd January, 1903, aged 82 years·

FRANK DREW, brother of the elder John Drew, died 1st Feb, 1903, aged 73 years.

HENRY A. WEAVER, senior, died 26th February, 1903. He was seventy years old and would have celebrated the fiftieth anniversary of his stage career the next week.

JOSEPH HAWORTH, in the full glory of a most brilliant career, was suddenly called apart at a time we had hoped to enjoy the maturity of his finest talents. The end came at Willoughby, Ohio, 28th August, 1903. The date of his birth has been written "1855" by most of his biographers, but the date given in my preceding sketch as 1858 is confirmed by a letter from Mr. Haworth to the writer some years ago. Mr. Haworth was inspired, in the early years of his public life, by the best actors of the period, and his ambition drove him to great exertion in the hope that he might some day be numbered among the greatest of American tragedians. That he did not quite reach the goal of his dreams was due, perhaps, more to the lack of public interest in the Shakespearean drama during the years of his best endeavours than to any shortcomings of his own. As it was, he grasped every opportunity to appear in the classic drama, and it is not too much to say that he was successful in every classic role that he undertook.

EMMA MADDERN STEVENS, for many years a prominent and much admired actress, died 16th Jan., 1903. Mrs. Stevens was one of the noted Maddern family of concert singers, that included also Mary. Elizabeth, mother of Mrs. Fiske. Richard, and Henry Maddern. Emma Maddern was the youngest of the family and the only one born in this country. Her birth occurred in Buffalo about fifty-seven years ago. About twenty years ago she married Robert E. Stevens, the well-known manager, then associated with Lawrence Barrett. Mrs. Stevens left three children—Emily, who is a member of Mrs. Fiske's company; James, a lawyer, and Robert who is engaged in mercantile business. Her sister Mary is also in Mrs. Fiske's support. Her life was ordered by a high sense of duty, and her good deeds and amiability were almost proverbial.

MRS. JEAN MARGARET DAVENPORT LANDER, known as an eminent actress for two score years in this country and in Europe, died 3rd July, 1903, aged seventy-four years.

OUR PORTRAITS.

The plates in this book, some of which have been executed from difficult originals, have international interest, inasmuch as not only the best half-tone engravers of Montreal have contributed, but also the leading firms of Philadelphia. the latter including Beck Engraving Co., Gatchell & Manning, Phila. Engraving Co., Standard Engraving Co., Universal Engraving Co., Commercial Engraving Co., Photo-Chromotype Co., Quirk Engraving Co. and the Week's Engraving Co.

Lightning Source UK Ltd.
Milton Keynes UK
UKHW012232110219
337137UK00006B/1150/P